RHETORIC BEY(

M000318122

Works of art in the Middle Ages were best experienced as communal, often multimedia events. Liturgies, books, song, architecture, prayers and poetry were performed as collaborative activities in which performers and audience together realized their work anew. Eleven essays by leading scholars of music, liturgy, literature, manuscript production and architecture analyse how the medieval arts invited and delighted in collaborative performances designed to persuade. The essays cast fresh light on subjects ranging from pilgrim processions within Chartres cathedral, to Hildegard of Bingen's hymns, to polyphonic song, to the oral delivery of diplomatic letters, and the 'rhetoric of silence' perfected by the Cistercians. Rhetoric is defined broadly in this book to encompass its relationship to its sister arts of music, architecture and painting, all of which use materials and media in addition to words – sometimes altogether without words. Contributors have concentrated on those aspects of formal rhetoric that are performative in nature: the sound, gesture and facial expressions of persuasive speech in action. Delivery (performance) is shown to be at the heart of rhetoric, that aspect of it which is indeed beyond words.

MARY CARRUTHERS is Remarque Professor of Literature, New York University, and a Fellow of All Souls College, Oxford.

CAMBRIDGE STUDIES IN MEDIEVAL LITERATURE

This series of critical books seeks to cover the whole area of literature written in the major medieval languages – the main European vernaculars, and medieval Latin and Greek – during the period *c.* 1100–1500. Its chief aim is to publish and stimulate fresh scholarship and criticism on medieval literature, special emphasis being placed on understanding major works of poetry, prose and drama in relation to the contemporary culture and learning which fostered them.

A complete list of titles in the series can be found at the end of the volume.

RHETORIC BEYOND WORDS

Delight and Persuasion in the Arts of the Middle Ages

EDITED BY

MARY CARRUTHERS

CAMBRIDGE
UNIVERSITY PRESS

CAMBRIDGE UNIVERSITY PRESS
Cambridge, New York, Melbourne, Madrid, Cape Town,
Singapore, São Paulo, Delhi, Mexico City

Cambridge University Press
The Edinburgh Building, Cambridge CB2 8RU, UK

Published in the United States of America by Cambridge University Press, New York

www.cambridge.org
Information on this title: www.cambridge.org/9781107647770

First published 2010
First paperback edition 2013

A catalogue record for this publication is available from the British Library

Library of Congress Cataloguing in Publication Data
Rhetoric beyond words : delight and persuasion in the arts of the Middle Ages /
[edited by] Mary Carruthers.
p.   cm. – (Cambridge studies in medieval literature; 78)
ISBN 978-0-521-51530-6 (hardback)
1. Rhetoric, Medieval.   I. Carruthers, Mary J. (Mary Jean), 1941–
II. Title.   III. Series.
PN183.R449   2010
808′.00902–dc22
2009053757

ISBN 978-0-521-51530-6 Hardback
ISBN 978-1-107-64777-0 Paperback

Contents

Illustrations

Contributors

MARGARET BENT is Emeritus Fellow of All Souls College, Oxford.

PAUL BINSKI is Professor of the History of Medieval Art at the University of Cambridge and Fellow of Gonville and Caius College, Cambridge.

MARTIN CAMARGO is Professor of English at the University of Illinois, Urbana-Champaign.

MARY CARRUTHERS is Remarque Professor of Literature at New York University and quondam Fellow of All Souls College, Oxford.

PAUL CROSSLEY is Professor of the History of Art at The Courtauld Institute of Art.

WILLIAM T. FLYNN is Lecturer in Medieval Latin at the Institute for Medieval Studies in the University of Leeds.

ELIZABETH EVA LEACH is University Lecturer in Music at the University of Oxford and Fellow of St Hugh's College, Oxford.

MONIKA OTTER is Associate Professor of English and Comparative Literature at Dartmouth College.

SUSAN RANKIN is Professor of Medieval Music at the University of Cambridge and Fellow of Emmanuel College, Cambridge.

LUCY FREEMAN SANDLER is Helen Gould Sheppard Professor of Art History, emerita, at New York University.

JAN M. ZIOLKOWSKI is Arthur Kingsley Porter Professor of Medieval Latin at Harvard University and Director of the Dumbarton Oaks Research Library and Collection in Washington, DC.

Abbreviations and primary sources commonly used

CCCM   Corpus Christianorum, continuatio medievalis
CCSL   Corpus Christianorum, series latina
CLS   Cistercian liturgy series
CSEL   Corpus Scriptorum Ecclesiasticorum Latinorum
LCL   Loeb Classical Library
MGH   Monumenta Germaniae Historica
OLD   P. G. W. Glare (ed), *Oxford Latin Dictionary* (Oxford
            University Press, 1982)
PIMS   Pontifical Institute for Medieval Studies Press, Toronto
PL   Patrologiae cursus completus, series latina
RLM   Carolus Halm (ed.), *Rhetorici latini minores* (Leipzig:
            Teubner, 1863)
TLL   *Thesaurus Linguae Latinae.*

The following editions and translations of texts discussed by more than one contributor have been used, unless otherwise specified in the notes.

Augustinus Aurelius. *De doctrina christiana*, ed. J. Martin. CCSL 32. Turnhout: Brepols, 1962. Trans. E. Hill, *Teaching Christianity*. Hyde Park, NY: New City Press, 1996.

M. Tullius Cicero. *De Oratore Dialogus*, ed. A. S. Wilkins. Oxford Classical Texts. Oxford University Press, 1902/1926. Trans. J. M. May and J. Wisse, *Cicero: On the Ideal Orator*. Oxford University Press, 2001.

Cicero. *Orator*, ed. and trans. H. M. Hubbell. Loeb Classical Library 342. London: Heinemann, 1962.

Cicero. *De inventione*, ed. and trans. H. M. Hubbell. Loeb Classical Library 386. London: Heinemann, 1949.

[Tullius Cicero]. *Rhetorica ad Herennium*, ed. and trans. H. Caplan. Loeb Classical Library 403. London: Heinemann, 1954.

Horace. *Satires, Epistles and Ars poetica*, ed. and trans. H. Rushton Fairclough. Loeb Classical Library 194. London: Heinemann, 1929.

M. Fabius Quintilianus. *Institutionis oratoriae libri duodecim*, ed. M. Winterbottom, 2 vols. Oxford Classical Texts. Oxford: Clarendon Press, 1970. Trans. D. A. Russell, *The Orator's Education*, 5 vols. Loeb Classical Library 124–7, 494. Cambridge, MA; London: Harvard University Press, 2001.

Editor's introduction

Mary Carruthers

Over sixty-five years ago, in an essay that has become a touchstone among students of medieval rhetoric, Richard McKeon observed that:

The history of rhetoric should have as subject an art which, although it has no special subject matter according to most rhetoricians, nonetheless must be discussed in application to some subject matter: rhetoric is applied to many incommensurate subject matters; it borrows devices from other arts and its technical terms and methods become, without trace of their origin, parts of other arts and sciences.[1]

This collection of essays explores some of the ways in which rhetoric, especially as performance or delivery (*pronuntiatio, actio*), has borrowed from other arts. Equally, the essays address how terms and methods of rhetoric were taken over into those same arts without a trace of their origin, so seamlessly indeed that the question of 'origin' is immaterial, at least to the focus of this book. The works of European rhetoric that survive in the Graeco-Roman tradition from classical and late antiquity, augmented in the Middle Ages by writers addressing specifically Christian situations, made analogies and parallels, and borrowed terms from the arts of music, painting, architecture and acting, and those arts, when they were theorized at all, did the same with rhetoric. Having no specific subject matter, rhetorical analysis was applied freely in the analysis of the other arts, those like music and poetry which formed part of the liberal arts curriculum, and also those which were 'mechanical', such as medicine and architecture.

The essays also remind us of Aristotle's fundamental distinction, at the start of his *Rhetoric*, among *epistēmē, téchnē* and *empeiría*, all signifying qualities of human knowledge.[2] *Epistēmē* is knowledge of a defined science, *empeiría* the sort of 'knowing how' that we might call having a 'knack' for specific tasks, a talent developed largely by personal experiment and by imitating the practical experience gained by others. *Téchnē*, 'art', is for Aristotle, a medial term. *Technai* extract from many particular practices a teachable system and method: system and method distinguish an art from a 'knack'. The other characteristic of an art is that it can be executed poorly or well. Someone with knack or 'talent' always does well; this is why we say they 'have a knack' for something. But an art can be performed badly without this affecting the excellence of the art itself.

There are actually two arts that have no definite subject of their own, but offer methods applicable to many. These are rhetoric and dialectic ('argument'); they stand in relation to one another as the two movements and voices of a Greek dramatic chorus, strophe and antistrophe. The first words of Aristotle's *Rhetoric* are: 'Rhetoric is the counterpart (*antistrophos*) of dialectic.' The metaphor is carefully chosen, for the heart of rhetoric, as of all art, lies in its performance: it proffers both visual spectacle and verbal dance to an audience which is not passive but an actor in the whole experience, like the chorus in drama. As an art, rhetoric is set by Aristotle in the practical social world, while dialectic is purer, more self-contained. In a witty metaphor, Jacques Brunschwig noted that 'dialectic is basically a greenhouse flower that grows and flourishes in the protected atmosphere of the school. … But rhetoric is a plant growing in the open air of the city and the public places.' Architecture, music, painting, literature and liturgy also all dwell in public places.[3]

In his essay, McKeon understood 'arts' to mean literature and language, and the academic disciplines developed from them, such as philosophy and law. He concluded that 'the many innovations which are recorded during [the Middle Ages] in the arts with which [rhetoric] is related suggest that their histories might profitably be considered without unique attachment to the field in which their advances are celebrated.[4] This suggestion for further research remains largely underdeveloped even now, as histories have been written largely without reference to the rhetorical methods and terminology in which such developments as formal logic are steeped.[5] Several contributors to this volume have taken on the task of considering methods directed to persuasion, from within the seemingly incommensurate boundaries of their own arts: chant, polyphony, architecture and the illumination of books.

As a result, rhetoric is defined broadly in this book to encompass its relationship to these sister arts which use materials and media in addition to words, sometimes altogether without words. From the subject area of the history of rhetoric itself, contributors have concentrated on those aspects that are performative in nature, the sound, gesture and facial expressions of persuasive speech in action. Delivery (performance) is not an aspect of rhetoric that has received much analytical attention from its students, certainly not as compared to invention and style, but it is at the heart of rhetoric, that aspect of it which is indeed beyond words. This was recognized aptly by the thirteenth-century Oxford Franciscan, Roger Bacon, who, attempting to classify the academic arts and sciences, identified rhetoric as something that was both of the linguistic arts and yet also beyond them, best considered, he thought, as music. In this he was newly articulating something Cicero and the antique rhetoricians had also observed, that there was in the performance of oratory a kind of hidden song (*cantus occultior*). Bacon observed:

For one who knows moral philosophy knows how to use persuasive speech, conforming as well with the appropriate gestures of pleasurable oratory. Likewise one who knows logic and grammar ... One who knows grammar uses [the relations of words] in an elementary way, but one who knows logic, with regard to what constitutes the form of argumentation, proceeds in these matters maturely and assigns their reasons and causes. But with respect to artful arrangement and eloquence and the persuasiveness of arguments, certainly neither a logician nor a grammarian can assign their causes, but one who knows music can; just as one who knows geometry is able to identify the reasons for the lines and angles and figures which a builder uses.[6]

The persuasiveness of artful language is exactly what Bacon identifies as lying beyond the definitional reach of grammar and dialectic (logic), the analytical tools of the trivium (which we now call 'the language arts' and Bacon here calls 'moral philosophy', the philosophy which relates to daily human life and social interaction). Rhetoric was traditionally defined as the art of persuasion, or rather, to paraphrase Aristotle, being able to discover, on a given political, judicial or diplomatic occasion, the appropriate means of persuasion and using them artfully and well. Bacon uses the word *suavis*, 'sweet', for the phenomenon of persuasion, recognizing as orators always had that persuasion is an action that occurs within the audience, the 'pleasure' which delights the mind and wins the confident consent of the will as well as the approbation of reason. It is this elusive but essential quality that the essays in this volume are especially concerned to examine.

Bacon identified the ultimate persuasiveness of the arts, their *suavitas*, with music, an extralinguistic art. Just as often, rhetorical pleasure was identified with variety and colour, on the analogy of painting and of sculpture – arts that were never placed within the traditional classifications of science (though geometry was considered to provide the theoretical rationale for architecture, as Bacon indicates).

Rhetoric and architecture have had a venerable dialogue. It is well-known that Vitruvius turned to rhetoric for many of his terms when composing his treatise *On Architecture*. And the language of architecture infused Christianity from the start, as it had Judaism – Jesus was himself likened to the keystone of the building which is the Church. The essays in this volume by Paul Crossley and Paul Binski both tease out many ramifications of this ancient connection in the theory and practice of church architecture in the Middle Ages. From their rich discussions I emphasize a single quotation from ancient rhetoric, among a great many possibilities. In his proemium to Book VII of *The Orator's Education (Institutio oratoria)*, Quintilian, turning to the subject of the arrangement of materials and arguments, likens his task to that of a builder: 'just as it is not enough in erecting a building simply to collect the stone and the timber and the other building materials, unless the hands of craftsmen are put to work to dispose and assemble them, so also in speaking, it will be nothing but a random accumulation unless Disposition organizes it, links it all up, and binds it together'.[7]

The link of rhetoric to painting was made most often as an analogy between the orator setting out his verbal *colores* and the painter his pigments. In addition, the traditional adages that 'poetry is a speaking painting (*pictura*), painting silent poetry', attributed to the Greek poet Simonides, and 'poetry is like a painting (*ut pictura poesis*)', found in Horace's *Ars poetica*, were known and admired throughout late antiquity and the Middle Ages. But the conflation of the crafts – the conceptual jump from verbal artifact as being like painting to the verbal artist being a painter in language – is found as well, and is perhaps more germane to the essays in this collection. The essential aesthetic quality called *enargeia*, 'bringing before the eyes', was esteemed not for its imaginative energy and vividness alone, but because it was crucial to rational demonstration, for it provides the *evidentia* needed to persuade judges (one's audience) of the moral veracity of one's argument.[8] Book 6 of Quintilian's *The Orator's Education* is devoted largely to this (he returns to it in Book 8). In order to be persuasive, proofs (*probationes*) need evidence (*evidentiae*), a word that has a quite different meaning in rhetoric than what we now assign it. As Quintilian says, 'Proofs may lead the judges to *think* our Cause the better one, but it is our emotional appeals that make them also *want* it to be so; and what they want they also believe [id quod volunt credunt quoque].'[9] The judge should 'no longer think that he is listening to a lament for somebody else's troubles, but that he is hearing the feelings and the voice of the afflicted'.[10]

In this way, the orator is a painter, for his words provide the 'evidence', the images 'brought-before-the-eyes' of imagination and reason which enable the judges to see feelingly the truth (not just the facts) of the situation they have been asked to analyse and decide. 'Liveliness' – the quality so praised in ancient painting – is a rhetorical value as well as the foremost pictorial value. The orator paints a scene with words so vividly before the inner senses of the mind that the judges can witness the event in full themselves; Zeuxis was valued for being so lively a painter that birds came to eat his painted grapes.[11] But it is not the lifelike mimesis alone, the fact of *trompe l'oeil*, that is significant. It is the effect which such vividness has on its audience; 'what they want, they also believe', they are persuaded. This is not a minor distinction to observe, for it involves the audience as agents together with the artist and the artifact in making a completed, whole work of art on each occasion that it is seen, read or performed. Seeing a painting is thus an occasion that can be rhetorically understood; its means is mimesis but its goal is persuasion and belief.

It is thus significant that, in recalling his own education as an orator, Cicero likens his method of apprenticing himself to different masters of rhetoric and philosophy in Athens and Rhodes to that of Zeuxis, the painter who selected features from five of the most beautiful young women of the city of Croton, in order to fulfil his commission to portray Aphrodite, the most excellent female beauty. In just such a way as Zeuxis, Cicero says, 'ex variis ingeniis excellentissima quaeque libavimus' [I extracted everything [that was] most excellent from various minds].[12] He models his own apprenticeship as that of a painter by training and by craft practice; it is no 'mere' metaphor or casual analogy. Similarly, characterizing the master Stoic orator, Cato, a statesman of great accomplishment though perceived as rather old-fashioned by Cicero's time, he wrote that 'his drawing was sharp and ... lacked only some brightness and colour which had not yet been invented.'[13]

But it was particularly in respect of evidence and character, the other figure (Greek *characterismōs*) deemed critical for setting out and judging the truth of a situation, that painterly 'vividness' is particularly emphasized in the rhetoric books. Rhetorical character was defined by the first-century AD Greek-trained rhetoric master, Rutilius Lupus, as painting of a kind: 'Just as a painter sets out his figures with colours, so an orator with this device paints the lineaments of the vices or virtues of those of whom he is speaking.'[14]

The inspiration for this collection of essays lies with two workshops held in 2004 and 2006, which focused on 'rhetoric and the nonverbal arts'. Enabled by generous financial support from New York University, each brought together a number of scholars from the fields of rhetoric, art history, musicology, Latin literature, medieval liturgy and theatre, whose knowledge also ranged across a wide temporal span in Europe from late antiquity to about 1600, when the Graeco-Roman rhetorical tradition was at its most influential. I am deeply grateful to all the learned and articulate participants in these workshops, one at New York University's Villa La Pietra in Florence and one at Balliol College, Oxford, for days of challenging conversation and non-stop exchanges. Though this collection does not by any means record the proceedings of those workshops, the writers were all part of one or both of them, and their essays reflect in part at least some of the richness of those gatherings.

These workshop conversations about medieval and early modern arts were entirely multidisciplinary, designed to focus on the question of why the vocabulary and model of rhetoric have held such force in the analysis of musical, liturgical and artistic performances more generally, and also to see if it still held valuable analytical power within arts other than literature alone. The collection of essays inspired by them is also deliberately multidisciplinary, bringing together the insights of musicologists, literary historians and historians of liturgy, architecture and manuscript painting, in an effort to explore the persuasive aspects of arts not typically thought of now as primarily either performative or persuasive. The analogies between rhetoric and music, architecture, painting and theatre are found from the beginnings of ancient writing on the subject of the arts; they continue to have been richly employed right through the Middle Ages. The task of the essays in this volume is to explore whether these analogies were simply deadened conventions, or whether they continued to have varied life and expression. It is also an intention of the authors to explore the possibilities of rhetorical analysis in theories of art more generally, in order to offer a lively and historically valid set of analytical terms to scholars working in a variety of medieval arts. Exploration of rhetoric and nonverbal arts is, of course, nothing new in theorizing the arts, forming indeed the foundation of that classicism against which the early nineteenth century so vocally rebelled. But we are trying to do something rather different. While seventeenth-century neoclassical theory, as applied to a variety of nonverbal arts including music and architecture, attempted to analyse the structures of completed works as imitating those of a classical oration, the efforts of the essayists in this collection are rather to examine forms dynamically as having their own implicit rhetoric, and to ask whether questions of audience, performance and invention can be considered rhetorically in a flexible sense, one in which the performance of a work on any given occasion is also the moment of its coming into full being. Rhetorical analysis models artistic experiences in terms of a mutually energized triad of composer (performer), composition (formal plan), and audience – Aristotle's *ethos, logos, pathos*.[15] None of these three is thought to be ever passive nor ever static; no work of art can fully exist apart from the occasion(s) of its performance(s), and no occasion can exist without all three components in constant interaction. Nor is persuasion possible without pleasure of some kind, as Cicero and Roger Bacon both recognized, for pleasure is what moves someone to some action, the final goal of all rhetoric. Finding and analysing that dynamism lies at the heart of each of the essays in this volume.

The essays are not grouped primarily by discipline, because a chief aim of the collection, gathering such an array of scholars to test in their own work some themes that appear common to rhetoric of both the verbal and non- or extraverbal sort, is to suggest connections that are not so obviously made across disciplines, and in the process to expand the ordinary restriction of rhetoric to the situation only of speaking aloud. Even when essays concern materials that have formed part of the 'normal' history of medieval rhetoric (such as the *artes epistolandi* and the category of delivery), their authors have emphasized aspects – such as relations of silence and voicing – that are unusual subjects in histories of rhetoric.

The collection begins with two essays that demonstrate the intellectual and social positions of two of the arts in addition to that of oratory. As one practising and capable of teaching *rhetorica* was an *orator* or *rhetor*, so a *musicus* was someone learned and capable of teaching the principles of music, and an *architectus* a learned professional, who gained this status late in the Middle Ages by claiming a science as intellectually principled as any other learned profession, including training in the liberal arts. The genre of the music treatise is much older than that of the architectural treatise (at least in the Middle Ages), but both claim their learned status to an important extent by borrowing terminology (though, as McKeon noted, often without attribution) from the long-established genres of grammar and rhetoric treatises. Paul Binski demonstrates how, during the thirteenth century in Paris especially, architecture, which had always been classified as a mechanical art, began to claim the dignity and status of a professional science, with an appropriate social dignity and intellectual seriousness. Music was one of the scientific arts from the beginning, like rhetoric, an art taught in schools and later in universities; one marker of this was the clear distinction made by Boethius (who wrote the text from which music was studied in schools through all the medieval centuries) between the *cantor*, who only 'sang the notes' without understanding the principles of what he sang, and the learned *musicus*, who not only could perform but understood and indeed could create within the boundaries of the art. Rhetoric was the pre-eminent art of composition, which was taught by masters in schools and learned according to principles instead of traditional practices alone, and supplied the obvious model for the pro-fessionalization of other arts seeking the status of science over mechanics. Margaret Bent demonstrates how the models of grammar and rhetoric served musical analysis and practice not only during the monastic period and in later Renaissance humanism, but during the crucial two 'scholas-tic' centuries between 1300 and 1500, when polyphonic song and motet came into their own. Musical treatises of the fifteenth century adopted a lexicon from rhetoric as well as grammar in order to analyse principles of musical composition, thereby reviving an old link between rhetoric and music, but also extending it considerably as the complexities of polyphonic music developed and, as well, the profession of (now named) composers, working in different locations and instructing others, as architects were also learning to do with patrons and workmen at about the same time. Like architecture, humanly created and performed music at this time also asserted its place as a learned craft, an Aristotelian-style *téchnē* which had system and method that could be taught as well as practised. When excel-lently accomplished, it could claim a dignity equal to that of oratory.

The two following essays examine the social and thus rhetorical situat-ing of compositions in arts not often thought to be rhetorical at all: late medieval polyphonic vernacular song, and the work of book-illuminating within a powerful late medieval household. Each in its way problematizes the idea of single authorship or idealized audience by demonstrating how invention could be a collaborative activity, self-consciously so in the case of polyphonic song. Elizabeth Eva Leach focuses on the case of 'perform-ing' one such song, with double texts and four singers, as requiring crea-tive collaboration among the performers, on the model of what is now sometimes called 'distributed cognition', a concept initially developed by social anthropologists and artificial intelligence designers, and lately taken up by some scholars of the Shakespearean theatre. In the situation she examines, the written song we now possess is the script of a perform-ance, the singers actually inventing their performance on the model of a trained orator speaking extemporaneously. Such performances are neither 'spontaneous' (*improvisus*, 'unprovided', being a negative term in both music and rhetoric) nor 'rehearsed', because the singers, like an orator, invent for the occasion from their learned store of principles and common places (or conventions), exhibiting their status as *musici*, masters of the complete science of musical art. The point of the written melodic line is indeed to provide the opportunities for variation, but according to science not ignorance, and the delight of such singing for the singers lay in responding immediately but appropriately to one another, as a social unit in which each's contribution made up a whole greater than its parts.

Lucy Freeman Sandler studies a different sort of sociable 'authoring', in this case a group of painters who, during the fourteenth century primarily, illuminated a number of books for the household of the Bohuns, a powerful English aristocratic family with many royal connections. The group of Bohun manuscripts, chiefly psalters and prayer books, were illuminated by a group of painters, led by John de Teye, an Augustinian friar, as were some of his assistants. Though historians assume, on good evidence, that the households of the great included artists and scribes as well as chaplains, confessors, clerks and many other learned men, it is unusual to have such a group identified in a way that we can know something about their education and background, and observe their work as artists over three generations of the Bohun family. In the design of these manuscripts, Sandler demonstrates how John de Teye's group responded to the particular sensibilities of the Bohun patrons for whom they worked, not thoughtlessly but rhetorically, varying the decoration in ways that responded to and guided the owners, in some cases young children, for whom the books were made. These books are consciously collaborative in a manner that includes not only the painters and scribes, but the patrons as well in a delightful intellectual game. Making art is fun, a quality as much (perhaps even more) a part of medieval art as of modern, though too often ignored by the moralists among us, or those who seem to believe that delight is not quite intellectually respectable.

Leach's and Sandler's essays also remind us that rhetorical composition is social in its essence, often imagined as a conversation (the original meaning of Latin *sermo*) about some common topic, taking place among people of similar education, who are well-disposed and confident with one another (*benevolentia*), the situation of Cicero's *De oratore* and Plato's *Phaedrus*, and replicated in the late medieval work (1463) known as *Les douze dames de rhétorique*, an illustration for which (made by one of its learned authors) is reproduced for the cover of this book. This poem is about the nature of rhetoric, but is not cast in the form of a manual – rather it is a learned conversation and *débat,* though conducted in written verse epistles, among a group of courtiers in the households of the dukes of Burgundy and Bourbon.[16] This should remind us that an understanding of art conditioned by rhetoric will stress situation and participation over object and individual response. And it is with a rhetorical understanding of the arts that medieval artists created their work.

The next set of essays looks at the traditional aspect of rhetoric known as delivery, or *pronuntiatio*. All of them focus on its extraverbal aspects of *vultus*, facial expressions, and *gestus*, the gestures (including clothing) used in oral delivery as an important means of persuasion. As Jan Ziolkowski notes in his review of how the traditional manuals treated *pronuntiatio*, the importance of these aspects is always emphasized but then given very short shrift in the text. It is in delivery, also called *actio* (as in the first-century BC manual, *Rhetorica ad Herennium*), that oratory comes closest to acting, a link that rhetoric both exploited and repudiated. Monika Otter addresses this anxiety in her elegant analysis of rhetorical *vultus*, with respect to the medieval understanding of *persona*. Examining the manuscripts of Terence, the Roman dramatist who was a major poet of the medieval curriculum, though not as a playwright but as an object of grammatical analysis, she demonstrates how the traditional masks of the actor focused the concerns over true and false speaking that are at the heart of rhetorical delivery. Jan Ziolkowski foregrounds the Cistercian legend of 'Our Lady's Tumbler' to analyse a completely mute art of persuading by means of gesture and expression alone, a story particularly apt to the silent religious order which gave it life. Martin Camargo pays attention to the cultivation and training of voice and vocal delivery in the medieval teaching of rhetoric, especially in manuals of *artes epistolandi*. These three essays together touch all the bases of rhetorical delivery: *vultus*, *vox* and *gestus* – tones and rhythms of voice, gestures, and facial expressions – in ways that expand their influence over medieval performance practices far more profoundly than is evident from their cursory treatment in the manuals.

The final four essays deal with performance as well, but instead of using categories taken from anthropology or psychology, employ a concept from rhetoric that is historically more appropriate (at least in these contexts) – *ductus* or (as it later and expansively became) *modus agendi*. While not unknown to ancient rhetoric, *ductus* was more developed in medieval rhetorics. My essay traces the enrichment of this useful concept during the medieval centuries, as it was analysed and employed in works about rhetoric, poetry and literary interpretation (exegesis), arguing that it basically addresses the persuasive effect of disposition and style as a dynamic process, the way in which a work guides those experiencing it through itself. The medieval analytical category of *intentio auctoris* considered 'intention' as a quality of the composed work itself, derived only at a remove from a particular, historical personage. This 'intention' of a work is expressed through its varying modes of stylistic performance, the *modi agendi*. Style, of course, is something shared by all the arts.

In a detailed examination of the routes contained within the architecture of Chartres cathedral and identified by the placement of its furniture and ornament – altars, passages, sculpture, stained glass – Paul Crossley demonstrates how in one great public building voiceless artifacts collaborate in a complex, multiple design to guide those walking through it in a set of possible journeys, each offering creatively meaningful experience to those who discover how to follow them both intellectually and physically – one must walk its routes in order to comprehend them. In Chartres, such performances are the intended completion offered by the work, and each performance completes it anew. Such a building presented the medieval pilgrims entering it with situations that had to be worked through; it could not be fully experienced as an object only.

The two final essays examine liturgy as an artistically satisfying and profoundly rhetorical use of *ductus*, 'journeying through' a work. Considering particular liturgies composed by known people for particular groups – Abelard's composition, at Heloise's commission and direction, of a liturgy for her convent of the Paraclete, and Hildegard of Bingen's liturgy for her nuns – William Flynn demonstrates how Abelard's own mastery of rhetorical theory directed his composition, and how Hildegard's extraordinary liturgy for St Ursula, including her hymn *Cum uox sanguinis*, bespoke the celebration of that feast within the Rupertsburg convent, using for his analysis the categories of *ductus subtilis* and *figuratus*.

Susan Rankin demonstrates how one particular Roman liturgy, for the feast on 13 May of 'Sancta Maria ad martyres', came into being as the vehicle to persuade the Roman populace that the Pantheon, that temple to all the pagan gods which had stood for Rome itself at one time, could be re-connected and reintended as a chief Christian church in Rome. She reconstructs the liturgy as it was performed by the pope, Boniface IV, and all his clergy with the Roman people inside the Pantheon on 13 May 609. In a major act of persuasion, Romans' attitude towards the building – and perhaps their city as well – was reconciled with God as a place not of demons but a fitting *templum Domini*. The conscious rhetoric of the occasion makes a proper end for this collection of essays, bringing together 'the available means' provided through multiple arts in one grand action of successful, lasting 'persuasion'.

NOTES

1 R. A. McKeon, 'Rhetoric in the Middle Ages', *Speculum*, 17 (1942): 1–33, at 3. The use of rhetorical terms in early modern theorizing about visual art has been more extensively studied, since Michael Baxandall, *Giotto and the Orators* (Oxford University Press, 1971); see, recently, Caroline van Eck, *Classical Rhetoric and the Visual Arts in Early Modern Europe* (Cambridge University Press, 2007).

2 Aristotle, *Rhetoric*, I.1.354a; a more extensive discussion of the types of human knowledge and definition of *téchnē* occurs at the beginning of his *Metaphysics* (I.1–2). Relevant to artistic practice also is the discussion of 'excellence' (*aretē*) in the *Nichomachean Ethics*, II.5 especially. All these texts were well-known and commented on from the late twelfth century.

3 J. Brunschwig, 'Rhetoric as a "counterpart" to Dialectic', in A. O. Rorty (ed.), *Essays on Aristotle's Rhetoric* (Berkeley; London: University of California Press, 1996), 34–55, at 51.

4 McKeon, 'Rhetoric', 33.

5 Notable exceptions include E. Stump, *Dialectic and Its Place in the Development of Medieval Logic* (Ithaca, NY: Cornell University Press, 1989), and her translation with commentary of the *De differentiis topicis* of Boethius (Ithaca, NY: Cornell University Press, 1978).

6 Roger Bacon, *Opus tertium*, c. 75, in *F. Rogeri Bacon opera quaedam hactenus inedita*, ed. J. S. Brewer, Rerum Britannicarum medii aevi scriptores 15 (London: Longman,1859), 306–7: 'Nam moralis philosophus scit uti sermone suavi, et gestibus convenientibus orationi delectabili conformandis. Similiter logicus et grammaticus. ... Grammaticus igitur utitur his pueriliter; sed logicus quantum ad formam arguendi quam constituit, in his procedit viriliter, et causas et rationes assignat. Sed quantum ad decorem et ornatum et suavitatem argumenti, certe non potest logicus, sicut nec grammaticus, causas et rationes assignare, sed musicus; sicut geometer causas linearum, et angulorum, et figurarum, quibus carpentator, habet dare.' See the essay below by Margaret Bent for some further discussion of Bacon's views.

7 Quintilian, *Inst. Orat*, VII, proem. 1.

8 On *enargeia* (and the related term *energeia*), see K. Eden, *Poetic and Legal Fiction in the Aristotelian Tradition* (Princeton University Press, 1986), and S. Newman, 'Aristotle's Notion of "Bringing Before the Eyes": Its Contributions to Aristotelian and Contemporary Conceptualizations of Metaphor, Style, and Audience', *Rhetorica*, 20 (2002): 1–23; for a discussion of *enargeia* in the early Christian traditions as well, see M. Carruthers, *The Craft of Thought: Meditation, Rhetoric, and the Making of Images, 400–1200* (Cambridge University Press, 1998), 130–50.

9 Quintilian, *Inst. orat*, VI.2.6.

10 *Ibid.*, VI.1.26.

11 The story is in Pliny, *Natural History*, 35.65. There are many tales like it – that Apelles painted a horse so lifelike that other horses neighed in recognition (35.95); that the triumvir, Lepidus, bothered by noisy birds, had a painting

made of a snake so lifelike it frightened them into silence (35.121). Pliny also recounts narrative paintings depicted with such vivid emotions that their onlookers experienced them as well (35.63–75), a clear parallel with rhetorical *enargeia* as discussed by Quintilian.

12 Cicero, *De inventione*, II.1–2; the quotation is at II.2.1. The story is also told by Pliny, *Natural History*, 35.65.

13 Cicero, *Brutus*, trans. G. A. Hendrickson, LCL 342 (London: Heinemann, 1962), 298 'Intelleges nihil illius liniamentis nisi eorum pigmentorum, quae inventa nondum erant, florem et colorem defuisse.' On the change in Roman taste that this comment reflects, see B. A. Krostenko, *Cicero, Catullus, and the Language of Social Performance* (University of Chicago Press, 2001).

14 Rutilius Lupus, *Schemata lexeos*, II.7, *RLM* 16.1–3: 'Quem ad modum pictor coloribus figuras describit, sic orator hoc schemate aut vitia aut virtutes eorum, de quibus loquitur, deformat.' Rutilius Lupus was contemporary with the Emperor Tiberius.

15 See Aristotle, *Rhetoric*, I.2.3–7, but these three terms recur throughout the treatise.

16 There is some uncertainty, as one might expect, about the exact division of labours among the poets of the *Douze dames*: see the introduction to *Les douze dames de rhétorique*, ed. D. Cowling (Geneva: Droz, 2002). See also C. Brown, 'Du nouveau sur le "mystère" des Douze Dames de Rhétorique: le rôle de Georges Chastellain', *Bullétin de la Commission Royale d'Histoire*, 153 (1987): 181–221.

CHAPTER I

'Working by words alone'

The architect, scholasticism and rhetoric in thirteenth-century France*

Paul Binski

In this contribution I want to suggest that thirteenth-century scholastic and rhetorical discourse informed, but more importantly was informed by, ideas about architects. Arguably a new edifice of thinking about the master builder was being raised at the great theological universities of northern Europe, principally Paris. It rose slowly, there were obstacles, and it is not clear how durable it proved to be. Nevertheless, within scholastic thinking of the period *c.* 1240–1300 something like a new departure in thought about architects as authors and professionals can be traced. The fundamental structure of this thought was ancient in origin: we find it in Vitruvius, and again later in the Florentine Renaissance; but we also encounter it refreshed and developed by the Aristotelianism of the thirteenth-century schools. The spirit of my observations is perhaps best introduced by Alexander Murray: 'Most of us were taught at school that Florentine Renaissance culture appeared, as if bubbling up from a hole in the ground, just before 1300. What we may not have been taught … is that the main tributary to that culture had gone *into* the hole from the scholasticism of the university of Paris, which reached the apogee of its medieval influence just before the Florentine Renaissance began.'[1] I do not for one moment wish to suggest that the Renaissance of the visual arts began in Paris; yet I believe that something important in the articulation of ideas about what architects and other makers of art actually were was going on in that city and especially the university towards 1300, and that this entailed a significant, but as yet not entirely recognized, shift of perspective apparent at the intersection of scholasticism and rhetoric.

At no point in this essay do I want to suggest that attitudes towards the practice of architecture were ever straightforward. Moral ambivalence was always a potential issue given that architecture could be linked to excess. No text concerning architects and their works written in the twelfth and thirteenth centuries possesses the irresistible rhetorical power, the

magnificent indignation, of St Bernard's *Apologia* (c. 1125) and its sono-
rous assault on *sumptuositas* and *curiositas* in the visual arts.[2] Bernard did
not openly attack architects so much as corruption of thought; but master
builders were a common target for censorious opinion. The monastic historian Gervase of Canterbury, on the face of it an ally of William of Sens,
the cathedral's new French architect, includes in his celebrated account
of William's lethal fall from the scaffolding of the Gothic church in 1178
the mysterious remark, 'In solum magistrum vel Dei vindicta, vel diaboli
desaevit invidia' [the master alone was the object of the vengeance of
God or jealousy of the Devil].[3] Perhaps Gervase had in mind the 'ruinous
skills' of Daedalus, the universal model of high-born, high-flown ingenuity come to grief in Ovid's *Metamorphoses*.[4] The image of the fall of Pride
was not uncommon in Gothic churches.[5] In his critique of pridefully
tall churches in the widely cited *Verbum abbreviatum* of the 1190s, Peter
the Chanter of Notre-Dame had explicitly warned against striving to be
like Daedalus: 'Non assimileris arte Daedalo in aedificando domo, non
gigantibus altitudine'.[6] We note Matthew Paris' characterization of the
architect Hugh of Goldclif as 'vir quidem fallax et falsidicus sed artifex
praeelectus' [a deceitful man and a liar, but a pre-eminent craftsman].[7]
The Peterborough Abbey chronicle ascribes the fall of the central tower
at Lincoln in 1237 to the 'builder's arrogance,' 'insolentia artificii'.[8] Even
earthbound painters could be accused, as they are in *Pictor in Carmine*, of
'nefanda presumptio' and 'licencia', 'criminal presumption' and 'licence'.[9]
Commentators of an ascetic and especially monastic turn of mind were
plentiful enough, and their targets were those who were coming to represent greedy, ambitious, devious, suspiciously able and, above all, secular
professions, including architects and art-makers.[10] Such professions were
in turn honing their own assault, theoretical and social, on ancient vested
interests.[11]

   While it would be quite wrong to claim that an age of positive consensus about the architect only dawned with the era of High Gothic – great
and favoured craftsmen had always existed – the thirteenth century does
seem to have witnessed some new thinking. Daedalus' example had long
been summoned as a measure of praiseworthy ingenuity: if any myth of
individual architectural *auctoritas* existed for medieval masons, it was
his.[12] It is difficult to see the introduction of giant labyrinths into the naves
of the great High Gothic cathedrals of France as anything other than a
sign of a deliberate defiance of the sort of thing represented by Peter the
Chanter's opprobrium, at least so far as the secular clerical corporations
were concerned. These churches, now speaking openly with a voice that

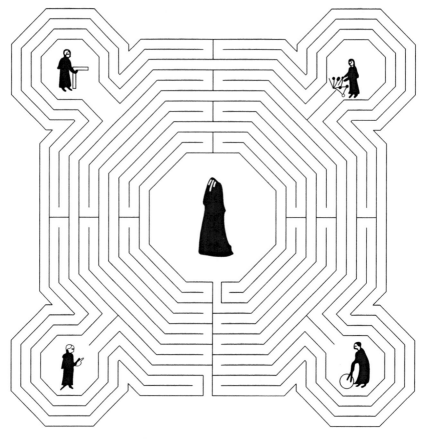

Figure 1.1 Reims cathedral, former nave floor labyrinth, after the drawing by J. Cellier (*c.* 1550–*c.* 1620), showing the cathedral's earliest masters identified in the labyrinth's inscriptions (namely Jean d'Orbais, Jean le Loup, Gaucher de Reims and Bernard de Soissons) and a central, unidentified figure

some of their members had once tried to silence, consciously deployed the labyrinth not in order to depict Theseus or the Minotaur, or for that matter Jerusalem, but rather, to judge from the only secure epigraphic evidence we have, at Reims (Figure 1.1) and Amiens (Figure 1.2) (at Amiens the labyrinth was explicitly called *le maison dedalus*), as magnificent public monuments to their architects.[13] These men were Christian 'types' for Daedalus. We note the Christian integument of meaning that could be spread over the troublesome pagan core of the story of Daedalus, as in the *Ovide Moralisé* in which Theseus' defeat of the Minotaur is interpreted as a figure of Christ's victory over Satan.[14] A metamorphosis had taken

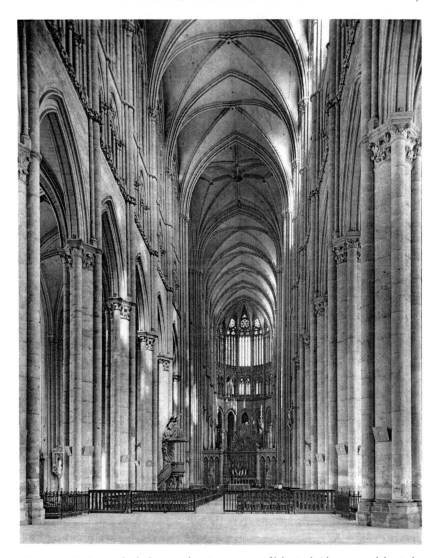

Figure 1.2 Amiens cathedral, nave, showing context of labyrinth (the present labyrinth is a modern reconstruction)

place: moral perspective was set aside, at least for the cathedral churches. No other Gothic culture in thirteenth-century Europe produced such huge and confident memorials, let alone buildings. The moderns really had outstripped the ancients, and these 'moderns' were French architects, the producers of that great export, *Opus francigenum*.[15] It is obvious that their monuments, placed in the public part of the cathedrals, constitute a proud assertion of the Church's surpassing power to command a professional resource, indeed an entire technology.

Even so, the practice of architecture enjoyed an interesting and ambivalent position for reasons other than its association with excess or devious ingenuity. One issue was, so to speak, social. The thirteenth century had inherited from the ancient and Early Christian worlds a distinction between the socially superior liberal arts and the inferior mechanical arts, between theory or science, and practice: Vitruvius (*De Architectura libri decem*) and Augustine are our witnesses, and the authority of Augustine was not superseded.[16] In regard to this ultimately classical distinction, the impression given by the sources before the thirteenth century is that craftsmen and architects were understood as being nearer to practitioners of the mechanical, i.e., manual arts. Hugh of St Victor's *Didascalicon* veers in this direction in its discussion (Book II) of the distinction between art, i.e., craft, and discipline. Thus, knowledge is an art when it consists of rules and precepts based on accumulated experience, rather than on the fixed laws of something like mathematics; rules are either a matter of opinion or experience on the one hand, or more abstract fixed certainties or truths on the other which are capable of demonstration and which are more properly indicative of knowledge as a discipline. A craft, says Hugh, requires the manipulation of a material, as in architecture, whereas abstract reasoning, as in logic, requires no such medium. Hugh's Book III groups architectural writers such as Vitruvius with authorities on agriculture, under mechanical science.[17] But there was a second, less social issue, namely the question of in virtue of what exactly a craft might be thought to operate. Here there was another, perhaps more optimistic, viewpoint: a craftsman of necessity both plans and executes, preconceives or thinks something through before making it, and so possesses a foreknowledge which is vital to the realization of his ends. Such a view of craft, *ars* or τέχνη, was entirely dignified, and its application broad. It could be taken for granted, for example, that poetry – the most discussed art – was a form of craft: poet-craft, as in Horace's *Ars Poetica*.[18] It followed from this that, throughout the Middle Ages, there was a highly respectable tradition of looking to the crafts, and to building especially, for rhetorical and epistemological models. Hugh of St Victor regarded architecture formally as a mechanical art, but also saw in building a model for memory as a mode of visualization: in this, he was heir to Quintilian and the use by the orator of mental building in composition. An idea about preconception before manufacture in the crafts originated in rhetoric and poetic theory, and it elevated the whole notion of craft, including building, as a serious mental activity. To it we will return.[19]

The twelfth and thirteenth centuries also witnessed significant changes in the way social, and especially professional, types were understood: in a number of spheres, a new discourse of the professions was emerging.[20] Issues of category before about 1250 are in part what make figures such as Elias of Dereham of Salisbury (d. 1245) so interesting, since he was evidently a polymath (administrator, *rector fabricae* and *artifex*).[21] Polymaths are hard to pin down at any time. But in a case such as his (or of Villard de Honnecourt, in some ways equally difficult to 'place'), the notion of ideas-driven specialism had as yet to find a sure foundation.[22] The age of the expert was about to dawn. In due course the architect was to switch sides. By 1300 in northern France, his position was clearer: the architect, in theory at least, possessed science (i.e., knowledge of fixed abstract principles or causes) and hence the capacity to teach; he possessed authorial responsibility; he did not get his hands dirty; and he was understood as an appropriate analogue for other aspirant professions, whether academic or lucrative. Architecture itself had grown more important in relation to the other visual arts. Figures such as Elias or Villard must by then have seemed old-fashioned.

One route to understanding how this happened was offered, albeit controversially, by Erwin Panofsky in his *Gothic Architecture and Scholasticism*: '… there exists between Gothic architecture and Scholasticism a palpable and hardly accidental concurrence in the purely factual domain of time and place'.[23] The builders of Gothic cathedrals were not likely actually to have read Gilbert de la Porrée or Thomas Aquinas, but they were exposed to 'the Scholastic point of view' in innumerable other ways, not least because they, like academics, worked within a social system 'rapidly changing toward an urban professionalism'.[24] According to this model, Gothic architecture developed a formal dialectic which aimed at the 'ultimate reconciliation of contradictory possibilities'. This dazzling technique, this intellectual magic, of reconciling the apparently irreconcilable was the same mental habit which informed academic instruction and analysis in the scholastic disputation.

Panofsky was making two related but distinguishable claims, one formal (there exists an analogical and causal relation between the *modus operandi* of formal design in Gothic and the disputation) and one sociological (the nature and standing of the architect might be understood increasingly within the context of urban professionalism). The first of these is not at all susceptible to proof; the second is more justifiable and is of more interest to us. We recall that it was Heinrich Wölfflin who noted sensibly and many years earlier (in his *Renaissance and Baroque*) that 'we still have to find the path that leads from the cell of the scholastic philosophers to the mason's yard'.[25] Social history was not really Panofsky's thing. All he offered to corroborate his contention was the caption on fol. 15 of Villard de Honnecourt's sketchbook of *c.* 1230 stating that Villard had arrived at an ideal plan for the east end of a church with Petrus de Corbeia 'inter se disputando': architecture could be the product of a schoolroom-like disputation.[26] The caption was added later in the century to the original Picard inscriptions. Panofsky has received much criticism of his thesis, not all of it justified.[27] In his search for formal congruence, however, it must be admitted that Panofsky made an error of emphasis: he set aside the fact that scholasticism (the term is imperfect and modern, and used here for convenience only) had content as well as form, substance as well as method. Yet there can be no doubt that, in regard to architects at least, he was onto something.

SCHOLASTICISM, POET-CRAFT AND THE WORDY ARCHITECT

I wish to pursue the architecture and scholasticism nexus by examining, first, the penetration of the concept of the architect (or the architectural) into scholastic and rhetorical discourse, so setting aside both Panofsky's problematic assertion about the formal implications of the scholastic 'mindset' for Gothic design, and his understanding of the relation of cause and effect. Here the substantive content of discourse matters. As A. J. Minnis has shown, in the course of the thirteenth century there was a shift to the self-conscious analysis, identification and propagation of correct form: the period became one of the 'expert' not least in academic practice.[28] Theological speculation, like secular literature, was increasingly brought under a new Aristotelian regime which displaced allegorical understanding as the central objective of study, and laid greater stress on literal meaning and 'style'. Minnis states: 'If twelfth-century exegetes had sometimes ignored stylistic considerations in their search for allegorical meanings, their successors placed a premium on the right meaning in the right literary form'.[29] Harnessed to this notion was an attendant and clearer sense of specifically human authorship, *auctoritas*. Minnis showed how a type of academic prologue that introduced Bible commentary in the schools of the mid thirteenth century came to be based on a specifically

Aristotelian theory of causality: this was known as the 'Aristotelian pro-logue', which replaced the so-called 'type-C' prologue used earlier.[30] Its theory was derived especially from commentaries on Aristotle's *Physics* and *Metaphysics*.

Aristotle had made a distinction between the efficient cause of a thing (the thing that first brings something into being), the material cause (the materials or sources used), the formal cause (that which provided, or literally informed, the thing acted upon) and the final cause (the end to which the thing was directed). For our purposes the important parts of this causal theory were the formal cause, or *causa formalis*, and the efficient cause, or *causa efficiens*. A distinction was made within the cat-egory of the efficient cause between a primary *moving* cause, and a sec-ondary *operating* cause: thus, as Guerric of St Quentin demonstrated *c.* 1240 in a commentary on Isaiah, while Isaiah was the operating cause of his writing, the Holy Spirit was the primary moving cause. The distinc-tion is fundamental, and it was known as the 'twofold efficient cause' or *duplex causa efficiens*.[31] In terms of Bible authorship it meant that God was the unmoved mover, the first *auctor*, whereas the human *auctor* was both 'moved' (by God) and 'moving' (in producing the text). Within this hierarchy of causes, human authorship was in effect analogous to divine authorship, except that it differed in relation to God's authority in being instrumental (since God cannot be moved extrinsically). Still, it was possible to see that the hierarchical relation between divine and human *auctoritas* might be rehearsed by analogy to ordinary human conditions. Though the Aristotelian scheme of causality was familiar long before – Philo uses it – the much more widespread derivation from it of analogies based on ordinary human experience was a practical achievement of the thirteenth century.[32]

The Aristotelian scheme of causality began to make its impact *c.* 1240 on theological commentary writings by Richard Fishacre at Oxford (*c.*1241–8), Robert Kilwardby (1248–61) and Guerric of St Quentin at Paris (1233–42) as well as in the circle of Alexander of Hales and Albertus Magnus.[33] But it was almost immediately evident that this powerful and versatile scheme justified its wider application, including the introduction of the word *auctor* into the discourse of the *artifex*. In his disputations held at Paris between 1276 and 1292, Henry of Ghent argued that God alone can be called the *auctor* of the science of theology. Following Aristotle's *Metaphysics* I, Henry reasoned that in the manufactured arts, in those cases where there is an art-maker or craftsman (*artifex*) who directs and regulates, and another who works by hand to put these things into effect, the *artifex* and not the manual operative is said to be the author (*auctor*) of the work. Since the true author understands underlying reasoning and principles and is able to demonstrate them to others, he alone should be called the principal author ('debet dici auctor principalis').[34] Thus, within a generation of the 1240s, it was possible to deploy an analogy from the creative arts to show how in them, as in theology, an author (art-maker or architect) was the *primary* efficient cause of a thing, and the mere mechanic or artisan the *instrumental* efficient cause. A hierarchy was envisaged which separated the form-giving originator from the form-receiving manual operator: one came up with the fundamental concept, the other was a tool which implemented it. An idea formulated for the verbal arts had jumped across to the nonverbal arts. And so it became possible in academic circles to think of authors as originators who gave form to something in 'their way', who created their own *modus tractandi* or way of treating subject matter.[35]

Though it appears to have been generally overlooked by art historians, the entry of the image of the *artifex* into scholastic theory of authorship had a corollary for the understanding of architects and art-makers themselves as *auctores*, especially because much scholastic use of the idea of the *artifex* prioritizes the example of architects. To begin its exploration, one well-known and frequently cited instance may be given. France must be grateful to Victor Mortet for rooting out texts from unexpected quarters, which would not at the time have been admitted into the debate by English architectural historians. Mortet's admirably inclusive policy placed in the domain of historians texts such as sermons. Sermons may be read in a spirit of generic expansiveness, as texts not always admitted by empiricists into the evidential domain of history. Though their audiences are not always known, in general sermons, because they follow and cannot lead, 'are the surest index of the prevailing religious feeling of their age'.[36] A sermon can only work, can only drive home rhetorically the moral point, if the similitudes or *exempla* it deploys are in some sense plausible or realistic. In his admirable survey of mendicant preaching in thirteenth-century Paris, David d'Avray makes a few revealing remarks about the preacher Nicolas de Biard (d. 1261): Biard was a mendicant, probably a Franciscan, and there are grounds for connecting this 'obscure' man to Paris.[37] His audience consisted in part of 'young secular clerics, possibly in an academic milieu' and his works were included in a *pecia* list of the Paris university stationers.[38] His use of market imagery implies a connection to the urban milieu – the 'language of the friars was permeated with a market-place vocabulary'.[39] Victor Mortet spotted part of a sermon by Biard in a short note on the expression 'Par ci le me taille', published in 1889.[40] Gaston Paris had used the sermon to suggest that this expression, of which he noted half a dozen examples, probably originated in the *ateliers* of the master masons with reference to the cutting not of cloth, but of stone. To this sermon, Mortet added a similar *distinctio* in a collection in Paris Bib. Nat. MS lat. 16490 (fol. 30) ascribed to Biard by, among others, Leopold Delisle[41]. These texts are widely cited as 'social' evidence for the status of the architect; but it is arguable that they suggest something richer. The extract from the sermon:

Magistri cementariorum, virgam et cyrothecas in manibus habentes, aliis dicunt: *Par ci me le taille*, et nihil laborant; et tamen majorem mercedem accipiunt, quod faciunt multi moderni prelati.

The master masons, holding rod and gloves in their hands, say to the others 'Here's where to cut it for me', and yet they themselves do not work; nevertheless they receive the greater fees – as do many modern Churchmen.

The *distinctio*:

Operantur aliqui solo verbo. Nota: In istis magnis aedificiis solet esse unus magister principalis qui solum ordinat ipsa verbo, raro aut numquam apponit manum, et tamen accipit majora stipendia aliis. Sic multi sunt in Ecclesia qui habent pinguia beneficia, et Deus scit quantum faciant de bono; operantur in ea solum lingua, dicentes 'Sic debetis facere' et ipsi nihil horum faciunt.

Some work by words alone. Observe: in these large buildings there is wont to be one chief master who orders matters only by word, seldom or never putting his hand to the task but who nevertheless receives higher wages than the others. So there are many in the Church who have rich benefices, and God knows how much good they do; they work with the tongue alone, saying 'Thus should you do' and they themselves do nothing.

There can be no doubt that at one level these oft-quoted sentiments are simply another friar's attack on lazy, overpaid and hypocritical clerics, presented in terms of a liberal–mechanical social split. As the schools had grown hugely in size, there arose a lively literature of estates satire by those who saw vain worldly ambition in fine dress, learnedness and leisure: Biard's *prelati moderni* (clerical upstarts?) seem to be one such target.[42] Yet the Biard texts are manifestly not solely about petty class resentment. Biard was not wholly against the feudal order or the virtuous deployment of wealth.[43] The *distinctio* is part of a miscellany including work by the connoisseur of sermons Peter of Limoges, Innocent III's *De vilitate conditionis humane*, Boethius' *De disciplina scolarium*, a *Vita Aristotelis*, *De morte Aristotelis*, *Aristotle ad Alexandrinum*, Seneca's *Exordia*, *De anathomia humani corporis* and *De studio puerorum*, suggesting a compiler engaged in some way with the severities and subtleties of paideia, and certainly a fairly highbrow, not populist, audience interested among other things in Aristotle.[44] What matters for our purposes is the implicit relation in the two passages of those who speak to those who cut. Before the thirteenth century, the notion that what architects say might matter in the creative process had little circulation: the 'dictation' of the design of a church was much more likely to be a divine prerogative. In his eleventh-century account of the building of St Augustine's at Canterbury, Goscelin mentions the *artifex* Blitherus, who was not only outstanding but in effect the notable *dictator* of the church, a usage related surely not only to his managerial station but also to his role as a 'composer' which has stylistic or poetic connotations (or, alternatively, serving as ironic comment on Blitherus as a source of 'blither' or 'blather', i.e., loquacious nonsense).[45] Biard's hierarchical image of the well-dressed authoritative man bearing his rod or ruler, presumably pointing superciliously to instruct the social inferior or mechanical, and above all working by distinctly tart words alone – we will not here speak of grandiloquence so much as of effective speaking – is, in contrast, an image of the *duplex causa efficiens* in action in thoroughly human terms. By word and indication, the act of stone-cutting is 'informed' by the words of an unmoved mover who seldom or never puts his hands to the task. Biard's understanding of cause and effect is the same as Henry of Ghent's, but Biard has added a socially telling 'spin': the architect is a 'cut above' the mere mechanic. His image is obviously not that of a scholastic or rhetor at work, but of a professional whose activity is construable in scholastic terms.

This admittedly limited instance brings us to Nikolaus Pevsner's wider study of the term 'architect' published in 1942, in which Biard's words are cited.[46] Pevsner arrived at his own Aristotelian moment with guidance from the mendicants, the Dominicans especially, who for him connected the translation and assimilation of Aristotle's *Politics* and *Metaphysics* with the eventual spread of the word 'architect' in a more modern (and more ancient) sense to Italy as well as France.[47] Panofsky did not note Pevsner's useful study; von Simson, approaching the Gothic from an unremittingly Platonic–Augustinian position, simply dismissed it.[48] Pevsner himself was presumably ignorant of the historical priority of the *accessus* literature in the Paris and Oxford schools and of the extent to which Aristotle's *Physics* and *Metaphysics* had penetrated curricular study much earlier in the thirteenth century.[49] (The relevance of the *Physics* will have been assured by Aristotle's use of the example of a builder and the art of building in exposition of his doctrine of causality.[50]) As a result, Pevsner de-scholasticized the question. Still, his focus on Aquinas helps us to arrive again at the position we have located in regard to the prologue literature. In the *Summa contra gentiles*, Aquinas defines the architect as possessing the same relation to those who work by hand as philosophy does, as a superordinate subject, in relation to other forms of knowledge. Thus superordinate subjects like philosophy are architectonic, and architects lay claim to be called wise 'architectonicae nominantur, quasi principales artes: unde et earum artifices, qui architectores vocantur, nomen sibi vindicant sapientium'.[51] Again, in his *Summa theologiae*, Thomas proceeds from Aristotle's *Ethics*, on which he commented, to form a distinction between the role of the architect and manual activity.[52] Aristotle's *Metaphysics* and *Politics* had made the same distinction in contrasting master craftsmen with servants or helpers.[53] Aquinas' commentary on the *Politics* states that the architect 'directs and commands craftsmen who work manually in the same way that a prince governs his subjects'.[54]

Thomas' position, like Biard's, takes for granted the long-held distinction between the liberal theorist and the mechanical operative, but translates it into Aristotelian terms. The extent to which any of this resulted from conscious direct allusion to the formulae of, say, Vitruvius, is questionable: in a study published in 1950, Eden for instance suggested that Aquinas' use of Vitruvius was limited to sections of the *Libri decem* which are prudential, not theoretical, relating to *phronēsis* not *epistēmē*.[55] In fact there is no need to dwell systematically on the prosaic issue of actual access to Vitruvius in the original, because Thomas' position entails a major formulation not found in Vitruvius.[56] Following Aristotle, Aquinas had in effect developed a quasi-political image of the architect as sovereign and empowered to direct and command, as *princeps* not *subditus*. Aristotle helped scholastics to understand that the 'sapiens architectus' of 1 Corinthians 3:10 also possessed the intellectual dominion enjoyed by superordinate sciences over subordinate ones: 'It is the function of the wise man to order' ('sapientis est ordinare') in Aquinas' words.[57] Here the notion of the 'subordination of the sciences', which Bonaventura, Aquinas and others developed in different ways, was fundamental.[58] The 'unmoved' architect is superordinate in virtue of his possession of science, not just craft; discipline, not just craft knowledge. In the Aristotelian dispensation (e.g., *Ethics*, VI.3) scientific knowledge is a demonstrative state, i.e., a state of mind capable of demonstrating what it knows; in regard to Aristotle's *Metaphysics*, Aquinas additionally reminds us that since science is teachable, those may teach who understand demonstrable causes.[59]

So to be an art-maker, a superior craftsman as it were, is also to enjoy a dominion over the forms proper to that particular person as an intentional agent. Such forms take shape in the mind, not in the hand. Form is a particular conceptual possession of the architect as author. Here we return to the dignified notion of the craftsman possessing foreknowledge, as in poet-craft. The *Poetria nova* of Geoffrey of Vinsauf of *c.* 1210 states: 'If one should lay the foundation of a house, his rash hand does not leap into action; an internal string of one's heart premeasures the work, and the inner person will draft the series in a particular order, and the hand of the heart rather than of the body figures the whole thing; and it is a mental rather than a physical thing ... When in the secret recess of the mind order has distributed the *res*, poetry may come to clothe the matter with words'.[60] Vinsauf's image, perfectly congruent with poet-craft and the rhetorical tradition of mental 'building', appears to echo the discussion of form in Aristotle's *Metaphysics*.[61] A similar idea to Vinsauf's is also found in the pastoral correspondence of that eminent Aristotelian, Robert Grosseteste (d. 1253).[62] Vinsauf's intent as a rhetorician is to show what invention consists of and how, with the aid of memory, it is to be attained; yet he also discloses something important about the role of invention in architecture. It is a conceptual or 'liberal' activity, a thing of the mind or the heart not the body, and as such enables an analogy to be drawn between the master builder and poet. That which is preconceived might well be nothing more than a plan. Yet when the expression *id quod bene concepi* was attributed to a thirteenth-century architect employed by the abbey of St-Trond, it seems likely that what was meant was a conception or design which was not simply correct, as in *recte loquendi*, but which was done well, *bene*, in the rhetorical sense.[63]

Rhetoric and the monastic tradition of visionary invention had therefore already suggested the possibility that master builders formed (or were granted) concepts prior to actual building.[64] Scholasticism did not create this understanding. In its Aristotelian form it achieved a sharpening or intensification of the notion of authorial responsibility, and then a generalization of it through ordinary social analogy. Scholastic comment on rhetorical theory similarly provided, in Fredborg's words, 'a widened and more precise range of arguments for the exact nature, function and means of rhetoric among the other arts and sciences'.[65] In particular, it enabled altogether larger claims to be made about master builders. First, such master builders were, in effect, a particular sort of craftsman whose power of preconception consisted not just of foreknowledge of the rules or precepts of a particular craft based on accumulated human experience,

but of knowledge of the more fixed certainties of 'science' more generally (in other words, to return to the distinction made by Hugh of St
Victor in the *Didascalicon*, knowledge as a discipline and not as an art).
Second, this power of preconception did not entail the direct manipulation of material, and was a hands-off activity in which the theoretician
was now split off from the implementer. Third, in virtue of their possession of science, master builders were analogous not only to poets but also
theologians, which is not to say that they actually were theologians, but
that their stance in relation to their operatives was proportional to that of
theologians in regard to theirs.

At this point we may at last turn Panofsky's hypothesis on its
head: what is striking about contemporary discussions is the extent to
which the image of the architect has penetrated scholastic or rhetorical
discourse. In noting (with reference to the passage cited earlier in the
Summa contra gentiles) that 'On at least one occasion a scholastic did use
an architectural metaphor to discuss intellectual matters', Erik Inglis (a
critic of Panofsky) continues with the claim that 'The absence of medieval
evidence that intellectual metaphors were applied to architecture, and the
rarity of architectural metaphors applied to thought, make it much harder
to credit Panofsky's thesis with any explanatory power'.[66] There are serious
grounds for questioning these assertions, regardless of what we conclude
about Panofsky. In the first place, the notion of building spiritually, of
ordering mentally, of 'edification' in terms of architectural metaphor was
widespread: 1 Corinthians 3:10 was itself key to the privileged notion of
the building as a structuring principle in medieval epistemology.[67] Such
currency will have been indebted in part to the use of the 'builder' image
not only in Aristotle but also, as we have already noted, in rhetoric and
poet-craft.[68] In such cases building metaphors are tropes for invention.
Scholastic use of the image of the builder or architect as an *exemplum* followed suit, and it is to be found not least in discussion of the definition
of the roles of professional groups. It occurs in Godfrey of Fontaines, in
whose discussion of the care of the physical Church the role of the theologian or cleric is subordinate at the practical level to that of the craftsman.[69] In one of his quodlibetal discussions in 1269, Aquinas, with perfect
consistency, drew an analogy between the architect and the theologian in
contrast to the ordinary priest and the jobbing builder; naturally, architects received higher wages.[70] His observation, noted earlier, that architects lay claim ('vindicant') to be called wise was therefore socially astute.
We have already drawn attention to Henry of Ghent's Aristotelian discussion of the *auctor*. Henry uses this same analogy between the architect

and masters of theology, since the architect, like the masters of theology, teaches the principles to be applied ('Architecton enim docet regulas operandorum') while the mason, like the lower clergy, merely puts the rules into effect, even though he may not understand their underlying thinking. An architect who behaved as if he were merely a stone-cutter would be worthy of reproach.[71] In the 1280s Gervase of Mont-Saint-Éloi provides us with an especially telling case: the disputation in the schools was superior to the act of preaching because disputation was 'architectonic', whereas preaching was merely operative: 'Unde ars disputaria est architectonica et predicatoria est manu operativa et ideo minus nobilis et minus meritoria, manu operativi minus merentur quam architectonici'.[72] In the light of the sentiment 'ars disputaria est architectonica' it seems at least marginally more possible that the caption 'inter se disputando', added to the ideal church plan in Villard's sketchbook, was put there by a cleric with the same sort of conception in mind.

THE ARCHITECT AS TEACHER AND MODEL PROFESSIONAL

By 1300, I suggest, schoolmen and rhetoricians had arrived at a clearer sense of the intellectual role of the master builder and of its capacity to provide analogies for other forms of creative and intellectual activity. The evidence for this lies in ordinary social comment of the sort we meet in Biard, and also in higher speculation which saw in the role of the architect to command subordinates something akin to actual teaching. Such material would have been nourishing grist to Panofsky's mill: the pathway between the scholar's cell and the mason's yard may not, in fact, be so very hard to trace for the simple reason that it is set out by the scholastics themselves. However, the steps taken here have followed it from the concept of the architect and the architectural to the scholar's cell (if cells they had), and not the other way round. Architecture, or at least the role of the architect, was 'good to think with' scholastically or rhetorically, and its impact on doctrines that are now considered 'scholastic' was demonstrably greater than the impact of those doctrines, generally considered, on actual architecture.

Yet the question arises – an important and difficult one – as to whether these developments had any practical implications at all for architects, or whether they were restricted much more narrowly to academic discourse itself.

In regard to this issue the evidence to hand is far more patchy and ambivalent, and no strong hypothesis could possibly be advanced from it about the actual station of architects in general at this time. Such material as we have for the image of the architect in the key period (let us say between *c.* 1240 and *c.* 1300) when the new discourse of authorship was establishing itself, is limited, though arguably presenting a more coherent and reasoned image of the profession than it is usually credited with. The instances are again familiar, but they remain instances rather than components of a much wider and demonstrable pattern of change. One such is the well-known incised tomb slab of the master mason of the abbey church of Saint-Nicaise at Reims, Hugues Libergier (d. 1263), now in the cathedral (Figure 1.3). Hugues was the first architect of Saint-Nicaise, begun in 1231. He probably conceived the remarkable west front and nave, and it was in the nave that his tomb was eventually placed. He was followed by Robert de Coucy who built the chevet.[73] His burial in the nave of the church near the portals is striking because *c.* 1260 such a position might be associated, as it was at Amiens, with an episcopal *fundator* such as Evrard de Fouilloy (d. 1222).[74] Evrard's tomb was to be joined around 1288 by the great labyrinth nearby. Hugues Libergier is shown on his tomb slab as a smartly dressed citizen in a coif and cape, clutching a model of the church of Saint-Nicaise to his breast as if he were indeed its *fundator*, and supporting a long staff-like ruler in his left hand; to either side are a set square and pair of dividers, the implements representing his expertise, and all around is the usual panoply of canopy and censing angels associated with noble tombs. The little church he holds is a fine exemplification of the wider purchase of the term 'patron' to include 'design': Hugues owns the design and has dominion over it because he is its *auctor*. Christopher Wilson is quite correct to argue that, though Hugues wears something very like the academic cap or *pilleus*, his tomb is a monument first to professional station, not the academic pretension one might expect from Panofsky's assertion that 'the architect himself had come to be looked upon as a kind of Scholastic'.[75] Yet it is obvious from the instruments shown on the tomb that this man is, in effect, a *sapiens* in regard to his art. These are attributes, 'regalia', symbolic representations.[76] The set square, dividers and ruler symbolize the science of geometry; the notched ruler could be said to indicate his conceptual and 'political' sovereignty as an *auctor*: together, the instruments signify the principles that regulate the act. This man possesses 'art'; but his image is very clearly not that of a don. The fact that Hugues is called *maistre* in his epitaph is incidental since the term was usual for master masons. Such tombs of teachers or academics as survive from the period invariably show the instructor with his pupils in a lecture-room context, with the teacher seated and making a speaking or teaching gesture. The Bolognese

Figure 1.3 Incised tomb slab of Hugues Libergier (d. 1263), Reims cathedral, formerly in the Abbey Church of Saint-Nicaise, Reims

instances are most well-known, while an incised slab of *c.* 1260 at Arpajon (Essonne) commemorating a schoolmaster, shows him seated in the guise of a grammarian holding a switch over a (now missing) pupil.[77] Hugues Libergier's tomb is in a sense more 'courtly' in showing a man at rest, not at work, being based on tombs of those of superior station such as Evrard de Fouilloy's.[78]

However, the epithet *doctor* is explicitly linked with the iconography of the ruler on the lost but documented tomb of the distinguished master mason Pierre de Montreuil (d. 17 March 1267) in the chapel he built at Saint-Germain-des-Prés in Paris. Like Hugues, he was accorded the right to burial in 'his' edifice. The description is given by Félibien, among others, but it is seldom given in full:

... il est figuré sur sa tombe tenant une règle & une compas à la main, avec cette epitaphe:

> Flos plenus morum vivens doctor lathomorum
> [Istius ecclesiae regis sanctaque Maria] (given by Verlet)
> Musterolo natus jacet Petrus tumulatus
> Quem rex caelorum perducat in alta polorum
> Christi milleno bis centeno duodeno cum quinquageno quarto decessit in
>   anno[79]

[he is depicted on his tomb holding a ruler and compass, with the following epitaph:

> In life a flower of courtesy, teacher of masons
> (Of this church of the King and Our Lady)
> Montreuil-born, Peter lies buried
> Whom the King of the high heavens leads above
> Who died in the year of Christ one thousand two hundred and twelve
>   and fifty-four.]

We are very familiar with the tag *doctor lathomorum* which is generally taken out of context, but not with the expression *Flos plenus morum*, which is to say that Pierre is not only *doctus* but also a gentleman, his possession of *mores* being the ethical virtue of a prudent man of social distinction. The smart garb of Hugues Libergier likewise indicates elegance of bearing. Biard's picture of the worker by words also fits. Biard's architect precisely does not work with his hands ('raro aut numquam apponit manum'): his gloves are carried, not worn, and signify wealth and social delicacy as fashion accessories.[80] 'Speaking well' will have been a recognized element in the attainment of social position and good *mores*.[81] Likewise Pierre de Montreuil is not only *doctus*, but one who, in virtue of his command of the science symbolized by his implements, may 'inform' the work of others in keeping with Henry of Ghent's notion that the architect 'teaches'. He is gentle, not horny-handed, and he is sovereign in his art. This notion of sovereign authorship prompts further thoughts

Figure 1.4 *Sapientia* directs her masons (Proverbs 9:1). Moralized Bible, Paris Bib. Nat. MS lat. 11560, fol. 46

about patronage, causes and lines of command. Biard's representation of the glove-holding architect who instructs is one shared by at least one image of a glove-clutching royal patron instructing his masons (as in the French prose Saint Graal, London, BL MS Royal 14.E.III, fol. 85v); this makes it clear that Biard's critique is at least in part one of social difference. Again, patrons issuing mandates to their architects by pointing gestures which are in turn passed on to the operatives by architects who themselves point, are surprisingly common.[82] The same line of command might be expected of other creative arts, especially 'bookish' ones. In the Paris Moralized Bible (Paris, Bib. Nat. MS lat. 11560, fol. 46) *Sapientia* herself points to a mason who hews out the seven pillars of her house

(Proverbs 9:1–5) (Figure 1.4).[83] The colophon miniature from the Toledo Moralized Bible of *c.* 1220 (New York, Pierpont Morgan Library MS. 240, fol. 8) depicts its royal patrons (above) with (below) a stern tonsured clerk pointing instructively to the implement-wielding scribe or illuminator. A similar formula is found on fol. 1 of the English fourteenth-century Holkham Bible Picture Book (London, BL MS Add. 47682) showing a Dominican handing out instructions to the scribe or illuminator.[84]

Public inscriptions commemorating architects form an important resource. One such was placed on the south transept of Notre-Dame in Paris marking the start of the work in 1257 by a named architect, Jean de Chelles, an associate of Pierre de Montreuil, as recorded by Félibien.[85] It is not impossible that such inscriptions formed part of the mini-renaissance that characterizes some important French work of the period such as the sculpted facade at Auxerre.[86] Easily the grandest statements were the now lost Reims and Amiens labyrinths (*c.* 1290? and 1288 respectively), for which these tombs and inscriptions seem like rehearsals; their inscriptions recorded either the succession of master masons (Amiens) or which masons were responsible for which part of the church (Reims).[87] These labyrinths were set down at the completion of both churches, though it is tempting to see a touch of triumphalism in their insertion only a few years after the nemesis at Beauvais in 1284, after which its choir stood in ruins. Reims was given to large-scale depictions of its distinguished personnel.[88] Both cathedrals' labyrinths harnessed an ancient mythological archetype to the ideal of the heroic architect of the Christian dispensation. Was there also a protohumanist element to this new version of the doctrine of the liberal art-maker? It is reasonable at first sight to see in the Notre-Dame inscription a response to the longer-standing Italian practice of erecting prominent texts commemorating sculptors and architects. Claussen has shown that from the twelfth century such Italian inscriptions were also starting to speak of architects or sculptors in such terms as *doctus, magistri doctissimi Romani, doctissimus in arte, doctor ... summus in arte*, and *doctus in arte*: Claussen indeed writes of 'Die Phase des akademischen Anspruchs'.[89] We should note that the term *doctor* in twelfth-century Italy appears to have been most closely associated with the Faculty of Law at Bologna, and pertained to the possession of intellectual (not mechanical) knowledge; but as an academic term denoting the ability to teach civil law, its usage really begins in the thirteenth century.[90] Indeed, as Baxandall reminds us, in regard to artists some caution may be necessary, given the semantic ambivalence of the word *doctus*: it can mean absolutely learned (i.e., possessed of science, knowledge of universal certainties), or, alternatively, learned in regard to those rules needed for a particular practice, i.e., *doctus in arte*, which is more like 'crafty' or 'cunning'.[91] This second usage seems to be common in the Italian inscriptions, and the likelihood that in such cases it was understood to have a mechanical, not necessarily a liberal, meaning is strongly suggested by the inscription about Nicola Pisano dated 1259 in Pisa stating that he possessed a '*docta manus*', i.e., a 'learned hand'.[92]

This understanding is compatible with the Italian understanding of the relation of *ars* and *scientia* implicit in the Milan cathedral chapter records as late as 1400, to which we return in a moment. The rhetoric of learnedness thus varied according to context. In that of Paris, the term 'doctor' provably did not carry a mechanical association, quite the reverse. Because scientific knowledge was demonstrative (we recall Aquinas' statement 'Signum scientiae est posse docere') the term *doctor* had obvious cultural capital in scholastic circles, and all the tendencies of the time were pointing to stricter and more jealous definitions and uses of a word associated principally in Paris, that most theological of universities, with the theologians.[93] The Dominican Peraldus in his *summa* had stressed the value of the *doctores*, whose learning 'yielded more than that of a thousand others'.[94] We saw earlier that Henry of Ghent states in absolutely Aristotelian terms (compare *Metaphysics* I.1) that the architect is one possessed of reasoned rules, who teaches. In such a context it is reasonable to suggest that the term *doctor* could only have been used with thought. But we need not go so far as to claim that Hugues Libergier or Pierre de Montreuil regarded themselves, or were regarded as, scholastics. Henry of Ghent helps us here. He sees the relation of architect to scholar-theologians as one of analogy or proportion: architects stand in the same relation to stone-cutters as masters of theology to ordinary clergy or preachers. These sovereign architects did not literally pass on scientific principles to their underlings in the same way as a scholastic teacher did to his disciples: Henry makes it clear that the stonemasons who are taught might very well not know or understand the principles derived from reason or science. But it is of course precisely this understanding that renders the architect, as a very special sort of craftsman, a 'cut above' his inferiors.

In the face of this very fragmentary evidence about actual architects at this time, we might more profitably see the connection of architecture and scholasticism in terms of the discourse or coinage relating to professional groups more generally. Our purpose is not to map a new, academically driven, conceptual scheme onto the social reality of the architect, but instead to consider a subtler form of engagement at a time when French architecture enjoyed European supremacy. To what extent were concepts of the professions actually coming to be coloured, even shaped, by academic language and by the power of repeatedly drawn analogies between such professions and thinkers? Were the conspicuous signs of social promotion evident on the few memorials we have in part a function of a new recognition of the station of the architect as a 'model' professional possessed of *scientia* who thereby could make claims, albeit ones of very uncertain practical consequences? The term *doctor* emerges as of interest at least in part because of its capacity to act as a mediating term between different spheres of professional activity, in specific contexts. One might think of emergent 'para-academic' features. Practically speaking too, patrons of major master builders will undoubtedly have been interested in their standing as creators, and in the possibility that their claims to possess a *personal* style, conferring advantages in the 'market', might have had some theoretical substance.

We might examine this notion of mediation by considering the view of the architectural profession adopted by other aspirant professions in France at this time. The masters of theology, as discussed by Ian Wei, formed one such profession.[95] Others were medicine and surgery. We note in passing that the term *doctor* in Paris spread from the practitioners of theology to those of law and medicine in the thirteenth century.[96] Medicine is an especially interesting case. Though architectural practice is often associated with the term 'mystery', medicine differed in principle because it dealt with people and disease, not buildings, and ideally possessed interpersonal charisma, as in theory it still should. Like architecture, medicine had been squeezed into the binary mechanical–liberal divide (again, on the mechanical side) by Hugh of St Victor in his *Didascalicon*, but it is obvious from John of Salisbury's critique of the verbosity of doctors that, as with architects, wordiness here too was a symptom of an inherent disdain for manual work on the part of an up-and-coming profession that regarded itself as 'liberal' and possessing charismatic authority.[97] In fact this disdain worked itself out in the course of the thirteenth century as medicine and surgery split across the liberal and mechanical duality. In his celebrated treatise on surgery, Henri de Mondeville (died *c.* 1320) implicitly recognized the 'turn to theory' on the part of medical elites, and engaged in a form of estates satire of the type we meet in Biard, in which loquacious doctors (not surgeons) 'know nothing and do nothing except talk at their patients'.[98] Mondeville maintained that in order for the surgeon to rise professionally, he would have to reconcile theory and practice within himself, and become an *artifex scientificus* in contrast to those who merely 'cut' mechanically, like tailors and furriers (or, we might add, stonemasons).[99] The thinking is again like that of Aquinas, since in Petrus de Alvernia's continuation of the commentary on the *Politics* we read in connection with the practice of medicine that the *artifex principalis* understands all causes and principles.[100] Mondeville does not appear to consider building a science. Nevertheless Pouchelle observes that, in terms of professional analogy, 'Mondeville's favourite model is the architect' because (and we have already met this in Vinsauf) the architect can conceive a plan of action prior to its execution.[101] The lucrative art of medicine provides an analogy for our model of the definition of the architect as a professional, which was clearly not free of the stresses and strains of social ambition and mobility.

ORDINATIO, DISPOSITIO AND 'ACADEMIC' STYLE

Near the start of Aristotle's *Rhetoric* a connection is made between rhetoric and such arts as medicine and geometry, because they can instruct or persuade about their own subject matter.[102] Since at least the twelfth century (e.g., Gundissalinus' *De divisione philosophiae*), geometry had been annexed on Aristotelian lines to the sphere of teachable theory prior to its implementation in practice.[103] Though a practical affair for masons, geometry as an art or science clearly had an elective affinity with its academic quadrivial counterpart (Villard refers to 'li ars de iometrie', Hans Schmuttermayer to 'diser hohen und freyen kunst', and the English Cooke manuscript to the 'worthy sciens of Gemetry').[104] Its discipline, based on certitude of causes, established the fundamental ordering of a plan, section or elevation. Biard in his *distinctio* uses the word *ordinare* to describe what a master mason does in regard to the establishment of these fundamentals. The term was part of the Vitruvian tradition: *ordinatio* was the first term of architecture and was achieved through quantity, the establishment of modules, a preliminary geometrical grid or matrix. It derived ultimately from the warp of the loom, though it carried the senses both of orderliness and 'soundness'.[105] Its aim was to establish a satisfactory relation of part to whole in any aspect of architecture. The English fourteenth-century Dominican John Bromyard in his *Summa* used the terms *ordinatio* and *dispositio* to refer to the setting-out of a cloister as the foundation of its (moral and spiritual) beauty.[106] Here the influence of the 'prescriptive dynamic of Ciceronian *dispositio*' in the *artes praedicandi* will be evident.[107] The term *dispositio* (the second of the five canons of rhetoric) in architectural language presumably came from the post-Vitruvian divisions of architecture proposed by Isidore of Seville (i.e., *dispositio, constructio, venustas*) which showed strong affinity with rhetorical compositional procedure, though it should be noted that Vitruvius too uses the term.[108] In rhetoric the terms were sometimes interchangeable, and according to Nims, Vinsauf uses *ordo* not *dispositio* only for metrical reasons.[109]

Illuminated books too necessitated a form of *ordinatio*, namely the grid of ruling on a page preparatory for script (the term itself was used with reference to monumental inscriptions in the ancient world).[110] The Toledo Moralized Bible colophon page mentioned earlier shows the scribe or illuminator poised to mark a ruled page, presumably following the *ordinatio* of the pointing advisor. But in the realm of the scholastic book especially, *ordinatio* entailed something more ambitious than just design. Malcolm Parkes has shown that by the thirteenth century *ordinatio* referred to the logical ordering of information on a page in terms of the nature of the subject to be studied, and as an aspect of the formal cause or *forma tractatus* of a work.[111] Kilwardby had stated in his *Notule super Priscianum*, that the 'Causa formalis consistit in modo agendi et in ordinatio partium doctrine', and 'In such circumstances', concludes Parkes (in, we note, Panofskian vein) 'the structure of reasoning came to be reflected in the physical appearance of books': books, chapters, *quaestiones, distinctiones*, running titles, tables of contents, alphabetical indices and so on.[112] This too was a means of establishing a coherent and self-evident relationship of part to whole. We find the term used in the sacrist's rolls at Ely cathedral in the 1320s with reference to the setting out of the *novum opus* there, and in the planning of wall paintings, as in the case of painters working 'ad ordinandum ... diversis historiis' in the Palace of Westminster in 1307–8.[113] The term clearly had a range of meanings, from the workaday to the highbrow, and there is no evidence that an elevated, scholastic doctrine of *ordinatio partium* necessarily formed part of the routine discourse of a mason or art-maker at this time, though so far as paintings are concerned it is interesting to note that in a tradition going back to the *Rhetorica ad Herennium* (III.9.17) the term *ordo* was commonest in relation to narrative order.

Still, it might be worth exploring the potential of the concepts of *ordinatio* or *dispositio* to illuminate architectural styles that manifestly placed exceptional emphasis *as styles* on the strict controlling matrix of the vertical and horizontal tracery grid, and the use of the detailed preparatory drawings which mediated between architects and patrons. The obvious instance is the 'academic' style of Rayonnant which emerged in Paris in the 1230s (Figure 1.5) in tandem with the new professional discourse of the architect, and which gained European supremacy towards 1300. French Rayonnant was par excellence the style of a dry, overarching, integrative *ordinatio* whose unitary character established an absolutely coherent and measured relation of whole to part, and the subordination of the related arts, especially stained glass and sculpture, to the sovereign stature of architecture and to the architect as impresario of these arts. Jean Bony writes of a stiffening of 'Rayonnant orthodoxy' and the 'academic codification' of Rayonnant forms in French architecture towards 1300, Wilson of a 'creative sclerosis' in which French architects had become 'upholders of a tradition which had attained perfection'.[114] The notion of the professional sovereignty of architects which emerged in France at this time is in keeping with this analysis. The dialectic between a strict *ordinatio* of the sort practised in France and the traditional virtues (rhetorical, theological, etc.) of a flexible openended *varietas* which formed part of *venustas*, the eloquent clothing of architectural form typical of English architecture of the same period, is arguably constitutive of the dynamic of much late medieval Gothic architecture in Europe as a whole.

Finally, we consider some thoughts and hypotheses. First, key to our discussion of the emergent French professional discourse of the architect as a *magister, doctor* or *artifex scientificus* is the relationship between science (that which possesses certitude and which is teachable), loquacity and the words which teach, and the 'moved' operator or implementer who is inarticulate or 'uninformed' without the shaping guidance of one sovereign in his art. We are not suggesting that the eloquence of the master builder consisted of anything like rhetorical high art; in the first instance, its role was to pass on the results of that which was knowable (*scientia*) to those charged with implementation. 'Speaking well' will have been an aspect of professional expertise and social promotion.[115] It must have had a major role in regard to patrons: such eloquence not only passed on that which was knowable, but rendered compelling that which was as yet unknown, because unbuilt. Eloquence was thus a form of *representation* of that which had yet to be realized and in which faith had to be placed, namely the gigantic capital investment entailed by a great building. Should the notion that master masons were 'dictators', possessed of eloquence in the sense of originating 'style,' prompt us to look more closely at the (pre-scholastic?) persuasiveness of William of Sens at Canterbury, or even – to fly a kite – at the (post-scholastic?) family name of one of the great dynasties of central European architects of the late Middle Ages, namely Parler: had the notion of eloquence become a dynastic label?[116]

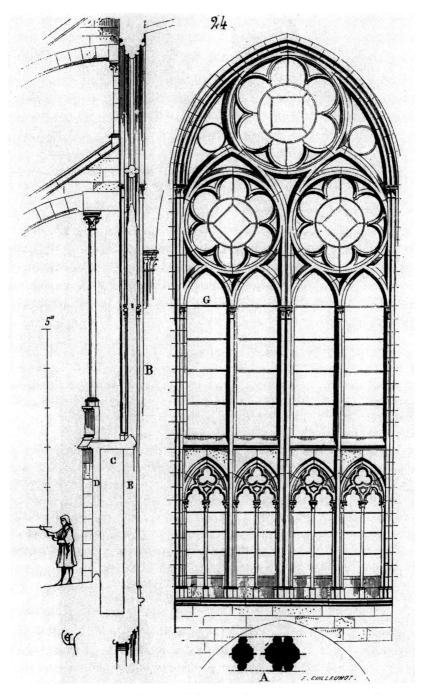

Figure 1.5 Saint-Denis, triforium and clerestory, showing strict Rayonnant *ordinatio*, including 'linkage' of elements by mullions, designed *c.* 1231

Second, in practical terms, did the implicit social and intellectual separation of the master from the mechanic not encourage the emergence
of what we might call 'theoretical oversight', i.e., the remote controlling
of more than one architectural project by a 'hands-off' master architect
relying on deputies on site who were themselves sufficiently eloquent and
versed in routine methods of construction to pass on his concept?[117] Third,
was the rise of 'legalistic' notions of the human *auctor* which entailed an
idea of authorial responsibility in any way related to the practice, much
more fully documented from the second half of the thirteenth century, of
issuing contracts to artists or architects?[118]

And finally, what was the basis of the doctrine expressed (gnomically, as
recorded in cathedral chapter minutes) by the Parisian expert Jean Mignot,
namely 'ars sine scientia nihil est', which he offered as a retort to Milanese
pragmatism during the contentious chapter debate at Milan cathedral in
January 1400?[119] Was Ackerman correct to suggest that this embodied
a French Platonic or Augustinian theory about the absolute primacy of
geometrical form, to which the Milanese responded with their own, half-
baked, Aristotelianism? Or was Mignot in fact stating no more than that
ars (i.e., the *technē* of *Ethics*, VI.4) must be informed by the demonstrable
principles and causes (i.e., *epistēmē*) which constitute *scientia* (geometry
especially), so being, in effect, a good Aristotelian? *Scientia* was an important term in scholarly discourse; and it seems at least possible that Mignot
was appealing to a scholar's sense of intellectual order in claiming scientific
status for his art. In this sense, his utterance could ultimately bear the
stamp of the schools of Paris.[120] It is interesting to learn that he was eventually dismissed by the duke of Milan for arrogance and insubordination.

Much in this essay is necessarily tentative, and concerns an emergent
realm of ideas and language rather than a demonstrable revolution in the
practical activity of architects. It is no part of the present case to suggest that the conceptual shift I have mentioned was understood widely, or
implemented seriously, in northern Europe at this time, though I would
suggest its future in Italy after 1300 was considerable. Yet in the long run
ideas and language matter. It has been well said that 'The clearest sign
that a society has entered into the self-conscious possession of a new concept is ... that a new vocabulary comes to be generated, in terms of which
the concept is then articulated and discussed'.[121] Whatever the *concept* of
the architect may have been earlier in the Middle Ages, I have argued
here, doubtless unfashionably, that a new *conception*, and an attendant
and reinforcing coinage, emerged in mid thirteenth-century French academic and professional culture as to the nature and capacity of architects

as a result of the development of ideas more generally, not least in regard to a sharpening of definition of what professional roles were. It is not coincidental that this way of thinking developed at a time when architecture began to enjoy supreme authority as the source of design in all media. The question 'Was Panofsky absolutely right or wrong?' has distracted us from a different and perhaps more important issue, namely whether the notion that a 'scientific' architect, in whom theory and practice were reconciled, owed its particular formulation in Gothic France in the period 1250–1300 to ideas that were Aristotelian in character and scholastic in formulation. All this will have been enhanced by the actual splendour of the Gothic style and by the increasing socio-professional status of its conceivers. It may also, I suggest, have provided a new language for eventually recuperating the ancient concept of the liberally educated architect combining *ratiocinatio* and *fabrica* as formulated by Vitruvius and reiterated in the preface of Alberti's *De re aedificatoria*.[122] Scholasticism was not useless in this process, for Paris, in this regard at least, had anticipated Florence.

NOTES

* Aspects of this paper were first presented in one of the Oxford University Slade Lectures delivered in 2007. I am extremely grateful to Professor Paul Crossley, Professor Marvin Trachtenberg and Dr Noël Sugimura for reading an earlier draft with the greatest thoroughness and for providing numerous references. I am indebted to Dr Annabel Brett and particularly to Dr Ian Wei for guidance on matters scholastic, and to Professor Martin Kemp for stimulating thoughts in my mind about the relationship between architecture and medicine. I owe a great debt to Mary Carruthers for many editorial suggestions.

1 A. Murray, *Reason and Society in the Middle Ages* (Oxford University Press, 1978), 21.

2 C. Rudolph, *The 'Things of Greater Importance.' Bernard of Clairvaux's* Apologia *and the Medieval Attitude Toward Art* (Philadelphia: University of Pennsylvania Press, 1990), 278–85.

3 *Historical Works of Gervase of Canterbury*, ed. W. Stubbs, 2 vols., Rolls Series 73 (London: Longmans, 1879–80), vol. I, 20.

4 Ovid, *Metamorphoses V–VIII*, ed. and trans. D.E. Hill (Warminster: Aris and Phillips, 1992), 112–13, line 215.

5 W. Sauerländer, *Gothic Sculpture in France 1140–1270*, trans. J. Sondheimer (London: Thames & Hudson, 1992), plate 125, third col. bottom (Chartres cathedral, south portal); copied by Villard de Honnecourt, see H. R. Hahnloser, *Villard de Honnecourt – Kritische Gesamtausgabe des Bauhüttenbuches, ms. fr 19093 der Pariser Nationalbibliothek* (Vienna: A. Schroll, 1935), plate 6 and figures 50–1.

6 Petrus Cantor, *Verbum abbreviatum*, PL 205, col. 258.

7 H. T. Riley (ed.), *Gesta abbatum monasterii Sancti Albani*, 3 vols., Rolls Series, 28 (London: Longmans, 1867–9), vol. I, 218–20, at 218; the episode is discussed by X. Muratova, '"Vir quidem fallax et falisidicus, sed artifex praeelectus": Remarques sur l'image sociale et littéraire de l'artiste au moyen âge', in X. Barral I Altet (ed.), *Artistes, artisans et production artistique au Moyen Age*, 3 vols. (Paris: Picard, 1986), vol. I, 53–72; and by P. Binski, *Becket's Crown. Art and Imagination in Gothic England 1170–1300* (New Haven: Yale University Press, 2004), 46–51.

8 O. Lehmann-Brockhaus, *Lateinische Schriftquellen zur Kunst in England, Wales und Schottland vom Jahre 901 bis zum Jahre 1307*, 5 vols. (Munich: Prestel, 1955–60), no. 2,407: *Ruina ecclesiae Lincolniensis, propter artificii insolentiam.*

9 M. R. James, 'Pictor in Carmine', *Archaeologia*, 94 (1950) [2nd series 44]: 141–66, at 142.

10 Binski, *Becket's Crown*, 43–51; for critiques of clerical vanity in France, see K. H. Tachau, 'God's Compass and *Vana Curiositas*: Scientific Study in the Old French *Bible Moralisée*', *Art Bulletin*, 90 (1998): 7–33, 22–7.

11 I am generally indebted to Murray, *Reason and Society*.

12 See for example P. C. Claussen, 'Früher Künstlerstolz: Mittelalterliche Signaturen als Quelle der Kunstsoziologie', in K. Clausberg, D. Kimpel *et al.* (eds.), *Bauwerk und Bildwerk im Hochmittelalter* (Giessen: Anabas, 1981), 7–34, at 17–18; Lehmann-Brockhaus, *Lateinische Schriftquellen*, nos. 4,691, 4,694, 4,841.

13 Among the more useful general studies are: P. R. Doob, *The Idea of the Labyrinth: From Classical Antiquity through the Middle Ages* (Ithaca, NY: Cornell University Press, 1990); C. Wright, *The Maze and the Warrior: Symbols in Architecture, Theology and Music* (Cambridge, MA: Harvard University Press, 2001); H. Kern, *Through the Labyrinth: Designs and Meanings over 5,000 Years* (Munich; London: Prestel, 2000). The arguments assembled by Wright against the 'pilgrimage' hypothesis seem conclusive, though the idea is reiterated unconvincingly by D. K. Connolly, 'At the Center of the World: The Labyrinth Pavement of Chartres Cathedral', in S. Blick and R. Tekippe (eds.), *Art and Architecture of Late Medieval Pilgrimage in Northern Europe and the British Isles*, 2 vols. (Leiden: Brill, 2005), vol, I, 285–314. For Reims and Amiens see, *inter alia*, L. Paris, 'Notice sur le dédale au Labyrinthe de l'Église de Reims', *Bulletin Monumental*, 22 (1856): 540–51; R. Branner, 'The Labyrinth of Reims Cathedral', *Journal of the Society of Architectural Historians*, 21 (1962): 18–25; S. Murray, *Notre-Dame, Cathedral of Amiens: The Power of Change in Gothic* (Cambridge University Press, 1996), 78–9, 85–6, 128–9 (Appendix A, no. 2), 212 nn. 1–2; Kern, *Through the Labyrinth*, 149–50, 160–1. The Minotaur appears at the centre of the labyrinth in the *Liber Floridus* MS in Ghent, A. Derolez (ed.), *Lamberti S. Audomari Canonici, Liber Floridus* (Ghent: In aedibus Story-Scientia, 1968), 41 (fol. 20); A. Derolez, *Liber Floridus Colloquium* (Ghent: E. Story-Scientia, 1973), 21, 26 n. 46.

14 The literature is extensive: see *Ovide moralisé, poème du commencement du quatorzième siècle, publié d'apres tous les manuscrits connus,* ed. C. de Boer and M. G. de Boer and J. Th. M. van 't Sant, Verhandelingen der Koninklijke Akademie van Wetenschappen Afdeling Letterkunde, n.s. 30 (Amsterdam: J. Müller, 1931), 109–213 (Book VIII); *Ovide moralisé en prose (texte du quinzième siècle),* ed. C. de Boer Verhandelingen der Koninklijke Nederlandse Akademie van Wetenschappen, Afdeling Letterkunde 61..2 (Amsterdam: J. Müller, 1954), 227–9; E. Panofsky, *Renaissance and Renascences in Western Art* (Stockholm: Almqvist and Wiksell, 1960), 75–8, 78 n. 2; N. Rudd, 'Daedalus and Icarus (i) From Rome to the end of the Middle Ages', in Charles Martindale (ed.), *Ovid Renewed: Ovidian Influences on Literature and Art from the Middle Ages to the Twentieth Century* (Cambridge University Press, 1988), 21–35.

15 R. Branner, *St Louis and the Court Style in Gothic Architecture* (London: Zwemmer, 1965), I, 112–37.

16 Vitruvius, *Ten Books on Architecture,* ed. T. N. Howe, trans. I. D. Rowland, (Cambridge University Press, 1999); O. G. von Simson, *The Gothic Cathedral: Origins of Gothic Architecture and the Medieval Concept of Order* (New York: Harper & Row, 1956), 21–58. See also the survey in R. Suckale, 'La théorie de l'architecture au temps des cathédrales', in R. Recht (ed.), *Les Batisseurs des Cathédrales Gothiques* (Strasbourg: Édition Les Musées de la Ville de Strasbourg, 1989), 41–50.

17 *The Didascalicon of Hugh of St Victor,* trans. J. Taylor (New York: Columbia University Press, 1961), 84; cf. also Giraldus Cambrensis, *Liber de principis instructione,* in Lehmann-Brockhaus, *Lateinische Schriftquellen,* no. 5,131.

18 See the penetrating discussion in R. G. Collingwood, *The Principles of Art* (Oxford University Press, 1938), 15–41.

19 M. J. Carruthers, *The Book of Memory: A Study of Memory in Medieval Culture* (Cambridge University Press, 1990), 43–5, 122–55; M. J. Carruthers, *The Craft of Thought: Meditation, Rhetoric, and the Making of Images, 400–1200* (Cambridge University Press, 1998), 221–76.

20 The literature on this issue is extensive and I am grateful to Ian Wei for advising me about it, not least in regard to the evidence of *ad status* preaching. See P. Michaud-Quantin, 'Le vocabulaire des catégories sociales chez les canonistes et les moralistes du XIIIᵉ siècle', in D. Roche and E. C. Labrousse (eds.), *Ordres et Classes: Colloque d'Histoire Sociale. Saint-Cloud 24–25 mai 1967* (Paris: Mouton, 1973), 73–92, at 82–5; D. L. D'Avray and M. Tausche, 'Marriage Sermons in *ad status* Collections of the Central Middle Ages', *Archives d'Histoire Doctrinale et Littéraire du Moyen Age,* 47 (1980): 71–119, at 71–5; G. Constable, *Three Studies in Medieval Religious and Social Thought* (Cambridge University Press, 1995), 329–31; C. Muessig, 'Audience and Preacher: *ad status* Sermons and Social Classification', in C. Muessig (ed.), *Preacher, Sermon and Audience in the Middle Ages* (Leiden: Brill, 2002), 255–76.

21 A. Hastings, *Elias of Dereham, Architect of Salisbury Cathedral* (Much Wenlock: R. J. L. Smith and Associates, 1997); N. Vincent, 'Master Elias of Dereham (d. 1245): A Reassessment', in C. M. Barron and J. Stratford (eds.), *The Church and Learning in Later Medieval Society: Essays in Honour of R. B. Dobson*, Harlaxton Medieval Studies 11 (Stamford: Shaun Tyas, 2002), 128–59.

22 For an 'aristotelianized' Villard, see J. Bugslag, '"Contrefais al vif": Nature, Ideas and Representation in the Lion Drawings of Villard de Honnecourt', *Word & Image*, 17 (2001): 360–78. Bugslag comments, at 374: 'Secular professionalism was another contested practice of the age, and Villard's social position may appear so uncertain to us exactly because clearly defined social paradigms and values had not yet encompassed it.'

23 E. Panofsky, *Gothic Architecture and Scholasticism* (New York: Meridian Books, 1951), 2.

24 *Ibid.*, 24.

25 H. Wölfflin, *Renaissance and Baroque*, trans. Kathrin Simon (London: Collins, 1964), 76–7; M. Podro, *The Critical Historians of Art* (New Haven: Yale University Press, 1982), 100.

26 Hahnloser, *Villard de Honnecourt*, 69–72, 195–8, plate 29a: 'Istud bresbiterium invenerunt Ulardus de Hunecourt et Petrus de Corbeia inter se disputando'; Panofsky, *Gothic Architecture and Scholasticism*, 87–8, 108 n. 62.

27 See P. Frankl (rev. P. Crossley), *Gothic Architecture* (New Haven: Yale University Press, 2000), 295–7; summaries and recent critiques are E. Inglis, 'Gothic Architecture and a Scholastic: Jean de Jandun's *Tractatus de laudibus Parisius* (1323)', *Gesta*, 42 (2003): 63–85; R. Branner, 'A Note on Gothic Architecture and Scholars', *Burlington Magazine*, 99 (1957): 372–5; C. M. Radding and W. W. Clark, *Medieval Architecture, Medieval Learning: Builders and Masters in the Age of Romanesque and Gothic* (New Haven: Yale University Press, 1992).

28 A. J. Minnis, *Medieval Theory of Authorship*, 2nd edn (Aldershot: Wildwood House, 1988), 85.

29 *Ibid.*, 131.

30 *Ibid.*, 15–33, 73–159.

31 *Ibid.*, 76–9.

32 C. Whitehead, *Castles of the Mind: A Study of Medieval Architectural Allegory* (Cardiff: University of Wales Press, 2003), 9.

33 Minnis, *Medieval Theory of Authorship*, 78–9.

34 *Ibid.*, 81, after Henry of Ghent, *Summae Quaestionum Ordinarium*, 2 vols. (Paris, 1520), fols. 71^r–71^v (*art. 9 qu.* 2): '... in artificialibus ubi est unus artifex qui opus dirigit et regulat, et alius manu operans secundam regulas ab artifice traditas, manu operans non dicit auctor operis, sed artifex'.

35 For the *modus tractandi*, see Minnis, *Medieval Theory of Authorship*, 29, 119–45; see also R. H. Rouse and M. A. Rouse, '*Statim invenire*: Schools, Preachers, and New Attitudes to the Page', in R. L. Benson and G. Constable

(eds.), *Renaissance and Renewal in the Twelfth Century* (Oxford: Clarendon Press, 1982), 201–25, at 224.

36 D. L. D'Avray, *The Preaching of the Friars: Sermons Diffused from Paris before 1300* (Oxford University Press, 1985), 259 (citing M. Pattison).

37 *Ibid.*, 161–2; for his Franciscan identity, B. Hauréau, *Notices et extraits de quelques manuscrits latins de la Bibliothèque Nationale*, 6 vols. (Paris: Klincksieck, 1891), vol. 2, 91, after Paris, Bib. Nat. MS lat. 12419, fol. 120.

38 D'Avray, *Preaching of the Friars*, 113–14, 280; M. W. Bloomfield *et al.* (eds.), *Incipits of Latin Works on the Virtues and Vices, 1100–1500 A.D.* (Cambridge, MA: Medieval Academy of America, 1979), 168–9, no. 1,841.

39 D'Avray, *Preaching of the Friars*, 211; see B. H. Rosenwein and L. K. Little, 'Social Meaning in Monastic and Mendicant Spiritualities', *Past and Present*, 63 (1974): 4–32, at 23–31.

40 G. Paris, 'Par ci le me taille', *Romania*, 18 (1889): 288–9; V. Mortet, 'La maîtrise d'ouevre dans les grandes constructions du XIIIᵉ siècle et la profession d'appareilleur', *Bulletin Monumental*, 70 (1906): 263–70, at 267–8; V. Mortet, *Recueil de textes relatifs à l'histoire de l'architecture et à la condition des architeectes en France au moyen âge*, 2 vols. (Paris: Picard, 1911–29), vol. II, 290–1, no. cxxxvii, 1.

41 Mortet, *Recueil*, vol. II, 290–1, no. cxxxvii, 2; L. Delisle, *Inventaire des manuscrits de la Sorbonne conservés à la Bibliothèque Impériale* (Paris: A. Durand, P. Lauriel, 1870), p. 62, nos. 15,176–16,718.

42 Murray, *Reason and Society*, 213–33; for the *prelati* see P. Frankl, *The Gothic: Literary Sources and Interpretations through Eight Centuries* (Princeton University Press, 1960), 135–6 n. 56.

43 D'Avray, *Preaching of the Friars*, 215–16, 219–20.

44 Delisle, *Inventaire*, 62.

45 Lehmann-Brockhaus, *Lateinische Schriftquellen*, no. 703; E. R. Curtius, *European Literature and the Latin Middle Ages*, trans. W. R. Trask, Bollingen Series, 36 (Princeton University Press, 1953), 75–76, 'ars dictaminis.'

46 N. Pevsner, 'The Term "Architect" in the Middle Ages', *Speculum*, 17 (1942): 549–62, Biard cited at 561.

47 *Ibid.*, 559–62.

48 von Simson, *Gothic Cathedral*, 30–1.

49 Minnis, *Medieval Theory of Authorship*, 29.

50 Aristotle, *Physics*, II.3195b, 22–5; see J. Barnes (ed.), *The Complete Works of Aristotle*, 2 vols., Bollingen Series 71.2 (Princeton University Press, 1984), vol. I, 334.

51 Thomas Aquinas, *Summa contra Gentiles*, I.1 ('Quod sit officium sapientis'), in *Corpus Thomisticum*, ed. E. Alarcón, (website), 2000–7, www.corpusthomisticum.org; Pevsner, 'The Term "Architect"', 559–60. Thomas surely sees the claim (*vindicia*) to be called wise as a legitimate consequence of the standing of 'architectonic' subjects; cf. however Frankl, *The Gothic*, 135, who (inexplicably) considers it surprising.

52 Aristotle, *Nicomachean Ethics*, VI.8 (Barnes (ed.), *Aristotle*, vol. II, 1,802–3); Thomas Aquinas, *Summa theologiae*, II.2, *quaestio* 47, art. 12: 'Unde manifestum est quod prudentia quidem in principe est ad modum artis architectonicae, ut dicitur in VI Ethic., in subditis autem ad modum artis manu operantis', in *Corpus Thomisticum*.

53 Aristotle, *Metaphysics*, I.1; *Politics*, I.4 (Barnes (ed.), *Aristotle*, vol. II, 1,553, 1,989); Pevsner, 'The Term "Architect"', 560.

54 Thomas Aquinas, *Sententia libri Politicorum*, I, *lectio* 10, no. 10: 'Sicut enim principalis artifex dirigit et imperat ministris artis qui manu operantur, ita princeps dirigit suos subiectos', in *Corpus Thomisticum*.

55 W. A. Eden, 'St. Thomas Aquinas and Vitruvius', *Mediaeval and Renaissance Studies*, 2 (1950): 183–5.

56 For Vitruvius manuscripts, see C. H. Krinsky, 'Seventy-Eight Vitruvius Manuscripts', *Journal of the Warburg and Courtauld Institutes*, 30 (1967): 36–70; few date to the thirteenth century, none coming from Paris in that period; also Frankl, *The Gothic*, 86–103.

57 For 1 Corinthians 3:10, see Pevsner, 'The Term "Architect"', 550, 554; Minnis, *Medieval Theory of Authorship*, 146.

58 Minnis, *Medieval Theory of Authorship*, 146.

59 Thomas Aquinas, *Sententia Metaphysicae*, I, *lectio* 1, no. 29 [81595]: 'Sicut igitur signum caliditatis est quod possit aliquid calefacere, ita signum scientis est, quod possit docere, quod est scientiam in alio causare. Artifices autem docere possunt, quia cum causas cognoscant, ex eis possunt demonstrare' (cf. *Sententia libri Ethicorum*, VI.3, no. 6 [73851]), in *Corpus Thomisticum*.

60 M. F. Nims, *Poetria Nova of Geoffrey of Vinsauf* (Toronto: IMS, 1967), 16–17; for the text as adapted here, see M. J. Carruthers, 'The Poet as Master Builder: Composition and Locational Memory in the Middle Ages', *New Literary History*, 24 (1993): 881–95, at 889.

61 Aristotle, *Metaphysics*, VII.1,032a–34a; *Physics,* II.3.195b (Barnes (ed.), *Aristotle*, vol. II, 1,630–1, also vol. I, 334).

62 Lehmann-Brockhaus, *Lateinische Schriftquellen*, no. 5,086 (Grosseteste to Master Adam Rufus): 'Imaginare itaque in mente artificis, artificii fiendi formam, utpote in mente architecti, formam et similitudinem domus fabricandae, ad quam formam et exemplar solummodo respicit, ut ad eius imitationem domus faciat.'

63 C. Wilson, *The Gothic Cathedral* (London: Thames & Hudson, 1990), 142.

64 Carruthers, 'Poet as Master Builder'; for the divine dictation of a plan or design, see C. Rudolph, 'Building-Miracles as Artistic Justification in the Early and Mid-Twelfth Century', in Wolfgang Kersten (ed.), *Radical Art History: internationale Anthologie. Subject: O. K. Werckmeister* (Zurich: ZIP, 1997), 398–410.

65 K. M. Fredborg, 'The Scholastic Teaching of Rhetoric in the Middle Ages', *Cahiers de l'Institut du Moyen-Âge Grec et Latin*, 55 (1987): 85–105, at 89. See also K. M. Fredborg, 'Rhetoric and Dialectic', in V. Cox and J. O. Ward

(eds.), *The Rhetoric of Cicero in its Medieval and Early Renaissance Commentary Tradition* (Leiden: Brill, 2006), 165–92.

66 Inglis, 'Gothic Architecture and a Scholastic', 76–7.

67 An important pointer is H. de Lubac, *Exégèse médiévale: les quatre sens de l'écriture*, Part II, vol. II Théologie 59 (Paris: Aubier, 1962), 41–60; for specialist studies, see R. D. Cornelius, 'The Figurative Castle: A Study in the Medieval Allegory of the Edifice with Especial Reference to Religious Writings', unpublished PhD thesis, Bryn Mawr College, 1930; Carruthers, *Book of Memory*, 122–55; B. E. Kurtz, 'The Small Castle of the Soul: Mysticism and Metaphor in the European Middle Ages', *Studia Mystica*, 15 (1992): 19–39; J. Mann, 'Allegorical Buildings in Mediaeval Literature', *Medium Aevum*, 63 (1994): 191–210; Carruthers, *Craft of Thought*; D. J. Cowling, *Building the Text: Architecture as Metaphor in Late Medieval and Early Modern France* (Oxford University Press, 1998); L. F. Sandler, 'John of Metz, The Tower of Wisdom', in M. J. Carruthers and J. Ziolkowski (eds.), *The Medieval Craft of Memory: An Anthology of Texts and Pictures* (Philadelphia: University of Pennsylvania Press, 2002), 215–25; Whitehead, *Castles of the Mind*; A. Wheatley, *The Idea of the Castle in Medieval England* (York Medieval Press, 2004).

68 Quintilian, *Inst. Orat.*, VII, Proem., 1.

69 I. P. Wei, 'The Self-Image of the Masters of Theology at the University of Paris in the Late Thirteenth and Early Fourteenth Centuries', *Journal of Ecclesiastical History*, 46 (1995): 398–431, at 404.

70 *Ibid.*, 409.

71 Henrici de Gandavo, *Quodlibet I*, ed. R. Macken (Leuven University Press, 1979), *questio* 35, 195–200, at 199, cited by Wei, 'Self-Image of the Masters of Theology', 415; cf. Minnis, *Medieval Theory of Authorship*, 81.

72 Wei, 'Self-Image', 419 n. 45.

73 D. Kimpel and R. Suckale, *L'Architecture Gothique en France 1130–1270*, trans. F. Neu (Paris: Flammarion, 1990), 346.

74 Sauerländer, *Gothic Sculpture in France*, 467 and plate 174.

75 Wilson, *Gothic Cathedral*, 143; cf. Panofsky, *Gothic Architecture and Scholasticism*, 26. For images of patrons holding churches or windows dating to the 1260s, e.g. the piscina at Saint-Urbain (Troyes), see J. Gardner, 'Cardinal Ancher and the Piscina in Saint-Urban at Troyes', in C. L. Striker (ed.), *Architectural Studies in Memory of Richard Krautheimer* (Mainz: von Zabern, 1996), 79–82, and J. Gardner, '"Sepulchram ... permagnificum et sumptuosum inter omnia sepulcra vicina." A Note on Cardinal Guillaume de Bray and his Tomb in Orvieto by Arnolfo di Cambio', in K. Bergdolt and G. Bonsanti (eds.), *Opere a giorni: Studi su mille anni di arte Europa dedicati a Max Seidel* (Venice: Marsilio, 2001), 85–90, and also, for a window at Rouen cathedral, see L. Grodecki and C. Brisac, *Gothic Stained Glass 1200–1300* (London: Thames & Hudson, 1985), figure 148.

76 N. Wu, 'Hugues Libergier and His Instruments', *Avista Forum*, 11 (1999): 7–13.

77 E. Panofsky, *Tomb Sculpture* (London: Thames & Hudson, 1964), 70–1, figures 289–90; F. A. Greenhill, *Incised Effigial Slabs: A Study of Engraved Stone Memorials in Latin Christendom, c. 1100 to c. 1700*, 2 vols. (London: Faber and Faber, 1976), vol, II, 109, figures 43a–b; R. Grandi, *I monumenti dei dottori e la scultura a Bologna (1267–1348)* (Bologna: Istituto per la Storia di Bologna, 1982).

78 Panofsky, *Tomb Sculpture*, 53.

79 A. Félibien, *Entretiens*, intro. A. Blunt (1725; rpt. Farnborough: P. Gregg, 1967), 229–30; variant in H. Verlet, 'Les bâtiments monastiques de l'abbaye de Saint-Germain des Prés', *Paris et L'Ile-de-France – Mémoires*, 9 (1957–8): 9–68, at 20.

80 Frankl, *The Gothic*, 136 n. 57; cf. however R. Bechmann, *Villard de Honnecourt: la pensée technique au XIIIe siècle et sa communication* (Paris: Picard, 1991), 28.

81 On speech and manners, see M. D. Johnson, 'Ciceronian Rhetoric and Ethics: Conduct Literature and "Speaking Well"', in Cox and Ward (eds.), *The Rhetoric of Cicero*, 147– 64.

82 Examples, including the Saint Graal MS, are conveniently illustrated in P. du Colombier, *Les Chantiers des Cathédrales* (Paris: Picard, 1973), figures 15, 19, 22, 23, 27, 58, 74, etc.; and see also H. M. Colvin (ed.), *The History of the King's Works, vol. I, The Middle Ages* (London: HMSO, 1963), plate 1.

83 Comte A. de Laborde, *La Bible Moralisée Illustrée conservée à Oxford, Paris et Londres*, 5 vols. (Paris: Pour les membres de la Société, 1911–27), vol. II, plate 270.

84 Both are illustrated in J. J. G. Alexander, *Medieval Illuminators and their Methods of Work* (New Haven: Yale University Press, 1992), 54 and figures 76–7; the images of patronage and authorship in the Moralized Bibles are discussed by J. Lowden, *The Making of the Bibles Moralisées, vol. I, The Manuscripts* (University Park: Pennsylvania State University Press, 2000), 87–90, 127–32, figure 34 and colour plates II, III, X.

85 Félibien, *Entretiens*, 228 (Recueil, IV): 'Anno Domini M° CC° LVII mense Februario Idus secundo hoc fuit inceptum Cristi genetricis honori kallensi Lathomo vivente Johanne magistro'; M. Aubert, *Notre-Dame de Paris* (Paris: H. Laurens, 1920), 138, gives a variant.

86 P. Binski, 'The Cosmati and *romanitas* in England: An Overview', in L. Grant and R. Mortimer (eds.), *Westminster Abbey: The Cosmati Pavements* (Aldershot: Ashgate, 2002), 116–34, at 120–3.

87 See n. 13 above.

88 R. Hamann-Mac Lean and I. Schüssler, *Die Kathedrale von Reims*, Part I, vol. II (Stuttgart: Steiner, 1993), plates 290–1; Gardner, '"Sepulchram …"', 85, figure 3.

89 Claussen, 'Früher Künstlerstolz', 14, 25, 26, 27, 30, in general 21–31.

90 See *inter alia* R. Feenstra, '"Legum Doctor", "Legum Professor" et "Magister" comme termes pour designer des juristes au Moyan Age', in O. Weijers(ed.), *Actes du colloque Terminologie de la vie intellectuelle au Moyen Age*, Études

sur le vocabulaire intellectual du Moyen Age 1 (Turnhout: Brepols, 1988), 72–7; also M. Teeuwen, *The Vocabulary of Intellectual Life in the Middle Ages*, Etudes sur le vocabulaire intellectual du Moyen Age 10 (Turnhout: Brepols, 2003), 76–8 and bibliography.

91 M. Baxandall, *Giotto and the Orators* (Oxford University Press, 1981), 124.

92 Claussen, 'Früher Künstlerstolz', 30.

93 See n. 85 above, and in addition O. Weijers, 'Terminologie des universités naissantes', in A. Zimmermann (ed.), *Soziale Ordnungen im Selbstverständnis des Mittelalters,* 2 vols. Miscellanea Mediaevalia 12 (Berlin: De Gruyter, 1979–80), vol. 1 I, 258–80, at 267–9, observing (at 268) that in view of the 'Doctors of the Church' the term tended to be used 'avec une certaine révérance'; and also O. Weijers, *Terminologie des universités au XIIIᵉ siècle* (Rome: Edizioni dell'Ateneo, 1987). Frankl, *The Gothic*, 137, simply connects the term with geometry, however.

94 Murray, *Reason and Society*, 265–6.

95 Wei, 'Self-Image'.

96 Teeuwen, *Vocabulary of Intellectual Life*, 77.

97 Murray, *Reason and Society*, 224; M.-C. Pouchelle, *The Body and Surgery in the Middle Ages*, trans. R. Morris (Cambridge: Polity, 1990), 19–20; G. Horobin, 'Professional Mystery: the Maintenance of Charisma in General Medieval Practice', in R. Dingwall and P. Lewis (eds.), *The Sociology of the Professions: Lawyers, Doctors and Others* (London: Macmillan, 1983), 84–105.

98 Pouchelle, *Body and Surgery*, 13–15, quotation at 15.

99 *Ibid.*, 15–16.

100 *In Politicam continuatio*, III, *lectio* 9, no. 6: 'Ulterius dicit quod medicus triplex est: unus quidem est qui non novit artem, sed ordinata ab aliis aliqualiter scit applicare ad opus. Alius est artifex principalis, qui novit simpliciter omnes causas et principia medicinae; et tertius est expertus qui aliqua novit, sed non simpliciter', in *Corpus Thomisticum*. Pevsner, 'The Term "Architect"', 560, takes this passage out of context.

101 Pouchelle, *Body and Surgery*, 103.

102 *Rhetoric*, I.2 (Barnes (ed.), *Aristotle*, vol. II, 2,155). See also D. Hutchinson, 'Doctrines of the Mean and the Debate Concerning Skills in Fourth-Century Medicine, Rhetoric, and Ethics', *Apeiron*, 21 (1988): 17–52.

103 L. R. Shelby, 'The Geometrical Knowledge of Mediaeval Master Masons', *Speculum*, 47 (1972): 395–421, at 402–3 and n. 24: 'Finis enim theorice est aliquid docere; finis vero practice est aliquid agree ... Artifex vero theorice geometer, qui plane novit omnes partes geometrie et eam docet' (etc.).

104 Hahnloser, *Villard de Honnecourt*, plate 36, caption; Shelby, 'Geometrical Knowledge', 418 and n. 63; D. Knoop, G. P. Jones and D. Hamer (eds.), *The Two Earliest Masonic MSS* (Manchester University Press, 1938), 71, lines 37–8.

105 Vitruvius, *Ten Books on Architecture*, 24, 149 n. 35.

106   P. A. Olson, 'John Bromyard's Response to the Gothic', *Medievalia et Humanistica*, 15 (1963): 91–4, at 92–3: 'Sicut etiam pulchritudo domus religiosorum consurgit ex bona ordinatione claustri & aliorum edificiorum. ... Iterum cordis pulchritudo, quod debet esse domus religiosa consurgit ex debita dispositione claustri, videlicet quatuor virtutum Cardinalium.'

107   M. Jennings, 'Medieval Thematic Preaching: A Ciceronian Second Coming', in Cox and Ward (eds.), *The Rhetoric of Cicero*, 313–34, cited at 321.

108   Pevsner, 'The Term "Architect"', 550–1; Carruthers, *Craft of Thought*, 230.

109   Nims, *Poetria nova*, 100 n. 56; see Fredborg, 'Rhetoric and Dialectic', 170.

110   Mallon developed the use of the term in epigraphy on the basis of one early inscription, but he did not associate it with Vitruvius: J. Mallon, 'Pour une nouvelle critique des chiffres dans les inscriptions latines gravées sur pierre', *Emerita*, 16 (1948): 14–45, especially 27.

111   M. B. Parkes, 'The Influence of the Concepts of Ordinatio and Compilatio on the Development of the Book', in J. J. G. Alexander and M. T. Gibson (eds.), *Medieval Learning and Literature: Essays Presented to Richard William Hunt* (Oxford University Press, 1976), 115–41, at 116–21.

112   Parkes, 'Ordinatio and Compilatio', 121.

113   F. R. Chapman (ed.), *Sacrist Rolls of Ely*, 2 vols. (Cambridge University Press, 1907), vol. II, 45: 'Item dat. cuidam de Londonia ad ordinand. novum opus ...'; for Westminster, see P. Binski, *The Painted Chamber at Westminster* (London: Society of Antiquaries, 1986), 21, after London, PRO E101/468/21, fol. 72; see also the accounts for St Stephen's Chapel, Westminster, in E. W. Tristram, *English Wall Painting of the Fourteenth Century* (London: Routledge, 1955), 282.

114   J. Bony, *The English Decorated Style: Gothic Architecture Transformed 1250–1350* (Oxford: Phaidon, 1979), 2–3; J. Bony, *French Gothic Architecture of the 12th & 13th Centuries* (Berkeley; London: University of California Press, 1983), 377, 461; cf. Panofsky, *Gothic Architecture and Scholasticism*, 10. For a more general re-evaluation of Rayonnant and diversification more generally in European architecture *c.* 1300, see A. Gajewski and Z. Opačič (eds.), *The Year 1300 and the Creation of a New European Architecture* (Turnhout: Brepols, 2007), from which I cite the paper by C. Wilson, 'Not Without Honour Save in its Own Country? Saint-Urbain at Troyes and its Contrasting French and English Posterities', 107–21, at 118.

115   The major late-fourteenth-century English architect Henry Yevele was presumably not just a trusted architect but also a reasonable conversationalist, to judge by his documentation as a dinner guest of important patrons such as William of Wykeham; see J. H. Harvey, *Henry Yevele* (London: Batsford, 1946), 46–7 and figures 42–5.

116   A. Legner, (ed.), *Die Parler und der schöne Stil 1350–1400: europäische Kunst unter den Luxemburger: ein Handbuch zur Ausstellung des Schnütgen-Museums in der Kunsthalle Köln*, 5 vols. (Cologne: Museen der Stadt Köln, 1978–80), *passim*.

117 Wilson, *Gothic Cathedral*, 140.

118 Minnis, *Medieval Theory of Authorship*, 94–103.

119 J. S. Ackerman, '"Ars Sine Scientia Nihil Est": Gothic Theory of Architecture at the Cathedral of Milan', *Art Bulletin*, 31 (1949): 84–111, at 100–2, and document no. III at 109–10; Frankl, *The Gothic*, 62–83.

120 Frankl, *The Gothic*, 108–9, persists, I believe inadvisably, in seeing Mignot's dictum as evidence that he himself regarded architecture merely as a mechanical art.

121 Q. Skinner, *The Foundations of Modern Political Thought*, 2 vols. (Cambridge University Press, 1978), vol. I, x.

122 Pevsner, 'The Term "Architect"', 549, 552; Leon Battista Alberti, *Ten Books on Architecture, ed. J. Rykwert* (London: A. Tiranti, 1955), ix; Frankl, *The Gothic*, 79 and n. 19.

CHAPTER 2

Grammar and rhetoric in late medieval polyphony

Modern metaphor or old simile?[1]

Margaret Bent

Consider a treatise whose six chapters are headed *de voce, de littera, de syllaba, de pedibus, de tonis, de posituris* (or *distinctionibus*). Musicologists would recognize these as musical terms and might expect musical content. But they are the headings of Book I of the *Ars major* by Aelius Donatus, the fourth-century tutor of Jerome, the grammatical treatise that was standard throughout the Middle Ages. They form but one example among many of the closeness of musical terminology to that of verbal grammar and rhetoric. Medieval music treatises acknowledge the arts of the trivium in a variety of ways:

1. through a large shared vocabulary of technical terminology; this area is eloquently addressed in a number of important studies;[2]
2. by modelling musical definitions on those of verbal grammar and rhetoric. The verbal definitions of ancient authors, including Horace and Quintilian (respectively in the first centuries BC and AD), associate rectitude or correctness with grammar, *recte scribendi* or *recte loquendi* (writing or speaking correctly); and they associate qualitative judgement with rhetoric, which can be done more or less well, *bene loquendi* (speaking well, or eloquence). *Recte* and *bene* recur throughout late antique and medieval definitions of musical procedures, thus recognizing that the structures and principles are, *mutatis mutandis*, the same as for verbal grammar and rhetoric, and that only the medium is changed;
3. by simile and metaphor, in both directions, from verbal to musical contexts as well as from musical to verbal. Grammar is not merely a simile or metaphor, though it is those too. Late medieval music theory is peppered with similes associating music with the verbal arts of the trivium, *sicut in grammatica, sicut in rhetorica,* and, less often, *sicut in dialectica,* notably in the anonymous thirteenth-century *Summa*

musice, which mentions three kinds of fault in chant, one of which is compared to those solecisms in grammar which arise from incoherence in the accentuation of words, the others to faults in rhetoric and dialectic.[3] Significantly, these are independently judged as faults of purely musical composition; they are faults neither because of the relationship of words to music, nor because of the dependency of music on its associated verbal text;

4 by emulative modelling of music treatises on their verbal counterparts, not only in language and definitions but also in the structure of the treatises themselves. The clearest example is the late-fifteenth-century counterpoint treatise of Johannes Tinctoris, to be discussed below.

The choice of the trivial arts of grammar, rhetoric and dialectic to make parallels with music is striking, given that at least speculative music theory, *musica*, with its basis in the ancient science of harmonics, belongs with the mathematical arts of the quadrivium. Rhetoric was aready invoked by Augustine, who in defining music as the *scientia bene modulandi*[4] clearly locates it in the rhetorical tradition, insofar as that is separable from the grammatical, while also acknowledging its foundations in number, then synonymous with rhythm. But a relationship between practical music theory and the trivial arts also flourished throughout the later Middle Ages, explicitly invoking them alongside music's quadrivial status as a university discipline, and setting it up as an art to which grammar and rhetoric apply. It is one example of a blurring of boundaries between the seven liberal arts, as found in informal 'trivia' of practical arts, such as Grocheio defines for grammar, computus and (practical) music.[5] Remigius of Auxerre writes in the ninth century that '*vox* [with a wider connotation than our 'voice'] is the material or beginning of music, and it exercises the same power in music as the point in geometry, the monad in arithmetic, the letter in grammar'.[6] This analogy is fulfilled in the use of letter names for musical sounds (*voces*). He invokes grammar from the trivium as well as arithmetic and geometry, companions with music in the quadrivial disciplines. *Poetria*, as the art of metrics, is part of *musica*, at least from St Augustine onwards if not before: the numerical, counted aspects of poetry were thus added to the quadrivial status of music. Music and poetry together form a kind of bridge between the arts of the trivium and quadrivium; a link between music and the verbal arts is increasingly emphasized in the later Middle Ages. The fourteenth-century theorist Petrus dictus Palma Ociosa combines words that are used to define both grammar and rhetoric;

music is 'ars sive scientia bene et recte modulandi', the art or science of making music both well and correctly.[7]

The fourteenth-century Abbot Engelbert of Admont recognizes the principle of analysis or construal for the intelligible communication of sung chant: 'Just as in the other senses the delight in what is perceived proceeds from perception, and perception from observing distinctions (*distinctiones*), so in the hearing of song there will be no pleasure unless the song is clearly perceived, nor can it be clearly perceived unless it is correctly parsed (*distinguatur*).'[8] 'Distinguere' is also used for the articulation of verbal parsing by punctuation, and of graphic musical equivalents to verbal punctuation: signs to separate units by dots, or colour (red notation) to distinguish duple from triple groupings.[9] These uses of dots and colour are ubiquitous in musical sources of the fourteenth and fifteenth centuries for rhythmic clarification; the dots are sometimes essential to a correct reading, sometimes corroborative of a reading that could have been arrived at without them. Just such parsing is specific to the musical grammars of particular cultures or periods, and applies not only to these rhythmic examples but even more to interval successions, how musical pitches are ordered according to the grammar of counterpoint. The idea that music can be 'understood' in this way, that heard music can be construed against the norms of an internalized grammar, may be foreign to listeners for whom the sole subject matter of music is emotional mirroring, mood painting, response, by means of stimulating, soothing or uplifting sounds. Musical languages may have some claim to universality at a deep structural level, but that lies beyond my concern here, and beyond my competence to investigate.[10] At the surface level of musical understanding or hearing in real time, music is by no means a universal language, as is immediately apparent when a Western musician is exposed to a high musical culture, such as Japanese music, that stands as far as can be imagined from Western traditions. The distinction may be subtler when one travels back in time to an antecedent tradition of the music with which we are more familiar. In the case of western medieval music, similar sound progressions in more recent styles may be as deceptively different as the changed meanings of Chaucerian words such as 'lewd' or 'nice'.

The most striking instance of such potential misunderstanding affects closure. The interval of the major third, which for us gives a sense of resolution or arrival, was for fourteenth-century musicians a point of maximum tension, not achieving closure but demanding it: it needs resolution onto the – to us – bare-sounding interval of a perfect fifth. Example 2.1

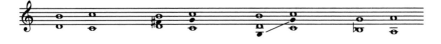

Example 2.1 Examples of cadential progressions

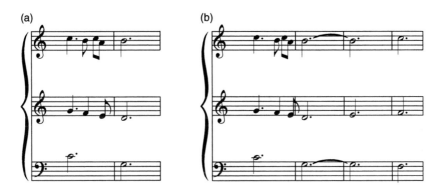

Example 2.2 (a) Incomplete cadential progression (b) Progression completed

gives examples of normal cadential (closural) progressions in two parts, always with a semitone step (whether or not so notated) joining the imperfect interval (the third or sixth) to the perfect (unison, octave or fifth). Where a third (grammatically subsidiary) voice is included, it is in black note-heads.

Example 2.2 is a progression (a) which may sound as if it had arrived on at least a temporary resting-place. Its continuation (b), normal and necessary by the standards of c. 1400, may sound to a modern ear as though it is tacked on to something that had already arrived. The real possibility of confounding closure and onward movement (exemplified in many recordings of this repertory) serves to illustrate a fundamental difference between musical grammar – and sense – then and now.

The marking up of a written verbal text with punctuation has close parallels with auxiliary signs such as dots and accidentals in a musical text. Words for written musical signs, *virga* (*virgula*) and *punctum* (*punctus*), are again related to the terminology of punctuation. As Malcolm Parkes observes, punctuation is a function of written language, of which it eventually became an essential component in order to resolve structural uncertainties in a text, and to signal nuances of semantic significance. In music too, signs which appear only sporadically in early notation later came to be essential. Many early verbal texts gave little help to the reader with respect to sentence or even word division, and musical texts like-wise generally lacked articulation marks for both the rhythmic divisions and pitch inflections that could have helped the inexperienced reader by separating sense units. Parkes makes a distinction between grammatical punctuation, which marks boundaries of sentences and sense units within them, and rhetorical punctuation which marks periodic structure, and *cola* and *commata,* within them; but there is some agreement between the two types with respect to complete and incomplete sense. Almost every-thing Parkes says has a parallel in musical signs and in what is expected in their absence. While punctuation is by definition a written art, and may be authorial, it is the responsiblity of the singer or the verbal ora-tor to compensate in performance for underprescriptive notation; the implementation of absent punctuation is in large measure a performer's art, usually without the need to write it, though the performer may sup-ply written markings to supplement or even to supersede what is already notated.[11]

Late medieval notation is underprescriptive with respect to what we call 'accidentals' (sharps and flats), signs which have become essential in modern notation. Singers of the time, conversant with the musical gram-mar, supplemented or supplied them as part of the process of reading and singing, as readers of semitic languages supply vowels, and orators supply inflections, whether or not helped by punctuation. These musical inflec-tions (notated or not) are often discussed by theorists under the heading of *musica ficta,* for whose 'invention' they give two reasons; *causa neces-sitatis* and *causa pulchritudinis.* Various explanations for these terms have been put forward, of which the notion that the former has largely to do with simultaneities ('vertical') and the latter with melodic ('horizontal') reasons comes close to what I here propose. I think that the models of grammar and rhetoric give us a helpful framework for this distinction by medieval writers. *Causa necessitatis* would then correspond to *recte,* as meaning grammatical criteria, essential inflections to ensure the cor-rection of perfect intervals and the appropriate marking of sense breaks, which can be judged objectively as correct or incorrect. *Causa pulchritud-inis* corresponds to *bene,* rhetorical reasons for inflections, which are often elective, and can be done in different ways, better or less well, accord-ing to taste and judgement. They will depend on the particular inflection or interpretation that performers wish to communicate about precisely how they understand ambiguous musical sense, its points of closure or caesura. Some inflections are essential at the grammatical level; others are open to equally valid alternatives. Unwritten punctuation and its equivalents in vocal inflection, whether spoken or sung, assume the orator's ability to construe text, and the musician's to construe musical sense units. Punctuation need not be fully notated in a verbal text, nor indeed did notated music require 'accidentals' to be signed, whether they were essential or elective in performance. The musical performer will inflect cadences or closural formulae, thus signalling sense breaks, just as the reader of text may supply punctuation or compensate for the lack of it, inflecting the voice to mark *cola* and *commata*; beyond that, orators, like musical performers, will communicate their understanding of ambiguities of sense and nuance within those units, and propose a reading that resolves them one way or another.

In 1477, a thousand years after Augustine, Johannes Tinctoris invites the reader to see his *Liber de arte contrapuncti* as an *Ars grammatica* by starting it with a quotation from Horace, 'Scribendi recte sapere est et principium et fons',[12] a standard definition of grammar as correct writing, but Tinctoris' use of this definition for the musical discipline of counterpoint implies a musical parallel and a musical application. He negotiates the same written–oral paradox as the grammarians, by defining counterpoint, which will be sung, as a rational and planned procedure ('moderatus ac rationabilis concentus') that can be made in writing or in the mind. Ronald Woodley's was perhaps the first of a number of studies exploring Tinctoris' emulation of humanist models; he convincingly demonstrates that the language of the proemium of the *Proportionale* is based on the prologue of Cicero's *De oratore*.[13] Reinhard Strohm has written magisterially on Tinctoris' humanist agenda in relation to ideas of rebirth and renewal in the absence of a musical tradition from antiquity capable of revival.[14] Leofranc Holford-Strevens has evaluated his arsenal of classical authorities.[15] Rob Wegman has contributed a number of important studies.[16] Alexis Luko has related Tinctoris' stance on *varietas* in Book III of the *Liber de arte contrapuncti* to *De oratore*, the *Rhetorica ad Herennium* and Alberti's *De pictura*.[17] In both its successful and its over-ambitious manifestations, his language invites such identifications, especially in the prefaces to the *Proportionale* and the *De arte contrapuncti*.[18] What has been less noticed is the way in which the form and content, especially of the counterpoint treatise, are, in addition, closely modelled on the standard grammar treatises. But first we need a brief digression to define what counterpoint meant in the fourteenth and fifteenth centuries. Counterpoint was what we might now call two-part harmony, a succession of dyads. It was not triadically based, as later harmonic theory came to be. Harmony was not a separate discipline, except in the quite different sense of harmonics (the physical basis of sound calculated proportionally). Counterpoint is now often defined as the combination of melodic lines, the horizontal strands of music, but originally it meant, literally, the placing of one point or note against another.[19] The dyadic skeleton is no more an obstacle to the fleshed-out composition of music in three, four or five parts than triadic harmony is to polychords containing ninths and thirteenths; it is just the basis of the grammar that governs the underlying interval progressions, on which multi-part music can be built, and back to which it can be analysed or parsed. The normal closural progressions were given in Example 2.1.

In Book I of the counterpoint treatise, Tinctoris grinds exhaustively through the consonant dyadic (i.e., two-part) intervals, and all their octave replications, the raw materials of which counterpoint is formed, unmeasured before being animated by rhythm in composed music. This closely parallels the way in which Donatus sets out the parts of speech, the fundamental ingredients of verbal composition, in Book II of the *Ars major*, where he proceeds in similarly laborious detail through the eight parts of speech. (These are treated more briefly as the sole contents of his *Ars minor*, a much shorter grammatical treatise.) Book III of the *Ars major* deals with barbarisms, solecisms, other 'vices' and 'tropes'. This corresponds to Book II of the *Liber de arte contrapuncti*, which deals with dissonance. Dissonance must never be used 'in counterpoint', that is, in the strict underlying dyadic contrapuntal relationship which is equivalent to verbal grammar; but it nevertheless has a controlled place in composed music, as do vices and tropes in verbal composition. The materials of contrapuntally based composition are the consonant two-part interval progressions (dyads) of medieval counterpoint theory. These consonances are presented as equivalent to the parts of speech, and dissonances are presented as the equivalent of linguistic 'vices'. Tinctoris' message is similar to that of Donatus; barbarisms and solecisms which are in principle forbidden can have some controlled or regulated use. Handled with care, they can indeed be desirable ornaments. Donatus cites uses of these forbidden fruits by ancient authors; Tinctoris cites uses by modern composers. Donatus gives examples above all from Virgil, but also from Terence, Horace, Livy and other authorities. Tinctoris refers to these classical authors, but in the absence of recoverable musical literature from antiquity, his musical authorities are his admired contemporaries, from whom he draws his examples for both praise and blame: 'As Virgil took Homer for his model, so I have used these composers as models for my modest works, and especially in the arrangement of the concords, I have plainly imitated their admirable style of composing.'[20] In the absence of ancient composers, Tinctoris' Homer, Virgil and Cicero were Dunstaple, Du Fay and Binchois, and the newer great composers of his own century.[21] And yet, despite praising the great compositional luminaries of the preceding generation, and his own contemporaries Ockeghem, Busnois, Regis and Caron, in the dedicatory prefaces of these two treatises (the *Proportionale* and the *Liber de arte contrapuncti*, when Faugues is added), he proceeds to the apparent anomaly later in the same treatises of taking them to task, poking his critical finger at them for sharply observed minor compositional errors. Tinctoris was here providing the ingredient of 'literary criticism' or *enarratio auctorum* found in grammar treatises. I think his criticisms should be seen as showing that his revered colleagues deserved such scrutiny, not as detracting from his high regard for Ockeghem and Busnois when they do not merely obey the rules. Even Homer nods, and Tinctoris cites precisely that famous image.[22] The grammarians likewise chastise the masters, but rather in order to enhance their authority than to diminish it.

For music, as for literature, we are totally dependent on written survivals. In both cases we are cut off from the performing traditions by which they were realized in sound, and strain to recover the content of musical and verbal literature, and to make of it what we can in modern performance. Music was more fleeting, fast-changing, its content less fully captured in writing and more dependent on those lost traditions; our endeavours with respect to music would have made little sense to Tinctoris, for whom music older than forty years was not regarded by the learned as worth hearing.[23] This stance marks a significant difference between the value set by humanists on the recovery of ancient literary texts, and the attitude to high-art music of the same men and their contemporaries: they valued the latest styles, whose composers and singers usually came from the north, and constantly updated their repertories.

From antiquity, the relationship between grammar and rhetoric was a complex and partly overlapping one. Quintilian covers both arts in the same treatise, but separates their functions: as already said, grammar is the art of writing or speaking correctly, *recte*; rhetoric is the art of speaking or writing well, *peritus* or *bene*: what James J. Murphy has called 'a complete system of speech invention and presentation'.[24] Grammar also includes interpretation of the poets, *enarratio poetarum*; it is in this area that Quintilian departs from the strictly grammatical, and enters the sphere normally reserved for rhetoric, and it is here that Tinctoris follows classical models in subjecting the work of his admired contemporaries to close and sometimes critical scrutiny. Historians of rhetoric are now realizing that a strict separation between grammar and rhetoric, particularly at the higher levels of practice, is not tenable in practice. As also with dialectic, they lie on a graded spectrum of skills and are not discrete or separable. A similar continuum also applies to the quadrivial arts; Boethius' *De arithmetica* is a prerequisite for the *De musica*.

Grammar has frequently been employed as a metaphor by modern writers on music to connote precisely the underlying rules and functions of different musical languages and dialects, and there have been few objections to this self-evidently sensible usage.[25] But 'Grammar and Music' has, as yet, no entry in the *New Grove Dictionary of Music*, a missed opportunity to show the primacy of verbal grammar among the various language models that music theorists, from the middle ages to the present day, have applied to musical structures, and to reflect the now very considerable secondary literature on this subject, especially for the period up to about 1300. The *New Grove* does, however, have an excellent article on 'Rhetoric and Music', albeit representative of the older, received view of this subject. Rhetoric is generally understood (and here I simplify) as a verbal art to which music may be a subservient and non-autonomous embellishment, underpinning, enhancing or expressing verbal sense.

But it should not be assumed that music is always the junior or dependent partner in the word-music relationship. It is a two–way street. The early motet began life with the addition of words to existing wordless melismas, and a longstanding tradition of writing new words to existing music (transferable hymn tunes, or the *cantasi come* tradition, providing words to be sung 'to the tune of …'). Writers on grammar and rhetoric frequently reached out to musical images to convey what they meant. Quintilian states that the orator must know the principles of music. He also uses the simile 'sicut in modulatione'.[26] There are many less well-known musical references in verbal treatises: Gilles Rico has drawn my attention to passages in Roger Bacon's works dealing with music and rhetoric, where in the *Communia mathematica* he affirms: 'the musician has reasons and causes to give demonstrations of all these things, and teachers of grammar, poetry, logic and rhetoric take from him (the *musicus*) each according to his usage'.[27] Three points are commonly invoked for the relation of rhetoric to music:

1 consideration of rhetorical figures or special effects, as outlined by Burmeister in his famous analysis of a Lasso motet (1607),[28] or Vicentino's advocacy in 1555 of parallels with ancient oratory that were to form the basis of the *seconda pratica*[29]

2 relating parts of a musical structure to those of a formal oration, especially as drawn from Quintilian, wordless musical compositions that can be judged to have *exordia*, and so on. The first notable modern application of this analogy between oratory and music was the identification of sections corresponding to the parts of an oration in Bach's *Musical Offering*.[30] The rhetoric of textless music is usually related to one or other of these two cases: either large-scale structures that mirror the sections of an oration, or figures or gestures that parallel or mimic verbal rhetorical figures (following Burmeister); but

3 more generally and most pervasively, musical rhetoric is usually understood mainly as what happens when words are purposefully set to music, and the music tailored to reflect those words, rather than cases where words are added to music that was composed without taking them into account. Specifically, it connotes how music supports, underpins and reflects a primary verbal meaning, how it enhances or expresses verbal sense. The primary rhetorical bond of words and music is treated as a humanistic marriage forged not until the sixteenth century, music usually being the junior partner.

This last category of musical rhetoric, at least, leaves aside the capacity of music to provide an independent self-contained structure valid without or beyond the words or verbal structures attached to it. There is indeed plenty of evidence to support a primary medieval understanding of rhetoric as closely related to the musical setting of words, especially in the centuries before polyphony was established and notated. The twelfth-century theorists of chant eludicated by Calvin Bower and others locate one function of music as a supporting handmaid to enhance the eloquent presentation of the verbal text, both as composed and as performed. But this, and the senses usually stated, are not the only ones. Bower has addressed grammatical models, structures and terminology in terms purely of music and music theory from the ninth to twelfth centuries. The liturgical chant he deals with is firmly wedded to words – and the musical structures do indeed mirror the verbal ones – but he brings out how the purely musical–grammatical structure of chant can be judged independently, and he shows that the musical structures follow their own laws.[31]

Current usage often treats rhetoric as a technique of special resort, not something inherent in all creation and performance, rather as it is now common in popular usage to treat 'rhetoric' as an exaggerated or negatively viewed style of presentation, a particular kind of persuasion or spinning, 'merely rhetoric', or 'empty rhetoric'. It is sometimes treated as detachable from content, as though 'rhetoric' were a special effect applicable to some kinds of discourse, but not inherent in all. Least of all is it now found in common parlance as a positive quality, something to be done well, *bene*.

According to a standard narrative, the rhetorical model disappears from music between its well-documented application to liturgical chant up to the thirteenth century, and the re-emergence of interest in rhetoric in a humanist context towards 1500. Thus, music is discussed in terms of grammar and rhetoric up to about 1300, and again from the late fifteenth century. The black hole in modern discussions of grammar and rhetoric in relation to music coincides with the fourteenth and fifteenth centuries. This period is considered dark if not downright barbaric with respect to text–music relations and expressiveness, and therefore a low point for 'rhetoric' understood primarily as dealing with text–music relationships – more often it is simply passed over in silence. The irony is that the highest artistic and intellectual accomplishments of medieval music are still often denigrated as dry and cerebral, waiting to be liberated and superseded by the humanizing and affectively sensitive Renaissance. That is another issue; I have dealt with a parallel aspect of it in a recent challenge to the monolithic and prescriptive concept of the isorhythmic motet, whose iron grip has distorted the historiography of the motet and the cyclic mass throughout the fourteenth and fifteenth centuries.[32]

But with respect to rhetoric two counter-claims can be made. First, music of this 'dark' period is indeed often closely related to its words, though not in a Romantic expressive way. This is done by juxtaposition of related or contrasting ideas, musical material either standing for its words or representing number, use of words as building blocks, and of musical motifs, rhythmic or melodic cells, voice crossings and various means to tag specific words, ideas, citations or structural points and moments of density. Some of these strands work both independently and together in some of the most artful compositions of the period; musical and verbal material had equally important foundational functions. If the music has its own structures, these need not merely support the text (self-fulfilling criticism by hindsight) but can also pull against it; there is room for contradiction, or even irony, as can be demonstrated in a number of motets.

Second, grammar and rhetoric do not simply disappear. The model moves sideways: I now believe that grammatical and rhetorical models may migrate from chant to polyphony at this time, specifically to the new discipline of counterpoint as formulated in the early fourteenth century. Counterpoint is the grammar of late medieval polyphony; it deals with the dyadic (two-note) intervals and the rules governing their succession. The fourteenth and fifteenth centuries saw the establishment of contrapuntally based part-music, and the development of rhythmic as well as pitch structures whose essentials could be sufficiently fixed in writing, thanks to a fast-evolving notational system. The rightness of a polyphonic musical structure was now almost as verifiable as a crossword, a framework against which one could as confidently diagnose a 'wrong note' as even untutored listeners can in hearing Mozart. It is in this period that counterpoint becomes established as a musical grammar, and it is in counterpoint treatises from the fourteenth and fifteenth centuries that we find the language, definitions and structures of grammar and rhetoric treatises already referred to. Polyphonic music becomes increasingly emancipated from the words that were so closely tied to it in the chant and chant commentaries of the preceding centuries: music that is complex both contrapuntally and rhythmically acquires (and is in turn enabled by) an autonomous structure that is in principle independent of its words. In practice, as in several fourteenth-century motets, the musical structures are sufficiently independent to 'talk back' at the words, to underline or to subvert them, all much more interesting than self-fulfilling prophecies of passive support. This also opens the way to a wide range of techniques for textual imaging and commentary that are clear, purposeful and vivid without recourse to the more obvious kinds of local mimetic word painting that we have come to expect in the sixteenth century.[33]

Of particular interest is the opening of *Cum venerint*, the *Ite missa est* motet of the fourteenth-century Mass of Tournai.[34] No editor or recorded version has dared to present this truly odd-sounding passage as both the clearly indicated manuscript accidentals and the musical sense demand, and as shown in Example 2.3a. At a first hearing, we think something must be wrong, either the written notes or the supplied inflections. The harsh dissonance results from superimposing two voice-pairs, each entirely logical within itself, shown reduced to their basic skeletons in Examples 2. 3b and 2. 3c. Precisely this passage is cited – in words only – by the mid-fourteenth-century theorist Johannes Boen, in an exceptionally rare critical comment which shows his recognition both of the unusual progression and of its rightness: 'the harshness is covered over with the surrounding

Example 2.3a Opening of *Cum venerint*

Example 2.3b Reduction of triplum and motetus of *Cum venerint*

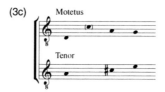

Example 2.3c Reduction of motetus and tenor of *Cum venerint*

sweetness'.[35] Sweetness is a standard epithet for consonance and aesthetic approval,[36] harshness for dissonance (not allowed in strict or simple counterpoint). Boen realized that this was a disturbing sonority, an apparently culpable dissonance. But the aural surprise, as shocking to him as to us, arises from the superimposition of two logical, overlapping pairings, and from appoggiaturas between them. He allows for auditory expectation, describing how imperfect consonances attract and allure the ear towards their resolution in perfect intervals. In other words, he is offering a critical justification of a surprising moment, a fourteenth-century *enarratio auctorum* to go with his grammatically and rhetorically self-conscious definition of music cited earlier – 'musica est ars sive scientia recte et bene modulandi'. Listening to this two-part foundation we can more easily hear that odd set of harmonies as a series of displacements. Arnulf of St Ghislain, writing around 1400, makes several references to how performers communicate musical understanding to listeners: 'Who will not marvel to see with what expertise in performance some musical relationship, dissonant at first hearing, sweetens by means of their skilful performance and is brought back to the pleasantness of consonance?'[37]

Medieval music is notated at relative, not absolute, pitch. It underprescribes accidental inflections, and gives no indication of tempo, dynamics or expression. Instrumental participation, if any, is never indicated, and it is often unclear whether words are to be attached to untexted parts. Performances can be made to sound so different from each other that definitions of music on the basis of what it sounds like to us, in a modern performance, are perilous. The sounding surface through which we encounter the music is its most fragile component. What does a performance that speaks to us, or seems to express our view of a poem, tell us about Du Fay or Machaut? All we can say about past tastes in the delivery (*actio, pronuntiatio*) of words or music, on the basis of common reactions to old recordings, is that we are unlikely to have liked the way they did it. Leaving aside questions of taste, the *judicium auri* invoked by medieval theorists licenses the exercise of appropriately trained judgement in when to inflect notes to achieve consonance and to signal sense boundaries. It does not license the imposition of anything that sounds good to anachronistically trained modern ears. Modern aural judgements may be formed circularly, and perhaps unconsciously, by uninformed performances, such as the many beautifully sung recordings which take the notated music at face value, avoiding inflections that would have been self-evident to a contemporary, on the mistaken premise that they are avoiding unnecessary change to the original, underprescriptive, notation, which demands active participation by the performer. Thus, performances are disseminated that in turn serve to normalize, and even to establish a taste for, wrong sounds (notably 'flat' leading notes), many of which have found their way into twentieth-century compositions that embody or reinterpret medieval and Renaissance compositions (especially works by Vaughan Williams, Peter Warlock, Maxwell Davies and other English composers). Instead of pretending to recover the irrecoverable actual sounds of medieval music, we ought to be devoting more effort to informing aural judgement by reconstructing their – at least partly recoverable – technical priorities; trying to learn the musical language in its own terms must be a first step towards internalizing aesthetic premises that are largely opaque to us. It is dangerous to assume that the notation means what it appears to mean, without understanding the training which complements it. That training would have led to an informed and idiomatic realization, including correction of those cadential progressions. Isidore of Seville famously said that sounds perish because they can't be written down. It is less often pointed out that that remains true of actual sounds even since notation became able to transmit some musical essentials: qualities of rhetorical delivery for words as well as music are impossible to describe and notate in such a way as to allow reconstruction.[38] It is a further paradox that music exists in sound, but that sound is its least stable element, not the only route by which it both reaches and expresses human understanding.

NOTES

1 This essay attempts to put a general frame around, and it partially overlaps with, a series of articles I have published over recent years, dealing with various aspects of musical grammar and rhetoric. These include: 'The Grammar of Early Music: Preconditions for Analysis', in C. C. Judd (ed.), *Tonal Structures in Early Music* (New York: Garland, 1998), 15–59; '"Sounds perish": In What Senses does Renaissance Music Survive?', in A. Grieco *et al.* (eds.), *The Italian Renaissance in the 20th Century: Acts of an International Conference, Florence, Villa I Tatti, June 9–11, 1999* (Florence: Olschki, 2002), 247–65; 'Sense and Rrhetoric in Late Medieval Polyphony', in A. Giger and T. J. Mathiesen (eds.), *Music in the Mirror: Reflections on the History of Music Theory and Literature for the 21st Century*, Publications of the Center for the History of Music Theory and Literature 3 (Lincoln: University of Nebraska Press, 2002), 45–59; 'Impossible authenticities', *Il Saggiatore musicale*, 8 (2001): 39–50.

2 These include: F. Reckow, '*Vitium* oder *color rhetoricus*? Thesen zur Bedeutung der Modelldisziplinen Grammatica, Rhetorica und Poetica für das Musikverständnis', *Forum Musicologicum*, 3 (1982): 307–21; 'Zwischen Ontologie und Rhetorik: Die Idee des *movere animos* und der Übergang vom Spätmittelalter zur frühen Neuzeit in der Musikgeschichte', in W. Haug and B. Wächinger (eds.), *Traditionswandel und Traditionsverhalten* (Tübingen: niemeyer, 1991), 145–78; Matthias Bielitz, *Musik und Grammatik* (Munich: Musikverlag Katzbichler, 1977); F. A. Gallo, 'Pronuntiatio: ricerche sulla storia di un termine retorico-musicale', *Acta musicologica*, 35 (1963): 38–46; C. M. Bower, '*Sonus vox, chorda, nota*: Thing, Name, and Sign in Early Medieval Theory', in M. Bernhard (ed.), *Quellen und Studien zur Musiktheorie des Mittelalters III*, Bayerische Akademie der Wissenschaften, Veröffentlichungen der Musikhistorischen Kommission 15 (Munich: C. H. Beck, 2001), 47–61; 'The Grammatical Model of Musical Understanding in

the Middle Ages', in P. J. Gallacher and H. Damico (eds.), *Hermeneutics and Medieval Culture* (Albany: SUNY Press, 1989), 133–45; W. T. Flynn, *Medieval Music as Medieval Exegesis* (Lanham, MD; London: Scarecrow Press, 1999); Don Harrán, *Word–Tone Relations in Musical Thought from Antiquity to the Seventeenth Century*, Musicological Studies and Documents 40 (Neuhausen-Stuttgart: American Institute of Musicology Hänssler-Verlag, 1986).

3 C. Page, *The Summa musice: A Thirteenth-Century Manual for Singers* (Cambridge University Press, 1991), 199–200, and K. Desmond, '*Sicut in grammatica*: Analogical Discourse in Chapter 15 of Guido's *Micrologus*', *The Journal of Musicology*, 16 (1998): 467–93.

4 *Aurelii Augustini De musica*, ed. Giovanni Marzi (Florence: Sansoni, 1969), I.2.

5 'Et quamquam omnes artes vel scientiae et omnis humana eruditio ad hoc tendat, quantum potest, tres tamen artes ad hoc propinquius ordinantur, puta grammatica, quae scribere cum modo loquendi et proferendi docet, et ars illa, quae temporum distinctionem et eorum computationem tradit, quam computum appellant, quae naturali vel astronomiae subiungatur, et cum his duabus concurrens musica, quae de cantu et modo cantandi discernit. Et istas tres non debet vir ecclesiasticus ignorare.' From *Der Musiktraktat des Johannes de Grocheo nach den Quellen neu herausgegeben mit Übersetzung ins Deutsche und Revisionsbericht*, ed. Ernst Rohloff, Media latinitas musica 2 (Leipzig: Gebrüder Reinecke, 1943), 58.

6 'Vox enim materies vel initium est musicae et eam vim obtinet vox in musica quam punctus in geometrica, monas in arithmetica, littera in grammatica.' From *Remigii Autissiodorensis Commentum in Martianum Capellam*, ed. C. E. Lutz, 2 vols. (Leiden: Brill, 1965): vol. 2, 336 (IX.499.14).

7 'Musica est ars sive scientia bene et recte modulandi sono cantuque congrua vel musica secundum quod dicit beatus Isidorus est peritia modulationis sono cantuque consistens.' From Petrus dictus Palma Ociosa, *Compendium de discantu mensurabili*. Johannes Wolf, 'Ein Beitrag zur Diskantlehre des 14. Jahrhunderts', *Sammelbände der Internationalen Musikgesellschaft*, 15 (1913–14): 505–34, at 507.

8 'In caeteris sensibus et sensibilibus delectatio fit ex perceptione, et perceptio ex distinctione, ita et in cantu et eius auditu non fit delectatio, nisi cantus bene percipiatur; nec poterit bene percipi, nisi recte distinguatur. Oportet ergo de necessitate cantorem volentem cantare delectabiliter per consequens cantare perceptibiliter: nec poterit cantare perceptibiliter, nisi cantet distinguibiliter et distincte: ergo ad debitum modum et morem cantandi summe necessaria est debita distinctio in omni cantu regulari.' Engelbert of Admont, *De musica, tractatus quartus. Scriptores ecclesiastici de musica sacra potissimum*, ed. Martin Gerbert, 3 vols. (St. Blaise, 1784; reprinted Hildesheim: Olms, 1963), vol. 2, 366.

9 Johannes Hanboys, *Summa*, gives examples of default rhythmic groupings which can be overruled ('unless otherwise indicated', *distinguatur*)

by a dot of division or a little stroke indicating division of the rhythmic mode: 'Tunc prima longa recta vocatur, secunda quoque alteratur, nisi per divisionis punctum distinguatur', and 'Tunc prima semibrevis vel valor pro recta habeatur, secunda vero alteratur, nisi per divisionem modi aliter distinguatur.' From Robertus de Handlo and Johannes Hanboys, *Regule and Summa*, ed. and trans. P. M. Lefferts, Greek and Latin Music Theory 7 (Lincoln: University of Nebraska Press, 1991), 232, 284 (in both cases with music examples). Similarly, Johannes Vetulus de Anagnia invokes dots to override what a dot-less reading would yield: 'Potest per modum perfectum alterari, nisi per divisionem modi aliter distinguatur.' From *Liber de musica Iohannis Vetuli de Anagnia*, ed. Frederick Hammond, Corpus scriptorum de musica 27 (Neuhausen-Stuttgart: American Institute of Musicology; Hänssler-Verlag, 1977), 66. The distinction of duple or triple measure by colour is attested in musical sources and by Johannes Boen: 'Solet aliquotiens cantor lascivia ductus in eodem cantu variare modum, ut nunc processus fiat per ternarium, nunc per dualitatem. Sed tunc oportet, quod huiusmodi cantus bene distinguatur per distinctos colores, ut in tenore moteti *In arboris emphiro.*' From Johannes Boen, *Ars (musicae)*, ed. F.A. Gallo, Corpus scriptorum de musica 19 ([Rome]: American Institute of Musicology, 1972), 20.

10 Two authoritative and very different studies are Harold Powers, 'Language Models and Musical Analysis', *Ethnomusicology*, 24 (1980): 1–60, and Jean-Jacques Nattiez, 'Linguistic Models and the Analysis of Musical Structures', *Rivista Italiana di Musicologia*, 35 (2000): 379–410.

11 See M. B. Parkes, *Pause and Effect: An Introduction to the History of Punctuation in the West* (Aldershot: Scolar Press, 1992), especially 1–12.

12 Horace, *Ars poetica*, 309.

13 Ronald Woodley, 'Renaissance Music Theory as Literature: On Reading the *Proportionale Musices* of Iohannes Tinctoris', *Renaissance Studies*, 1 (1987): 209–20. Further important published and unpublished articles are available, and a bibliography listed, on his Web site, www.stoa.org/tinctoris/tinctoris.html.

14 R. Strohm, 'Music, Humanism, and the Idea of a "Rebirth" of the Arts', in R. Strohm and B. Blackburn (eds.), *Music as Concept and Practice in the Late Middle Ages, The New Oxford History of Music*, vol. III, Part I, new edn (Oxford University Press, 2000), 346–405.

15 Leofranc Holford-Strevens, 'Tinctoris on the Great Composers', *Plainsong and Medieval Music*, 5 (1996): 193–9.

16 Rob C. Wegman, 'Johannes Tinctoris and the "New Art"', *Music & Letters*, 84 (2003): 171–88; '"Musical Understanding" in the 15th century', *Early Music*, 30 (2002): 46–66; '"Das musikalische Hören" in the Middle Ages and Renaissance: Perspectives from Pre-War Germany', *The Musical Quarterly*, 82 (1998): 434–55; 'Sense and Sensibility in Late-Medieval Music', *Early Music*, 23 (1995): 299–312.

17 Alexis Luko, 'Tinctoris on *varietas*', *Early Music History*' 27 (2008): 99–136, citing also Sean Gallagher, 'Models of *Varietas*: Studies in Style and

Attribution in the Motets of Johannes Regis and his Contemporaries', unpublished PhD thesis, Harvard University (1998), chapter 2.

18 Johannes Tinctoris, *Liber de arte contrapuncti* in *Johannis Tinctoris Opera theoretica*, ed. Albert Seay 3 vols., Corpus scriptorum de musica 22 ([Rome]: American Institute of Musicology, 1975), Vol. II. For a valuable new edition see Johannes Tinctoris, *Proportionale musices* [and] *Liber de arte contrapuncti*, ed. with introduction, commentary and Italian translation by Gianluca D'Agostino (Florence: Edizioni del Galluzzo, 2008).

19 Richard Crocker, 'Discant, Counterpoint, and Harmony', *Journal of the American Musicological Society*, 15 (1962): 1–21.

20 'Ea quoque profecto numquam audio, numquam considero quin laetior ac doctior evadam, unde quemadmodum Virgilius in illo opere divino Eneidos Homero, ita iis Hercule, in meis opusculis utor archetypis. Praesertim autem in hoc in quo, concordantias ordinando, approbabilem eorum componendi stilum plane imitatus sum.' From Johannes Tinctoris, *Liber de arte contrapuncti*, Prologus, 12–13.

21 Strohm's memorable perception, 'Music, Humanism', 380. His texts and partial translations of the Proemium to the *Proportionale* (which he dates c. 1473–4) and the Prologus to the *Liber de arte contrapuncti* (1477) are given in the appendix to that chapter, 395– 9.

22 'nullo prorsus alio modo eos excusandos arbitror quam per hoc dictum Horatii, "Quandoque bonus dormitat Homerius", id est ut Acro exponit, quandoque errat bonus poeta, unde et bonum etiam musicam aliquando errare non est mirandum.' From Johannes Tinctoris, *Liber de arte contrapuncti*, III.23, 144.

23 'Neque quod satis admirari nequeo quippiam compositum nisi citra annos quadraginta extat quod auditu dignum ab eruditis existimetur.' From Johannes Tinctoris, *Liber de arte contrapuncti*, Prologus, 12. This immediately precedes the passage quoted in n. 20 above. Strohm ('Music, Humanism') gives a masterly and nuanced account of the different form of humanistic 'rebirth' imagery developed by musicians, especially Tinctoris, and extends it to the idea of progress expressed in writings by Martin le Franc. For a somewhat different reading of Martin's own forty-year limit, see Margaret Bent, 'The Musical Stanzas in Martin le Franc's *Le champion des dames*', in J. Haines and R. Rosenfeld (eds.), *Music and Medieval Manuscripts: Paleography and Performance* (Ashgate: Aldershot, 2004), 91–127.

24 James J. Murphy, *Rhetoric in the Middle Ages* (Berkeley; London: University of California Press, 1974), 25.

25 Few objections, that is, until some recent sniping. See Daniel Leech-Wilkinson, 'Machaut's *Rose, lis* and the Problem of Early Music Analysis', in E. E. Leach (ed.), *Machaut's Music: New Interpretations* (Woodbridge: Boydell Press, 2003), 249–62, and my 'The "Harmony" of the Machaut Mass', in the same volume, 75–94, where I respond to a charge that, by daring to refer to right notes and wrong notes, I have made this a moral rather than a methodological issue.

26 *Quintilian, Instit. Orat.*, I.10.1–33. Book I was known throughout the Middle Ages. The importance of the rediscovery of a full text in 1416 has been somewhat exaggerated; see John O. Ward, 'Quintilian and the Rhetorical Revolution', *Rhetorica*, 13 (1995): 231–84.

27 'Musicus habet omnium istorum raciones et causas demonstrationes dare et grammatici, poete, logici, rethorici et alii ab eo accipiunt quilibet secundum usum suum.' From Roger Bacon, *Communia mathematica*, ed. R. Steele (Oxford: Clarendon Press, 1940), 55. At some other points he describes music and rhetoric as two disciplines responsible for a 'raptus animi'. See *ibid.*, 51–8; *Opus Tertium*, in *Fr. Rogeri Bacon opera quaeclam hactenus inedita*, ed. J.S. Brewer, 3 vols. (London, 1859), vol. 1, 307–9; *Opus Maius*, ed. John Henry Bridges, 2 vols. (Oxford, 1897), vol. I, 100–3, 178–9, 237–8. See also Gilles Rico, 'Music in the Arts Faculty of Paris in the Thirteenth and Early Fourteenth Centuries', unpublished D.Phil. thesis, Oxford University (2005).

28 Joachim Burmeister, *Musica Poetica* (Rostock,1606).

29 Nicola Vicentino, *L'antica musica ridotta alla moderna prattica* (Rome, 1555).

30 Ursula Kirkendale, 'The Source for Bach's "Musical Offering": The "Institutio oratoria" of Quintilian', *Journal of the American Musicological Society*, 33 (1980): 88–141. Similar ideas have now been extended to earlier repertory, notably by Patrick Macey in a number of publications, including 'Josquin and Musical Rhetoric: *Miserere mei, Deus* and Other Motets', in Richard Sherr (ed.), *The Josquin Companion* (Oxford University Press, 2000), 485–530.

31 Bower, 'The Grammatical Model', 143.

32 Margaret Bent, 'What is Isorhythm?', D. B. Cannata *et al.* (eds.), *'Quomodo Cantabimus Canticum?': Studies in Honor of Edward H. Roesner*, American Institute of Musicology. Micellanea 7 (Middleton, WI: American Institute of Musicology, 2008), 121–43. See also Bent, '"Sounds perish"', for some revision to a standard view of this medieval–Renaissance divide.

33 For some examples, see Margaret Bent, 'Words and Music in Machaut's Motet 9', *Early Music*, 31 (2003): 363–88; 'Polyphony of Texts and Music in the Fourteenth-Century Motet: *Tribum que non abhorruit/Quoniam secta latronum/Merito hec patimur* and its "quotations"', in Dolores Pesce (ed.), *Hearing the Motet: Essays on the Motet of the Middle Ages and Renaissance* (New York: Oxford University Press, 1997), 82–103. The essay by Elizabeth Eva Leach, also demonstrates the constant play of musical grammar and rhetoric in the performance of a French polyphonic song.

34 Published in *Polyphonic Music of the Fourteenth Century*, ed. L. Schrade *et al.*, 24 vols. (Monaco; Éditions de l'Oiseau-Lyre, 1956), vol. I, 129; discussed by Sarah Fuller, '"Delectabur in hoc auris": Some Fourteenth-Century Perspectives on Aural Perception', *The Musical Quarterly*, 82 (1998): 466–81, and Margaret Bent, 'Ciconia, Prosdocimus, and the Workings of Musical Grammar as Exemplified in *O felix templum* and *O Padua*', in Philippe Vendrix (ed.), *Johannes Ciconia: musician de la transition* (Trunhout: Brepols,

2003), 65–106. The latter study includes examples of elective alternative readings.

35 Johannes Boen, 'Ex quo concludo mothetum *Cum venerint* in principio secundi modi sui sub correctione tanti sui artificis esse defectuosum, ubi tertiam inter duas claves taliter disposuit: Inter quas notas tonus est una cum semitonio maiore et sic minus quam tertia dytonalis, que perfecta dicitur, plus vero quam semiditonalis, que imperfecta dicitur; nam si littera ♭ mi primam non precederet, esset inter eas prescise tonus, ad quam distantiam littera ♭ mi apposita addit semitonium maius per primam suppositionem partis precedentis. Pro excusatione tamen tanti artificis potest dici, quod debeat admitti, quia asperitas eius dulcibus circumstantiis et suffulta.' From Wolf Frobenius, *Johannes Boens Musica und seine Konsonanzenlehre* (Stuttgart: Musikwissenschaftliche Verlags-Gesellschaft, 1971), 67–8.

36 M. Carruthers, 'Sweetness', *Speculum*, 81 (2006): 999–1,013, makes the point that 'sweetness' is spoken of most often as containing in itself its opposite, 'harsh' or 'bitter'. See also Christopher Page, 'Reading and Reminiscence: Tinctoris on the Beauty of Music', *Journal of the American Musicological Society*, 49 (1996): 1–31; see n. 21 for the passage reporting the divine sweetness ('tantam suavitudinem') of his favoured composers.

37 Christopher Page, 'A Treatise on Musicians from ?c.1400: The *Tractatulus de differentiis et gradibus cantorum* by Arnulf de St Ghislain', *Journal of the Royal Musical Association*, 45 (1992): 1–21, at 16, 20.

38 See Blair Sullivan, 'The Unwritable Sound of Music: The Origins and Implications of Isidore's Memorial Metaphor', *Viator*, 30 (1999): 1–13.

CHAPTER 3

Nature's forge and mechanical production

Writing, reading and performing song*

Elizabeth Eva Leach

The forge was an important locus of 'making' in the Middle Ages, providing a metaphorical space for procreation, poetic creation, musical composition and – because of its coordinated production of sound – musical performance. That artistic creativity in various media is linked to a site of mechanical (if skilled) production usually involving several craftsmen, allows medieval creativity both to be seen as a collaborative practice and also to be inflected significantly by ideas of copying and imitation. Medieval song is thus a dynamic form that comes into full being only through a series of collaborative and performative processes that have their own implicit rhetoric and that are themselves subject to thematization and play within the corpus of composed works that have come down to us. This essay first explores the forge as a creative and performative space before examining one such thematization of the forging of song: Jacob Senleches' double balade, *Je me merveil/J'ay pluseurs fois*. The modern(ist) assumption of composers writing pieces that are then interpreted, realized or even merely executed by performers will be discarded in favour of viewing the musical trace as a series of more or less precise memorial *notae* from which trained singers invent a collaborative (simultaneous) performance. The modern concept of 'distributed cognition' will be used to describe this creative interaction of composer, notation, singers and memory, and to gain insight into the totality of the song's rhetoric.

MEMORY, THE FORGE, *INVENTIO* AND THE MECHANICAL

The image of artistic creativity taking place in a mint or a forge, through a mechanical process of stamping, minting or coining, has roots in late antiquity. In the Middle Ages it relies on the way in which natural procreation was already figured within the threefold hierarchy of creativity found in writers from Chalcidius to William of Conches. In this hierarchy, only God truly creates; nature's laws carry on God's creation by producing more creatures, and human artistic creativity strives – ultimately in vain – to imitate nature. Nature is most commonly personified as God's sub-vicar, turning out creatures in a forge according to the divine plan, as, for example, in the work of the twelfth-century Chartrist, Alan of Lille.[1] Human art – usually synecdochically represented by poetry – is adulterate, third degree creativity, but is modelled on that of Nature and thus shares in the image of the forge as its locus of the creative act. Contrasting nature and art in his continuation of the *Roman de la Rose*, whose Lady Nature is heavily indebted to Alan of Lille's, Jean de Meun notes that Art takes Nature's 'coins' as her models but 'her understanding is so weak and bare that she cannot make living things, however natural they seem'[2]. Nevertheless, artistic creativity is something to be celebrated because, as Alan of Lille (citing Boethius) notes, 'of all things composed of matter and form only the human mind has ever been able to stamp names upon things as it willed'.[3]

Although it is figured as a mechanical process, artistic creativity was an intrinsically human activity. As Mary Carruthers has noted, medieval people do not 'have' ideas, they 'make' them, much as medieval workmen make things in their more literal forges, using machines as tools.[4] *Memoria* serves as the machine for that creativity, for that part of memory called *inventio*.[5] While it is viewed as mechanical and physical, the medieval art of memory is not about rote memorization, but is instead a compositional art involving things we might more readily term creativity and imagination. That is, memory is a machine for making images through mechanical reproduction without that meaning unthinking, rote memorization. The memory creates artistic products much as a forge stamps coins and in both cases this image of mechanical reproduction is ultimately human, collaborative and can go awry.

Although the mechanical and artificial might now be held to be antithetical to the human, for premodern societies machines were fully human: Augustine says that knowledge is itself a kind of machine. This brings ideas forged 'mechanically' from memory closer to what we would call 'cognition' since the process involves emotion, imagination and cogitation within recollection.[6] Moreover, the making of cognitive pictures is not literally mimetic: the pictures that function as memorial *notae* do not literally copy the things they are of, but are rather a verbal–visual mix that can be as arbitrary as we would now consider the linguistic sign.[7]

It was not negative to see *inventio* as a mechanical process – a form of reproduction, and the human body itself was seen as a mechanism – not in the materialist and secular eighteenth-century sense, but quite literally reflecting the ingenuity of design in God's creation.[8] In music theory treatises, too, the whole human body – the natural instrument producing the sound of song – is sometimes referred to as a machine.[9] In Alan of Lille's story, Nature's forge malfunctions thanks to the subministrations of a meddling Venus; like Nature's creative arena, the human forge, too, was always at risk of going wrong.

CREATION AND PROCREATION: THE MORAL AMBIGUITY OF MEMORY

Since Nature's creativity is focused on producing the creatures of the sublunary world, it is a picture of *pro*creation. Nature's law allows animals to mate and continue their species. In Latin, the sparks that fly from an anvil when struck by a hammer were referred to using the word 'seed' (*semina*), the same used for the 'spark of life', semen. This idea derives from neo-Platonic thought transmitted from late antiquity to the Middle Ages via epitomists and commentary writers. For example, Macrobius' fifth-century Commentary on the *Dream of Scipio* notes that 'Once the seed has been deposited in the mint where man is coined, nature immediately begins to work her skill upon it so that on the seventh day she causes a sack to form around the embryo, as thin in texture as the membrane that lies under the shell of an egg, enclosing the white.'[10]

When coining is an image of sonic or linguistic artistic expression, the image on the coin is a name. When coining figures Nature's sexual creativity, the images stamped on the creatures coined in Nature's forge are their faces, their identity and their lineage.[11] Active masculine hammers creating life with seeds produced from their contact with passive feminine anvils fitted medieval medical ideas of sexuality and gender roles perfectly.

Between the phallic hammer and the passive sounding-block of the anvil is desire (often symbolized in pictures of Nature's forge by heart-shaped bellows or blazing furnaces). In Alan of Lille's *Complaint of Nature*, Lady Nature explains how she trained Venus to help her in the process of forging God's creatures and how Venus contravened Nature's rules, pairing the wrong hammers with the wrong anvils and even hammers with hammers. Alan describes procreation using grammatical imagery, the grammar of hammers and anvils. In his extended metaphorical equivalence between human procreation and poetic creation, the process of production in both cases is dangerously open to lustful distraction.[12] He implies that human art cannot convey truth in a way free from the influence of man's corrupting nature because human perversion is manifested in language as well as in sexuality.[13]

It is unsurprising that, like the machine for procreation, the machine for creation – memory – can also malfunction. Like other forms of mechanical reproduction, remembering can be led astray, it can be distracted. In mnemotechnical terms this does not lead necessarily to a failure of memory – to forgetting – but rather to its disorder, *curiositas*.[14] This is not a disinterested Ciceronian curiosity for knowledge, but an ocular kind of fornication, Augustine's 'lust of the eyes'; for Thomas Aquinas it is opposed to intellectual study.[15] Throughout the Middle Ages, singers are frequently urged to renounce this *curiositas*, which for them manifests itself in the pursuit of novelty, the over-elaboration of chant in performance, and the use of high pitches and excessively wide vocal ranges within a single melody.[16] Such singers are accused of sexual impropriety, lasciviousness, or turning Lady Musica into a harlot. They fail to employ their human capacity for reason in favour of deploying an ability to perform that is completely ungrounded in theoretical understanding. They do not learn anything, but merely copy the outside effect of the music-making of others.[17] One significant element in the theoretical foundations that such mere singers lack is symbolized by the forge itself. This is not Nature's forge, but one in which the proportions of musical consonance were discovered, by either a passing Pythagoras or the smith's biblical brother Jubal.

According to the neo-Platonists the rational principles of music were discovered by chance one day when Pythagoras was passing a blacksmith's shop. The sound of the smiths' different hammers striking in alternate and regular succession seemed to give musical intervals. Asking the men to swap hammers allowed Pythagoras to rule out the variables of speed or force of striking. He then recorded the weights of the hammers, eventually concluding that harmonious tones are produced according to a proportion of the weights: 6:8:9:12.

This story was reported by over a dozen classical authors and transmitted to the Middle Ages principally through the writings of Macrobius and Boethius. Certain writers rejected Pythagoras' pagan discovery in favour of a biblical one by Jubal (sometimes called Tubal), whose brother Tubalcain was a blacksmith.[18] Some writers combined both stories, reasoning that Jubal got there first and that Pythagoras was just a post-diluvian Johnny-come-lately, rediscovering principles that had once been known.[19]

SENLECHES (& CO.) AS THE HAMMER OF THE AMATEUR

The forge is therefore not just a place in which Nature procreates and poets create, but is also a symbolic location for the origins of the true understanding of the fundamental principles of *musica*. In effect Lady Nature's forge producing creatures is also Lady Musica's forge producing songs. Such an inference is made in Guillaume de Machaut's *Remede de Fortune* (before c. 1356).[20] After attending a sumptuous dinner with his lady, the lover-protagonist chronicles the various forms of after-dinner relaxation offered to the guests. The very beautiful room ('chambre moult belle') to which the company retires contains musicians who are:

> Milleurs assez et plus scïens
> En la vieus et nouvelle forge
> Que Musique qui les chans forge,
> Ne Orpheüs, qui si bien chanta
> Que tous ceaus d'enfer enchanta
> Par la douçour de son chanter.[21]

[better and more knowledgeable in the old and new forge than Music, who forges songs, or Orpheus, who sang so well that he enchanted all those in hell by the sweetness of his song.]

These musicians are better singers than Orpheus and better at forging music than Music herself. The published translation interprets 'forge' as a reference to the composition (writing) of music in contrast to the singers' singing of it. In modern musical practice we are used to composition and performance being distinct practices with different practitioners, one 'making' in notation (writing), the other 'making' in sound (performing). However, this division does not hold well for the Middle Ages, when the role of composer was a more specialized component of being a singer and when neither singing nor composition relied largely on notation. Yet in the late medieval context, newly available elaborate forms of music-writing played with their own possibility to prescribe practice, and with the ambiguity of creativity that song's written and sounding states enabled.[22]

A verbatim performance from late medieval notation is not possible, because the notes underprescribe certain elements of the music (of the pitch content in particular). The placing of pitches on a heighted staff (a set of lines signifying relative pitches) seems to fix them, but the translation of this into sound cannot be achieved without a memory of the relative difference between the pitches that are represented.[23] The relative intervals of an individual singer's part will be adjusted further on account of the counterpoint of the sounding polyphonic whole. The realization of these elements thus relies on the memory and education of the highly trained singer, who reads the arbitrary representation of sounds in graphic symbols – the memorial *notae* of musical notation. In a polyphonic song, the singers collaboratively invent the harmonies in performance, using a shared external memory (made up of written *notae*) that has been provided by a single individual (the composer). Only by remembering the sounds of particular intervals can the singer attempt to render his or her notation into sound. Only by responding to the sounds of the other singers (whose notated parts the individual singer cannot follow at the same time as his own) can the singer make decisions about the precise interval content of his or her own melody.

It is both because memory is a machine for making – for *inventio* – not a rote memorization of the thing made, and because writing is an external kind of memory, that the relationship between notation and its musical performance is similar to the relationship between human memory (the machine for *inventio*) and the rhetorical performances that it generates. In creating a written artifact – the notated music – the composer is merely providing something that provides a schedule for the initial performance and an external memory of the piece for later performances, which the singers (who probably included the composer in the earliest performances of most pieces of music in the Middle Ages) can use to invent (that is, to discover, to reveal or to find) the song again.

The poems of the double-texted song by the late-fourteenth-century harpist and composer Jacob de Senleches, *Je me merveil/J'ay pluseurs fois*, present two singers who deplore the state of contemporary music-making. Their shared refrain text – the moment of nodding verbal agreement between these two different voices singing at once – is presented as a canon (that is, the two upper voices effectively sing the same music as each other but with a small time lag between them). This highly 'composerly' technique is accentuated in its written presentation by being hidden from view: the two voices use different-looking notations to signal these similar musical lines.

This song is a piece by a named composer, in a notational form that is highly intricate and thus presents itself as primarily a textual object, a work, and one whose performance has been read as referring involutedly to its own being. The assumption of most modern commentators on this piece has been that it is concerned with composing music in the sense of making it in writing, criticizing less able composers, and maybe even critiquing the very same modern (notational and musical) style that it exemplifies itself.[24]

The focus on composition and composers in musicology has historically tended to result in the elision of performers in favour of a discussion of notated works. Musicologists have even talked about the way in which the composer-centred work concept that seems to have been born around 1800 caused the performer to be viewed as the instrument of the composer, mechanically following the increasingly precise notations that the composer leaves behind. On account of modern perceptions of mechanism, the performer then becomes a lifeless mannequin, only animated by the work.[25] In part this is because the usual way in which we access music today presents performer-free sound, seemingly allowing unmediated communion with the music of the composer.[26] But musicology is not alone in such emphasis on authors and works. Even within the discipline of theatre studies – whose performers are at least visible even when recorded – a similar treatment of plays as texts (and I am thinking here particularly of the Shakespearean canon) and focus on authors have only relatively recently come under sustained critique. One must probably conclude that the author-centredness of the academy (made up, as it is, of writers) has historically been the chief cause of the relatively scant regard accorded to performers.

As will be discussed below, the early modern theatre in fact makes an interesting point of comparison for medieval song in several respects: it is a collaborative performance act whose 'text' certainly has an 'author' but whose performed 'work' is somewhat flexible. It is also presented in a notation whereby each performer sees only his own part and must rely on aural cues that suggest certain 'movements' (in theatre these are cues or stage directions contained in the dialogue; in music, these are the succession of intervals between each upper-part singer and the tenor).[27]

Although writing is mentioned in the first stanza of Senleches' cantus text, and the cue for the refrain's 'joke' (see below) is based on very visual notational difference, any idea that the song voices only a *composer* (or composers) addressing amateur *composers* needs to be challenged. The central issue of this song seems, to me, to be more centrally the interplay between composer, notation and singers, especially when, as seems likely in this case, the medieval singers would have included the composer among their ranks.[28] The hammer and anvil of the musical forge are not pen and paper producing textual coin, but tongue and teeth, two parts of the natural instrument of a singer, producing the sound of coin being struck.[29] Senleches, like most music theorists who discuss these matters, most criticizes those who think they know about musical doctrine when they don't, because learning is not just a matter for composers.

Far from criticizing his compositional rivals, Senleches' song addresses the relationship between forging a song in writing as a composer and forging a song in sound as a singer – a relationship mediated by notation – in a period when the memory was a machine for invention, the mechanical was positively human, and being someone's instrument was a culturally approved career choice. In short, I suggest that a song is less an object than a collaborative rhetorical process which binds the composer, notation, singers and listeners within a machine, whose workings – when going well – should mirror in sonic ratios those that medieval thinkers posited in the heavens.

FORGING SONG

In the earliest performances of this song it seems likely that the composer was also one of the singers. Unlike other songs of the period, there is no evidence that this song was widely distributed and perhaps it was never performed outside the composer's immediate circle.[30] The song is a double balade with three musical parts: it has a textless tenor part (probably sung wordlessly to a vowel, or perhaps played instrumentally) and two upper voices performed simultaneously, each setting a different three-stanza balade text but sharing the same refrain (the texts and translations are provided in Figure 3. 1).[31] Both the singers of the texted upper voices despair of 'forging' and want to give it up, as the refrain text explains, 'because everyone is getting involved in forging' ['Puis que chascuns se melle de forgier']. In the lower-pitched texted voice (functionally the 'contratenor' part) the speaker tells how he often used to make virelais and rondels for his own amusement, but now wants to stop completely 'because everyone is getting involved in forging'. The only person who ought to forge, he maintains, is someone with such an acute understanding that one only knows how to 'remake' [*refayre*] what such a person fashions.[32] But instead everyone wants to go first, saying 'I know' in order to praise his own doings and to blame others in what they do, and so the speaker wearily concludes that he does not wish to get involved any more 'because everyone is getting involved in forging'. He reveals that some even go in secret to show their things to other people in order to get them properly finished [*pour parfayre*], although this is not done from good sense because such foolish wits have no clue whom to ask.

In the higher-pitched texted voice (functionally, the cantus), the speaker expresses his amazement at how often he sees someone who wants to get involved in copying [*contrefaire*] but fails to write the end or beginning

Cantus	Contratenor
Je me merveil aucune fois comment	J'ay pluseurs fois pour mon esbatement,
Homme se vuelt meller de contrefaire	Ou temps passé, heü playsir de faire
Ce dont n'escrit fin ne commencement	Un virelay de petit sentiment
Et quanqu'il fait, raison est au contraire.	Ou un rondel qui [bien] a moy puist playre.
Dorenavant voil ma forge deffaire:	Mais maintenant je me vueil tout quoy tayre
Englume ne mertell ne m'ont mestier	Et moy lesier ester et reparer
Puis que chascuns se melle de forgier.	Puis que chascuns se melle de forgier.
C'est soctie par peu devisament,	Forgier doit chilz qui son entendement
Car cel labour ne leur est necessaire;	A si agut c'on n'i sceit que refayre;
Je ne di pas pour celuy qui aprent	Mais chascuns vuelt aler primierement
Et qui connoist s'il seit bien ou mal faire:	Disant 'je sçay' pour loer son afayre
Celui doit on tenir a debonaire.	Et pour autruy blasmer en son repaire.
Mais je ne vueil plus faire ce mestier	Si ne me vuel je plus enpeschier
Puis que chascuns se melle de forgier.	Puis que chascuns se melle de forgier.
Quant on leur dit leur vice evidement,	Il en i a qui vont celeement
Qui cognoscent, se ne leur puet il plaire:	Moustrer lour fais a autruy pour parfayre:
Il respondent molt ourguelleusement,	Ce n'est pas fayt aseürement
Disant que de doctrine n'ont que faire!	Ne de bon sens, se leur on doit desplayre,
Il doinent aus nouvels fol exemplaire ...	Mais fol cuidier ne sceit ou il repayre!
Pour ce farai soppes en un panier	Pour ce m'estuet bouter en un poillier
Puis que chascuns se melle de forgier.	Puis que chascuns se melle de forgier.
I am sometimes amazed how man wants to get involved in composing [contrefaire] that of which he does not write end or beginning, and all that he does, reason is contrary to it. From now on I want to dismantle [deffaire] my forge – neither anvil nor hammer have need of me, because everyone is getting involved in forging.	I have many times, for my own amusement in the past, had pleasure in making a virelai of modest feeling or a rondel which might please me well. But now I want to keep completely silent and leave myself be and go home, because everyone is getting involved in forging.
It takes little reckoning to know it is folly, because this labour is not necessary for them. I am not talking about someone who studies and who knows if he can do it well or badly: such a person one must deem good [debonaire]. But I do not want to do this business any longer, because everyone is getting involved in forging.	Only he should forge who has such acute understanding that the knowledge of everyone else is limited to copying [refayre] his example. But everyone wishes to go first saying 'I know' so as to praise his own business and to blame others in what they do. So I do not wish to get involved any more, because everyone is getting involved in forging.
When one tells them of their evident vice, which they know, although it cannot please them, they reply most proudly, saying that they have no doctrine other than doing it! They give newcomers a foolish example, which is why I shall make soup in a basket [i.e., be engaged in an enterprise doomed to failure], because everyone is getting involved in forging.	There are those who go secretly to show what they've done to others so as to complete them. This is not done with surety nor from good sense (although one might displease them), but a foolish wit does not know where to go. This is why I must knock it on the head,[1] because everyone is getting involved in forging. [1] The literal sense of the idiom here is obscure, but the meaning is clear.

Figure 3.1 Texts and translations of Jacob Senleches' double balade,
Je me merveil / *J'ay pluseurs fois*

and disregards reason in everything. He vows henceforth to dismantle his forge – neither anvil nor hammer has need of *him* 'because everyone is getting involved in forging'. He implies that his own forging has involved a lot of labour for scant reward, labour these upstarts eschew. He specifically exempts from his critique those who put in the effort to learn good from bad, but denounces those who, when told of their errors, proudly reply that they have no training other than the very act of making songs (with this 'making' being unspecified as to whether it is through composing or singing).

Several of the terms here present problems of translation, but it is clear from the fact that the speaker of each poem himself forges in his forge and says that only the most acute understanding should attempt it, that 'forge' carries none of its modern associations of counterfeiting or duplicitously copying but rather signals – neutrally – the act of making, which can be done well or badly, with rational doctrine or without. But, like the forges of Nature (and Venus), or the machine of memory, the musical forge can become disordered if insufficient reason and understanding are exercised. The word 'contrefaire', similarly, is less negative than its modern equivalent, which is why I have not used the term 'counterfeit' in the translation. In this period it refers, as Stephen Perkinson has shown, to the copying of the outer appearance of a thing (rather than its inner essence).[33] While this might mean that the thing thus copied has the capacity to deceive, its fourteenth-century uses are closer to the idea of mindless (irrational) mimicking or mirroring than to the modern concept of duplicitous counterfeiting.[34] In music, the uses of the prefix 'contra' (Latin), 'contre' (French), or 'counter' (English) frequently imply not the faking of something, but rather something's counterpart. This is the sense of the prefix in counterpoint ('contrapunctus') – a musical technique in which a note in one voice is placed against (that is, simultaneously, *and* in harmony, with) a note in another. This is also the sense of the contratenor voice part as it relates to the tenor. The 'contratenor' is not a specific voice type (it is usually in the same pitch range as the tenor and would thus similarly be sung by a tenor or baritone voice type), but a description of function.[35] With a different word separation, the first two lines of the cantus here could even be read as saying that 'I often marvel how a man who wants to make *a contratenor part* [vuelt meller de contre faire] has not written the end or the beginning of it.' This might even relate to the then-contemporary vogue for providing existing songs with new contratenor parts, some of which are certainly of a noticeably lesser (or at least 'different') quality to the arguably authorial parts for the piece and thus could represent the work of the unlearned composers that the song lambasts.[36] The sense of 'contrefaire' is indicative of the fact that medieval creativity in this period was viewed as a continuum of productive incompleteness, with all texts effectively rewriting earlier texts.[37]

FORGING IRONY?

The song's texts participate in an irony found in lyric repertoire from the troubadours to Machaut and beyond – the claim *in sung performance* that one is not going to make music any more.[38] The song's notational and compositional features lend authority to the speakers of its texts, whose two voices are so congruent that they seem to represent a composite single voice, that of 'the song's maker(s)' with an elision between the single maker represented by the composer and the several 'makers' who present the song sonically in performance. As a composed double balade, the song is already showing the forging of the speaker(s) of its text(s) to be highly accomplished. The way in which the song is written down adds to this attestation with the most central moment being the point where both voices have the same text – in the refrain.

The refrain, as already mentioned, is a musical canon – that is, the singers don't just sing the same text but one after another they sing the same music – giving the audible sense of a second singer copying or remaking the music of the first. However, the canon is notated differently in each voice, using different time signatures and various combinations of full black, full red, and void black note shapes: the two notations are visually distinct.[39] This has led modern critics to see the rhetorical force of the song being that, however much the singers of the refrain think they are doing their own thing (because their notations look different), they end up copying one another. This fact is opaque to the singers looking at the notation, but is revealed in sound to the listeners.[40] However, I think this interpretation rests on a number of misapprehensions. Only the second singer – the former maker of virelais and rondels who is now going to keep quiet – is actually copying; the first singer is a true author. Yet the two voices' complete texts are saying broadly the same thing, so it would be hard to maintain that the first voice is the true artist and the second voice is one of those criticized (by both voices) in the refrain. Moreover, in a three-stanza piece, the fact of the imitation would not remain hidden from the singers, who are also listeners (and indeed *have* to listen to each other in order to sing correctly). Nor, as I discussed above, are they specifically or centrally criticizing imitation or copying. Rather they are disparaging a musical (that is, singing or composing) practice, whose practitioners lack understanding of their performance's theoretical basis, and blaming the misplaced pride of those who refuse to put in the mental work that making music (whether in writing or in performance) properly requires. The only possible mention of copying is in the second text, whose second stanza notes that those of acute enough understanding (the only people who ought to be allowed to forge) make such things that people in general don't know what to do with them short of remaking them. But even this is not direct copying but rather remaking [*refayre*], a creative process based on re-creation. Forging (that is, fashioning, or making) is simply what singers (and composers) do: at issue here is the ethical value of that action, based on the engagement not just of doing (*faire*) but doing with learning (*doctrine*). In short, this song enacts one of the basic discussions of music theory – the differentiation between mere *cantores* and true *musici* – in a text whose presiding metaphor obliquely makes reference to the locus of the discovery of music theory's basic tenets: the forge that revealed the rational basis of consonance.[41] In effect, the *musici* who base practice on understanding can order their memories, whereas the *cantores* whose practice has no basis in theoretical understanding are doomed to the vice of *curiositas*.

Although the modern editions represent the refrain as if the different notations give precisely the same result, Anne Stone has suggested that the notational differences could be interpreted as creating a number of small sounding differences in the length of the notes.[42] For those who see the meaning of the refrain as being bound up with a critique of imitation or copying, this adds a further layer of irony, since not only can these dunderheads only imitate but 'even their imitation is imperfect'.[43] Interpreting the rhythm in this way, the singer who goes second at first seems to rush to catch up, then corrects himself, then rushes again, corrects by holding a note a little longer, but not quite enough, and never quite manages to get his musical imitation exact. But nonetheless, the counterpoint works – the fabric of the music is stretched across its rhythmic frame, but not so much that it doesn't still hang together – and the voices finish the refrain together with the word 'forgier'.

Stone and Gilles Dulong speculate that the imitation's rhythmic inexactness forces the singers to depict the incompetence of the music writers being described by the poem. Forcing them to enact what they dispraise effectively shows the performers to be the mindless instrument of the composer. However, in my interpretation the song attests to the 'entendement ... si agut' of those who are not forced into slavish copying but can introduce workable changes and create something new out of something old.[44] This goes not only for composers but also for singers who are making anew an already performed composition each time they sing it. And an inexact canonic refrain would not be incompetent imitation on at least two counts: first, because it would still work; and second, because the same inexact canon would be repeated exactly, three times, once for each of the three stanzas. In a strophic song, the triple repetition of this joke would make it clear that a *seemingly* cobbled together inexact canon – as if the singers are not quite getting an exact canon right – is exactly what is intended by both composer and singers. The inexact imitation in performance shows instead (once the listener works out what is going on) that the singers are not mindless imitators, just as the varied musical script for the two similar melodic lines shows that the composer is not a mere imitator either.

It thus becomes clear that the singers of this song – in so far as they may be identified with the sentiments they express in words and the reading practices they employ in making their melodies – view and project themselves as radically distinct from the people being criticized by the text that they are singing. Rather they are – as is more usual in the expression of first person lyric – identified prosopopoeically with the first person speakers of their texts, who are so appalled by the downgrading of reason and understanding in the practice of making music that they are not going to make it themselves any more. The congruent views of the two texts mark them as the double expression of a single voice, emblematic, perhaps, of the multivoiced making of the composer's composition that a polyphonic song-setting makes necessary. In traversing the gap between the notational memorial cues of the song's written trace and its sounding performance, the singers deploy the very rationality and understanding whose lack they deplore in other forgers of song.

MUSICAL NOTES AS MEMORIAL *NOTAE*

This notation cues more content than it actually represents, so that once any performance of this song finally stops, its sounds are lost. Sounds cannot be written down per se, and the cognitive link between their external representation (the musical notes) and the now faded performance is held collectively in several memories. The understanding required to re-enact the song is thus 'distributed' across the group rather than owned by a single person. For modern performances of this song, this fact is a problem. The very complexity of this song – its play with the role of distributed cognition in its performative making – means the range of possible modern interpretations of the notation is far larger than that of most of its contemporaries. We are even less sure about the relative pitches, intervals, note lengths and durations here than in other songs of this period, even than in other songs by Senleches.[45] The memories of the singers who turn the music-writing of the composer into the music-making of their sonic performance are necessarily engaged in remembering a whole host of interactions in rehearsal, involving a number of decisions made together with the other singers, through discussion, doctrine, reason and understanding, none of which is represented directly in the notation.

The challenging nature of the notation in Senleches' song means that singers of the song cannot simply 'follow the instructions'; the musical notes are even more clearly closer to the nonlinguistic status of memorial *notae* than musical notation usually is; they point to what has to be remembered from the creation of the sonic product in performance. This is not just the case in the refrain. The notation as a whole cannot just be read off; it is rhythmically difficult and it requires the singers to realize, by sharpening or flattening certain pitches, a number of cadences that are deliberately deceptive. Each singer would have been performing not from a score where there was visual oversight of the entire musical piece, but from the individual line of a single part (whether visually present or imprinted in memory). In several places where the intelligent and experienced individual singer might expect that a certain kind of line is, given its contour, a cadence point, upon hearing the other two parts it proves not to be one. In rehearsal this would require a split-second adjustment, responding to the way in which hearing the musical whole confounds the expectations arising from reading one's own line. Perhaps these points would result in the singers stopping, (mentally) noting the problem, and repeating the phrase correctly; or perhaps the wrongly inflected phrase would be passed over, with the offending singer retrospectively acknowledging his error by some gesture.[46]

Alternatively, the rhythmic complexity of the song sometimes delays a contrapuntal resolution in the other voices so that the opposite occurs: the resolutions are correct but just don't sound right to start with – the individual singer must 'stick to his guns' until the others fall into line. In some places the singer is faced with the choice of either not placing a cadence where one obviously should go given what he can hear in the other two parts, or making the cadence by singing an extremely irregular interval.[47] The various ways in which singers negotiated these decisions depended on expert decision-making that was collaborative, flexibly hier-archical (with the tenor often having most control of the sonorities and, perhaps, with the composer having the most say overall),[48] and relied on external tools and representations (the visual aspect of the notation on the page or in memory, and the sound of the other voices).

So are we left thinking that this song, for all its cleverness, did its greatest cultural work in the rehearsal room? Did it serve only the social interaction of its singers? Is it just some kind of singers' in-joke? This certainly forms the central part of my argument, but this will only make us dismiss it if we introduce later categories of value, and import more modern performance situations and practices. Not much information about musical rehearsal in the Middle Ages can be gleaned directly from the sources but it is possible to posit early modern theatre as a useful comparison. As with early modern theatre, the composer of a medieval polyphonic song was often one of the performers; the performers worked principally from their own parts in isolation.[49] Simon Palfrey and Tiffany Stern have recently refocused the study of Shakespeare's plays through the fact of their having been originally copied into, learned from, and rehearsed using parts. The interaction of the individual play-ers in rehearsal and performance then becomes something with which a seasoned playwright – especially one who is, as was usually the case, also himself an actor – can work and play. This collaborative nature of rehearsal and performance has also been investigated by Evelyn Tribble using the modern psychological concept of distributed cognition. This combination of a focus on the division of a single work into separate parts and the use of distributed cognition as a way of investigating the collaboration necessary for the re-presentation of the work as a whole provides a useful way of imagining the rehearsal and performance of a song like *Je me merveil/J'ay pluseurs fois*.[50]

Analyses of expert thinking have traditionally focused on individ-ual cognition, whereas those that foregrounded instead the social and environmental nature of cognition typically led to qualitative analyses of 'everyday thinking' (about mundane activities such as supermarket shopping, for example).[51] Edwin Hutchins' study of maritime navigation on the USS *Palau*, by contrast, studied expert group cognition, thereby offering surprisingly close parallels to both the early modern theatre and, I would argue, medieval musical performance.[52]

Distributed cognition typically involves a hierarchical structure of individuals, using external objects to represent things difficult to represent mentally, in a process that necessitates collaboration.[53] The goal of analysis is to discover how 'distributed units are coordinated by analyzing the interactions between individuals, the representational media used, and the environment within which the activity takes place'.[54] Because the work in question involves more than a single toolless individual, the analysis involves a description of 'how mental activity is externalized into the world, as people create external representation to support their own activity or collaborative action' and, in its most rigorous use, a description of 'its application in elucidating the architecture of cognition, where the cognitive activity is not simply mentally represented'.[55]

For the early modern theatre the tools, artifacts and practices are the playhouse, the so-called plots (single folio summaries of actors' entries), actors' roles, plays' verbal structure, the apprentice system and the organizational practices of companies. These things constrain as a way of enabling because a cognitively rich environment has an effect on the agent operating within that system. The example Tribble gives is the use of oversize buttons and levers in a nuclear power plant as a way of orienting the employees to 'maximize "situation awareness"'.[56] In this song by Senleches, the cognitive richness of the elaborate visual notation does exactly this – it maximizes the singers' aural awareness of the canon, of its inexactness (if Stone's attractive interpretation of the rhythms is right) and thereby of its composedness.

Tribble argues that the early modern theatre strategically underloads its actors' rote memories by having them work from parts with minimal cues.[57] Medieval music is similarly copied in parts, usually with no visual cues because the cues are given aurally in conjunction with the basic counterpoint training of the singers.[58] Working from theatrical cues means that actors have to listen to the other actors rather than just reading the other parts silently; in medieval songs, singers have to listen to the other singers because they can't see the whole musical framework in score and need to know the intervals their notes make with the tenor to sing their parts correctly. If actors listen to the other parts, much of the information they need is contained in what is in them.[59] This is no less true of medieval songs: the contrapuntal hierarchy means that the context of the tenor in relation to one's own part contains, if one listens, all the information required for realizing the interval content of one's underprescriptively notated part. Component parts are not fully determined by the whole system, but neither are they independent of it because some (but not all) of their characteristics are changed by interaction with the system; as Tribble says, 'good writing' in itself – that is, writing which is designed to be highly memorable – provides the most effective 'cognitive scaffold'.[60] It is this concept of good writing that Senleches plays with so thoroughly and so aptly given that his song deplores the *bad* writing (and singing) of others. His song's notational play can only be experienced by those fluent in the distributed cognitive processes whose lack is the subject of the song texts' critique. Accentuating the difficulties of these processes as a way of drawing attention to the expert status of the singers (and through them, the composer), lends weight to their censure of the bad song-making (composition and singing) of others.

The 'fixed form' of the balade provides the equivalent of the early modern theatre plot – a schematic diagram of the shape of the performance as a whole. The singers' knowledge of pitch space and the conventions of movement within it (the making of correct progressions to perfect intervals by singing semitones in unusual places) enables them to realize the visual–spatial notation as audible–temporal music in much the same way as the space of the theatre and conventions of movement within *it* enable movement from a two-dimensional plot to a three-dimensional play. This kind of mechanism is a premodern one in which individual agency is directed, but not delimited, by these practices.[61]

The distance between the notation and its realization is the space in which creativity lives, not because the singers have to make anything up, nor necessarily because there is a huge difference between any two performances of the same piece. Instead, this gap allows the composer to play the singers as his instrument without that making them dehumanized; they become his machine, or the machine of him. In fact, if the composer is one of them, it effectively turns the performers into a corporate body – a social extension of the individual. This collective subjectivity fits with the fact that two singers voice two poems that seem to emanate from a single individual's point of view and are unified in the very refrain that throws up all the issues of copying, following, notation and memory. In medieval terms the three-part medieval musical machine – the three singers of this song – mirrors in microcosm the harmony of the engine in the sky – the music of the spheres – thereby signifying the rational and divine basis of human life itself. And although the singers act as a medium – like the coin that is stamped with hammers in the forge – like coin, they are not just a medium, a means of equating or translating one thought from composing mind to listening mind, but become themselves a commodity with its own particular value.[62]

NOTES

* I would like to thank Mary Carruthers and Eric Clarke for their helpful comments on earlier drafts of this paper.

1 See, in particular, Alan of Lille, *The Plaint of Nature*, trans. J. Sheridan (Toronto: PIMS, 1980), 146; G. Economou, *The Goddess Natura in Medieval Literature* (University of Notre Dame Press, 2002), 84; and N. Häring, 'Alan of Lille, *De planctu Naturae*', *Studi medievali*, 3rd series, 19 (1978): 797–879, at 840.

2 For the full passage, see Guillaume de Lorris and Jean de Meun: Le Roman de la Rose, ed. A. Strubel (Paris: Librairie Générale Française, 1992), lines 16,009–28; *The Romance of the Rose*, trans. F. Horgan (Oxford University Press, 1994), 247–8. See also Economou, *The Goddess Natura*, 106.

3 'Ut testatur Boethius rebus ex materia formaque constantibus solus humanis animus extitit qui prout voluit nomina rebus inpressit', quoted in J. M. Ziolkowski, *Alan of Lille's Grammar of Sex: The Meaning of Grammar to a Twelfth-Century Intellectual* (Cambridge, MA: Medieval Academy of America, 1985), 28, citing P. Glorieux, 'La Somme "Quoniam homies" d'Alain de Lille', *Archives d'histoire doctrinale et littéraire du moyen âge* 28 (1953): 113–364, at 141. See also Hugh of St Victor, *Didascalicon*, I.9, which notes that the human work is 'only imitative of nature' and is thus 'fitly called mechanical, that is adulterate', like a 'skeleton key', but goes on to argue that human reason 'shines forth much more brilliantly' in inventing things, from which the 'infinite varieties of painting, weaving, carving, and founding have arisen, so that we look with wonder not at nature alone but at the artificer as well'. From *The Didascalicon of Hugh of St. Victor*, trans. J. Taylor, rev. edn. (New York: Columbia University Press, 1991), 55–6.

4 M. Carruthers, *The Craft of Thought: Meditation, Rhetoric, and the Making of Images, 400–1200* (Cambridge University Press, 1998), 3–5.

5 Personified as the mother of the Muses, Memory is 'at the beginning, as the matrix of invention for all human arts, of all human making, including the making of ideas'. As Carruthers (*Ibid.*, 7) notes, this story 'memorably encapsulates an assumption that memory and invention, or what we now call "creativity," if not exactly one, are the closest thing to it'. In their opening chapters, medieval music theory treatises usually follow Isidore of Seville (*Etymologiae*, III.15) in deriving *musica* from the Muses; the relation between music and Memory is thus theoretically explicit.

6 Carruthers, *The Craft of Thought*, 22–3, 2.

7 *Ibid.*, 2–5.

8 As Carruthers (*Ibid.*, 7) says, 'In order to create, in order to think at all, human beings require some mental tool or machine, and that "machine" lives in the intricate networks of their own memory.'

9 A treatise for singers from around 1300 deems it fitting that 'the Saviour of the world, three persons in one, should receive the triple gift of our observance: the heart must yearn, the mouth sound, and the whole mechanism [*machina*] of the body strive which so devoutly prays to the Lord in this way [i.e., through singing chant]. Anyone who thoroughly strives in his praying

with mind, voice and works is deservedly called a *citharista* in the Temple of the Lord.' From *The Summa Musice: A Thirteenth-Century Manual for Singers*, ed. C. Page (Cambridge University Press, 1991), 59, 148–9. This division into thought, word and deed casts chant as a deed: singing is mechanical reproduction, but mechanical reproduction is an image of doing, of making, and thus of creativity.

10 Macrobius Ambrosius Theodosius, *Commentary on the Dream of Scipio*, trans. W. H. Stahl (New York: Columbia University Press, 1952), 112. *Commentarium in somnium Scipionis*, ed. Franciscus Eyssenhardt (Leipzig: Teubner, 1868), 498: 'uerum semine semel intra formandi hominis monetam locato hoc primum artifex natura molitur ut die septimo folliculum genuinum circumdet humori ex membrana tam tenui qualis in ouo ab exteriore testa clauditur et intra se claudit liquorem'.

11 This Aristotelian idea is frequent in medical and physiological treatises of the Middle Ages and surfaces in literary treatments of extramarital pregnancy; see Nancy Vine Durling, 'Women's Visible Honor in Medieval Romance: The Example of the Old French Roman du Comte de Poitiers', in Renata Blumenfeld-Kosinski (ed.), *Translatio Studii: Essays by His Students in Honor of Karl D. Uitti for His Sixty-Fifth Birthday* (Amsterdam: Rodopi, 2000): 117–32, at 126.

12 Ziolkowski, *Alan of Lille's Grammar of Sex*, especially 27–30 (on 'The Grammar of Hammers and Anvils') and 105–7 (on the relation of grammar, poetry, free will, natural goodness and discipline).

13 Economou, *The Goddess Natura* 86.

14 Carruthers, *The Craft of Thought*, 82.

15 See Cicero, *Tusculan disputations*, trans. J. E. King, LCL (London: Heinemann, 1927), I.44; Augustine, *Confessions*, VI.8; and Britton J. Harwood, 'Dame Study and the Place of Orality in Piers Plowman', *English Language History*, 57 (1990): 1–17, at 7, 15 n. 19.

16 See E. E. Leach, *Sung Birds: Music, Nature, and Poetry in the Later Middle Ages* (Ithaca, NY: Cornell University Press, 2007), 205, 239–54; William Dalglish, 'The Origin of the Hocket', *Journal of the American Musicological Society*, 31 (1978): 3–20; and E. E. Leach, 'Gendering the Semitone, Sexing the Leading Tone: Fourteenth-Century Music Theory and the Directed Progression', *Music Theory Spectrum*, 28 (2006): 1–21.

17 See Dalglish, 'The Origin of the Hocket'.

18 See Jean-Marie Fritz, *Paysages sonores du Moyen Âge: Le versant épistémologique* (Paris: Champion, 2000), 128–37, and E. E. Leach, 'The Unquiet Thoughts of Edmund Spenser's Scudamour', in Gioia Filocamo and M. J. Bloxam (eds.), *'Uno gentile et subtile ingenio': Studies in Renaissance Music in Honour of Bonnie J. Blackburn* Turnhout: Brepols, 2009, 513–20, at 515–18.

19 See the summary in Fritz, *Paysages sonores du Moyen Âge*, 128–37. The weight of hammers does not make much difference to the pitch of the struck anvil, as Vincenzo Galilei showed in the sixteenth century. The story continued to be told, however; it works with string lengths. See J. W. McKinnon, '*Jubal vel*

Pythagoras, quis sit inventor musicae?', *The Musical Quarterly*, 64 (1978): 1–28. Franchino Gaffurio, *Theorica Musice* (Milan, 1492), I.8.36–9, reports the priority of Jubal as an addendum to his telling of the Pythagoras tale. His source is Peter Comestor, *Historia Scholastica*; see *Petri Comestoris Scolastica Historia. Liber Genesis*, ed. Agneta Sylwan, CCCM 191 (Turnhout: Brepols, 2005), 53–5.

20 See *Guillaume de Machaut, Le Jugement du Roy de Behaigne and Remede de Fortune*, ed. J. I. Wimsatt *et al.* (Athens: University of Georgia Press, 1988). The date I've given (later than that usually offered) is the latest date ascribed to the earliest surviving manuscript of this poem. See also L. Earp, *Guillaume de Machaut: A Guide to Research* (New York: Garland, 1995), 212–15.

21 Guillaume de Machaut, *Remede de Fortune*, lines 4,002–7. Since the forge showcases music rudiments, the idea of an old and a new forge might differentiate between old and new bases for music, whether in terms of tuning (the century's invention of the leading note demanded a different tuning of the semitone; see Leach, 'Gendering the Semitone') or in terms of performance style, as seems to be suggested by comments in the final book of the compendious early-fourteenth-century music-theoretical work *Speculum musicae* by Jacques of Liège (see Frank Hentschel, 'Der Streit um die "ars nova" – nur ein Scherz?', *Archiv für Musikwissenschaft*, 58.2 (2001): 110–30).

22 See Leach, *Sung Birds*, chapter 3.

23 The inventor of the staff, Guido of Arezzo, is very clear about the ongoing need for memory within his system, saying that 'we need to implant deeply in memory the different qualities of the individual sounds and of all their descents and ascents' before being able to use his notation to learn an unknown melody; see Guido of Arezzo, Epistle Concerning an Unknown Chant', in James McKinnon (ed.), *The Early Christian Period and the Latin Middle Ages,* Source Readings in Music History (New York: Norton, 1998), 107.

24 Anne Stone, 'The Composer's Voice in the Late-Medieval Song: Four Case Studies', in Philippe Vendrix (ed.), *Johannes Ciconia: musicien de la transition* (Turnhout: Brepols, 2003), 179–87, and Gilles Dulong, 'Canons, palindromes musicaux et textes poétiques dans les chansons de l'ars nova', in Katelijne Schiltz and Bonnie J. Blackburn (eds.), *Canons and Canonic Techniques, 14th–16th Centuries: Theory, Practice, and Reception History* (Leuven: Peeters, 2007), vol. 1, 61–82, at 69. Ultimately Dulong reads the speaker as implicated in his own critique since he is deploring modernity and yet employing the features he decries (complex rhythms and notations). However, the poem says nothing against modern notation or musical style: instead it laments those who do without understanding, something that no singer or composer of this work could be accused of on account of its very complexity of notation. I would instead see the notation and style as further distinguishing the composer and singers here from the objects of their critique (see below).

25 See C. Abbate, 'Ouside Ravel's Tomb', *Journal of the American Musicological Society*, 52 (1999): 465–530, and E. Le Guin, '"One Says that One Weeps, but

One Does Not Weep": *Sensible*, Grotesque, and Mechanical Embodiments in Boccherini's Chamber Music', *Journal of the American Musicological Society*, 55 (2002): 207–54.

26 I am reluctant to see this mentality as a result of modality. Rather than seeing recording technology as the driving factor in our acousmatic appreciation of music, I would propose to see it as the logical outgrowth of Romantic aesthetic preoccupations with the performer playing 'as if from the soul of the composer'. See M. Hunter, '"To Play as if from the Soul of the Composer": The Idea of the Performer in Early Romantic Aesthetics', *Journal of the American Musicological Society*, 58 (2005): 357–98.

27 The cue is familiar but the outlining of stage directions in the speeches of other characters is often used as a prop for the least experienced members of the cast: for example, E. Tribble, 'Distributing Cognition in the Globe', *The Shakespeare Quarterly*, 56 (2005): 135–55, at 154: 'A boy who is told "here, sirrah, approach" knows what he is to do.'

28 Stone, 'The Composer's Voice', 182, considers only the possibilities that the speaker is a poet or composer.

29 On the parts of the natural instrument, see, for example, Marchetto of Padua, *Lucidarium*, ed. J. W. Herlinger (University of Chicago Press, 1985), 91. A reference to the 'anvil of the throat' can be found in the treatise of Arnulf of St Ghislain (who takes it from Alan of Lille – see E. E. Leach, '"The little pipe sings sweetly while the fowler deceives the bird": Sirens in the Later Middle Ages', *Music and Letters*, 87 (2006): 187–211, at 210). The striking of words by singers in their oral forges is made more explicit in the use of this metaphor in a much later song by Dowland. See Leach, 'Unquiet Thoughts'.

30 One copy of both text and music survives in a single source, the Chantilly codex (*F-CH* 564). This source unusually contains a large number of both *unica* and author attributions; see E. E. Leach, 'Dead Famous: Mourning, Machaut, Music, and Renown in the Chantilly Codex', in Y. Plumley and A. Stone (eds.), *A Late Medieval Songbook and its Context: New Perspectives on the Chantilly Codex (Bibliothèque du Château de Chantilly, MS. 564)* (Turnhout:Brepols, 2009), 63–93.

31 I am very grateful to Helen J. Swift for discussing these texts and my translations with me and making many helpful suggestions.

32 The implication is that lesser talents can do no better than remake the products of great talents. This remaking would not, however, be exact. Whether there is an oblique reference here to the remaking of Senleches' own composition in performance is difficult to assess. As I argue below, such remaking is not necessarily exact and is 'mechanical' only in the medieval sense of being human and rationally engaged. It, too, is a kind of forging, and composers in this period regularly remade songs (in the sense of using cited material) by themselves and others.

33 See S. Perkinson, 'Portraits and Counterfeits: Villard de Honnecourt and Thirteenth-Century Theories of Representation', in N. A. Rowe and

D. S. Areford (eds.), *Excavating the Medieval Image: Manuscripts, Artists, Audiences: Essays in Honor of Sandra Hindman*, (Aldershot: Ashgate, 2004), 13–36.

34 In contracts (written in French) for the making of tomb images for the English King Richard II (1395), for example, the images should 'contrefaire' the King and Queen; see P. Binski, *Medieval Death: Ritual and Representation* (London: British Museum, 1996), 103. This is a kind of portrayal, a representation, which is meant to be as close to the original as possible in its exterior representation.

35 See M. Bent, 'Naming of Parts: Notes on the Contratenor, c. 1350–1450', in Filocamo and Bloxam (eds.), *'Uno gentile et subtile ingenio'*, 1–12.

36 Maybe the accusation about such composers not writing beginnings and ends is true: of two non-authorial contratenors added to Machaut's works in the wider transmission, one (*On ne porroit* [B3]) lacks its beginning and the other (*Je sui aussi* [B20]) is missing its end. For the arguments in favour of seeing the late medieval added contratenors doing something with different parameters rather than being merely deficient, see P. Memelsdorff, *'Lizadra donna*: Ciconia, Matteo da Perugia, and the Late Medieval *Ars contratenor'*, in Philippe Vendrix (ed.), *Johannes Ciconia* 233–78.

37 See J. Cerquiglini-Toulet, *The Color of Melancholy: The Uses of Books in the Fourteenth Century*, trans. L. G. Cochrane (Baltimore: Johns Hopkins University Press, 1997), and H. J. Swift, '"Tamainte consolation / Me fist lymagination": A Poetics of Mourning and Imagination in Late Medieval *dits*', in C. E. Léglu and S. J. Milner (eds.), *The Erotics of Consolation: Desire and Distance in the Late Middle Ages* (New York: Palgrave Macmillan, 2008), 141–64.

38 We should note, though, that the singer mentions only his former pleasure in the composition of virelais and rondels, whereas this song is a (double) balade. On the topos in Bernart de Ventadorn, see S. Gaunt, *Gender and Genre in Medieval French Literature* (Cambridge University Press, 1995), 130–1. For the topos in Machaut's *Pour ce que tous* (B12), see E. E. Leach, 'Singing More About Singing Less: Machaut's *Pour ce que tous* (B12)', in E. E. Leach (ed.), *Machaut's Music: New Interpretations* (Woodbridge: Boydell and Brewer, 2003), 111–24; and Anne Stone, 'Music Writing and Poetic Voice in Machaut: Some Remarks on B12 and B14', in Leach, (ed.), *Machaut's Music*, 125–38. The related 'farewell to poetry' topos is similarly found in contemporary writers such as Chaucer and Froissart.

39 Publishing constraints prevent the colour reproduction that the notation demands. A colour facsimile can be seen, however, in Dulong, 'Canons', 68. Stone, 'The Composer's Voice', 184, Ex. 5 lays out in analytical score parallel diplomatic transcriptions of the two different notations.

40 'Each believes he is making his own personal work, but in reality each does nothing more than imitate the others' (Dulong, 'Canons', 68, translation mine).

41 On this topic, see E. Reimer, 'Musicus und Cantor: Zur Sozialgeschichte eines musikalischen Lehrstücks', *Archiv für Musikwissenschaft*, 35 (1978): 1–32;

and C. Page, 'Music and the Origins of Courtliness', in K. Busby and C. Kleinhenz (eds.), *Courtly Arts and the Art of Courtliness* (Cambridge: Brewer, 2006).

42 See Stone, 'The Composer's Voice', 184, Ex. 6 for a score showing a possible interpretation of small differences between the two.

43 *Ibid.*, 185; and G. Dulong, 'La ballade polyphonique à la fin du Moyen Age: De l'union entre musique naturelle et musique artificielle', unpublished PhD thesis, Université de Tours Francois-Rabelais/Conservatoire National Supérieur de Musique et de Danse de Paris (2000), 69. For Dulong this additional irony changes the tone of the critique from one of deploring the practice of the amateurs to one of mocking it.

44 Stone's negative interpretation of the verb 'forgier' (to forge) forces her to translate these lines differently, with 'entendement ... si agut' signalling 'intelligence so limited' rather than 'sharp'; see Stone, 'The Composer's Voice', 181. But the speaker here is referring not to the many who are getting involved in forging, but to the few who are worthy forgers (i.e., makers) of song.

45 Or, at least, I am when attempting to view the song through my understanding of medieval counterpoint as set out in E. E. Leach, 'Counterpoint and Analysis in Fourteenth-Century Song', *Journal of Music Theory*, 44 (2000): 45–79.

46 Such practice is common in small vocal ensembles today, especially when rehearsing long pieces. The erring singer typically raises a finger or hand to acknowledge his or her mistake so long as it is not catastrophic enough as to have caused a complete breakdown in the musical texture. The idea communicated by the gesture is in essence 'oops, *mea culpa* – I'll get it right next time and have made a mental (or pencil) note to remind myself'.

47 These cases involve approaches to the C sonority that is the terminal type in this piece. In the last minim (a quaver in the modern transcription) of bar 21, the resolution requires $a_\flat$ and $d_\flat$; the tenor might sing $D_\flat$ in bar 20 or not. (The resolution is held for a semibreve but the song is offset metrically at this point.) A similar case is at the end of the piece as a whole, although this instance could be negated if the tenor F were viewed as an error for D (this would not work in the case of bar 21 because such a correction would introduce parallel octaves between tenor and cantus). Another case is at the very outset of the B section where the initial tenor $b_\flat$ would lead to the cantus singing $f_\natural$, which would force the cadence to be made by a tenor $d_\flat$ at the end of bar 42.

48 Although the notation's syncopations give the sense of a singer's anticipation and delay of certain notes and resolutions, as if it is the singers who are teasing each other by withholding or pre-forcing certain progressions, the highly textual notational complexity suggests instead that this is built in by the plan of the composer. The complex rhythms are written using different time signatures in each part and at the point in the first section where the uppermost voice talks about everyone wanting to *contrefaire* songs, the melody of part of a famous song by another composer is cited without its text. See

Yolanda Plumley, 'Citation and Allusion in the Late *Ars Nova*: The Case of the *En Attendant* Songs', *Early Music History*, 18 (1999): 324–5.

49 S. Palfrey and T. Stern, *Shakespeare in Parts* (Oxford University Press, 2007), in particular, views the Shakespeare canon from the perspective of parts and cues, in the process elucidating various aspects of rehearsal and performance that are not clear from full play texts. The survival of theatrical parts from sixteenth-century England is extremely rare. Because of the more compact notation of music compared to play texts, individual voice parts are usually presented sequentially on the same manuscript opening in the surviving musical sources. However, additional or alternative individual parts are sometimes copied many folios from the parts with which they belong, and separate part-books survive from the fifteenth century onwards. I would suggest that singers might have owned their own parts in some more ephemeral form for the purpose of 'conning', much as was the case with play parts later. Correspondingly, a complete lack of survival for such putative musical material would hardly be surprising.

50 It should be noted, too, that the act of forging required distributed cognition in that it usually involved more than one smith with the blows of hammers on the anvil carefully coordinated. See, for example, the image from *Speculum Humanae Salvationis* (Österreichische nationalbibliothek s.n. 2612, fol. 25^v), c. 1330–40 at http://larsdatter.com/aprons-smiths.htm.

51 See, for example, S. Woll, *Everyday Thinking: Memory, Reasoning, and Judgment in the Real World* (Mahwah, NJ: L. Erlbaum, 2002).

52 E. Hutchins, *Cognition in the Wild* (Cambridge, MA: MIT Press, 1995).

53 Tribble, 'Distributing Cognition in the Globe', 141.

54 M. Perry, 'Distributed Cognition', in J. M. Carroll (ed.), *HCI Models, Theories, and Frameworks: Towards a Multidisciplinary Science* (Boston: Morgan Kaufmann, 2003), 196.

55 *Ibid.*, 197.

56 Tribble, 'Distributing Cognition in the Globe', 142, citing D. A. Norman, *Things That Make Us Smart: Defending Human Attributes in the Age of the Machine* (Cambridge, MA: Perseus, 1993), 142.

57 See also the comments in Palfrey and Stern, *Shakespeare in Parts*, 83–90.

58 See M. Bent, 'The Grammar of Early Music: Preconditions for Analysis', in C. C. Judd (ed.), *Tonal Structures in Early Music* (New York: Garland, 1998), 15–59.

59 See Palfrey and Stern, *Shakespeare in Parts*, *passim*, and Bent, 'The Grammar of Early Music'.

60 Tribble, 'Distributing Cognition in the Globe', 152.

61 *Ibid.*, 155.

62 For the full argument that the fourteenth century saw the beginnings of the recognition that money was not just a medium but a commodity in itself, see J. Kaye, *Economy and Nature in the Fourteenth Century: Money, Market Exchange, and the Emergence of Scientific Thought* (Cambridge University Press, 1998).

CHAPTER 4

Rhetorical strategies in the pictorial imagery of fourteenth-century manuscripts

The case of the Bohun psalters

Lucy Freeman Sandler

Pictorial imagery in medieval manuscripts can be and has been treated in several ways. In broad outline, one general approach may be called internalized in that the focus of study is the choice of subjects, their sequence, and the compositional devices used to construct the single image or the narrative or non-narrative cycle, usually in the context of a history of images, without reference to the books in which they are placed; a second general approach may be called externalized, in that attention is focused on single images and pictorial cycles in relation to verbal texts, whether the texts are physically present or not, an approach often employed by literary historians and recently popular among art historians devoted to text–image questions; yet another approach is further externalized, treating images in manuscripts as illustrations or reflections of medieval society, almost completely reversing the first focus on images-in-themselves. Nevertheless all three approaches are alike in that the analysis culminates in the completed images; they are viewed as *faits accomplis*.

Yet pictorial imagery can also be considered dynamically: how did illuminators structure their images and image cycles to affect book users and shape their responses? The strategies employed by artists to lead, persuade and move manuscript audiences – readers, listeners or viewers – may be called rhetorical. In most cases however the term 'rhetorical' can only be used generically, in that the audience addressed is known only in broad categories of date, gender and social status, and equally, the degree of awareness of a specific audience on the part of illuminators and consequently the rhetorical techniques they used can be defined only very generally.

On occasion however there is sufficient documentation of date, artist, place of production and patron to go beyond the generic. This is the case for a group of devotional books made in England during the second half of the fourteenth century for the Bohun family.[1] These manuscripts offer the opportunity to study a specific instance where the subject and design of manuscript images were purposely adjusted by the artists to their audience. The Bohuns were an important noble family, earls of Hereford, Essex and Northampton, hereditary constables of England, and knights of the garter. One male Bohun, Humphrey, the fourth earl of Hereford and Essex (c. 1276–1322), married Elizabeth (1282–1316), a daughter of Edward I; one female Bohun, Eleanor (1366–1399), daughter of Humphrey the seventh earl, married Thomas of Gloucester (1355–1397), last son of Edward III; and another, her sister Mary (c. 1369–1394), married Henry Bolingbroke (1366–1413), son of John of Gaunt, earl, then duke of Lancaster, third son of Edward III.[2]

The chief Bohun family residence was at Pleshey Castle in Essex. There, they maintained a large household, or *familia*, which included not only cooks, grooms and other domestic help, but chaplains, confessors, clerks, scribes and, over the years from c. 1360 to 1390, at least two, and then a third illuminator.[3] We know the names of two of these artists, and we know about their relatively high status in the Bohun *familia* from wills and other documents; and it is my conviction that the artists revealed their social position clearly in the images they painted in manuscripts they made for the Bohuns. John de Teye, the name of the first Bohun artist, was called 'our illuminator' in the will of Humphrey de Bohun, the sixth earl of Hereford and Essex, who died in 1361.[4] In the same will John was given the fairly large sum of ten pounds and asked, along with William Monklane, Humphrey's Augustinian friar confessor, to pray for Humphrey's soul.[5] We learn from this will and from other documents that John de Teye himself was an Augustinian friar, who was permitted to live outside his religious community.[6] Although he probably did not have a university degree, he was undoubtedly literate,[7] and his colleague William Monklane was theologically sophisticated, 'comme un maître de divinité' as Humphrey's will says.[8] In 1384, John de Teye, still working at Pleshey, but now probably for Joan Fitzalan (d. 1419), widow of Humphrey de Bohun, the seventh earl of Hereford, Essex and Northampton (1342–73), namesake and nephew of the sixth earl, asked permission of the order of Augustinian friars to train another Augustinian, Henry Hood, in the art of illumination, and Henry was still at Pleshey in 1389.[9]

Between c. 1360 and the mid 1380s John de Teye together with at least one other artist – anonymous – along with a number of scribes, who might also have been in the Bohun household, produced some ten luxury psalters and books of hours for the Bohuns.[10] We can turn quickly to the question of why these, or any, medieval books have images at all, beyond technical necessity at its basic level, that of providing information that words alone cannot supply, as, for example, in the illustrations of encyclopaedias and scientific works. For the Bohun books however, images are first of all visual punctuation: they articulate the structure of the text by placement and size. Other functions are more particularly rhetorical: when an image parallels the text, when an image comments on the text, when it subverts or ignores the text, when the reader goes back and forth between image and text, the result is to heighten the experience of using the book, to increase the time spent using the book, and to make the user think or act beyond the book.

It is of course self-evident that images in books were put there by illuminators. How did they decide on what subjects to paint, and how their pictures would look? There are several answers: they received instructions, either verbal, that is, written on or near the spaces for pictures or communicated orally, or visually, in the form of shorthand sketches or cues. Most of the time such instructions were cursory, *annunciatio* in Latin, or *annonciation* in Anglo-Norman, for the Annunciation, for example, or a kind of stick-figure sketch.[11] These were the counterparts of the catchwords and signatures used by scribes to make sure that pages and gatherings of manuscripts were in the right order. More importantly, we have to take into account that when an illuminator was told to paint an Annunciation, he knew how to make it look because he had an actual model in another manuscript, or a model book of drawings. Most often, he could depend on his own visual memory to recall, recreate or invent the necessary image.

In the fourteenth century general instructions for subjects came from patrons, occasionally from what are called 'scholarly advisors', and more usually from entrepreneurs in the book trade, those who commissioned the scribes and artists to produce the manuscript and who set the number and type of illustrations. Consequently, for the illuminator, subjects were largely prescribed. But not entirely, however. In one important area of the page, the areas around the text and the margins, whether treated decoratively or figurally, artists were generally free to paint themes and motifs of their own choice. Of course, they shared prevailing ideologies – social, religious and political – and these were expressed visually in the vast and heterogeneous marginal world of flora, fauna, drolleries, hybrids, parodies, genre scenes and nightmare fantasies. But, whether it was a matter of marginal or nonmarginal, the most consequential decisions in the hands of artists concerned how the image would actually look – that is, they lay in the formal areas of drawing, composition and colour. It seems to me worth emphasizing that close attention to how images – even those that appear to be formulaic – actually look is fundamental to any kind of interpretation.

Given the large sphere of artistic decision-making, we can turn to the role of the artist-as-rhetor, that is, as producer/creator/inventor of an effect on the user of the book. Artists may have been attuned to rhetorical techniques, having, for instance, heard sermons, attended mass and participated in great Church festivals, just as they were attuned to theology, having learned the catechism and the rosary. The Bohun artists were probably more sophisticated rhetorically and theologically than many illuminators because of their clerical status, but we have no evidence that they were readers of rhetorical treatises.[12] Terming their art 'rhetorical' is, I believe, a way that *we* can focus on how their images might conceivably work on the reader/viewer.

The Bohun manuscripts fall into two groups, first three large psalters with illustrations in the form of historiated initials for every psalm and in one case also for the subdivisions of the added Hours of the Virgin.[13] The earliest of these manuscripts was started around 1350 for Humphrey the sixth earl, but finished in the 1360s for Humphrey the seventh earl; the two others were started for the seventh earl but not completed until after he died in 1373.

The second group of Bohun psalters and hours is a series of four small manuscripts (approximately 175 × 130 cm) with illustrations – full-page miniatures, bas-de-page vignettes and historiated initials – articulating the main text divisions.[14] These were all made in the 1380s for Mary de Bohun, daughter of Humphrey the seventh earl, or her husband, Henry Bolingbroke. They were married at the end of 1380 or early in 1381. At the time, he was nearing fifteen and she was ten or eleven; Mary had her first child when she was about sixteen, and died in 1394 after giving birth to her sixth. Her husband usurped the throne in 1399, and was crowned as Henry IV.[15] The manuscripts were probably ordered for their destined owners, underage at the time, from the Bohun artists at Pleshey by Mary's mother, Joan Fitzalan, the dowager countess of Hereford. She outlived her daughters, her sons-in-law, and even some of her grandchildren, not dying until 1419.

Now it may be asked what the illustrations of the first group of manuscripts made for the male Bohuns reveal about the position of the artists in the Bohun *familia*, and how the artists conceived of their relationship with

Figure 4.1 Writing bear. London, British Library MS Egerton 3277, fol. 13ᵛ, detail

their fellow employees and with their employer. In a word, the familiar, intimate and playful tone of some of their images makes it evident that the artists were not outside professionals, but really knew their patrons, and consequently were in a position to create images that would work effectively.

Two examples can serve to demonstrate this point, both from one of the fully illustrated psalters begun for Humphrey the seventh earl, the manuscript now in the Egerton Collection at the British Library that was begun in the 1360s by the anonymous artist who generally worked alongside John de Teye. The first (Figure 4.1) is a decorative nodule at the bottom left corner of the border of the last page of the first text gathering of the manuscript, the page on which scribes would be expected to put a catchword as a link to the next gathering. In fact, the image shows a scribe, or rather a bear-scribe, standing at a lectern writing on a scroll. A pen is held in his right paw, and a pen-cleaning cloth is under his left paw.[16] The words inscribed on the scroll are a *double entendre,* to be read both in Latin and, in part, in English: 'scre*bere* Piers, Martin et Robinet'. Piers, Martin and Robinet appear to be the names of three scribes, perhaps not just of this manuscript, which seems to have been written by only two hands, but rather individuals who were also employed in other Bohun work, maybe clerical tasks such as record-keeping as well as book-writing.[17] It should not be overlooked that the bear is literally being 'goosed' by a goose-hybrid, a kind of naughty 'us boys' visual joke. Of course, it is the artist who is teasing the scribes; it is the artist who is in control. He painted the picture, and he is telling the reader/viewer about his fellowship with the scribes in the Bohun *familia.*

Figure 4.2 Psalm 42, Nabal's men before Abigail. London, British Library MS Egerton 3277, fol. 32ᵛ, detail

But the artist is also talking directly to Humphrey de Bohun, and this is borne out by the second image that is reproduced here from the Egerton psalter (Figure 4.2), the historiated initial for Psalm 42: 'Judge me O God and distinguish my cause from the nation that is not holy: deliver me from the unjust and deceitful man.' In the field of the initial is a biblical subject showing Nabal's armed men before Abigail (1 Kings 25:12; like all the illustrations of the manuscript, it is drawn from the Old Testament books of Kings). Immediately outside the initial, and in fact intertwined with its finials, are three animals playing with each other: a bear, an ape and a golden-tan lion. If we have already concluded that a bear is a pictorial nickname for a Bohun scribe, we can confidently suppose that the other animals also allude to particular individuals. Elsewhere, both in picture and in word, the Bohuns, as earls of Hereford, are designated by a golden lion, the emblem drawn from the gold lions on their coat of arms.[18] Here too, I believe that the lion refers to a Bohun, in this case, Humphrey the seventh earl, the destined owner of the Egerton psalter. I would also suggest that the ancient association of apes and art is a basis

Figure 4.3 Canticle of Anna, the Lord and the poor. Vienna, Österreichische
Nationalbibliothek MS 1826*, fol. 129, detail

for an identification of the ape with the artist.[19] It can be said then that
scribe, artist and patron 'play' with each other as equals, at least pictorially. What, however, did Humphrey de Bohun think of this? It was more
than a private joke just for the private pleasure of the artist alone. I think
that the artist did indeed expect Humphrey to 'get it', to appreciate his
audacity as a pictorial jester, and to give him permission to take liberties,
despite his subservient rank.

The social contract suggested by this image made it possible for the
artist to communicate a widely ranging visual commentary, not only limited as here to the small world of the castle, but expanded to the larger
spheres of politics and religion. The areas beyond the edges of the historiated initials were used to cultivate and reinforce the Bohun view of their
importance in the world, as for instance in cases where heraldic shields,
the historiation of the initials and the words of the text mutually enhance
each other. One example is the initial for the Canticle of Anna, the mother
of Samuel (Figure 4.3), from the Bohun psalter now in Vienna, a manuscript begun as early as 1350 for Humphrey the sixth earl, and completed
by John de Teye, probably before the death of Humphrey the seventh earl

in 1373. In the Vienna psalter all the psalms and canticles are illustrated
ad verbum.[20] The historiation of the Canticle of Anna, executed by John
de Teye, is a pictorial example developed from lines 7–8 (1 Kings 2:1–10,
'The Lord maketh poor and maketh rich, he humbleth and he exalteth.
He raiseth up the needy from the dust, and lifteth up the poor from the
dunghill'). It shows the Lord reaching towards one of the needy, an old,
crippled woman in the foreground. The background panel of the initial
is patterned with the arms of England. In the marginal extension from
the initial is a large shield with the Bohun arms; this, together with the
royal heraldry, responds to the triumphant opening lines of the canticle: 'My heart hath rejoiced in the Lord, and my horn is exalted in my
God: my mouth is enlarged over my enemies: because I have joyed in thy
salvation.'

These lines were sometimes understood during the fourteenth century to refer not only to biblical victories but to the recent military tri-
umphs of the king of England and his noblemen. In the early 1360s they
were quoted by John Ergom (died c. 1386), an Augustinian friar of York,
in his exposition of the long Latin political poem attributed to John of
Bridlington (d. 1379), known as the *Bridlington Prophecies*. Ergom dedicated his commentary to the same Humphrey de Bohun, the seventh
earl, for whom the Vienna psalter was completed. Interpreting the verse
'Exaltabuntur in Gallos cornua iusti' (*Prophecies*, 2.2) as a prediction of
the English victory at the Battle of Crécy (1346) in which Humphrey the
seventh earl's father, William de Bohun, earl of Northampton (d. 1360),
had participated, Ergom wrote: '"The horns of the just will be exalted
over the French", that is, the might and the strength of Edward, the just,
will triumph over the French in this conflict.'[21] So the image as a whole –
whose subject as well as composition were devised by John de Teye in his
dual capacity as cleric and as artist – takes the lesson of the text, makes
it vivid by pictorial example, and applies it personally to the user of the
book, and also, I might add, to his anticipated descendants, who, it was
expected, would inherit the manuscript.

In the Egerton psalter in the British Library, which had been commissioned for Humphrey de Bohun the seventh earl in the 1360s and executed
almost entirely by the anonymous associate of John de Teye, the biblical
subject of the historiation for the Canticle of Anna is linked with the
marginal representation of the arms of England and Bohun (Figure 4.4).
The initial itself shows the Israelites slaying 100,000 Syrians in Samaria
(from 3 Kings 20:29). Although the subject is in a normal position in the
pictorial cycle of this manuscript, which is drawn from the first three Old

Figure 4.4 Canticle of Anna, Israelites slaying Syrians. London, British Library MS Egerton 3277, fol. 99ᵛ, enlarged detail

Testament books of Kings, the particular moment of triumph depicted resonates reciprocally not only with the canticle text but also with the marginal arms, graphically and verbally setting out an equivalence between Anna's triumphant song of thanksgiving for the birth of Samuel, the military triumph of the Israelites, and the mighty power of England and her loyal Bohun supporters.

The manuscripts of the second Bohun group, the small-format psalters and hours made for Mary de Bohun or possibly her husband Henry Bolingbroke, were probably commissioned for their still underage owners by Mary's mother Joan. They have practically none of the witty political and social commentary that fills the margins of the large psalters made

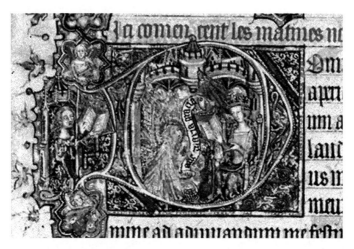

Figure 4.5 Matins of the Virgin, Annunciation. Copenhagen, Kongelige Bibliotek MS Thott 547.4°, fol. 1, detail

for the male Bohuns, although the borders are crammed with heraldry that proclaims the prominence of the Bohun dynasty by coupling Bohun arms with those of England, Lancaster and other noble families related by marriage. Joan, dowager countess of Hereford, was not 'one of the boys', but she certainly had her daughter's fortunes in mind, and the two chief Bohun artists, John de Teye and his anonymous associate, understood that well and acted on it.

In the small book of hours, now in Copenhagen, made for Mary de Bohun in the mid 1380s, possibly around the time of the birth of her first surviving son, Henry, eventually Henry V, John de Teye again used Bohun heraldry in conjunction with biblical imagery to reinforce the message of the opening illustration for Matins of the Virgin (Figure 4.5). As usual, the subject is the Annunciation, and, consonant with contemporary iconography, the Virgin Mary, golden-haired and crowned, is shown seated in a golden chair, in an interior suggested by the architecture above. She is approached by an angel in a shower of golden rays; he bears a scroll inscribed *Ave Maria gracia*. Diagonally above the head of the Virgin is another shower of gold, the symbol of the Holy Spirit. The Virgin acknowledges the angelic message with one hand, while she keeps her place in an open book with the other. The Virgin interrupted at her reading is a common motif of the Annunciation in contemporary manuscripts, although it is less common to represent her in so queenly a fashion at the same time.

The Bohun Annunciation, already layered in meaning, is to be read in conjunction with the image just outside the initial, which shows a golden-haired woman within a tower-like interior. She rests her hands on the pages of an open book, echoing the gesture of the Virgin. Her garment is patterned heraldically with the arms of Bohun and England, alluding to the past and present connections of the Bohuns with the royal house, and helping to identify her specifically as Mary de Bohun. And the holy subject of the Annunciation is itself projected against a background of the same armorials. The artist delivered a clear message in showing to Mary de Bohun a model of her own piety by depicting her imitating the piety of the Virgin Mary. The angelic salutation, *Ave Maria*, itself is recited at Matins of the Hours of the Virgin, that is, it is part of the text of the fictive books and the actual book; furthermore, the Virgin comes 'to life' in the form of a vision actualized in paint, which could be seen every time Mary de Bohun herself opened this actual book, and recited its prayers; and finally, even when the book was closed, the pictorial simulacrum of Mary de Bohun could continue to call up the vision of the Virgin Mary, the image serving as a surrogate vehicle of the prayers of the actual Mary de Bohun *in perpetuum*.[22]

Except for the Vienna Psalter, where the images are word-illustrations which respond directly to the texts of the individual psalms and canticles, the chief illustrations of the Bohun psalters are independent narratives, either from the Book of Genesis or the first three books of Kings. Although the actual words inspiring these illustrations are not present on the pages, the pictorial cycles, especially of the large-format psalters with hundreds of historiated initials, parallel the text of the selected biblical chapters very closely. But translation of verbal into pictorial is everything – and that is the operational sphere of the artist. The Bohun artists selected the biblical subjects themselves and both their choices and the details of the representations were adapted to the status and personalities of the books' intended owners in ways designed to move and persuade them in their devotions.

For example, we may consider the illustration of Psalm 52, marking one of the important text subdivisions, in the large-format Bohun psalter now in Exeter College, Oxford (Figure 4.6). The manuscript was begun by John de Teye and his associate for Humphrey the seventh earl, or possibly his uncle Humphrey the sixth, c. 1360, and completed by several later hands only c. 1390, following however a pictorial plan that did not change over this fairly long period.[23] The narrative scenes in the historiated initial

Figure 4.6 Psalm 52, scenes from life of Joseph. Oxford, Exeter College MS 47, fol. 32

and across the bas-de-page tell the story of Joseph from Genesis 37, 39 and 40 in nine vignettes crowded with small-scale figures in dramatic actions and gestures. In the initial, at top left, Joseph tells his brothers and his father Jacob of his dream that he saw the sun, the moon and eleven stars worshipping him (Genesis 37:9); the brothers envied him and Jacob rebuked him for suggesting that he was their king (Genesis 37:8, 10–11). The artist, John de Teye, visualized the words for 'telling', 'rebuking' and 'envy' with emphatic gestures. He also stressed the word 'king' by depicting kings in the vertical border niches, where they alternate with fools, a pictorial response to the opening line of the Psalm, 'The fool said in his heart: There is no God.'

The next compartment of the initial, at the top right, recounts pictorially how Joseph, sent to Sichem where his brothers were minding their sheep, to see how they were doing, finds them at Dothain, where, seeing him 'afar off', they plotted to kill him (Genesis 37:13–20). Joseph's journey is indicated by the travelling bag over his shoulder and his gesture of greeting at the very moment – that is, in the same picture-frame – when the brothers are clustered together secretively. Below, in two scenes in the left compartment, first, the brothers 'forthwith stript him', and next, they 'cast him into an old pit' (Genesis 37:23–4). And then, as shown in the lower right compartment, they dipped his coat in the blood of a kid – the lower left corner – and sent it to Jacob – seated on the far right – to look as if Joseph had been devoured by a beast (Genesis 37:31–3).

In the bas-de-page, the brothers are drawing Joseph out of the pit – on the far left – and making a deal to sell him to the Ishmaelite merchants, one shown reaching into his purse (Genesis 37:27–8); then, in the second compartment, he is sold in turn to Potiphar, shown crowned because he is the 'princeps' of the army of the Egyptian pharaoh (Genesis 37:36).[24] Then, on the central axis of the page, comes the attempted seduction of Joseph by Potiphar's wife, also crowned, as Joseph 'leaving the garment in her hand, fled' (Genesis 39:7–12). And then (after Potiphar's wife's false accusation to her husband, which is not shown) Joseph is pushed into prison (fourth compartment), where he gains custody of the prisoners (Genesis 39:20–2), including Pharaoh's butler and baker, and interprets their dreams (compartment on the far right), having said to them 'Doth not interpretation belong to God? Tell me what you have dreamed' (Genesis 40:1–8). The artist neatly began and ended the pictorial sequence with the interpretation of a dream.

In the earliest major study of the Bohun manuscripts, the distinguished manuscript scholar Eric Millar observed that in sequences such as these the Bohun artists 'seem to have invented their own compositions and read the text for this purpose'.[25] It is indeed quite possible that John de Teye, the artist here, could have read the text, and his resulting *inventions* are wonderfully vivid equivalents of the words of Scripture and the actions they describe. Of course, the question is how the manuscript recipient Humphrey de Bohun interpreted the pictures. Could he himself have read the Bible, was he familiar enough with Old Testament stories to recognize the pictorial narratives, or did he have guidance close at hand in the person of his clerical artists, his chaplain and his confessor? In this case, we know that the Bohuns owned Bibles in Latin, French and English, and a variety of biblical handbooks and summaries;[26] so if Humphrey had been literate in any of these languages he could have studied the sources. However it is still more possible that a competent member of his household expounded the images orally as I have in writing the paragraphs above, saying 'see, this is what is happening', quoting the biblical text and encouraging study, not of the words in another book, but of the pictures in this one.

The same chapters of Genesis were illustrated by John de Teye in a psalter made in the 1380s for the younger daughter of Humphrey the seventh earl, that is, Mary de Bohun, now at Lichtenthal Abbey in Baden-Baden (Figure 4.7). The Joseph cycle begins in the upper part of the letter S of the Psalm 68 initial at the same point as in Humphrey's psalter, with Joseph recounting his dream to his father Jacob while his brothers confer; in the lower part of the letter are three episodes, organized slightly differently than the comparable scenes in the Exeter College manuscript. First Joseph meets a man at Sichem who tells him that his brothers are at Dothain, and points the way; then, without a reappearance of Joseph, the brothers are plotting to kill him; and then they are stripping him. Below, in the bas-de-page, are two tightly overlapping scenes, first Joseph drawn out of the pit by one of his brothers, and then sold to two Ishmaelites. The next vignette shows a boat approaching a thin vertical shoreline, with a passenger depositing the small naked Joseph on land into the hand of a merchant. It is an inventive and apparently unprecedented response to the biblical phrase, 'and they led him into Egypt' (Genesis 39:1), perhaps drawing on knowledge that the route from Dothain in the land of Canaan to Egypt was by sea.[27] Then the last vignette shows the presentation of Joseph to Potiphar and a court official.

As similar as the individual compositions for the same subjects are in the two Joseph pages, there is one striking difference in the choice of subjects; the would-be adulterous wife of Potiphar, one of the most frequently

Figure 4.7 Psalm 68, scenes from life of Joseph. Baden-Baden, Lichtenthal Abbey
Archiv MS 2, fol. 67

Figure 4.8 Psalm 80, marriage of Moses and Zipporah. Baden-Baden, Lichtenthal
Abbey Archiv MS 2, fol. 83, enlarged detail

depicted characters in the Joseph story, is absent from the Lichtenthal
psalter. It is not for lack of space; indeed John de Teye invented an unca-
nonical space-filler in Joseph's sea-passage. Here I think is one of those
cases where the artist did not want to provide even a negative visual model
of a deceitful wife for a young and innocent bride.[28]

In this way the pictorial representations seem to have been adapted to
a particular person, to guide the eye and shape the sensibilities of the
owner of the manuscript, not only by avoiding negative ones, but also by
emphasizing positive models, persuading by attractive images with which
a young woman could identify. Several further instances can be pointed
to in the Lichtenthal psalter, for example, the representations of marriage
and motherhood. In the vignette of the marriage of Moses and Zipporah
(Exodus 2:21) in the bas-de-page of Psalm 80 (Figure 4.8), the wedding

Figure 4.9 Psalm 75, marriage of Moses and Zipporah. Oxford, Exeter College MS 47, fol. 49ᵛ, enlarged detail

takes place in a crenellated grey stone building with an arched entrance on the left and a traceried window above a wall buttress on the right. This exterior is cut away to reveal, on the left, the witnesses and the bride and groom facing, on the right, an altar and an Old Testament priest. Formally, the wedding is treated as a narrative, and read from left to right, thus diverging from the tradition of representing marriages axially with the priest in the centre and the spouses symmetrically on either side.

In the comparable scene of the marriage of Moses and Zipporah from the Exeter College psalter (Figure 4.9), also painted by John de Teye, the overall narrative design and the main action of the priest taking the hands of the bride and groom in his are similar. There are, however, telling differences. In the Exeter College psalter, the foreground spouse is Moses, whose body in fact almost completely hides that of Zipporah. In relation to each other, Zipporah is on Moses' left, and that is the standard positioning of bridal couples. But in the Lichtenthal psalter, Zipporah is clearly in the foreground, taking in fact the superior position, on the right of Moses. In a series of representations where headdresses are significant identifiers of station and status, Zipporah's long, pale unbound hair is crowned with a gold princess' chaplet. She is another visual model for the young Bohun bride who owned this manuscript.

At the same time, someone with a fair degree of theological sophistication, like the Bohun artist, might have been familiar with the idea that Zipporah was a type of the Church, and Ecclesia is always represented as crowned, although Zipporah almost never is. So potentially this crowned Zipporah, with whom Mary de Bohun could be expected to identify, could become part of the equation, Moses = Christ and Zipporah = Ecclesia, bride of Moses and bride of Christ, an equation capable of explication in the hands of one of the religious guides available to the Bohun household.[29]

In the Lichtenthal psalter John de Teye put a particular emphasis on Old Testament scenes of birth as well as marriage. The first such scene is on the Psalm 1 page, whose text and historiated initial are entirely surrounded by a historiated border. There are twenty-one Genesis episodes in all, from the beginning of Creation to the apocryphal account of Cain and Lamech,[30] and the pictorial layout was designed to articulate the various stages of this story. The birth of Abel is prominent at the lower left of the bas-de-page (Figure 4.10). It has some quite unusual features, including the cave setting, like that sometimes seen in the birth of Christ, and the nakedness of Eve, which is altogether unparalleled in the Bohun manuscripts (cf. Figure 4.12).

The second birth scene is of Esau and Jacob (Figure 4.11). Here the subject is in the historiated initial for Psalm 52, the primary focus of the page. Jacob, the second born (Genesis 25:25), is squirming out of Rebecca's bed. The image has one exceptional feature, that is, the woman standing on the left, a witness, indicating the action with a hand gesture. Elsewhere in the manuscript such witness figures, or announcers, stand outside the initial frame, but here one is incorporated in the composition. I think the woman may be intended to be Rebecca herself. In the biblical account, Rebecca consulted the Lord when she felt the infants struggling in her womb, and God answered with a prophecy, telling her: 'Two nations are in thy womb, and one people shall overcome the other, and the elder shall serve the younger' (Genesis 25:22–3). This prophecy was fulfilled in the birth of the twins Esau and Jacob. Rebecca was the only Old Testament

Figure 4.10 Psalm 1, birth of Abel. Baden-Baden, Lichtenthal Abbey Archiv MS 2,
fol. 8, enlarged detail

woman who had a direct conversation with God, and thus had a special
distinction as the recipient of God's prophecy and the instrument of its
implementation.

This Lichtenthal psalter birth scene may be compared with the less
dramatic composition painted by John de Teye's associate in the contemporary Bohun psalter, now in the Bodleian Library (Figure 4.12). The
comparison suggests that the Lichtenthal image was carefully thought
out to provide visual support for a particularly elevated view of women
that stresses their role as mothers 'of nations', a role confirmed by God's
promise to Rebecca's husband Isaac (Genesis 26:4), 'And I will multiply
thy seed like the stars of heaven: and I will give to thy posterity all these
countries: and in thy seed shall all the nations of the earth be blessed.'

The third birth scene in the Lichtenthal psalter is that of Moses,
shown on the Psalm 80 page (Figure 4.13). Here again, the page layout
is organized so that the birth of Moses (Exodus 2:2) is prominent, in the
upper part of the historiated initial. The mother lies in bed, the infant
is enfolded in the arms of a midwife, and the father acknowledges the
birth with a gesture. The abandonment and finding of Moses (Exodus

Figure 4.11 Psalm 52, birth of Esau and Jacob. Baden-Baden, Lichtenthal Abbey Archiv MS 2, fol. 54ᵛ, detail

Figure 4.12 Psalm 119, birth of Esau and Jacob. Oxford, Bodleian Library MS Auct. D.4.4, fol. 138, detail

Figure 4.13 Psalm 80, birth of Moses. Baden-Baden, Lichtenthal Abbey Archiv MS 2, fol. 83, detail

2:3–6) are depicted below, with some very unusual details. First of all it is not the mother, or even both parents, but the father alone who puts the infant in the water of the Nile, as if the image of a mother abandoning her child, no matter how justified, would be too painful for the recipient of this manuscript to contemplate. But another unusual detail turns bad fortune into good. Pharaoh's daughter, crowned as a princess – one of those young, blond, and in this case extremely fashionably dressed pictorial protagonists with whom Mary de Bohun could identify – draws Moses' basket out of the other side of the river and becomes his adoptive mother. In fact, in the most rare detail in the image, Moses himself is already crowned, both when he is put into and taken out of the river. In Exodus 2:13, Moses was later asked 'Who hath appointed thee prince and judge over us?' Taking licence to translate this biblical figure of speech literally, John de Teye seems to have constructed a visual lesson about the importance of women as mothers, as forces of dynastic continuity and the transmission of power, which could be understood by the living reader, easily able to relate to the attractive female models depicted in her book.

Looking at and reading these manuscripts were intended to be rewarding incrementally. For the Bohuns, reading and recitation of the psalms or the Hours of the Virgin, a devotional exercise that was repeated over and over, was associated with study of the fundamental narratives of human and sacred history in the Old and New Testaments in pictorial form. They were aware of the spiritual benefit of such study: in her will Mary de Bohun's sister Eleanor left one of her daughters 'with my blessing, a book, with the psalter, hours, and other devotions, with two gold clasps enameled with my arms, which book I have used a great deal', and she gave her son, another Humphrey, 'a well written and richly illuminated psalter with gold clasps enameled with white swans and the arms of my lord and father and other gold bands on the tissues [that is, the cloth cover] in the form of mullets, which psalter was left to me to be given to my heirs, and thus from aforesaid heir to heir'.[31] Why were these books significant enough to be passed from Bohun to Bohun? It was only their bindings, carefully described in the inventories as the quotations show, that had any substantial material value. But the artist-designed biblical images made study delightful and sweet, offering repeated moral and spiritual rewards for immediate and future owners; pictures of Bohuns in prayer served as owner-surrogates and as memorials, preserving images of past Bohuns for future generations; and finally, some images pictured the Bohuns to themselves, in the way they wished to be remembered in perpetuity. In all this the Bohun artists played a major, generative role, confirming their rhetorical power.

LIST OF BOHUN MANUSCRIPTS ILLUSTRATED BY JOHN DE TEYE AND HIS ASSOCIATE

1   Vienna, Österreichische Nationalbibliothek MS 1826*, Psalter, begun before 1350? for Humphrey de Bohun, sixth earl of Hereford and Essex, completed by 1373? for Humphrey de Bohun, seventh earl of Hereford, Essex and Northampton: fols. 1–6ᵛ (calendar), illustrations, John de Teye, and minor initials, associate of John de Teye, c. 1360–73; fols. 7–57ᵛ, 58ᵛ, 85ᵛ (Psalms 1–67, 68, 97), initials and borders, various hands prior to John de Teye, c. 1350?; fols. 51–160, initials and borders (Psalms

58–150, Canticles, Penitential Psalms, Litany and Memoriae), John de Teye, except as noted, c. 1360–73?

2   Oxford, Exeter College MS 47, Psalter, begun c. 1360, possibly for Humphrey de Bohun, sixth earl of Hereford and Essex, or after 1361, for Humphrey de Bohun, seventh earl of Hereford, Essex and Northampton, completed for unknown patron in a later campaign, c. 1390: (new foliation) fols. 1–6ᵛ (calendar), illustrations, later artist, c. 1390; fols. 7–81ᵛ (Psalms 1–113), historiated initials and borders, John de Teye, and most minor initials, associate of John de Teye, c. 1360–73; fols. 82–126ᵛ (Psalms 118–50, Canticles, fragmentary litany, Memoriae), minor initials, associate of John de Teye, c. 1360–73, historiated initials and borders, various later hands, c. 1390.

3   London, British Library MS Egerton 3277, Psalter and Hours, begun after 1361?, probably for Humphrey de Bohun, seventh earl of Hereford, Essex and Northampton, completed in the 1380s in a later campaign, possibly on commission from Joan Fitzalan, countess of Hereford, widow of the seventh earl: fols. 1–6ᵛ (calendar), illustrations, follower of John de Teye's associate, 1380s?; fols. 7–170ᵛ (Psalms, Canticles, Litany, Hours of the Virgin, Penitential Psalms and Litany, Office of the Dead, Memoriae, Confession of Robert Grosseteste), all initials and borders, except as noted below, and almost all verse initials and line-fillers, associate of John de Teye, c. 1361–73; fols. 29ᵛ, 46ᵛ, 67, 68ᵛ, 78, 87, 98ᵛ, 114, 120ᵛ, 123, 126ᵛ, 129, 133, 142, 145ᵛ (main divisions of Psalter, Hours of the Virgin, Penitential Psalms and Office of the Dead), large historiated initials and borders, anonymous artist over earlier drawings by John de Teye or his associate, 1380s.

4   Cambridge, Fitzwilliam Museum MS 38–1950, Psalter, made for Mary de Bohun or Henry Bolingbroke, c. 1380–94, with fifteenth-century additions for a male owner: fol. 1 (Psalm 1), miniature, historiated initial and bas-de-page, John de Teye; fols. 1ᵛ–217ᵛ (Psalms, Canticles, Penitential Psalms and beginning of Litany), miniatures, historiated initials, bas-de page illustrations and minor initials, associate of John de Teye; fols. 218–43ᵛ (part of litany, prayers and calendar), fifteenth century.

5   Oxford, Bodleian Library MS Auct. D.4.4, Psalter and Hours of the Virgin, made for Mary de Bohun, c. 1380–94, with fifteenth-century additions: fols. iiiᵛ–xiᵛ (prayers and calendar), fifteenth century; fols. xiiᵛ, 1, 181ᵛ, 243ᵛ (full-page miniatures, Psalm 1 miniature, initial and bas-de-page), followers of John de Teye; fols. 1ᵛ–274 (Psalms, Canticles, Penitential Psalms, Litany, Hours of the Virgin, Memoriae and prayers, Gospel

Sequences, Office of the Dead), full-page miniatures, half-page miniatures, historiated initials, bas-de-page illustrations, and minor initials, except as noted above, associate of John de Teye.

6 Baden-Baden, Lichtenthal Abbey Archiv MS 2, Psalter and Short Office of the Cross (in Anglo-Norman), made for Mary de Bohun or Henry Bolingbroke, c. 1380–94: fols. 1–158 (Calendar, Psalms, Canticles and Litany), calendar illustrations, historiated initials, borders and bas-de-page illustrations, John de Teye; fols. 160–164ᵛ (Short Office of the Cross), historiated initials and borders, assistant, over drawings by John de Teye; fol. 165 (prayer), historiated initial and border, John de Teye; almost all minor initials and borders, verse initials and line-fillers throughout, associate of John de Teye.

7 Copenhagen, Kongelige Bibliotek MS Thott 517.4°, Legends of the Virgin Mary, St Margaret and St Mary Magdalene, made for Mary de Bohun, c. 1380–94: fols. 1, 10ᵛ, 22ᵛ, historiated initials and borders, John de Teye; almost all minor initials and borders, associate of John de Teye.

8 Copenhagen, Kongelige Bibliotek MS Thott 547.4°, Hours of the Virgin, made for Mary de Bohun, c. 1380–94: fols. 1–66 (Hours of the Virgin, Penitential Psalms and Litany, Office of the Dead), historiated initials, borders and bas-de-page illustrations, John de Teye; almost all minor decoration, associate of John de Teye.

9 Pommersfelden, Gräflich Schönborn'sche Bibliothek MS 348 (2934), Memoriae and Gospel Sequences from a book of hours, made for Mary de Bohun or Henry Bolingbroke, c. 1380–94: fols. 1–9, 10ᵛ-14ᵛ, historiated initials, borders, minor decoration, associate of John de Teye; fols. 9ᵛ-10 (Instruments of the Passion, male and female saints), full page miniatures, John de Teye.

10 London, British Library MS Royal 20.D.iv, Romance of Lancelot, written and illustrated in France, c. 1300, possibly listed in the Pleshey inventory of 1397 (Dillon and St John Hope, 'Inventory', 301): fols. 1, 102ᵛ, miniatures overpainted by John de Teye, c. 1360–1380s.

NOTES

1 On the Bohun manuscripts in general, see the following: M. R. James and Eric G. Millar, *The Bohun Manuscripts* (London: Roxburghe Club, 1936); L. F. Sandler, 'A Note on the Illuminators of the Bohun Manuscripts', *Speculum*, 60 (1985): 364–72; L. F. Sandler, *Gothic Manuscripts 1285–1385*, 2 vols., A Survey of Manuscripts Illuminated in the British Isles V, ed.

J. J. G. Alexander, (London: Harvey Miller, 1986), vol. II, nos. 133–42; Lynda Dennison, 'The Stylistic Sources, Dating and Development of the Bohun Workshop, ca. 1340–1400', unpublished PhD thesis, University of London (1988); L. F. Sandler, 'Political Imagery in the Bohun Manuscripts', in A. S. G. Edwards (ed.), *Decoration and Illustration in Medieval English Manuscripts,* English Manuscript Studies 10 (London: British Library 2002), 114–53; L. F. Sandler, 'The Illustration of the Psalms in Fourteenth Century English Manuscripts: Three Psalters of the Bohun Family', in B. Muir (ed.), *Reading Texts and Images: Essays on Medieval and Renaissance Art and Patronage in Honour of Margaret M. Manion* (Exeter University Press, 2002), 123–52; L. F. Sandler, 'Lancastrian Heraldry in the Bohun Manuscripts', in J. Stratford (ed.), *The Lancastrian Court,* Harlaxton Medieval Studies 13 (Donington: Shaun Tyas, 2003), 221–32.

2 On the Bohun family, see, most recently, *ODNB: Oxford Dictionary of National Biography from the Earliest Times to the Year 2000*, online edition (Oxford University Press, 2004–), under Humphrey de Bohun, Henry IV, Thomas of Woodstock; also Ian Mortimer, *The Fears of Henry IV, The Life of England's Self-Made King* (London: Vintage Books, 2008).

3 The most detailed information comes from the will of Humphrey de Bohun, sixth earl of Hereford and Essex, d. 1361; see J. Nichols, *A Collection of all the Wills now Known to be Extant of the Kings and Queens of England, Princes and Princesses of Wales, and every Branch of the Blood royal from the Reign of William the Conqueror to that of Henry the Seventh* (London: J. Nichols, 1780), 44–56.

4 Nichols, *Wills*, 50. On John de Teye and the Bohun artists, see L. F. Sandler, 'A Note on the Illuminators of the Bohun Manuscripts', *Speculum,* 60 (1985): 364–72, and, with revised views on the identification of the artists' hands, L. F. Sandler, *The Lichtenthal Psalter and the Manuscript Patronage of the Bohun Family* (London: Harvey Miller 2004), 126–9.

5 Nichols, *Wills*, 50.

6 See Francis Roth, *The English Austin Friars 1249–1538*, 2 vols. (New York: Augustinian Historical Institute, 1961, 1966), vol. II, no. 559.

7 *Ibid.*, vol. I, 136–77, on the education of Augustinian friars.

8 Nichols, *Wills*, 50.

9 Roth, *English Austin Friars*, vol. II, nos. 559, 603.

10 See List of Bohun manuscripts above.

11 On instructions to illuminators, see J. J. G. Alexander, *Medieval Illuminators and their Methods of Work* (New Haven: Yale University Press, 1992), especially 52–71.

12 The well-known 1397 inventory of the books at Pleshey confiscated from Thomas of Gloucester, some of them volumes that must have been available earlier to John de Teye and his associates, includes more than eighty 'Livres de diverses rymances et Estories'. Among them are romances, chronicles, legal, medical, moral and devotional texts, encyclopaedias and dictionaries, but no works of classical authors or rhetorical treatises; see J. Dillon and

W. H. St John Hope, 'Inventory of the Goods and chattels Belonging to Thomas, Duke of Gloucester, and Seized in His Castle at Pleshy, Co. Essex, 21 Richard II (1397); with Their Values, as Shown in the Escheator's Accounts', *Archaeological Journal*, 54 (1897): 300–3. The kind of rhetorical treatises that might ideally have been available to artists trained as Augustinian friars may be ascertained from the medieval catalogue of the library of the Augustinian friars of York, many of the volumes bequeathed by Friar John Ergom (see above, 103); see K. W. Humphreys (ed.), *The Friars' Libraries*, Corpus of British Medieval Library Catalogues (London: British Library, 1990), under Rhetorica, Grammatica, Cicero, M. Tullius, and Galfridus de Vino Salvo.

13 Nos. 1–3 in the List of Bohun manuscripts.

14 Nos. 4–6, 8 in the List of Bohun manuscripts.

15 See *ODNB*, under Henry IV (entry by Henry Summerson).

16 See L. F. Sandler, 'Bared: The Writing Bear in the British Library Bohun Psalter', in S. L'Engle and G. B. Guest (eds.), *Tributes to Jonathan J. G. Alexander: The Making and Meaning of Illuminated Medieval and Renaissance Manuscripts, Art, and Architecture*(London: Harvey Miller, 2006), 269–80. In 'Bared' (270) I identified the marks under the bear's left paw as indecipherable letters, perhaps *lu* or *lii*, but closer study suggests a new identification as a bit of pen-cleaning cloth.

17 On clerks and scribes in noble households, see Kate Mertes, *The English Noble Household 1250–1600* (Oxford: Basil Blackwell, 1988), especially 23–74.

18 See Sandler, 'Political Imagery', especially 116 discussing John Ergom's commentary on the *Bridlington Prophecies*, dedicated by Ergom to Humphrey de Bohun, seventh earl.

19 On apes as artists in the Bohun manuscripts, see L. F. Sandler, 'Gone Fishing: Angling in the Fitzwilliam Bohun Psalter', in J. Cherry and F. A. Payne (eds.), *Signs and Symbols: Harlaxton 2006*, Harlaxton Medieval Studies 16 (Donington: Shaun Tyas, 2009), 168–79.

20 See L. F. Sandler, 'Word Imagery in English Gothic Psalters: The Case of the Vienna Bohun Manuscript', in F. O. Büttner (ed.), *Der illuminierte Psalter* (Turnhout: Brepols, 2005), 387–95.

21 John Ergom, commentary on the *Bridlington Prophecies*, in Thomas Wright (ed.), *Political Poems and Songs relating to English History*, 2 vols., Rolls Series 14 (London: Longman, Green, Longman and Roberts, 1859–61), vol. I, 123–215, esp. 156–57. See also Sandler, 'Political Imagery', 118–19.

22 On the various functions of images of the worshipper and the object of his or her devotion, see L. F. Sandler, 'The Wilton Diptych and Images of Devotion in Illuminated Manuscripts', in Dillian Gordon *et al.* (eds.), *The Regal Image of Richard II and the Wilton Diptych* (London: Harvey Miller, 1997), 137–54.

23 Who inherited the manuscript after the death of Humphrey the seventh earl in 1373, and who commissioned its completion, is unknown. In the late fifteenth century the book was owned by Elizabeth of York, wife of Henry VII, and subsequently, by Katherine of Aragon, first wife of Henry VIII; see

James and Millar, *Bohun Manuscripts*, 5–6. For division of hands, see the List of Bohun manuscripts above.

24 Cf. Genesis 39:1: 'Igitur Ioseph ductus est in Aegyptum, emitque eum Putiphar eunuchus Pharaonis, *princeps exercitus*, vir aegyptius, de manu Ismaelitarum a quibus perductus erat.'

25 James and Millar, *Bohun Manuscripts*, 8.

26 Among the books listed in the Pleshey inventory (see n. 12 above) are 'a medium size Bible with silver clasps', 'three large books covered with white leather with brass clasps, comprising the Bible', 'a medium size bible, well written, covered with cloth of gold of Cyprus, with two enameled gold clasps', 'a small Bible covered with old green leather, with two silver clasps', 'an English book of the Gospels covered with red leather', 'a small booklet with a verse kalendar of the chapters of the Bible, covered with cloth of gold', 'a Latin book of Holy Scripture covered with white leather', 'a book in French of the narratives of the Gospels' and 'a book of Bible narratives briefly summarized'. Some of these were categorized as *pro capella* (for use in the earl's chapel) but most were listed under the heading 'livres de diverses romances & estoires' (various books of romances and narratives).

27 Awareness of sea routes from the Holy Land to Egypt came from firsthand experience of pilgrimages and crusades, and from various written sources such as romances, travel accounts, encyclopaedias and maps. It may be significant that Humphrey de Bohun, the seventh earl, had participated in the capture of Alexandria from the Saracens in 1365, arriving by sea from Rhodes – see V. H. Galbraith, *The Anonimalle Chronicle 1333–1381* (Manchester University Press, 1927), 52, 170–1; and late in 1392, Henry IV, with many members of his *familia*, went on pilgrimage to Jerusalem via Venice, Rhodes and Cyprus (Mortimer, *Fears of Henry IV*, 110–15), but the date is too late to be relevant to the illustration in the Lichtenthal psalter; further, among the books listed in the Pleshey inventory of 1397 (see n. 12 above) are copies of Bartholomaeus Anglicus' thirteenth-century encyclopaedia, *De proprietatibus rerum*, which includes a large quantity of geographical information, the travels of John Mandeville (d. 1373?) to the Holy Land (although whether this could already have been at Pleshey during the time of John de Teye is uncertain), two copies in French of the *Gesta Tancredi*, a crusader romance, one identified as old, and a valuable copy of the crusader *chanson de geste* of Godfrey de Bouillon, 'I large livre de Godefray de Boilloun ove claspes dargent enorrez et enamaillez pris xiiis iiiid'.

28 In the same way, in the bas-de-page of Psalm 26 (fol. 29) John de Teye hid the nakedness of the drunken Noah (Genesis 9:20) by showing him from the rear, whereas in the small illustration for Psalm 12 in the Exeter College psalter (fol. 16ᵛ), he showed Noah in a more usual way, spreadeagled facing the viewer; see Sandler, *Lichtenthal Psalter*, figure 25, and James and Millar, *Bohun Manuscripts*, plate IIa (as fol. 14ᵛ, the folios having since been renumbered).

29 In the *Bible moralisée*, the marriage of Christ and the Church was paired
    with the explanation, 'Moses signifies Christ, his wife the Church'; see A. de
    Laborde, *La Bible moralisée conservée à Oxford, Paris et Londres: reproduc-
    tion intégrale du manuscrit du xiiie siècle*, 5 vols. (Paris: pour les membres de
    la Société, 1911–27), vol. I (of Oxford, Bodleian Library MS Bodley 270b.
    fol. 40).
30 See Petrus Comestor, *Historia scholastica*, PL 198, 1,078–9.
31 Nichols, *Wills*, 181.

CHAPTER 5

Do actions speak louder than words?

The scope and role of *pronuntiatio* in the Latin rhetorical tradition, with special reference to the Cistercians

Jan M. Ziolkowski

This investigation has two main, discrete aims. First is to offer a very brief survey of performance as it was treated formally in the Latin rhetorical tradition. This effort focuses upon what is stated in explicit discussions of *actio* and *pronuntiatio*, the two Latin technical terms for delivery, the first connected with gesture and the second with elocution. In this section, I focus wherever possible upon the involvement of nonverbal arts in the delivery of words, and I seek to identify the modifications that the concepts of *actio* and *pronuntiatio* underwent in the Middle Ages.

In the second part I consider ways in which Ciceronian traditions of performance metamorphosed among the Cistercians. I have chosen this context partly because the heavy use of sign language in this monastic order renders these monks singularly attractive candidates for an examination of nonverbal performance. Among the White Monks, Aelred (c. 1100–67), abbot of Rievaulx from 1146, holds special interest, because of the active role he played in conditioning the conduct and therefore the performance of Cistercian converts from the knightly class. I argue that Aelred shaped knights who took the cowl to be not just monks in general but (at least to a degree) Ciceronian monks in particular. This simultaneous Christianization and Ciceronianization entailed an adaptation of both a philosophy, especially about friendship, and a comportment, which was powerfully moulded by the application to life as a whole of what in rhetoric passed under the names of *actio* and *pronuntiatio*. Intellectuals of the twelfth century proved to be deeply concerned with the relationship between word and deed, especially in instruction: *docere verbo et exemplo* [to teach by word and example] became a shibboleth. This Ciceronian outlook also took hold outside monasteries in cathedral schools and led to what might be called a 'personality cult' connected with great teachers.[1] Furthermore, even without Aelred's contribution to the order, the Cistercians, owing to their sign language, had associations with nonverbal performance that encouraged the rise of a lore linking them with mimes. Well before St Francis (1181–1226) came to be regarded as a *jongleur*, the brothers from the order of Cîteaux were attracted to nonverbal communication – and persuasion – as a means of catching attention and stirring hearts. Thus the song and dance of the saint from Assisi would seem at first blush to have nothing Ciceronian about them, but they may have at least a bit of classical rhetoric in their lineage.

Before embarking upon a survey of the rhetorical tradition proper, I would like to relate a pair of anecdotes which suggest two directions in which oratory can tend. One deals with the relationship between formal speech and music, the other with that between formal speech and sign language. The first account comes from the hodgepodge of *exempla* that was assembled in the first half-century of the common era by Valerius Maximus (first half of first century AD), although it is also reported by Cicero (*De oratore*, III.225), Aulus Gellius (*Noctes Atticae*, I.11.10), Quintilian (I.10.27) and Plutarch (*Vitae*: 'Tiberius Gracchus', II.5). Valerius Maximus treats of it in a section entitled 'How much importance lies in elocution [*pronuntiatione*] and apt bodily movement', where he reports:

… whenever [C. Gracchus] spoke before the public, [he] had a slave skilled in the art of music stationed behind him. With an ivory pipe the man secretly shaped Gracchus' elocution. When the rhythm was too relaxed, he would heighten it, when over-agitated, he would tone it down; for the heat and impetus of his discourse did not let the speaker be himself an attentive judge of this balance.[2]

Music is often cast as being at the receiving end in the exchange between grammar and rhetoric, arrogating terminology and constructs from disciplines that formed the foundation of education and intellectual life throughout the period in which Latin held sway. Among other things, this little story about Gracchus – whether veracious or not, and however we decode its enigmatic concision about how the music guided the words – tells us not to be lulled into disregarding the mutual indebtedness of the two arts.[3]

The other anecdote has become known as the 'Debate in Signs'.[4] In its earliest and most common version it is attested in the famous gloss on Justinian's *Corpus juris civilis* (*Body of Civil Law*, sixth century) by the early-thirteenth-century Bolognese jurist Accursius (c. 1185–1263).[5] According to Accursius, the Romans once sought to acquire law from the Greeks. Before granting them this privilege, the Greeks wished first to test the Romans by staging a kind of debate between a Greek and a

Roman, so that they could determine if the Romans deserved the boon of law. The Romans chose an ignoramus to represent them, so that if he lost they would not be shamed. The debate had to take place in gestures, since the Greek knew no Latin and the Roman no Greek. First the Greek lifted one finger, to which the Roman answered by raising two. Then the Greek held out his hand flat, to which the Roman reacted by clenching his fist. Thereupon the Greek declared himself defeated and the Romans entitled to Greek law. The explanation for the verdict of the Greeks is that to them one finger signified one God; two fingers, God the Father and Son; the flat hand, the all-encompassing grasp of God; and the fist, the all-powerful might of God. But to the Romans the gestures were devoid of theological significance and instead threatened different types of physical violence: one finger was a menace to put out one of his eyes; two fingers, to put out both eyes of his opponent; the flat hand, to slap; the fist, to punch.

This legend, which appears in many later sources, reminds us amusingly of the extent to which rhetoric, even within the realm of Christian theology, could involve nonverbal expression. At the same time the anecdote constitutes a caveat against any hasty or simplistic interpretation of gestural expression. Two of the most influential rhetoricians, Cicero (*Orator*, 56) and Quintilian (*Inst. orat.*, XI.3.65–6), referred to gestures as a linguistic system.[6] As with any other language – and maybe even more so, since for so long this language had neither a dictionary nor a grammar – gestures were and are susceptible to mistranslation. In the *De doctrina Christiana* (Book I) Augustine of Hippo (354–430) differentiates between voluntary and involuntary *signa*. Even within the realm of voluntary signs, communication is subject to many of the same misunderstandings as could occur in speech or writing.

THE LATIN RHETORICAL TRADITION OF *ACTIO* AND *PRONUNTIATIO*

In the terminology of Latin rhetoric both *actio* and *pronuntiatio* apply to the realization of a speech by vocalization (*figura vocis*, which covers breath and rhythm) and accompanying physical movements (*motus corporis*).[7] In turn those movements are subdivided (Cicero, *De oratore*, III.57.216) into gestures (*gestus*) and facial expressions (*vultus*). Although at times *pronuntiatio* is restricted to the features of the voice and *actio* to gestures and facial expressions, usually the two terms are approximately synonymous.[8]

Both *actio* and *pronuntiatio* correspond to the Greek *hypocrisis*, which relates to the techniques of actors (Greek *hypocrites*, 'actor'). *Hypocrisis* had been introduced into the terminology of rhetorical theory by Aristotle (*Rhetoric*, III.1.1403b). The dual histrionic and oratorical associations of the Greek word reflect the ambivalence, perhaps even hypocrisy, about the relationship between speech-delivery and acting that pervades the Roman rhetorical tradition.[9] On the one hand, rhetoricians make untold pronouncements against oratory that bears too strong a resemblance to acting. Cicero in particular takes pains to distinguish between the actor and the speaker.[10] On the other hand, examples abound of orators, from Demosthenes through to Cicero and beyond, who hone their skills by observing and imitating actors.[11] Indeed, Cicero is even alleged to have competed with an actor named Roscius: Cicero would use words to convey a thought, while Roscius would employ gestures.[12] Somewhat rarer are alleged incidents in which actors would watch orators in the Forum in order to copy from them gestures that they could employ on the stage.[13]

The equivalent of *actio* and *pronuntiatio* in modern English is *delivery*. German has maintained *actio* in the phrase *rednerische Aktion*, whereas the Romance languages have preferred their derivatives from *pronuntiatio*. It should be noted that *performance* (from English) has been coming on strong in other languages. The verb *perform*, which derives ultimately from Old French *par –*, 'completely' and *fornir*, 'to provide', evolved from its initial meaning 'to do, carry out, finish, accomplish' to develop at the latest in the early seventeenth century (the first attestation dates to 1610) its modern-day theatrical and musical sense.[14] In recent times *performance* has been used so often and applied to so many different areas as to justify the desperate-sounding question 'Is there anything outside the purview of performance studies?'[15] Because the topic of performance has attracted keen attention for a number of years, and because the line between performance in a theatrical sense and performativity in a broader meaning has been crossed repeatedly, paying heed to definitions seems all the more important in trying to delimit the scope of meanings we attach to performance.

By whatever name we designate it, the phenomenon under discussion constitutes the fifth and final of the major divisions or canons (Latin *officia*) of the rhetorical art. It is preceded by *inventio, dispositio, elocutio* and *memoria*. To judge by the treatment of *pronuntiatio* in a resource of modern rhetorical scholarship such as Heinrich Lausberg's (1912–92) *Handbook of Literary Rhetoric: a Foundation for Literary Study*, one would be encouraged to infer that delivery occupied a negligible niche in the

Graeco-Roman rhetorical tradition.[16] Consequently, it has been asserted in the entry on delivery in a recent English-language encyclopaedia of rhetoric that, 'During the medieval and Renaissance periods, delivery declined greatly because rhetoricians ignored it in favor of other rhetorical issues. The political and religious systems at work in this long period did not make delivery a compelling function of rhetoric.'[17] Yet leaping to such a conclusion would be mistaken. No lesser a source than Pliny the Younger (c. AD 61 to c. 112) observed pertinently that when we receive words, we are affected much more deeply by words heard and seen than by those merely read.[18] Furthermore, the treatment of memory and delivery in classical rhetoric has been examined for its applicability to speech composition and delivery today.[19]

For reasons that hardly demand glossing, delivery has usually occupied a prominent place in the practice of oratory. In the second century BC Athenaeus related the story that Demosthenes, the greatest Athenian orator (384–322 BC), when asked what was most important, next most important, and third most important in rhetoric, had replied in each case 'delivery', almost like the mantra of realtors, 'location, location, location'. Cicero repeated the anecdote, as did Valerius Maximus.[20] C. Iulius Victor, a rhetorician of the fourth century AD who leaned heavily on Cicero, includes a capsule form of the legend in his *Rhetorica*.[21] Proficiency in delivery commanded sufficient respect that a profession developed for teachers of elocution and singing, who were known as *phonasci*.[22]

But however significant delivery may have been in practice, and however often lip service was paid to it in the treatises in its capacity as the final *officium*, it was not salient in rhetorical theory. Although Aristotle emphasized the importance of delivery, he devoted little space to it.[23] The first detailed exposition appears to have been a tractate on *hypocrisis* by Theophrastus of Eresus (c. 371–287 BC), but the treatise is no longer extant.[24] During the Middle Ages the *Rhetorica ad Herennium* was thought to be the work of Cicero, but it is now ascribed to an anonymous called, for convenience's sake, Tully. This text contains the oldest surviving account of delivery (III.11.19–III.15.27) and probably the one best known during the Middle Ages. Its author claims that many writers had emphasized the indispensability of delivery but that to date no one had written carefully on the topic.

Cicero, whose impact on the later tradition of formal rhetoric was (and remains) paramount, calls delivery the most essential aspect of a speech. At the same time his Stoicism led him to restrict *actio* more than might otherwise have been the case. The rhetorico-cultural movement known as the Second Sophistic (c. AD 60–230), which in practice took *actio* to an opposite extreme of florid excess, had no exponent among rhetoricians whose expositions of theory shaped the Latin tradition.

The other main influence on the Latin rhetorical tradition alongside Cicero was Quintilian, whose *Institutio oratoria* (XI.3.1–184) offers the fullest ancient treatment of delivery, especially of oratorical gestures and their use.[25] In his discussion of gesture (68–149) Quintilian proceeds from head to feet, describing how each limb can be used, which motions are allowed, and what emotion is conveyed by each movement; he is very sensitive to the effect of delivery style on the emotional reception of a speech (2).[26]

After Cicero and Quintilian, other minor Latin rhetoricians dealt with the topic of delivery. C. Iulius Victor, who has been noted already for his mention of Demosthenes, devotes a few pages to *pronuntiatio*.[27] Another theorist of the fourth or fifth century AD, Consultus Fortunatianus, covers all five canons of rhetoric in his three-book *Ars rhetorica*.[28] Huge changes in attitudes towards *actio* and *pronuntiatio* as constituents of formal rhetoric did not occur among the early Christians. Not worlds apart from the Stoic Cicero, Jerome (c. 345–420) spoke out against the exaggerated *actio* of secular orators. Augustine did not delve into *actio* explicitly in *De doctrina Christiana*, although he touched upon *modus proferendi*, a different phrase to express the same concept. Elsewhere he gave only cursory advice on delivery.

Thanks to the fundamental conservativism of education in the period, late antique and early medieval rhetoricians in the Latin West hew closely to the lines evident already in the *Rhetorica ad Herennium*, Cicero and Quintilian. Thus Martianus Capella follows Quintilian and Fortunatianus (who himself was beholden to Cicero and Quintilian) in two triads.[29] He divides *actio* into voice, mimicry and gesture, and he sees *actio* as having the threefold objective of securing the good disposition of listeners, convincing them and motivating them. The fullest analysis of *actio* to survive from the early Middle Ages is in the *Dialogus de rhetorica et virtutibus* by Alcuin (c. 730–804).[30] Alcuin relies heavily on Cicero's *De oratore* (III.56.213) and *Orator* as well as on C. Iulius Victor.

As a final note on the status of delivery in the medieval arts of eloquence, it is worth underscoring that *pronuntiatio* found a niche not only in rhetoric but also in grammar. Since the two arts (which along with logic composed the trivium, the three verbal arts of eloquence) overlapped so much, this is not surprising. In any event, we find *pronuntiatio* at the centre of the five constituents of *lectio*, itself one of the four divisions of grammar in its capacity as the *scientia interpretandi*.[31]

From the mainstream of grammar and rhetoric, the *actio* of recitation did not pass evenly into all the new branches of rhetoric that developed from the very end of the eleventh century and later. To take one example, *actio* is not an issue in the *Ars lectoria* (Art of Reading [Aloud]), composed in 1086 by Aimeric of Angoulême, or in the other works that followed it.[32] Such treatises offer guidance on the quantity and accentuation of Latin syllables and words for those who need to enunciate properly when reading aloud. Or, to turn to another instance, *actio* tended to be covered minimally, if at all, in *artes praedicandi*. An isolated exception is found in Thomas Waleys, *De modo componendi sermones cum documentis* (first half of fourteenth century).[33] But in general, although comments are to be found here and there on the unseemly flamboyance of chanting, delivery of sermons, or reading by this or that individual, manuals furnish few explicit directives about how to achieve effects of voice or body, regardless of whether those effects might be deemed to be either decorous or not.

In contrast, recitation receives treatment in the *artes versificandi* that survive from the second half of the twelfth century and later. In times when much of what was written was meant to be read aloud, the composers of texts would have had considerable incentive to think beforehand about the accompanying gestures that the words in their compositions might elicit. The effects of these possibilities on the works that have come down to us, from antiquity and the Middle Ages alike, deserve much further exploration.[34]

In the twelfth-century *Ars versificatoria*, Matthew of Vendôme limits himself to a stock observation, capped by a quotation from Martial (*Epigrams*, I.38.2), on the importance of attending properly to recitation.[35] In the later and much more influential *Poetria nova*, Geoffrey of Vinsauf (died c. 1210) relies on the *Rhetorica ad Herennium* and Quintilian in expounding at considerably greater length upon the topic of delivery.[36] The title of the *Poetria nova* encapsulates Geoffrey's ambition to synthesize in a form suited to his own era Cicero's rhetoric and Horace's art of poetry. Geoffrey's indebtedness to Cicero in regard to *actio* elicits remark from commentators. The same aspiration is evident in Geoffrey of Vinsauf's *Documentum*, which in its handling of delivery is more explicitly indebted to both Cicero and Horace.[37] An indebtedness to the identical pairing can be found in comments on delivery in other sources from the early thirteenth century, as for example in the commentary on Alan of Lille's *Anticlaudianus* by Ralph of Longchamps.[38]

A very late and major shift from the traditional pairing of Cicero and Horace comes in Matthias of Linköping (Mathias Ouidi or Övidsson), a Swede who was born about 1300 and died about 1350. In his *Poetria* (Poetics) and *Testa nucis* (Nutshell), written between 1318 and 1332, Matthias reveals that, unlike all other authors of *artes poeticae*, he regards as his master Aristotle, as mediated through the commentary of Averroes. Consistent with this alignment, Matthias adheres to standard procedure in the commentary tradition by examining the essentials and accidentals of his topic, namely, poetry.[39] This scrutiny leads him to indicate explicitly that he does not need to give full treatment to the accidentals, since Geoffrey of Vinsauf and Horace have already done so. Matthias' Aristotelianization represents a radical departure from the approaches that prevailed in the twelfth and early thirteenth centuries. But although novel in many regards, Matthias stays close to traditional discussions of *pronuntiatio* in his treatments of gesture and intonation.[40]

THE INFLUENCE OF CICERONIAN *ACTIO* ON CISTERCIANS

At the outset I promised to consider the ways in which the Ciceronian tradition of recitation and performance played out among the Cistercians. These issues call out for attention to a topic the relevance of which to recitation and performance may seem paradoxical, namely, silence. In graphic systems to represent sounds silence fulfils a fulcral function, but it is a fulcrum that is not identified explicitly until after the conventions for the representation of sound have already developed quite far. Just as in mathematics the concept and sign for the essential absence that is designated by zero came to be recognized only late,[41] so likewise the silences between words or the pauses in music acquire form long after their sonic opposites.[42] Thus word spacing is not indicated systematically until centuries after words are written in *scriptio continua*, and rests become routine in musical notation only after first notes and then staves have been standardized. *Benedict's Rule* enjoins upon monks that they hold their tongues in the chapel, refectory and dormitory,[43] and the times and places of silence were only broadened among the Cistercians. The long twelfth century may be seen to have had a special predilection for silence, embodied most remarkably in the visual peculiarities of the romance about a character who bore this (in)activity as her name.[44] Even against the backdrop of this widespread predisposition to the topic of silence, the Cistercians showed a special affinity for this practice in their writings. It is no coincidence that the earliest expression of the Seven Sages cycle, in which the protagonist takes an oath to hold his tongue that nearly costs him his life, emanates from the pen of a Cistercian author.[45]

Although both silence and prayer may be considered *artes* and perhaps even nonverbal *artes*, the Cistercians circumvented words to find other modes of self-expression. Even among the Benedictines and Cluniacs, those who wished to communicate in places and in times when words were not permitted sometimes used hand signs known in Latin as *signa loquendi*.[46] The *Rule* makes reference to signs that can be heard, when Benedict prescribes that at meals silence should be preserved: 'If, however, any is required, it should be requested by an audible signal of some kind rather than by speech.'[47] In contrast, the *signa loquendi* are visible rather than audible. An early and intriguing reference to them appears in the life of Odo of Cluny (878/9–942) written soon after his death by John of Salerno:

For, whenever they had to ask for things they needed, to accomplish it they exchanged various signs, which I think grammarians would call *notae* of the fingers and eyes. In fact this arrangement had grown up to such an extent among them that I think if they had been without the use of tongues, these signs could suffice for signifying everything they needed.[48]

Another famous example from among the Cluniacs appears in Bernard of Cluny's *Customary*, which sets forth that in the scriptorium a monk who hankered after a pagan text should communicate as follows: 'If he wants a school book written by a pagan, he should make the usual sign for a book [palms open before him] and then he should touch his ear with a finger, just as a dog scratches with his foot, since the infidel may well be compared to an animal.'[49] Most of the signs designate what would be nouns, but they involve mimesis of actions. Thus the sign for beer is to grind one hand against another, while that for the schoolmaster is putting two fingers to the eyes (to signify watching) and holding up the little finger (to indicate a small one – a child).[50]

Lists of these monastic signs have been compiled since the eleventh century. They vary from order to order, with those of the Cistercians being by far and away the most elaborate.[51] The Cistercian lists tend to comprehend roughly 250 keywords.[52] They have continued to expand their vocabulary. Although most of their signs designate nouns, the lists could nonetheless permit a rich range of expression.

The reason for the fullness of their lists is not hard to deduce. Of twelfth-century monastic orders, the Cistercians were the most restrictive of speech. In addition to the chapel and dormitory (where the need for silence went, so to speak, without saying), Cistercians specified the cloister, refectory and infirmary as sites where signs rather than voices were to be employed.[53]

To come to grips with the Cistercian application of signs, a good first step is to consider the sensitivity of Aelred of Rievaulx to both Cicero and nonverbal expression – what we could call altogether appropriately 'body language'. Aelred's exposure to Cicero's *De amicitia* as a young man began a lifelong engrossment in that text, in the topic of friendship, and in the ideal of exploring and performing friendship through philosophical dialogue about it with friends. But the Cistercian's knowledge of the Roman author was not restricted to the single dialogue. Rather, it extended to Cicero's rhetorical writings. In particular, Aelred derived from Cicero a sensivity to reading nonverbal communication, which he adapted to a Cistercian setting.

Aelred corresponded with Bernard of Clairvaux (c. 1090–1153), who was his elder by roughly a decade. Both migrated from aristocratic backgrounds into the monastery, where they seem to have exercised considerable magnetism over their fellow monks. Aelred came from a good family that had close ties to both the Church and the royal court of Scotland, and he had an equally good career in the Church. The lineage of both Bernard and Aelred may help to explain the prominence of gesture in Cistercian life. Peter Abelard, only slightly older than Bernard and also of noble birth, viewed the move from being a knight to being a cleric as an exchange of the sword of Mars for that of Minerva.[54] Aristocrats who rose within the ranks of Cistercianism had to make a similar transition, but their conversion was not from military to dialectic contention. Rather, they retained vestiges of the *vita activa* they had left behind. As an order, they had economic dealings with the 'real world' that made them both extraordinarily successful and extraordinarily suspect: their understanding of 'work' in the imperative 'ora et labora' that went back to the ur-monk, Benedict, was much more physical and material than that held by most of their peers, especially the Benedictines. More important for the present purposes, they may have unhanded the swords wielded by their doppelgänger, the Knights Templar (whose order was shaped by Bernard himself),[55] but their hands remained in restless and eloquent motion. Like the great masters in education of their day, the leaders of the Cistercians achieved their preeminence not so much through their words alone as through the overall physical presence of which their words were but a part.[56]

Walter Daniel, Aelred's boon companion and later hagiographer, related that after the saint's death on 12 January 1157 he anointed three fingers of his abbot's right hand, namely, the thumb, index and middle finger 'because it was with these that he had written many things about God'.[57] Walter's gesture warrants reflection. In depictions of Gregory the Great, he receives inspiration from a dove that whispers in his ear, but it is his scribe who waits to write down the words and notes. Cistercian writers could not be like Gregory, even less like Thomas Aquinas, who was renowned for his ability to occupy multiple scribes as he dictated almost simultaneously two or three texts he had composed in his mind. In times of silence they had to write or speak with their hands.

Twelfth-century Cistercians had their own, characteristic attunement to the physical, and it expressed monastically the same impulses that were leading to the creation of courtesy books and books of manners as well as of 'cults of personality' that grew up around both the physical persons and the minds of great school masters.[58] From the fusion of Aelred's Ciceronianism with his own genius (as writer and friend alike) emerged the stage-setting that leads us into both Books I and II of his *De spiritali amicitia*. These scenes – and they are truly scenes, not just passages – show Aelred's literary persona as an entity caught between the secular and the monastic, the physical and the spiritual, the vocal and the silent, the inner and the outer, the self and society.

The first of these tableaux appears at the opening of Book I (1–3), when Aelred, in speaking alone with his friend Ivo, conjures up the presence of Christ between them; recalls the busy scene of talking, questioning and arguing with other monks in which they had participated earlier – and which had left Ivo feeling neglected by Aelred; and confronts his friend about the moody (and jealous) silence he had rightly detected in him, through gestures and other behaviours. The second comes at the opening of Book II (1–2), when Aelred speaks with Walter, who had reacted with a similar jealousy to the attention his abbot had to pay the men of the world with whom he had been meeting earlier. In these two passages we read about not only the utterance of words but also the interpretation of physical bearing. We receive an exposure to friendship not solely through a learned philosophical disquisition but also – in a tradition that stretches back beyond Cicero's *De amicitia* at least all the way to Plato's *Lysis* – through an enacted dialogue.[59] At the same time the detail provided in *De spiritali amicitia* transcends what is found in any of its dialogic predecessors: the textual and the performative are wedded with an unprecedented intimacy.

In secular settings roughly contemporaneous with Aelred, *actio* and *pronuntiatio* become a matter not merely of the words but of the entire person of the communicator. *Actio* came to encompass many other things beyond language and language-related style, such as physical comportment, manners and clothing.[60] Aelred takes the development in a different direction, since he expresses himself not solely in his words and bearing but also in his attunement to the words and bearing of others.

Reading as it developed in the Middle Ages has come to be seen as a highly active process. The fallacy that text and performance stand in opposition to one another has been dispelled as theories of performativity have grown rampantly over the decades since J. L. Austin (1911–60).[61] Although the reading that took place in medieval grammatical culture was textual, the texts were very much works in progress.[62] The functions that we would know as authorship and editing were shared elaborately among those who composed texts and those who wrote them, while readers knitted together the threads and added more of their own. All of these categories – texts, authors, scribes and readers – carried possibilities for what goes now under the name of performance.

Aelred shows himself the most active of readers, engaging with Cicero's *De amicitia* by bringing it into his own Cistercian context as both a text to be read and a script to be re-interpreted and reenacted among his own friends. The success of his rereading also hinged upon his ability to interpret (which is to read in another guise) his friends through his knowledge of a gestural language much subtler than a few hundred words in Cistercian sign language, but undoubtedly conditioned by it. And Aelred was also an active writer. For more than three decades the term 'performing self' has been used to identify writers whose texts are centrally concerned with the act of their own writing.[63] In a manner at once self-effacing and self-promoting, Aelred makes his dialogue on friendship into a demonstration – a staging – of himself and his intimates as they perform the formations, deformations and ends of friendships. In a manner that epitomizes much of what is truly spectacular about the twelfth century, Aelred makes each of the books in *On Spiritual Friendship* an act in a play – a spectacle – that dramatizes different aspects of his self as a friend.[64]

The heavy use of sign language by the Cistercians did not pass unnoticed or uncriticized. Although the signs were intended to avoid the dangers of speech, they had the capacity of any language to be overused and misused. As any parent or teacher can attest, quiet does not necessarily mean that work is going on or that mischief is not taking place. Lulled by a mistaken sense that the problems and pitfalls of communication lie solely or mainly in the spoken word, and reassured by the unlikelihood of being caught in the act (certainly not overheard), monks and lay brothers who were ignorant or irresolute in their profession seem to have overindulged themselves in the *signa loquendi*.[65] Consequently the Cistercians were taken to task by other orders for their overuse of signs. In a sermon the Augustinian canon Jacques de Vitry (c. 1160/70–1240) related:[66]

> I have heard of certain monks who were enjoined to maintain silence and not even to make signs with their hands, for the reason that they revealed idle and fanciful things to their friends through signs with their hands; since they did not dare do so in another way, they spoke in turn with their feet, confiding to their friends the battles of kings, deeds of warriors, and almost all the news and rumours from the whole world.

Even within their own ranks the Cistercian propensity to what would now be called 'signing' garnered criticism. Bernard of Clairvaux himself had warned strenuously against the use of signing at inappropriate times, such as during Lent, since he had urged: 'Let the hand fast from idle signing and from all activities which have not been enjoined', an exhortation that equates the *signa loquendi* with finger food that the Lenten faster must eschew.[67]

But the warnings apparently fell on deaf ears – or blind eyes. Helinand of Froidmont (d. after 1229) related in one of his sermons how a visionary saw the dead punished in the limbs with which they had sinned.[68] Those who had resorted needlessly to *signa loquendi* for idle and childish conversations had the skin torn from their fingers and had their fingers laid on anvils, where they were pounded to pieces by hammers. The same story seems to be related as an *exemplum* in Paris, Bib. Nat. MS Latin 15912, fol. 64[r], which gives a thirteenth-century account of a Cistercian novice who saw the torments suffered by dead monks as a result of excesses, such as relying upon signs to express 'trifling and playful things': 'On account of the unnecessarily numerous signs with which they communicated to each other certain trifling and playful things, the fingers of the heedless [monks] were flayed and shattered by repeated blows.'[69] Last but not least, Caesarius of Heisterbach (c. 1180–1240), who became in 1199 a monk and eventually prior of the Cistercian monastery from which he takes his name, tells of a lay brother (*conversus*) who returned to life after undergoing a vision of purgatorial punishments. Upon recovering, he cautioned his brothers against immoderate use of speech and sign language.[70]

Religious ritual and performance often intertwine in the Middle Ages. In the reports of these Cistercian visionaries and revenants, the overlaps between the two are only intensified by the circumstance that texts recording these rituals and performances are *exempla* – illustrations to be incorporated in sermons. But the intricacy of the relationship between ritual and performance in the sermon and exemplum pales beside that of my final case study.

From the reality of their sign language to lore about other forms of nonverbal performance was evidently only a short step or two, in this case a pas de deux that takes us from the hellish aftermath of excessive sign language to salvation through the truly histrionic. A narrative, preserved in both Old French and Medieval Latin, describes how a professional entertainer who has turned Cistercian dances rather than chants his praise of God.

The French version of this tale is called an *essamplel* (line 3) – *exemplum*. Written in rhyming octosyllabic couplets, this poem is known as *Tombeor Nostre Dame* or *Our Lady's Tumbler*. Its story runs as follows: an acrobat tires of the world, sells his belongings and joins the monks of Clairvaux. He finds the ways of the monastery alien, both because of its liturgy and because of its *signa loquendi* and silence. Silence is the sole means at his disposal for demonstrating his devotion, but it earns him only derision from his fellow monks, who do not regard him as a true peer. Eventually the tumbler falls into despair over his uselessness in performing the liturgy. In his despondency, he calls upon the Virgin repeatedly for her help and wanders the monastery until he happens upon a subterranean chapel with an altar and above it a statue of the Virgin. Upon hearing on the level above him the sounding of the summons to a mass, he resolves that he will celebrate Mary in the only way he knows: he will tumble. He takes off his monastic habit, which leaves him in simple undergarments. At first he performs leaps and genuflects. Later he somersaults, vaults, walks on his hands and weeps. He fits all of these actions within a pattern that includes embellishments and variations equivalent to the chants of praise that he can hear his fellow monks producing above him. It is punctuated by bows and prayers to the statue. The tumbler promises to adore the Virgin with his body. After performing until he collapses, the tumbler vows to the image of Mary to return to fulfil all the canonical hours in this form of devotion.

For years and years the tumbler repeats his performance at all the canonical hours. Eventually God wills it that the secret should come out, so that everyone might know that God rejects no one of any trade whatsoever, provided that the person loves God rightly. A fellow monk notices that the tumbler never comes to mass, blames him for his absence, and follows him to the crypt, where he sees the acrobatic divine office. The monk finds the performance laughable, but also stirring (lines 360–4).

Accordingly, he reports on the incident to the abbot, who comes with him to watch. When the sweat-covered acrobat collapses at the end of this performance, the abbot and monk witness a miracle: the statue of the Virgin Mother steps down from her plinth with a company of angels, mops the brow of her faithful servant, and finally goes off.

The abbot and monk watch the same sequence on various other occasions, delighted that the poor minstrel has won the favour of God and his mother. The monk repents of his earlier attitude towards the tumbler and agrees to abide by the abbot's command for him to keep the matter silent. Finally the abbot invites the entertainer to come to him. The tumbler fears that his performance has been discovered, and his anxiety only heightens when the abbot asks him how he had earned his living before joining the monastery. Soon the minstrel confesses, expecting the worst, but instead the abbot kisses him, solicits his friendship, and tells him to continue performing the divine office as he has been doing. The tumbler falls ill from joy but continues to enact his devotions and pushes himself until he nears death. As he lies on his deathbed, a marvel is witnessed by the abbot and all the monks: the archangels of God are arrayed on one side and the devils on the other, waiting to claim the dying man's soul, when the Mother of God appears and takes the soul heavenward, in the company of the angels. Thereupon the body is buried and the abbot reveals to one and all the story of the gymnastic monk, which brings great joy and culminates in praise to God for his miracles. The poet closes the poem with a call to prayer.[71]

This text contains all the elements that make performance in the Middle Ages a fascinatingly difficult but promising area to explore. It offers ritual, with liturgical song, space and audience. But even this characterization of the tale makes matters seem too straightforward.

For instance, consider the location of the events that unfold. The summons to prayer and chant of the liturgy are not seen but only heard faintly from above, background noise to what is wordless dance, punctuated solely by weeping that functions within the language of gestures as the tearful equivalent of a stage whisper. The weeping of the acrobat simultaneously substitutes for the liturgy of monastic chant and vouches for his spiritual repentance, partly by planting him firmly in the lineage of redemptive weeping that leads from the desert fathers through John of Fécamps, Aelred of Rievaulx and beyond.[72] The space where the tumbler moves through his routine constitutes a parallel universe to the chancel of the church, which we never see. It is a chapel, but a subterranean chapel, as unreal-seeming as the mysterious chambers where Tristan and Isolde take refuge in some of the romances named after them or where the title character hides his lover in Chrétien's *Roman de Cliges*.

Even the question of audience is not so straightforward. To the best of his knowledge the tumbler performs for no living person, but only for the Virgin who is unseen except in the guise of a statue. Would the *exemplum* have been conceivable outside the lush emotiveness with which Mary was shown in the twelfth century to become involved in human affairs? Elsewhere in miracles of the Virgin when statues come to life, they also respond to a combination of prayers or entreaties and actions: once again, we encounter the powerful fusion of *verbum* and *exemplum* that is a hallmark of twelfth-century culture.[73] Furthermore, the role of the statue makes the tumbler into a typically medieval Pygmalion, using his humble human art to vivify a man-made image.

Beyond Mary, a flesh-and-blood audience attends, but it is one of which the tumbler is unaware. Since not only the lurking abbot and monk but also the statue of the Virgin become embroiled in the course of events, the story lends support to performance theories which maintain that observers of performances cannot be detached and must participate.[74] By this token, the behaviour of the tumbler must be a true performance, since it forces beings both human and divine to participate.

The ironies of the tale are rich. At the outset performance and ritual appear to be irreconcilable. A skilful performer (although designated *tumeor*, 'tumbler', in the title, within the poem itself he is first called [line 9] a *menestrel*, 'minstrel') is humiliated at his inability to express himself through a language he does not comprehend, in songs and rituals he has not mastered. A lower-class monk feels constrained to mark his devotions on a plane palpably below that of all others in his community.

The physical agility associated with his social origins elevates him ultimately, but until then he is kept down (literally) by his inferior command of the words and gestures that make a monk. And what of silence? The tumbler, thwarted in part by monastic silence, embarks upon a path of wordless action. Initially he merely mimes the ritual of silence he witnesses among the monks. Later he enacts the canonical hours in a performance that may not make the mute stones speak but at least animates a lifeless statue. As a result, the excellence – both physical and spiritual – of his performance constrains his monastic antagonist to express the error of his ways through a silence imposed upon him by the abbot.

Is the performance rhetorical? If rhetoric is indeed the art of persuasion, then, yes, the tumbler's dance must be regarded as supremely and effectively rhetorical. It persuades the most important of its spectators, to wit, first the Virgin and later the abbot. The tumbler's persuasion has such power that it moves even an inanimate statue. The exception that proves the rule is the onlooking monk who fails to be persuaded – who fails to comprehend the true nature of the ritual. To the unpersuaded monk the dance remains initially what it would have been in the world outside, a performance that is capable of bringing solace and that has its own piety, but that is ultimately a very humble equivalent to the more strenuous, and meaningful, devotions of the brethren in their chant. It is the spiritual father of the monastery whose presence enables this monk to move beyond his initial response of laughter and to apprehend the power, the spiritual power, of the unspoken rhetoric that informs the perform-ance. And the abbot helps the monk participate more fully in the rhetoric by enjoining silence upon him.

In the concentric circles that radiate out from the dancer, the first and most important ring joins him to the Virgin, as embodied in the statue. Once he has persuaded her of his sincerity, a chain reaction begins that leads next to the abbot. Outside the monastery is the larg-est audience of all, which helps to explain why the poem was set down in the vernacular. Those of us who read the events – and when they were written, they were meant to be heard rather than read – have enforced upon us a silence as we experience simultaneously the rhetoric of the poet's words and the rhetoric of the tumbler's wordless dance. We are the final circle of the social activity that has at its centre the silent speech of the ritual dance and that takes its cue from the Virgin, who tells us how she has been moved and how we should be in turn. If we had been recipients of the story as an *exemplum* or poem in the Middle Ages, we might even have experienced it as delivered to the accompaniment of gestures that drew upon the repertory of performers like the tumbler himself.

While the whole story extols the tumbler for the sincerity of his devo-tion through acrobatic performance, it also constitutes a caution to monks that wherever they go and whatever they do, they will be seen. Not only is God himself watching (or at least a close relative), but so too are fellow monks who can and will go to their superiors. Implicit is the message that nothing – not even physical movements executed in silence – escapes the notice of the authorities, abbatial and heavenly. They supervise in the full etymological sense of the verb, since they look down from a higher plane. But the message is not ultimately a pessimistic one of the need to adhere to the status quo. In fact, the Virgin Mary is shown to be acces-sible everywhere to human beings of all statures, and it is the abbot who comes down to the crypt from the heights of the choir. Both Virgin and abbot assume places as members of the tumbler's audience, which means at least temporary parity with him. In a sense, they are even subordinated to him, insofar as they are persuaded by his power.

A remarkable feature of *Our Lady's Tumbler* is the poet's effort to convey in detail the sequence of movements that the dancer-gymnast executes as his devotion to the Virgin. The passage in question is a tour de force of technical terms to designate particular gymnastic turns the tumbler makes. Whether all the vocabulary would have had precise meanings to professional entertainers when the poem was composed or whether some of it existed only in the poet's imagination cannot be determined definitively. In either case the description constitutes a reminder of the ephemerality that many nonverbal arts suffered (and continue to suffer) when not video-recorded. If not seen by a capable dancer with a good eye and a better memory, the best dance will disappear the moment after being performed. The poet of *Our Lady's Tumbler* endeavoured gamely to preserve the unpreservable when he put into metre the motions of the devout tumbler. The fragility of the tumbler's art is no less characteristic a trait of his humility than are his lack of Latin, his inability to perform the liturgy, and his ignorance of *signa loquendi*.

Unlike Aelred of Rievaulx's *On Spiritual Friendship*, the tale of *Our Lady's Tumbler* has nothing to do with the 'performing self' if we understand the performance as the authorship of a text that dramatizes the self of the author. Then again, maybe the jongleur of the Old French text was also a tumbler: the common origins of the words 'jongleur' and 'juggler' open the door to such an interpretation. Whether the acrobat is a performing self or a performing other, he is engaged in a truly tacit renegotiation of power relationships that pit the lowly against those higher in the patriarchal hierarchy – between humanity and God, between vernacular and Latin, between lay brother and abbot. The humble agent succeeds, both within the narrative and in the (re)performance of the narrative, by competing through physical movement for the attention of the minds exposed to the narrative.[75] If the rhetorical situation is one in which power is exercised and transferred (as seems often to be the case in Cicero),[76] and if the power is specifically that of moving and persuading by oratory, then the jongleur's dance may be considered in a sense a silent oration that accomplishes effectively the aim of persuasion. At the same time it is of course liturgical, but liturgy and rhetoric are by no means inherently contradictory, since rites are in some sense also persuasive, both of the human participants and the divine audiences – as here.

A final fact worth observing is that at the very end of the twelfth and beginning of the thirteenth centuries, the Cistercian order seems to have been embroiled in an internal controversy over the appropriateness of allowing troubadours/trouvères and joglars/jongleurs and their songs and performances within a monastic context.[77]

The tale of *Our Lady's Tumbler* is not merely a blip on the chart of *exempla*. On the contrary, it came into being in the middle of the stretch, more or less coincident with the so-called long twelfth century, when the Cistercians extended the compass of self-expression to reach beyond words spoken and written to embrace not only silence but also specific motions and general carriage of the body. The development among the White Monks of what could be styled a rhetoric of silence and of comportment demonstrates amply that the distinctively twelfth-century pre-occupation with the relationship between interiority and exteriority was playing out in a special fashion within the Cistercian context, not only within the liturgy (where one would expect intersections of words, music, gestures and even dance-like processions) but even within those precincts of monastic life where wordlessness prevailed.[78] In *De doctrina Christiana* Augustine referred famously to gestures and facial expressions as *verba visibilia*.[79] Aelred of Rievaulx and the *exempla* that deal (both favourably and unfavourably) with the monastic sign language of his order show how complex those 'visible words' had become. But the tours de force of 'visible words' are literally the turns that the acrobat performs in *Our Lady's Tumbler* after he has transcended the art of silence to return to his original craft. His sequence assembles the best moves ever contrived by the acrobats of Metz, France, Champagne, Spain, Brittany, Lorraine and Rome, since all these place names are used to describe leaps and somersaults that he performs: his performance is a koiné of movements no less expressive than the words of a highly skilled orator or preacher.

The complexity of such 'visible words' was not recognized and influential only within the cloisters. The physicality of the communication – between monks as well as between monks and God or saints – in which such verbalization was used could fairly be called histrionic, in reference to both the etymological connection of the adjective with professional entertainers and the emotional connotations it conveys. Another appropriate adjective would be jongleuristic, which would have the advantage of signalling how the Cistercians anticipated the Franciscans. The *Legend of Perugia* tells that after Francis had composed his celebrated *Canticle of Brother Sun* (*Laudes creaturarum*), he wanted a former secular poet, Brother Pacificus, to lead through the world friars skilled in preaching and singing. After singing 'as true jongleurs of God', the preacher would proclaim 'We are the jongleurs of God' and would ask 'Who are, indeed, God's servants if not jongleurs who strive to move men's hearts in order to lead them to the joys of the spirit?'[80] Although in due course the silence that the Cistercians had inherited from the Cluniacs lost its appeal, other aspects of their song and dance lived on in unending action; and in surviving and perhaps even thriving, their rhetoric lived on as well, since Francis' intentness on moving men's hearts abides by the emphasis on persuasion that typifies classical rhetoric.

Disputes have raged endlessly about the relative weight assigned to speech and writing in Western culture. We as historians and literary historians, like the authors whom we study, articulate our views of the past verbally, and under the sway of our words and faith in words, we may be predisposed to underestimate deeds: verbalization comes more readily to us than action as we ponder the pairing of *verbum et exemplum*. The trivium-based culture of the Western Middle Ages – of the culture that went by the name of *omnis Latinitas* – rested upon an enactment of words long *avant la lettre* (or *parole*) of speech-act theory; but it built equally upon an *actio* that paralleled or even supplanted words. Rhetorical persuasion had from the beginning nonverbal aspects, which could draw audiences to the performer's message, which could translate or amplify words in gestures, or which could replace words altogether. The nonverbal aspects have bound rhetoric, sometimes comfortably, sometimes less so, to performers, such as actors and musicians, and they have also permitted the representation of the verbal in images. By virtue of their religion, medieval Christians had no choice but to be caught up in the paradoxical relationship between word and Word as well as between word/Word and deed. Ultimately the nonverbal allowed the representation of their deepest beliefs, as any painting of the Annunciation will confirm. In this Word-filled wordlessness, both speaker/actor and spectator/participant play essential roles. The tumbler, however humble he may be, belongs to this same rich and complex negotiation, the fulfilment of a distinctively medieval turn in what was designated in technical language as *actio* and *pronuntiatio*.

NOTES

1 C. Stephen Jaeger, *The Envy of Angels: Cathedral Schools and Social Ideals in Medieval Europe, 950–1200* (Philadelphia: University of Pennsylvania Press, 1994), and Peter Godman, *The Silent Masters: Latin Literature and Its Censors in The High Middle Ages* (Princeton University Press, 2000).

2 Valerius Maximus, *Factorum ac dictorum memorabilium libri IX*, ed. and trans. D. R. Shackleton Bailey, LCL (Cambridge, MA: Harvard University Press, 2000), 248–51: 'Quantum momentum sit in pronuntiatione et apto motu corporis' (VIII.10.1).

3 On reciprocal influences between the two arts (particularly in antiquity) in the usage of *pronuntiatio*, see F. Alberto Gallo, 'Pronuntiatio: Ricerche sulla storia di un termine retorico-musicale', *Acta musicologica*, 35 (1963), 38–46.

4 Laurence De Looze, '"To Understand Perfectly is to Misunderstand Completely": The "Debate in Signs" in France, Iceland, Italy and Spain', *Comparative Literature*, 50 (1998), 136–54.

5 *Glossa ordinaria* (also known as *Glossa glossarum*) to Book I, Tit. 2 of the *Institutiones iuris civilis* (Lyon: Apud Antonium Vincentium, 1556–8).

6 Compare Lucretius, *De rerum natura*, V.1,031.

7 For *actio* as a *terminus technicus* for the delivery of a speech, see TLL, 1.440.18–83 (and compare 1.443.75–444.40). For *pronuntiatio*, see TLL, 10/2.1,918.13–1,919.56, with categories that reveal the complex scope of the word: A *actio oratoris*, B *lectio, actio recitantis*, C *actio scaenica*, D *usus loquendi, latinitas*, E *musica*.

8 Quintilian, *Inst. orat.*, III.3.1: 'the system of oratory ... consists of five parts: invention, disposition, elocution, memory, and delivery or performance; both terms are used'. Contrast *Inst. orat.*, XI.3.1, 11.3.14; Fortunatianus, *Rhetorica*, XIII; and Martianus Capella, V.540 – and note TLL, 1.440.84–441.13.

9 Gregory S. Aldrete, *Gestures and Acclamations in Ancient Rome* (Baltimore: Johns Hopkins University Press, 1999), 169–71; Jody Enders, *Rhetoric and the Origins of Medieval Drama* (Ithaca, NY: Cornell University Press, 1992), 19–35; Fabio Rosa, 'Le voci dell'oratore: Oratoria e spettacolo nell'excursus Quintilianeo *De pronuntiatione*', in Lia de Finis (ed.), *Scena e spettacolo nell'antichità: atti del Convegno internazionale di studio, Trento, 28–30 marzo 1988* (Florence: Leo S. Olschki, 1989), 253–67; Carl Sittl, *Die Gebärden der Griechen und Römer* (Leipzig: Teubner, 1890), 199–211.

10 See *De oratore*, III.56.214–57.215 and *Orator*, 86: 'there is also delivery, neither melodramatic nor theatrical, but with moderate motion of the body, though accomplishing many things with the face'.

11 On Demosthenes and the actor Andronicus, see Quintilian, *Inst. orat.*, XI.3.7. On Cicero's attendance of theatrical performances in his youth, see Plutarch, *Cicero*, 5.3.

12 Macrobius, *Saturnalia*, III.14.11–12.

13 Valerius Maximus, *Factorum ac dictorum memorabilium libri IX*, VIII.10.2.

14 C. T. Onions (ed.), *The Oxford Dictionary of English Etymology* (Oxford: Clarendon Press, 1966), 668.

15 Richard Schechner, 'What Is Performance Studies Anyway', in P. Phelan and J. Lane (eds.), *The Ends of Performance* (New York University Press, 1998), 357–62, at 361. The sentence is quoted by Bruce W. Holsinger, 'Analytical Survey 6: Medieval Literature and Cultures of Performance', *New Medieval*

Literatures' 6 (2003), 271–311, at 274. Holsinger provides an excellent overview of recent developments in performance theory as applied to medieval literature.

16 Much more attention has been accorded to delivery by F. Rebmann, 'Pronuntiatio', in G. Ueding (ed.), *Historisches Wörterbuch der Rhetorik*, 10 vols. (Darmstadt: Wissenschaftliche Buchgesellschaft, 2005), vol. XII 212–47, and Georg Wöhrle, 'Actio: Das fünfte officium des antiken Redners', *Gymnasium*' 97 (1990): 31–46.

17 Kathleen E. Welch, 'Delivery', in T. O. Sloane, (ed.), *Encyclopedia of Rhetoric* (Oxford University Press, 2009), 218.

18 Pliny the Younger, *Epistles*, II.3.9 'In addition, it is commonly said that the spoken word makes a much greater impression, for though what you read may be much keener, all the same what the delivery, demeanour, appearance and gestures of the speaker imprint remains the more deeply in the mind.'

19 J. F. Reynolds (ed.), *Rhetorical Memory and Delivery: Classical Concepts for Contemporary Composition and Communication* (Hillsdale, NJ: L. Eribaum Associates, 1993).

20 See Cicero, *Orator*, 56, and Valerius Maximus, *Facta*, VIII.10.1.

21 Cap. 24; *RLM*, 373–448, at 440 (lines 32–3).

22 *OLD*, under *phonascus*, and *TLL*, 10/1.2,051.62–2,052.1, with particular reference to Quintilian, *Inst. orat.*, II.8.15 and XI.3.19 (compare XI.3.22).

23 Aristotle, *Rhetoric*, III.1.3–5, III.7.10, III.16.10. For discussion, see W. W. Fortenbaugh, 'Aristotle's Attitude toward Delivery', *Philosophy and Rhetoric*, 19 (1986): 242–54.

24 See W. W. Fortenbaugh, 'Theophrastus on Delivery', in W. W. Fortenbaugh (ed.), *Theophrastus of Eresus: On his Life and Work* (New Brunswick, NJ: Transaction Books, 1985), 269–88. The existence of the treatise is confirmed, among others, by Diogenes Laertius, *Vitae*, V.2.48, 'Theophrastus'.

25 For a quick overview, see Richard von Volkmann, *Die Rhetorik der Griechen und Römer, in systematischer Übersicht*, 2nd edn. (Leipzig: Teubner, 1885), 573–80. On Quintilian's indebtedness to the Greek rhetorical tradition in his section on *pronuntiatio* and *actio*, see Maddalena Vallozza, 'La tradizione greca nella teoria della pronuntiatio di Quintiliano', in Graziano Arrighetti (ed.), *Letteratura e riflessione sulla letteratura nella cultura classica: atti del convegno: Pisa, 7–9 giugno 1999* (Pisa: Giardini, 2000). On his theory of gestures, see Peter Wülfing, 'Antike und moderne Redegestik: Eine frühe Theorie der Körpersprache bei Quintilian', in Gerhard Binder and Konrad Ehlich (eds.), *Kommunikation durch Zeichen und Wort* (Trier: Wissenschaftlicher Verlag Trier, 1995), 71–90.

26 Elaine Fantham, 'Quintilian on Performance: Traditional and Personal Elements in *Institutio* 11.3', *Phoenix*, 36 (1982): 243–63, and Ursula Maier-Eichhorn, *Die Gestikulation in Quintilians Rhetorik* (Frankfurt am Main: P. Lang, 1989).

27 Cap. 24; *RLM*, 440 (line 30) to 443 (line 19).

28 III.15–23; *RLM*, 130 (line 4) to 134 (line 19). The same in *Consulti Fortunatiani Ars rhetorica*, ed. Lucia Calboli Montefusco (Bologna: Pàtron, 1979).

29 Cap. 43; *RLM*, 484 (line 7) to 485 (line 6).

30 *RLM*, 523–50, at 546 (lines 9) to 547 (line 2); *The Rhetoric of Alcuin & Charlemagne*, ed. and trans. W. S. Howell (Princeton University Press, 1941).

31 Martin Irvine, *The Making of Textual Culture: 'Grammatica' and Literary Theory 350–1150* (Cambridge University Press, 1994), 69.

32 Aimeric, *Ars lectoria*, ed. H. F. Reijnders, *Vivarium*, 9 (1971): 119–37, 10 (1972): 41–101 and 124–76; Magister Siguinus (Seguin), *Ars lectoria: un art de lecture à haute voix du onzième siècle* (composed 1087–88), ed. C. H. Kneepkens and H. F. Reijnders (Leiden: Brill, 1979); John of Garland, *Ars lectoria ecclesie*, ed. E. Marguin-Hamon, *L'ars lectoria ecclesie de Jean de Garlande: une grammaire versifiée du XIIIe siècle et ses gloses* (Turnhout: Brepols, 2003).

33 In T. M. Charland (ed.), *Artes praedicandi* (Paris: Vrin, 1936), 328–403, at 331–4. Other shorter passages are identified by Martin Camargo, 'Medieval Rhetoric Delivers; or, Where Chaucer Learned How to Act', *New Medieval Literatures*, 9 (2008): 41–62, at 45–6.

34 The possibility of such effects was suggested by Robert P. Sonkowsky, 'An Aspect of Delivery in Ancient Rhetorical Theory', in D. W. Prakken (ed.), *Proceedings, American Philological Association, Ninety First Annual Meeting, and Philological Association of the Pacific Coast, Fifty-Seventh Annual Meeting*, 90 (1959): 256–74.

35 Matthew of Vendôme, *Ars versificatoria*, IV.40, in Edmond Faral; (ed.), *Les arts poétiques du XIIe et du XIIIe siècle: recherches et documents sur la technique littéraire du moyen âge* (Paris: E. Champion, 1924, rpt. 1958), 189; trans. Aubrey E. Galyon (Ames: Iowa State University Press, 1980), 108.

36 Geoffrey of Vinsauf, *Poetria nova*, lines 2,031–65, in Faral (ed.), *Les arts*, 259–60; *Poetria nova of Geoffrey of Vinsauf*, trans. Margaret F. Nims (Toronto: PIMS, 1967), 90–1.

37 *Documentum de modo et arte dictandi et versificandi* (short version), II.3.170–5, in Faral (ed.), *Les arts*, 318–19; trans. Roger P. Parr (Milwaukee: Marquette University Press, 1968), 94–5. On the ascription and title of the long version, see Martin Camargo, '*Tria sunt*: The Long and the Short of Geoffrey of Vinsauf's *Documentum de modo et arte dictandi et versificandi*', *Speculum*, 74 (1999): 935–55.

38 Radulphus de Longo Campo, *In Anticlaudianum Alani commentum*, XXI.146, ed. Jan Sulowski (Wrocław: Zakład Narodowy im. Ossolińskich, 1972), 143 (line 25) to 144 (line 4).

39 On the scholasticizing of rhetorical commentaries after about 1285, see John O. Ward, *Ciceronian Rhetoric in Treatise, Scholion, and Commentary* (Turnhout: Brepols, 1995).

40 The older edition is *Poetria och Testa nucis av Magister Matthias Lincopensis*, ed. Stanislaw Sawicki, *Samlaren*, n.s. 17 (1936): 109–52, at 135 (lines 9–21) and 138 (line 17) to 139 (line 19). The newer is *Poetria*, in *Testa nucis and Poetria*,

ed. and trans. Birger Bergh (Arlöv: Berlings, 1996), 58–61 (sects. 52–4) and 68–73 (sects. 78–88).

41 Robert Kaplan, *The Nothing That Is: A Natural History of Zero* (Oxford University Press, 2000).

42 M. B. Parkes, *Pause and Effect: An Introduction to the History of Punctuation in the West* (Aldershot: Scolar Press, 1992), and Paul Saenger, *Space Between Words: the Origins of Silent Reading* (Stanford University Press, 1997).

43 Rudolf Hanslik (ed.), *Benedicti Regula*, 2nd edn (Vienna: Hoelder-Pichler-Tempsky, 1977), chapters 6, 38.7, 42, 48.5, 48.18, 52.2.

44 Heldris de Cornuälle, *Silence: A Thirteenth-Century French Romance*, ed. and trans. Sarah Roche-Mahdi (East Lansing: Michigan State University Press, 1999).

45 See Jan M. Ziolkowski, 'Vergil as Shahrazad: How an Eastern Frame Tale was Authorized in the West', in Franco Fido, Rena A. Syska-Lamparska and Pamela D. Stewart (eds.), *Studies for Dante: Essays in Honor of Dante Della Terza* (Florence: Edizioni Cadmo, 1998), 25–36.

46 Walter Jarecki, *Signa loquendi: die cluniacensischen Signa-Listen* (Baden-Baden: Koerner, 1981).

47 Hanslik (ed.), *Benedicti Regula*, 98; Timothy Fry (ed.), *The Rule of St. Benedict in English* (Collegeville, MN: Liturgical Press, 1982), 60. For further information, see Ambrose G. Wathen, *Silence: the Meaning of Silence in the Rule of St. Benedict* (Washington: Cistercian Publications, 1973).

48 John of Salerno, also known as Iohannes Italus and by various other names, *Vita Odonis*, I.32, PL 133: 57 (my translation).

49 *Ordo Cluniacensis per Bernardum*, I.27, in M. Herrgott (ed.,) *Vetus disciplina monastica* (Paris, 1726), 133–364, at 172; Jean Leclercq, *The Love of Learning and the Desire for God: A Study of Monastic Culture*, trans. Catharine Misrahi, 3rd edn (New York: Fordham University Press, 1982), 145–6, n. 46.

50 D. Banham, (ed.), *Monasteriales Indicia: The Anglo-Saxon Monastic Sign Language* (Pinner, Middx.: Anglo-Saxon Books, 1991), 23–4, no. 22, and 38–9, no. 85.

51 On Cistercian sign language see Scott G. Bruce, first in the article 'The Origins of Cistercian Sign Language', *Cîteaux: Commentarii cistercienses*, 52 (2001): 193–209, and later in the book *Silence and Sign Language in Medieval Monasticism: The Cluniac Tradition c. 900–1200* (Cambridge University Press, 2007). For texts, see Bruno Griesser, 'Ungedruckte Texte zur Zeichensprache in den Klöstern', *Analecta Sacri Ordinis Cisterciensis*, 3 (1947): 111–37; Walter Jarecki, 'Die "Ars signorum Cisterciensium" im Rahmen der metrischen Signa-Listen', *Revue bénédictine*, 98 (1988): 329–99; G. Müller, 'Die Zeichensprache in den Klöstern', *Cistercienser Chronik*, 21 (1909): 243–6; and Axel Nelson, 'Teckenspråket i Vadstena Kloster', *Nordisk Tidskrift för Bok-och Biblioteksväsen*, 22 (1935): 25–43.

52 Paul Gerhard Schmidt, 'Ars loquendi et ars tacendi: Zur monastischen Zeichensprache des Mittelalters', *Berichte zur Wissenschaftsgeschichte*, 4 (1981): 13–19, at 17.

53   Bruce, 'Origins', 203 n. 54.

54   Letter 1, 'Abaelardi ad amicum suum consolatoria', para. 2, in *Abelardo ed Eloisa: Epistolario*, ed. and trans. Ileana Pagani (Turin: Unione Tipografico – Editrice Torinese, 2004), 104–233, at 108; *The Letters of Abelard and Heloise*, trans. Betty Radice, rev. M. T. Clanchy (London: Penguin 2003), 3–43, at 3.

55   For a recent history of the order, see Helen J. Nicholson, *The Knights Templar: A New History* (Stroud, Gloucs.: Sutton, 2001). On Bernard's role in founding the order, see Franco Cardini, *I poveri cavalieri del Cristo: Bernardo di Clairvaux e la fondazaione dell'Ordine Templare* (Rimini: Il Cerchio, 1992).

56   Here I extend arguments made by Jaeger, *The Envy of Angels*, and Godman, *The Silent Masters*.

57   *Vita Aelredi*, chapter 59, ed. and trans. F. M. Powicke, *Walter Daniel's Life of Aelred, Abbot of Rievaulx* (London, 1950), 63.

58   Once again, see Jaeger, *The Envy of Angels*, and Godman, *The Silent Masters*.

59   On the tradition, see Jan M. Ziolkowski, 'Twelfth-Century Understandings and Adaptations of Ancient Friendship', in Andries Welkenhuysen, Herman Braet and Werner Verbeke (eds.), *Medieval Antiquity* (Leuven University Press, 1995), 59–81.

60   Joachim Bumke, *Courtly Culture: Literature and Society in the High Middle Ages*, trans. Thomas Dunlap (Berkeley: University of California Press, 1991), 181.

61   J. L. Austin, *How to Do Things with Words*, 2nd edn, ed. J.O. Urmson and Marina Sbisà (Cambridge, MA: Harvard University Press, 1975).

62   See Jan M. Ziolkowski, 'Text and Textuality, Medieval and Modern', in Barbara Sabel and André Bucher (eds.), *Der unfeste Text: Perspektiven auf einen literatur- und kulturwissenschaftlichen Leitbegriff* (Würzburg: Königshausen & Neumann, 2001), 109–31.

63   Richard Poirier, *The Performing Self* (New York: Oxford University Press, 1971).

64   Although the article touches upon Aelred of Rievaulx in only one phrase, Martin Stevens, 'The Performing Self in Twelfth-Century Culture', *Viator*, 9 (1978): 193–218, at 198, remains essential reading on application of 'the performing self' to medieval culture.

65   For firsthand reference to the pitfalls of hand signs in monastic life, see Müller, 'Die Zeichensprache in den Klöstern', 245.

66   Jacques de Vitry, *The Exempla or Illustrative Stories from the Sermones Vulgares of Jacques de Vitry* (London: Published for the Folk-lore Society by D. Nutt, 1890), 19, no. 48 (my translation), quoted by Schmidt, 'Ars loquendi', 19.

67   *Sermones in quadragesima*, Sermo 3, para. 4, in *Bernardi opera*, ed. J. Leclercq and H. M. Rochais, 7 vols. (Rome: Editiones Cistercienses, 1957–74), vol. IV, 353–80, at 367.

68   Sermo 22, *In nativitate B. Mariae Virginis 2*, PL 212: 668.

69 Bruce, 'Origins', 206 n. 73. This manuscript seems to have been produced not long before or after 1200 in a Cistercian house in the Beauvaisis, most likely in Beaupré. On this manuscript see Léopold Delisle, *Inventaire des manuscrits de la Sorbonne* (Paris, 1870), 28, no. 15912, and Brian Patrick McGuire, 'The Cistercians and the Rise of the Exemplum in Early Thirteenth-Century France: A Reevaluation of Paris B.N. MS lat. 15912', *Classica et mediaevalia*, 34 (1983): 211–67.

70 Caesarius of Heisterbach, *Libri miraculorum*, II.32, in *Die Wundergeschichten des Caesarius von Heisterbach*, ed. Alfons Hilka, 3 vols. (Bonn: P. Hanstein, 1933–7), vol. III, 115; cited by Bruce, 'Origins', 204 n. 59.

71 The most convenient means by which to approach the Old French (extant in five manuscripts) is through *Le jongleur de Notre-Dame*, trans. Paul Bretel (Paris: H. Champion, 2003). On the reception of the poem, see Jan M. Ziolkowski, 'Juggling the Middle Ages: The Reception of Our Lady's Tumbler and Le Jongleur de Notre-Dame', *Studies in Medievalism*, 15 (2006): 157–97. The only recent mention of the tale in the context of performance has been made by Domenico Pietropaolo, 'Improvisaton [sic] in the Arts', in Timothy J. McGee (ed.), *Improvisation in the Arts of the Middle Ages and Renaissance* (Kalamazoo: Medieval Institute Publications, Western Michigan University, 2003), 1–28, at 11–12.

72 For information on the texts and for analysis, see Piroska Nagy, 'Religious Weeping as Ritual in the Medieval West', in Don Handelman and Galina Lindquist (eds.), *Ritual in Its Own Right: Exploring the Dynamics of Transformation* (New York: Berghahn Books, 2005), 119–37.

73 Albert Poncelet, 'Miraculorum B. V. Mariae quae saec. VI–XV latine conscripta sunt Index postea perficiendus', *Analecta Bollandiana*, 22 (1902): 241–360, no. 1,668.

74 Ronald Grimes, *Beginnings in Ritual Studies* (Columbia: University of South Carolina Press, 1995), cited by Mary A. Suydam, 'Background: An Introduction to Performance Studies', in M. A. Suydam and J. E. Ziegler (eds.), *Performance and Transformation: New Approaches to Late Medieval Spirituality* (New York: St Martin's Press, 1999), 1–25, at 8. Suydam's piece offers a very approachable introduction to performance studies, aimed specifically at medievalists.

75 Poirier, *Performing Self*, 86–7.

76 Matthew Fox, 'Rhetoric and Literature at Rome', in W. Domink and J. Hall (eds.), *A Companion to Roman Rhetoric: Expansion, Resistance, and Acculturation* (Malden, MA: Blackwell, 2007), 369–81, especially 375–7.

77 William D. Paden, Jr, '*De monachis rithmos facientibus*: Helinant de Froidmont, Bertran de Born, and the Cistercian General Chapter of 1199', *Speculum*, 55 (1980): 669–85.

78 On the topic of interiority during this period, see Ineke van 't Spijker, *Fictions of the Inner Life: Religious Literature and Formation of the Self in the Eleventh and Twelfth Centuries* (Turnhout: Brepols, 2004), and Jan M. Ziolkowski, '*Amaritudo Mentis*: The Archpoet's Interiorization and Exteriorization of

Bitterness in Its Twelfth-Century Contexts', in C. S. Jaeger and I. Kasten (eds.), *Codierungen von Emotionen im Mittelalter / Emotions and Sensibilities in the Middle Ages* (Berlin; New York: Walter De Gruyter, 2003), 98–111.

79 Augustine, *De doctrina christiana*, II.5 (in the numbering of the CSEL edition, which corresponds to II.3.4 in the old numbering), ed. and trans. R. P. H. Green (Oxford: Clarendon Press, 1995), 58: 'Some of the signs by which people communicate their feelings to one another concern the eyes; most of them concern the ears, and a small number concern the other senses. When we nod, we give a sign just to the eyes of the person whom we want, by means of that sign, to make aware of our wishes. Certain movements of the hands signify a great deal. Actors, by the movement of all their limbs, give certain signs to the *cognoscenti* and, as it were converse with the spectators' eyes; and it is through the eyes that flags and standards convey the wishes of military commanders. All these things are, to coin a phrase, visible words.'

80 *Legend of Perugia*, 43, in M. A. Habig (ed.), *St. Francis of Assisi, Writings and Early Biographies: English Omnibus of the Sources for the Life of St. Francis* (Chicago: Franciscan Herald Press, 1973), 1,021–2.

CHAPTER 6

Vultus adest *(the face helps)*

Performance, expressivity and interiority

Monika Otter

The title of this essay cites a much discussed line in Hildebert of Lavardin's so-called 'Rome elegy', written about 1100. The poem apostrophizes Rome, admiring her greatness even in ruins; in a companion poem, a personified Rome replies that despite her discomfiture, she is now better off, having found Christian truth. Towards the end of the first of the two poems, Hildebert turns to a feature that greatly intrigued medieval visitors to Rome: its ancient statuary.

Here even the gods themselves admire the shapes of the gods and wish they were equal to the artificial faces. Nature could not create gods with such a face as these admirable *signa* of gods created by men: *vultus adest his numinibus*, and they are venerated for the work of the craftsmen rather than for their divinity.[1]

Line 35, 'vultus adest his numinibus' (which I am leaving untranslated for now), had always been translated as 'these godheads have faces' and interpreted as a prime example of Hildebert's 'humanism': his sincere recognition of the beauty of art, of the human face, even of modern personhood and individualism. In a 1976 note, Otto Zwierlein balked at the standard interpretation, objecting in part to the anachronistic projection of 'humanism', in part simply to the oddness of the verse itself.[2] What precisely is it supposed to mean? Hildebert has just spent several verses commenting on the statues' faces, so why would he now inform us that they *had* faces in the first place? And would it not be rather more surprising if they did not? It seemed a weak line in an otherwise masterfully crafted poem. Therefore, admittedly against unanimous manuscript consensus, Zwierlein proposed emending 'vultus' to a less problematic 'cultus', and translating it something like, 'these gods have cults', or 'these gods are venerated'. He pointed out that the emendation would improve the flow of the sentence (from *cultus* to *coluntur* – 'these gods have cults, and they do because …'), and that 'vultus' would be an exceedingly easy copying mistake to make, given its similarity to 'cultus' and the context.

In a published reply, Peter von Moos quickly disposed of this suggestion by pointing to the verse's source in Lucan, which shows that 'vultus'
has to be the right reading. It is the word 'adest' that has been misleading
most readers: it must be 'adesse' not just in the sense of 'being there' but
of 'helping'. The phrase in Lucan, said of Cleopatra, is 'vultus adest precibus', that is, 'her face supports her entreaties', or perhaps one could say,
'reinforces her entreaties'.[3] This is a well-known line; John of Salisbury also
cites it, as a key quotation in Book III of the *Policraticus*.[4] Reading *vultus*
more broadly as 'aspect' or even 'beauty', Moos therefore suggests that the
line might mean something like, 'these gods are helped by their looks'.[5]

Textually, there is no need to reopen the question, if only because
Moos has the manuscripts on his side. But Zwierlein could have pointed
out that, as far as textual reminiscences go, 'cultus adest' is also a memorable tag. In a textual culture in which the normal mode of serious study
involved memorization, a metrical foot or a clausula is very likely to stick
in one's mind and be recalled in oblique and strange and semi-conscious
as well as more straightforward ways. Ovid uses 'cultus adest' in the *Ars
Amatoria*, to contrast modern times with the rusticity of past times, something like 'today we have culture'.[6] But since it occurs in connection with
women's makeup, it is understandable that John of Salisbury recalled it
in a slightly different meaning of 'cultus', namely 'grooming' or, indeed,
makeup: he says in the *Entheticus Maior* that personified Truth is better
where no 'cultus adest', without makeup or varnish, with her own true
face.[7] And in fact a quick search of the searchable text databases we now
have at our disposal (the Patrologia Latina, the Perseus Project or the
Brepols Library of Latin Texts) shows that collocations of both 'cultus
adest' *and* 'vultus adest', or wordplay on 'cultus and vultus', or even combinations of all three, are not so rare. Even in the rhetorical textbooks we
shall presently look at, *vultus* (facial expression) and *cultus* (study, practice)
occur in close proximity. When we ask what Hildebert's line 'means', we
may really be asking how to translate it. As long as it is left in its original
language, the line can happily 'mean' the intersection or the aggregate
of all the meanings the words allow and all the reminiscences they call
up – especially in such an intertextual, citation-happy culture as the Latin
Middle Ages. Even though Hildebert wrote 'vultus adest', 'cultus adest'
may very well be in play, by the exact same mechanisms (the rhyme, the
near-homophony, the context, the proximity of the related verb *coluntur*) that suggested it to Otto Zwierlein. And one might note that 'cultus
adest' also makes a relevant thematic contribution here, contrasting the
true face with the artificial face, genuine with artificial expression.

But let us entertain 'vultus adest' for a moment. Moos is surely right in pointing us to the Lucan parallel, but how much does the reminiscence help us in stabilizing the meaning of Hildebert's line? Several attempts at translating it with Moos' suggestion in mind – C. Stephen Jaeger's 'carved likenesses improve these deities' or Jean-Yves Tilliette's 'ces divin- ités tirent bénéfice de leur apparence' – at best select one narrow path among a whole field of possibilities, and not the most obvious one, to the neglect of all others.[8] First of all, the very broad reading of *vultus* is not the first that comes to mind. If it means 'aspect' it surely retains a strong semantic component, as it does in the Lucan verse, of 'facial aspect', even 'facial expression'. Moreover, how exactly are the gods and their *vultus* like Cleopatra in Lucan? Cleopatra matches insincere words with an insincere expression. Kurt Smolak, making the same objection, goes as far as to declare the quotation thematically irrelevant.[9] Without altogether reject- ing the Lucan reminiscence, he proposes a more proximate source for Hildebert's poem: an Ottonian hymn that anticipates both the conceit of apostrophe and prosopopoeia, an address to Rome and a reply by Rome, but also – repeatedly – the phrase 'vultus adest'. It is best to cite it in the original, to show the artful deployment of that key phrase:

> En, ubi vultus adest, querens oracula matris
> Pro natis hominum, en, ubi vultus adest,
> Vultus adest Domini, cui totus sternitur orbis.
> Signo iudicii vultus adest Domini.[10]

It must be said that this parallel, convincing though it is, also does not yield an easy or altogether appropriate meaning. The first two occur- rences of 'vultus adest' are obscure in their precise reference. (Smolak, acknowledging the text's difficulty and suspecting textual corruption, does not offer a translation.) And in the second distich, as Smolak points out, 'vultus adest' refers to the Lord, echoing a common biblical usage. If the *vultus domini* is in play in Hildebert's poem, the allusion surely has to be heavily, even daringly, ironic. If God's *vultus* is a synecdoche for His benevolent and self-identical presence, the pagan gods – reduced in the companion poem to 'numina vana' – are anything but self-identically present. Or, rather, they are self-identical, but only in the empty sense of idols, which short-circuit any notion of both reference *and* presence; only in the sense that there is nothing for the images to be identical *to*: the stone faces are all there is.

However one reads it, Lucan's 'vultus adest' sits a bit awkwardly in Hildebert's poem, not firmly tied in syntactically or semantically, and not exactly parallel to how Lucan uses it. It is not hard to see how Cleopatra's facial expression can 'help', 'support' or 'coincide with' her words, however mendacious. Words and face coincide and one 'helps' the other. But in Hildebert's construction there is nothing that exactly corresponds to 'precibus'. The gods' *vultus* aids or reinforces – what? The gods themselves? Their numinosity? The vagueness, it seems to me, is not accidental, and not inappropriate. *Vultus*, as Maurizio Bettini has shown, is a fairly charged word for 'face'.[11] More neutral words were available in Latin to designate the face simply as a part of the body. *Vultus* carries strong implications of intentionality, of turning towards somebody (both these things have been suggested as its etymology – akin to either *volvere*, 'to turn', or to *volere*, 'to want').[12] It is also a technical term in rhetoric: Quintilian explains in Book XI of the *Institutiones* how an orator should use his *vultus*, meaning deliberate, studied facial expression, to help make his point. In short, *vultus* is about intention, about expressing, communicating, as Cleopatra does with her *vultus*.

If we admit some unstable combination of some or all of these meanings and echoes, and concur with Moos in hearing Lucan's verse above all, Hildebert is playing a complicated game. On the one hand, he declares the statues empty, material things. They may have a likeness of a face, of facial features; if they have an expression it is a simulation, an illusion of one. They cannot have an 'expression' in the literal sense of 'expressing' an inner state, a meaning, an intention. On the other hand, such an intention *is* implied by the Lucanian reminiscence of 'vultus adest' – where the face or facial expression is specifically said to correspond to, 'aid' or communicate an intention, a speech of Cleopatra's. Thus Hildebert lends his gods a quasi-interiority but one that remains paradoxical, circular and incomplete. It is the *vultus* that makes these statues 'gods', conscious quasi-persons, in the first place, yet it does so precisely by implying a consciousness behind the face. No wonder the sentence is shaky, in itself and as a quotation from Lucan.

The larger conceit – discussed in some detail by both Jaeger and Michael Camille – is that the gods envy their own representations.[13] But the joke is not simply that they are less beautiful or less perfect; that is the least of these deities' problems. It is nothing compared to the awkward fact that they do not exist. These are, as the companion poem stresses, *numina vana*, vain or 'empty' images: they represent nothing.[14] There are no gods. Hildebert's gods do not envy the statues their beauty or perfection so much as their reality. Another way of saying the same thing, of course, is that the images *are* the gods – the classic definition of 'idol'.

To the extent that the statues have referents, entities that can be said to 'admire', 'envy' or 'wish', they are created by the images themselves. The statues and their referents coincide. Hildebert's clever joke is that he pretends to pull them apart again, to grant the gods a limited, temporary independent existence – a fictional existence – just long enough to call them as witnesses to their own non-existence. See? They are not real. They said so themselves.[15]

I have dwelt on Hildebert's verse and its many polysemies because it engages a number of considerations and uncertainties about *vultus*, 'face', a recognized subcategory of rhetorical *pronuntiatio*. These considerations can be traced in a number of high medieval texts (roughly from the ninth to the twelfth centuries). Although there is no sustained discourse or coherent theory of *vultus* in that period, any more than there is in classical culture,[16] the scattered yet interconnected references can be valuable clues to medieval attitudes towards performance, rhetorical and theatrical, textual and physical.

Hildebert's poem uses the conceit of the statues' faces in two ways. First, *vultus* functions as an interface between oneself and an Other, or, metaphorically (and here I agree with C. Stephen Jaeger) a reader and a textual Other.[17] The face appears solid and well-delineated, the outer surface of an inner life. Thus, it functions as an absolute divide between a speaker and an interlocutor; yet, as a projection of the Other's interiority, it also holds out the promise of a glimpse into the inner life it both covers and reveals. The face is, after all, par excellence that feature of the body by which we meet, recognize and know a person. We speak of face-to-face encounters rather than, say, body-to-body encounters. The twelfth-century Cistercian Guilelmus Abbas considers the face-as-interface in an extended meditation on 'the multiple face of man' in encountering God: 'For as many affects as the human soul has, it has as many faces towards you.' The soul's many faces meet the *vultus domini*, the face of the Lord, in a mirroring (God's face of mercy meeting the soul's face of humble contrition), in a substitution (His face is spat upon and slapped so that hers may appear radiant and dignified), and in a fusion, the 'kiss of the groom and the bride'.[18]

Despite its apparent solidity, *vultus* is experienced in all my sample texts as a problematic, paradoxical interface. It sets up a number of seemingly straightforward relations: I and thou; inside and outside; inward feeling and outward expression. But all these relationships are liable to blurring and even dissolution. It is never entirely certain who or what (if anything) is behind a face; whether the face expresses the affect, or the essence, of

the person within, or on the contrary gives rise to that inner life or constitutes it; whether, even, what we are encountering comes from behind the
face or, mirror-fashion, from ourselves.

Second, for Hildebert – and, as I shall argue, for other writers – *vultus*
is also an interface in an encounter with classical culture as the Other.
The learned culture of the earlier and high Middle Ages, with the various
'Renaissances' from the Carolingians to the twelfth century, sees itself
very self-consciously as heir and successor to the ancients, usually seeking
to stress proximity and continuity, to the point of treating the ancients
as present and contemporary. But occasionally, in medieval face-to-face
encounters with antiquity, particularly with traces of its self-performance
(statuary, oratory, theatre), we sense a profound feeling of estrangement,
and not only for the reason usually stated, namely the ancients' paganism.
This anxiety of reception, however, also provides the medieval heirs with
spaces for performing themselves, creating, that is, their own culture.

The treatment of *vultus* in the ancient arts of rhetoric is vexing in the
same way as their treatment of *pronuntiatio*, performance, in general.
Like delivery in general, *vultus* is said to be absolutely vital, yet not much
is said about it. Both Cicero and Quintilian proclaim, 'the face is everything' ('dominatur autem maxime vultus'), yet deal with it in a single
paragraph. To make matters worse for us, these two crucial sources were
not widely read in our period; though *Ad Herennium*, one of the most
widespread rhetoric texts, does have a fairly detailed section on delivery,
where facial expression is discussed together with 'vocis figura' – voice
quality.[19] *Ad Herennium* supplies the basic formula 'vox, vultus, gestus',
which is repeated in the numerous rhetorics that essentially excerpt and
summarize *De oratore* and Quintilian. (For instance, Fortunatianus in his
catechism-like style: 'What elements make up *pronuntiatio*? Voice, *vultus*,
gesture. What is added to them? *Cultus* or *habitus*.'[20]) That is, medieval
students were presumably still taught that *vultus* is essential, but given
even less detail to substantiate this wisdom than Cicero or Quintilian
provided. They may well have come away feeling somewhat vague and
puzzled as to the precise significance of the term, let alone its practical
applicability.

Nonetheless, it is instructive to observe the two main classical sources,
which, for all their brevity, manage to present us with an astonishing
range of conflicts and slippages, some acknowledged, some not. First of
all, there is some slippage between your face as quintessentially you, that
by which we can stably recognize you; and your face as mobile, adaptable,
consciously manipulable, therefore also able to conceal or deceive. To

some extent, that semantic distinction is distributed between the words *facies* and *vultus*. *Facies* comes from *facere*, as ancient and medieval etymologists point out. Hence it denotes the way one is made, one's 'features' (French *faiture*); *vultus*, thought to be etymologically linked to *volere* (to desire), carries the charge of 'facial expression'.[21] Quintilian makes the distinction most memorably when he describes, by analogy, the human voice as having both a *facies* (a stable set of characteristics, a unique configuration by which we can recognize a given individual under most circumstances) and a *vultus* (the expression or inflection the speaker chooses to give it in a particular instance).[22] But that distinction is far from absolute, and both *facies* and *vultus* can freely assume both meanings.

Moreover, *vultus* shares in the ambivalence that suffuses the entire discussion of *pronuntiatio*: it has much in common with the art of the actor, and young orators are even advised to learn from famous actors. Yet the association with acting, a base profession miles away from the high status the orators claim for themselves, is also to be avoided.[23] That the body is expressive, and that this expressivity can and should be harnessed, is acknowledged but eyed with suspicion: expressivity can too easily slide into the showy and 'effeminate' gestures of stage business. To the extent that the orator is to craft his body language and facial expression at all, the artifice must never be apparent. The orator must walk the very fine line that marks the proper performance of rhetorical manliness – a manliness that is undermined and negated as soon as its performance becomes at all visible. One performs rhetorical masculinity by appearing not to perform it at all.

The second difficulty that leads the orator to invoke but also disavow the actor's art has to do with sincerity and authenticity. If *vultus* is supposed to be the true and spontaneous expression of inner states, or of character (a Stoic idea),[24] both the actor and the orator have the peculiarity of displaying 'inner states' that are not properly theirs, that are adopted and performed in a theatrical, forensic or civic context, on someone else's behalf, with motives and goals that are not properly the performer's. In that sense, the oratorical *vultus* is as empty as the theatrical (or the statuesque). It corresponds to no inner state; it suggests and therefore fictitiously creates one. While Cicero and Quintilian have no problem defending the probity and social usefulness of this performance, it is at the heart of the gravest charge against rhetoric: its hollowness, its lack of true ethical commitment. The good orator can advocate any position and defend any side in a conflict with equal persuasiveness. This is an accusation orators know how to answer (by partially embracing it), but it does imperil the ideal of the rhetor as the *vir bonus* par excellence.[25]

Quintilian's answer, in Book XII of the *Institutio*, is to collapse the distinction between inward and outward, between intention and expression, and with it the whole idea of a correspondence between them, of representation; and to declare the orator's performance, as well as his ethical integrity, tautologically self-identical. A good speech act carries its intentions within it; the good orator is by definition a *vir bonus* and vice versa. (Cf. *Inst. orat.* XI.3.182–3: oratory, unlike acting, is an 'action', not an 'imitation'). Structurally, this is not unlike Hildebert's sly manoeuvre of making the statues not truly representations of gods but identical with gods – but the very different ethical thrust of that manoeuvre shows up the slipperiness of the rhetor's self-defence.

With all these ambivalences, it is unsurprising that Cicero's and Quintilian's brief treatments of *vultus* are somewhat contradictory and not easily applicable to rhetorical practice. Cicero, with deceptively clear logical connectors, oscillates between *vultus* as a natural index of inner intentions, and *vultus* as a sign system to be carefully manipulated:

For delivery is wholly a matter of the soul (*Animi est enim omnis actio*), and the face is an image of the soul, while the eyes reflect it. The face is the only part of the body that can produce as many varying signs as there are feelings in the soul … Consequently (*quare*), it is quite important to regulate the expression of the eyes (*oculorum esto magna moderatio*). We should not alter the appearance of the face itself too much, so as to avoid distorting it or acting like a fool. It is the eyes that should be used to signify our feelings in a way suited to the actual type of our speech, by an intense or relaxed, or a fixed or cheerful look. Delivery is, so to speak, the language of the body (*Est enim actio quasi sermo corporis*), which makes it all the more essential that it should correspond to what we intend to say; and nature has actually given us eyes, as it has given the horse and the lion their manes, tails, and ears, for indicating our feelings.[26]

This ambiguity, coupled with the urgent admonition to avoid exaggeration of any sort, may well leave the student in doubt as to what, if anything, he is actually to do with his face.

Quintilian helps with somewhat more specific advice, albeit mostly of the negative sort (do not ever flare your nostrils or bite your lips, XI.3.80–1; eyebrows should be 'neither too fixed, nor too mobile', XI.3.78). But, if anything, he exacerbates Cicero's underlying paradox. He cheerfully mixes voluntary and involuntary facial motions. Tears, given by nature as 'mentis indices', share a sentence with advice on how to move one's eyes appropriately. Blushing or turning white is mentioned in one breath with the manipulation of the eyebrows. He twice explicitly uses the word *fingere*:

In the face itself, the most important feature is the eyes. The mind (*animus*) shines through especially in these. Even unmoved they can sparkle with happiness or be clouded over with grief. Nature has given them tears as well, as an indicator of feelings; and these either burst out in grief or flow for joy. And when the eyes do move, they become intent, relaxed, proud, fierce, gentle, or harsh; these qualities should be assumed (*fingentur*) as the pleading demands.[27]

Quintilian's ambivalence is most tellingly encapsulated in his uncertain treatment of masks. Where Cicero makes a clear distinction between an actor playing with a mask (hence limiting his facial expressivity) and without a mask (therefore able to use his acting skills more fully, and perhaps more admirably), Quintilian has it both ways. Masks are a metaphor for the orator's conscious selection of the proper facial expression: 'Therefore in plays composed for the stage, artists in delivery borrow extra emotion from the masks (*a personis*). Thus in tragedy, Aerope is sad, Medea fierce, Ajax mad, Hercules truculent.'[28] That donning a 'mask', however well chosen, conflicts with the advice to keep one's eyes and eyebrows mobile, is not noted, but perhaps highlighted by Quintilian's special mention of the comic mask that 'has one eyebrow raised and the other not, because he is sometimes angry and sometimes calm, and the actors regularly turn towards the audience that side of the mask which suits the particular part they are playing'.[29] This trick allows for some change of expression, but it hardly makes up for the enforced immobility he otherwise deplores.

If *vultus* gives us an additional register of para-linguistic signs to be employed like words or gestures, there is also the possibility of fraudulent use, of dissimulation. This, in fact, is the essence of the Lucan allusion that figured so prominently in our discussion of Hildebert's poem. Cleopatra's face does indeed match her words (*vultus adest precibus*), but we know her intentions are insincere. John of Salisbury quotes the sentence in that sense.[30] On the other hand, if the face is also a natural index of inner states, one may ask if dissimulation is even possible; and there are famous classical loci in which *vultus* functions both ways, actively trying to deceive or conceal, *and* involuntarily displaying the true emotion within.[31] Here, the two senses of *vultus* as an assumed, artificial rhetorical expression, and *vultus* as the involuntary, spontaneous and natural reflex of an inner state are powerfully and paradoxically telescoped.

The Stoic ideal that underlies to some extent the polysemy in Cicero and Quintilian, of the *vultus* that corresponds equably and stably to one's inner state, shows up in the high Middle Ages in the genre of court satire, where the assumed, dissimulated *vultus* is the ultimate expression of the court's inauthenticity and its tyrannical power over the individual courtier, who has no choice but to play along and inflict that quintessential self-alienation on himself. In fact, besides satirically condemning the *vultus alienus* (notably in John of Salisbury's *Policraticus*, Book III), writers also prudentially recommend manipulating one's face, as a sad necessity perhaps, but also a self-protective, adaptive skill. John himself counsels his book in the *Entheticus minor* (a kind of extended *envoi* that precedes the *Policraticus*), to approach Becket, the dedicatee, with great care. It is to attempt no deception – 'You will please him by virtue only'; but at the same time the book is also exhorted, with no great sense of contradiction, to watch its face and reveal itself only slowly and strategically, risking no displeasure on the great man's part. The Chancellor's face, too, may or may not be 'veiled'.[32] Even more pointedly, Abelard counsels his son, 'In all things the wise man considers the time and the place, and assumes many faces, as they fit the circumstances.'[33]

In the *Policraticus*, sincerity, or its impossibility, is a constitutive element of John's political theory. The hypocrisy of courtly self-alienation is not only a sign of the times, an evil or vice among many, but a contradiction that underlies, for better or for worse, the political system John knows and tries to capture in his writings. He gives it an entire book of its own (Book III), whose elaborate theatre metaphor is among the most interesting and well-informed discussions of classical theatre the high Middle Ages produced.

The association of theatre and the need for public role-playing has a long satirical tradition, particularly in Juvenal, which John knows well and cites liberally. Yet for him the metaphor must have assumed a certain exotic flavour – quite appropriate to its intended meaning of artifice and alienation. For the Roman theatre, as has frequently been discussed, is another locus where the Middle Ages find themselves face to face with classical culture – yet also perhaps the aspect of the classical inheritance that is most fundamentally alien to medieval readers.[34] Terence's comedies were well-established school reading; they came with prefatory material about Terence's life and about the Roman theatre, and with Donatus' commentary, which quite frequently remarks on matters of performance. The late classical illustrations, featuring scenes with masked characters, continued to be reproduced until the thirteenth century, if with varying degrees of comprehension.[35] Medieval readers were certainly acquainted with multiple forms of theatricality and performativity, as several recent studies have stressed.[36] Yet they had no active or clear knowledge of theatre as a building or as a cultural institution, and these notions partially eluded them, filtered as they were through late antique sources that are already culturally distant from the classical theatre, as well as through their quite different practical experience of plays and mummings in their own culture. In addition, there is a certain theoretical and practical indifference to some concepts that strike both the ancients and us as constitutive of theatre – such as a sharp distinction between textual, narrative diegesis and theatrical representation, or the notion of a more or less stable impersonation, where an actor 'stands in' for a character with his body and speaks that character's words and no others. Medieval theorists, even more than their classical counterparts, tend to lump narrative and theatrical genres together; and some medieval plays, in particular the so-called 'Latin elegiac comedies' of the twelfth century, notoriously mix narrative commentary with character speeches.[37] This indifference allows medieval commentators, at times, to tolerate conflicting notions that strike us as quite incompatible, or to hold on to a 'mistaken' notion of classical theatre despite quite good information to the contrary.[38] The short explanation for this puzzling attitude is that classical drama – and in practice, this means above all Terence – is seen as a text to be read and studied in school, not a performance to be staged or watched in a theatre. Yet, as we have been learning recently, we should not be too hasty in excluding performance from medieval reading culture – particularly in a school context.[39]

In a 1950 article, Mary Hatch Marshall turned to a set of medieval comments on the word *persona* – commentaries on Boethius' 'De duabus naturis et una persona Jesu Christi, contra Eutychen et Nestorem' – in hopes of showing that these writers, of the ninth to thirteenth centuries, actually had a far more developed idea of ancient theatre than is often supposed.[40] These texts are not specifically interested in theatre but in theology: they are concerned with the theological term *persona*, not primarily trinitarian in this case but Christological, that is, how precisely we are to conceive of the doctrinal statement that Christ is both human and divine, and what precisely is wrong with those conceptualizations that have been labelled heretical. In so doing, they feel the need to help us understand the polysemy of the word *persona*, but at the same time take advantage of it. Apart from its meanings in grammar and rhetoric, *persona* means 'theatrical mask', 'character' as in *dramatis personae*, and also 'person' in our sense – what the commentaries often call the 'substance' of an individual human being, close to what we would call 'identity'. Historical accuracy or conceptual clarity about the ancient theatre is not their priority, and indeed the comments are interestingly muddled. They are extraordinarily difficult to read, and often obscure rather than elucidate the passage in Boethius upon which they expand. Their linguistic uncertainty reveals a tenuous grasp on the concepts – and, perhaps more than confusion, a certain indifference to the directionality of both the etymological and the ontological argument Boethius makes: whether *persona*, 'individual, person', is derived from *persona*, 'mask', or the other way around; and whether primacy belongs to the mask or to the actor speaking through it or to the character represented – that is, the very nature of theatrical representation.

Here is Boethius himself.

> The name *persona* seems to have been transferred from elsewhere, namely from those 'personae' that in the comedies and tragedies represented those people of whom [the play] treats. *Persona* comes from *personare*, therefore from 'sound', because through the hollowness itself the sound necessarily had to become louder. The Greeks, too, call these personae *prosopa* from the fact that they are put on the face and cover the countenance before the eyes [of onlookers] … But because with the imposition of the personae the actors, as I have said, represented the people of whom the tragedy or the comedy treated, that is Hecuba or Medea or Simo or Chremes, therefore other people, too, who could be securely identified through their appearance, were named 'personae' by the Latins and 'prosopa' by the Greeks.[41]

Apart from repeating the familiar notions that masks were used to amplify sound and that their etymology links them to *per-sonare*, or sounding through – both ideas that predate Boethius by a good bit even though they are no longer accepted by most scholars today – Boethius asserts that the theatrical use of *persona* as 'mask' and then as 'character' precedes the extended use of *persona* as 'any human individual'; and that this notion of the individual had to do with secure identification and outer appearance.

Let us take one of the commentaries – from the ninth century, perhaps by Johannes Scotus and perhaps by Remigius of Auxerre – as an example of the rich but uncertain readings this passage occasioned:

> *Personis* that is, face masks [*larvae*]. For among the ancients the custom of actors was to ridicule in the theater whoever they wanted, with their bare faces. But since this was not well received, they put on masks, in which because of the hollowness the sound came out louder, and no one was openly ridiculed. These masks were called *personae* because the actors were called *personae*, because they represented in them the substance of individual people. Hence also they are called *personae* as in 'per se sonantes', sounding of themselves. And you should know that they ridiculed the sayings and deeds of those whose substances they represented with fables and the gesticulation of their bodies. And from these *personae*, that is face masks, it was transferred so that the individual substances of all humans are called *personae*. … *Quorum interest* that is, between whom there is a difference of sex or status; or, to whom the performance pertains. …

Quorum intereat, that is, between whom there was some difference. *Hecubam* wife of Priam. *Medeam* whore of Colchis. *Simonem vel Chremetem*: these are comic characters.[42]

The commentator sees three terms in the theatrical meanings of *persona*: the mask; the actor (or role); the persons represented. Interestingly, he seems somewhat indifferent to the direction of the etymology, or seems to have it both ways: masks were called personae because they represented what we would call 'persons' – and vice versa. The glossator also introduces another insight into masks and characters, by somewhat wilfully misreading the phrase 'quorum interest': he gives the correct translation as a second option, 'those to whom the play pertains', but neglects this in favour of another meaning of 'interest', namely, 'there is a difference between': that is, masks permit actors to represent characters somehow 'distant' from them, such as lowly actors portraying people of high status, or males performing female roles. But he also works in another key idea of these Boethian commentaries: that masks work to differentiate the characters on the stage, to make them identifiable and distinguishable from each other. In this sense, it is the mask that gives its name to the individual, and the mask that creates the character, not the actor 'sounding through' it. The glossator's 'per se sonantes' etymology just about reverses Boethius' 'per-sonantes': Boethius' masks channel what is behind them, i.e., the actors (or characters?) sound 'through' the masks. The glossator's *personae* 'sound of themselves', i.e., assume an autonomy that would be the exact opposite of the instrumentality Boethius implies. Furthermore, the glossator cannot seem to conceive of this representation except as a satirical aping, a lampooning, apparently of individuals in the audience, and the mask somehow mitigates the offence. Without the mask, actors would face spectators and barefacedly imitate them. Contrary to most configurations of mask versus face, the *nuda facies*, the naked face, would here be *too* directly representational. This idea challenges the directionality of the representation the glossator had first set up. Instead of the mask representing the actor, who stands for a fictional character, the actor is now conceived of as offensively representing those who look on. Instead of a transparent medium that channels a reality behind him, he becomes a mirror, with nothing behind him, only throwing back what is before him. And the mask, rather than reinforcing this unwelcome representation, muffles and mitigates it.

What, then, might medieval students of Terence have made of the masks staring at them from the illustrated Terence codices? Or, by extension, what might they have made of Terence's dramatic form and their sketchy and fluctuating knowledge of how it was performed? Looking at the invaluable scene-by-scene compilation of Terence illustrations by Leslie Webber-Jones and C. R. Morey, it seems clear that some of the illustrators realized that the characters' odd, simian faces were supposed to be masks, whereas others did not, or not quite. Of the manuscripts that have a fairly full set of illustrations, P (Parisinus Latinus 7899, ninth century), C (Vat. Lat. 3868, ninth century) O (Bod. Auct. F.2.13, twelfth century) clearly depict masked figures; Tur. (Turonensis Lat. S24, twelfth century), and L (Leidensis Lipsianu 26, tenth century) apparently do not. It is harder to say in other instances: N (Leidensis Vossianus 38, tenth century) has ape-like faces, but is it aware that those are masks?[43] On the other hand, many of the miniatures show figures touching or gesturing to the face, their own or someone else's, which might just be an attempt to draw our attention to masks.[44] F (Ambros. Lat. H. 77 inf., ninth–tenth century) seems to have more than one illustrator at work, of whom at least one is more aware of masks than the others.[45] F also appears to misunderstand the standard opening picture of most comedies, an *aedicula* (booth) with masks on shelves. The faces on the shelves in F's miniatures are not clearly masks: very oddly, they have necks and even shoulders attached.[46] Evidently, the masks qua material objects – as props used in actual theatres – are of so little interest to these medieval recipients of Terence as to become almost unintelligible. They must, however, have contributed greatly to the sense of strangeness of the ancient theatre – marked also, as has frequently been noted, by the emphatic past tense of almost all medieval comments on the theatre.[47]

The famous frontispieces to the illustrated codices – which, remarkably, survive well into the age of printing – are helpful in that they attempt to render a more general conceptualization of Terence's theatre.[48] Based on Isidore's somewhat unclear description of the classical stage, they show the *auctor* hidden in a booth at the centre of the stage (the *scaena* proper, according to Isidore) reciting his poetry, while actors, masked or not, mime the action on stage. Later versions of this description sometimes specified that the mimes would be hiding inside the booth along with the poet and come forth as needed.

Whatever resonances this description might have had for either Isidore or his later medieval readers – whether or not they were familiar with some form of recitation-plus-miming – the emphasis of this Isidorian iconography is clearly on the author, a figuration not so much of theatre as of text. It is a visual representation of the poet's 'voice', present but

hidden, and projected through a variety of 'masks'.[49] This is nicely consonant with a standard medieval approach to literary genre, derived from
Servius, that turns entirely on voicing – but not on performance as such.
There are genres in which only the poet speaks (such as most lyrics, or
third person narratives); genres in which only the characters speak (tragedy and comedy, but also certain kinds of poems); and mixed genres, in
which we hear sometimes the poet and sometimes the characters (epic or
pastoral, for instance). This classification does recognize a special status
for plays, although they do not occupy their category exclusively; and neither stages, actors nor any of the realities of theatrical performance enter
into their definition.[50]

This interest in the author's voice, as an almost autobiographical self-
statement, helps explain the medieval fascination with Terence's prologues,
sometimes at the expense of the actual plays. Terence opens each of his
comedies with a defiant counterattack on unnamed opponents who have
publicly criticized him. What to us reads like extraneous and somewhat
tedious prefatory material evidently engaged the medieval imagination a
great deal. A c. 1100 manuscript, Vat. Lat. 3305 ('S' in Webber-Jones and
Morey) has an idiosyncratic opening picture, a revealing variation on the
standard drawing of the Isidorian stage.[51] It does depict dramatic scenes
in the lower register; but these are dominated by the larger top portion,
which is inspired by the prologues of Terence's plays and the scholia on
them. We see Terence seated on the left. On the right is his opponent,
whose name, Luscius Lavinius, was supplied by the early commentaries
(properly 'Lanuvius'). Presiding over the scene is 'Calliopius', the name
of an early redactor of Terence's play preserved in the colophons of many
medieval Terence manuscripts. To this medieval illustrator, Calliopius
has become a kind of literary judge, mediating between the two opponents, as his strange cross-armed gesture indicates, and reading from a
book – the prologue to *Andria*, not the play. The Roman public in the
middle register is watching *that* spectacle, not the theatrical scenes below,
which figure perhaps as arguments, as the content of the *disputatio* that
is the top register. By privileging the prologue, quite analogously to the
Isidorian pictures of the poet in his booth, the illustrator here seems to be
more eager to get a handle on Terence's voice than on actors and scenes.

The oft-cited but hard-to-place playlet *Delusor Terentii* ('Terence and
his critic') is also a take on Terence's combative prologues.[52] It is hard
to date (datings have ranged from as early as the seventh to the tenth
century), and it is fragmentary; only the beginning survives. It is clearly
a schoolroom skit. There are elaborate stage directions which leave no

doubt that it was performed; and the 'Delusor' not only mentions but almost obsessively insists that he is very young. He first attacks Terence from the audience, then is challenged by Terence to come up on stage and debate him. The boy follows the invitation but does not have much to say; most of the humour comes from the Delusor's asides to the audience that he does not know what to say and wishes he had not got himself into this fix. Apart from charging that Terence's verse is so hard to scan that it is not even clear whether it is supposed to be verse or prose – a remark which comes from the standard commentaries – he merely keeps repeating that Terence is so very old, quite irrelevant to a young boy like himself. Always keeping in mind that we do not know how the skit went on, in the surviving portion it has little or nothing to say about Terence as a dramatist, or about the plays. It does take some cues from the plays, such as the comic technique of the confidential aside to the audience. But apart from that, for their end-of-year performance, the masters and students of that particular school chose not to put on a Terentian comedy but the introduction and the footnotes.

In this decidedly textual climate, it is probably fair to say that the *dramatis personae*, the masks on the shelves in the Terence codices, stood not so much for material objects, something medieval readers knew the Romans had used; nor did they stand metonymically for the actors or the roles. They are images of the author's voices. Yet might they not also depict the reader's encounter with these voices? Whether or not medieval students and teachers sometimes felt the urge to get up and physically act their Terence (and surely they must have),[53] even in the driest of grammar lessons they would have recited and declaimed him. Donatus' commentary, which accompanies the Terentian text in most manuscripts, concentrates on difficult words and grammatical structures. But it does quite frequently include stage directions of sorts, helping readers picture how the characters must have moved, how they might have modulated their voices – and even, in a small but significant number of instances, their faces: 'this is said with a jocular face'; 'this is said in jest, with a face like a supplicant's'.[54] One recent critic, John Barsby, notes in passing that evidently Donatus must be assuming that performances in the theatre were by and large done without masks.[55] But that, as Rainer Jacobi notes, scarcely follows. Donatus is not thinking principally of the theatre, but of the classroom; the performance notes are not stage directions but aids for young readers in understanding and processing the text.[56] Donatus' notes tell us little about how he envisioned the public stage. They do provide clues on how he envisioned reading in schools: ideally at least, potentially at least, as quasi-performative, quasi-impersonating. Readers may not fully recite, fully inhabit the roles; they may remain firmly settled in their objective, distant role as readers – or, indeed, in the case of schoolchildren, bored, patient, mechanical or assiduous parsers of Latin words and construers of sentences. But they are also invited to imagine, and maybe try out with their voices or even their bodies, how one might do the role. The voice heard in the text, which can split itself into however many characters, is in that sense the shared property of the author and the reader, with the masks providing an interface, a point of encounter.

Such a reading model implies nearness as well as distance, an imagined presence as much as a felt absence. Even the Isidorian image of the stage articulates this double experience: the author is 'present' yet hidden from view. And the ambivalence is fully acted out in the *Delusor Terentii*, where a medieval person – the hapless schoolboy – quite literally comes face to face with the ancient author. Terence is very present, in the flesh (played, one presumes, by the master?), to take the boy to task for his impudent remarks. His presence, his antiquity, his authority weigh heavily on the boy. Yet the entire dialogue – so far as we have it – revolves around the boy's estrangement from this hoary old author/auctoritas/voice. In the end, the skit is a sort of exorcism: a *modernus*, a child, confronting an all-too-present Ancient Author and bravely telling him where to go.

NOTES

1 hic superum formas superi mirantur et ipsi
   et cupiunt fictis vultibus essere pares.
   non potuit Natura deos hoc ore creare,
   quo miranda deum signa creavit homo.
   vultus adest his numinibus, potiusque coluntur
   artificium studio quam deitate sua.
   > *Hildeberti Carmina minora*, ed. A. B. Scott, 2nd edn (Munich: Saur, 2001), no. 36, lines 31–6. The companion poem is no. 38. My translation.

2 O. Zwierlein, 'Par tibi, Roma, nihil', *Mittellateinisches Jahrbuch*, 11 (1976): 92–4.

3 *M. Annaei Lucani De Bello Civili Libri X*, ed. D. R. Shackleton Bailey (Stuttgart: Teubner, 1988), X.105, 269.

4 John of Salisbury, *Policraticus*, ed. C. C. I. Webb, 2 vols. (London, 1909; rpt. Frankfurt: Minerva, 1965), III.10 vol. I, 200.

5 P. von Moos, 'Par tibi, Roma, nihil – Eine Antwort', *Mittellateinisches Jahrbuch*, 14 (1979): 119–26.

6 Ovid, *Ars Amatoria*, III.127, in *Ovid: The Art of Love and Other Poems*, ed. and trans. J .H. Mozley 2nd edn (Cambridge, MA: Harvard University Press, 1979).

7 *John of Salisbury's Entheticus Maior and Minor*, ed. J. van Laarhoven (Leiden: Brill, 1987), vol. I, 104–5, line 14.

8 C. S. Jaeger, 'Charismatic Body – Charismatic Text', *Exemplaria*, 9 (1997): 117–37, 118; J.-Y. Tilliette, 'Tamquam lapides vivi: Sur les "élégies romaines" d'Hildebert de Lavardin (ca. 1100)', in C. Nicolet (ed.), *'Alla Signorina': Mélanges offerts à Noëlle de la Blanchardière* (Roma: École française, 1995), 379. I want to stress that both essays, as well as Smolak's (n. 9 below), nonetheless offer splendid readings of the poem, to which I am very much indebted. The point is not that their translations are wrong, but that the line is essentially untranslatable.

9 K. Smolak, 'Beobachtungen zu den Rom-Elegien Hildeberts von Lavardin,' in M. W. Herren, C. J. McDonough and R. G. Arthur (eds.) *Latin Culture in the Eleventh Century: Proceedings of the Third International Conference on Medieval Latin Studies, Cambridge, September 9–12, 1998*, 2 vols. (Turnhout: Brepols, 2002), vol. 2, 380 n. 26.

10 My tentative translation: 'Behold where *vultus adest*, lamenting the mother's oracles / For the children of men, when *vultus adest* / The face of the Lord is present, before whom the whole world lies prostrate; / In the sign of Judgement, the face of the Lord is present.' 'In assumptione Sanctae Mariae in nocte, quando tabula portatur', in W. von Giesebrecht, *Geschichte der deutschen Kaiserzeit*, 5th edn, 2 vols. (Leipzig: Duncker and Humblot, 1881), vol. I, 899.

11 M. Bettini, 'Guardarsi in faccia a Roma: Le parole dell'apparenza fisica nella cultura latina', in *Le orecchie di Hermes: Studi di antropologia e letterature classiche* (Torino: Einaudi, 2000), 313–56.

12 G. L. Cohen, 'Latin voltus/vultus= Face, Expression (on Face)', *Latomus*, 38 (1979): 337–44.

13 Jaeger, 'Charismatic Body', 119; M. Camille, *The Gothic Idol: Ideology and Image-Making in Medieval Art* (Cambridge University Press, 1989), 36–7.

14 *Hildeberti carmina minora*, no. 38, line 1.

15 We may compare an epigram on a Venus statue that has a certain tradition – Ausonius' version is modelled on an earlier Greek version – in which Venus is upset that the sculptor must have seen her naked to represent her so well, and wondering how this could have happened; see *The Works of Ausonius*, ed. R. P. H. Green (Oxford: Clarendon Press, 1991), 82. The conceit is a witty take on the lifelikeness topos, especially if one does not believe in Venus as a real entity, like the late classical authors who believed at most in a very attenuated sort of way. (In Ausonius' version, Praxiteles' saucy answer is not something one would say to a real goddess.) There is no Venus except qua statue – yet here she steps out of her own image, so to speak, to register both admiration and vexation at having been depicted. The surprising feat is not that the image has matched its original so closely – there is no original; it is that it has given the original its very existence.

16 On classical reflections on *vultus*, see the important essay by Bettini, 'Guardarsi in faccia'; and F. Frontisi-Ducroux, *Du masque au visage: Aspects de l'identité en Grèce ancienne* (Paris: Flammarion, 1995).

17 Jaeger, 'Charismatic Body'. My debt to Jaeger's brilliant reading of Hildebert's poem will be readily apparent. To Jaeger, the poem marks the transition – which is also the subject of his book *The Envy of Angels: Cathedral Schools and Social Ideals in Medieval Europe, 950–1200* (Philadelphia: University of Pennsylvania Press, 1994) – between an early medieval, embodied, 'charismatic' ideal of text, teaching and culture, characterized by a strong sense of presence; and a later, textual mode, governed by the 'absence' we now take for granted as the fundamental condition of written text. In this argument, I would question only – but crucially – the strong epochal divide between the two modes; both presence and absence, embodiment and representation, seem to me to coexist (in various mixtures) in texts both before and after Jaeger's dividing line of c. 1100. It seems significant to me that Hildebert's poem is an elegy; he places *both* the embodied and the representational view of the statues – Jaeger's 'before' and 'after' – firmly in the past.

18 'Meditatio VIII: De multiplici facie hominis, et osculo atque amplexu sponsi et sponsae', PL 180: 229–32.

19 *Rhetorica ad Herennium,* III.11.20–15.27. On the availability of *De oratore* and Quintilian (the section under discussion, Book XI, is absent from practically all medieval manuscripts), see L. D. Reynolds, *Texts and Transmissions: A Survey of the Latin Classics* (Oxford: Clarendon Press, 1983), 102–9, 332–6.

20 'Pronuntiatio quibus modis constat? voce, vultu, gestu. His quid accedit? Cultus sive habitus': *RLM*, 130. Similarly, Martianus Capella, 'De Rhetorica', in *RLM*, 484.

21 R. Maltby, *A Lexicon of Ancient Latin Etymologies* (Leeds: Francis Cairns, 1991), under *facies* and *vultus*.

22 Quintilian, *The Orator's Education*, XI.3.47.

23 E. Gunderson, *Staging Masculinity: The Rhetoric of Performance in the Roman World* (Ann Arbor: University of Michigan Press, 2003), 111–48; A. Richlin, 'Gender and Rhetoric: Producing Manhood in the Schools', in W. J. Dominik (ed.), *Roman Eloquence: Rhetoric in Society and Literature* (London: Routledge, 1997), 90–110; A. Arellaschi, 'Sur trois aspects comparés de l'art oratoire et de l'art dramatique d'après Cicéron (de Orat. III) et Quintilien (de Inst. Orat. XI)', *Vita Latina*, 100 (1985): 26–34.

24 See E. C. Evans, 'A Stoic Aspect of Senecan Drama: Portraiture', *Transactions and Proceedings of the American Philological Association*, 81 (1950): 169–84; and E. C. Evans, *Physiognomy in the Ancient World* (Philadelphia: American Philosophical Society, 1960), 26–8.

25 B. Cassin, '"Philosophia enim simulari potest, eloquentia non potest", ou: le masque et l'effet', *Rhetorica*, 13 (1995): 105–24.

26 Cicero, *On the Ideal Orator*, III.221–3, 294; my emphases.

27 Quintilian, *Inst.orat.*, XI.3.75. See also the use of *finguntur* at XI.3.79.

28 *Ibid.*, XI.3.74.

29 *Ibid.*, XI.3.74, 122–5.

30 John of Salisbury *Policraticus*, III.10, vol. I, 200.

31 For some examples, see R. Funari, 'Sul contrasto tra il volto e l'animo: un motivo sallustiano in Plutarco, *Vita Luculli* 21,6', *Maia*, 55 (2003): 313–16; M. Bettini, 'Guardarsi in faccia', 332–6.

32 *Entheticus maior and minor*, vol. I, 232–5, lines 43–85. Laarhoven's comments on this passage (vol. II, 431) seem needlessly complicated – perhaps he is tripped up by the contradictory sentiments.

33 Quoted in C. S. Jaeger, *Medieval Humanism in Gottfried von Strassburg's 'Tristan and Isolde'* (Heidelberg: Winter, 1977), 94; my translation.

34 S. Pietrini, 'Medieval Ideas of the Ancient Actor and Roman Theater', *The Early Drama, Art and Music Review*, 24 (2001): 1–21; S. Pietrini, *Spettacolo e immaginario teatrale nel Medioevo* (Roma: Bulzoni, 2001), 115–22, 165–93; L. Allegri, *Teatro e spettacolo nel Medioevo* (Bari: Laterza, 1988), 255–74; C. R. Dodwell, *Anglo-Saxon Gestures and the Roman Stage* (Cambridge University Press, 2000). Several of the essays collected in F. Mosetti Casaretto (ed.), *La scena assente: Realtà e leggenda sul teatro nel Medioevo* (Alessandria: Edizioni dell'Orso, 2006) also address this topic.

35 L. Webber-Jones and C. R. Morey, *The Miniatures of the Manuscripts of Terence Prior to the Thirteenth Century*, 2 vols. (Princeton University Press, 1954).

36 See for instance C. Symes, 'The Appearance of Early Vernacular Plays: Forms, Functions, and the Future of Medieval Theater', *Speculum*, 77 (2002): 778–83, and *A Common Stage: Theater and Public Life in Medieval Arras* (Ithaca, NY: Cornell University Press, 2007); Allegri, *Teatro e spettacolo*, 34–54; D. Dox, *The Idea of the Theater in Latin Christian Thought: Augustine to the Fourteenth Century* (Ann Arbor: University of Michigan Press, 2004), especially 53, 143 n. 43.

37 I. Thompson, 'Latin "Elegiac Comedy" of the Twelfth Century', in P. G. Ruggiers, *Versions of Medieval Comedy* (Norman: University of Oklahoma Press, 1977), 51–66. Of course, in classical as in more recent theatre, it was not uncommon for one actor to play more than one role in a given play, but this does not change the fundamental principle of representation.

38 Much could be gleaned, for instance, from the treatise by Evanthius that often preceded commented Terence manuscripts; or, to some extent, from Donatus' commentary itself – Donatus, *Commentum Terentii*, ed. P. Wessner, 3 vols. (Leipzig: Teubner, 1902). See also M. H. Marshall, 'Boethius's Definition of *Persona* and Medieval Understanding of the Roman Theater', *Speculum*, 25 (1950): 471–82; and M. H. Marshall, 'Theatre in the Middle Ages: Evidence from Dictionaries and Glosses', *Symposium*, 4 (1950): 1–39; 5 (1951): 366–89.

39 See for instance J. M. Ziolkowski, *Talking Animals: Medieval Latin Beast Poetry, 750–1150* (Philadelphia: University of Pennsylvania Press, 1993), 131–97, and *Nota Bene: Reading Classics and Writing Melodies in the Early Middle Ages* (Turnhout: Brepols, 2007); C. D. Lanham, 'Freshman Composition in the early Middle Ages', *Viator*, 23 (1992): 115–34.

40 Marshall, 'Boethius's Definition'.

41 'Nomen enim personae uidetur aliunde traductum, ex his scilicet personis quae in comoediis tragoediisque eos quorum interest homines repraesentabant. Persona uero dicta est a personando ... idcirco autem a sono, quia concauitate ipsa maior necesse est uoluatur sonus. Graeci quoque has personas prosopa uocant ab eo quod ponantur in facie atque ante oculos obtegant uultum ... Sed quoniam personis inductis histriones, indiuiduos homines quorum intereat in tragoedia uel in comoedia ut dictum est repraesentabant, id est Hecubam uel Medeam uel simonem uel Chremetem, idcirco ceteros quoque homines, quorum certa pro sui forma esset agnitio, et Latini personam, et Graeci prosopa nuncupauerunt.' Boethius, *The Theological Tractates and the Consolation of Philosophy*, ed. and trans. H. F. Stewart and E. K. Rand, LCL (Cambridge, MA: Harvard University Press, 1936), 84–6; (my translation); this passage is discussed in Marshall, 'Boethius's Definition', 472–3.

42 '*Personis* id est larvis. Apud enim antiquos mos fuit histrionum ut in theatris hominibus quibuscumque vellent nuda facie illuderent, sed hoc cum displicuisset, adhibitae sunt larvae, in quibus et maior sonus propter concavitatem ederetur et nulli aperte illuderetur. Hae ergo larvae personae dictae sunt eo quod histriones personae dictae sunt, eo quod historiones in his singulorum hominum substantias repraesentabant. Unde et personae quasi per se sonantes sunt dictae. Et sciendum, quia quorum substantias repraesentabant, eorum dictis et factis fabulis et gesticulatione corporis illudebant. Ab his itaque personis, id est larvis, translatum est, un omnium hominum substantiae individuae personae vocarentur ... *Quorum interest* id est inter quos distat sexus vel qualitas vel ad quos pertinet ipsa praesentatio ... *Quorum intereat* id est inter quos distabat aliquid. *Hecubam* uxor Priami. *Medeam* Colchica meretrix. *Simonem vel Chremetem* comicae sunt personae.' Marshall, 'Boethius's Definition', 473.

43 See Weber-Jones and Morey, figures 61, 141, 335.

44 E.g., *ibid.*, figures 115, 136, 190, 214, 219, 274, 321, 342.

45 Compare for instance, *ibid.*, figures 409 and 561 (masks) with 441 (no masks), 532 (uncertain).

46 *Ibid.*, figures 450, 680.

47 Allegri, *Teatro e spettacolo*, 33.

48 Pietrini, *Spettacolo*, 165–85. Pietrini reproduces a generous selection of medieval and Renaissance versions of the image both here and in her essay 'La memoria del teatro antico nell' iconografia tardomedievale', in Mosetti Casaretto (ed.), *La scena assente*, 215–27. See also the comprehensive collection of Terentian images in Webber-Jones and Morey, *Miniatures*.

49 R. Jacobi, *Die Kunst der Exegese im Terenzkommentar des Donat* (Berlin: de Gruyter, 1996), 151.

50 Pietrini, *Spettacolo*, 111–12; see also Frontisi-Ducroux, *Du masque au visage*, 40–1.

51 Discussed in detail by D. H. Wright, 'The Forgotten Early Romanesque Illustrations of Terence in Vat. Lat. 3305', *Zeitschrift für Kunstgeschichte*, 56 (1993): 183–206. R. Raffaelli, 'Un prologo medievale di Terenzio: Per l'esegesi dell'illustrazione del Vat. Lat. 3305, f. 8v', in C. Questa and R. Raffaelli (eds.),

Due seminari plautini: La tradizione del testo; I modelli (Urbino: Quattro Venti, 2002), 89–101, takes issue with Wright but is actually not very far at all from his reading. The picture has been frequently reproduced, among other places in Wright's essay; in Webber-Jones and Morey, *The Miniatures*, vol. I, figure 10; in Pietrini, *Spettacolo*, figure 42.

52 *Hrotsvithae Opera*, ed. P. von Winterfield, MGH Scriptores Rerum Germanicorum in usu Scholarum (Berlin: Weidmann, 1965), XX–XXIII. See M. Giovini, 'Elementi poetici e drammatici nel *Delusor* (X sec.)', *Studi umanistici piceni*, 26 (2006): 129–47; Allegri, *Teatro e spettacolo*, 257–8; C. Villa, *La lectura Terentii, Vol. 1: Da Ildemaro a Francesco Petrarca* (Padova: Antenore, 1984), 67–98.

53 For some clues to a recited (and sung!) performance of Terence, see Villa, *La Lectura Terentii*, 4 and n. 7.

54 'hoc ioculari uultu dicitur', 'hoc quasi supplicanti uultu ad irrisionem dicitur' (my translation). Donatus, *Commentum*, Eunuchus, 236, 281, 316, 328. Cited in J. Barsby, 'Donatus on Terence: The *Eunuchus* Commentary', in E. Stärk and G. Vogt-Spira (eds.), *Dramatische Wäldchen: Festschrift für Eckard Lefèvre zum 65. Geburtstag* (Zürich: Olms, 2000), 512.

55 Barsby, 'Donatus on Terence', 511–12.

56 R. Jacobi, *Die Kunst der Exegese*, 10–12.

CHAPTER 7

Special delivery

Were medieval letter writers trained in performance?

Martin Camargo

When we think of the production, transmission and reception of letters, we envision a solitary individual composing a text that will be read silently by another individual. The technological innovations that have allowed email and texting to replace traditional letter writing as the preferred mode of written communication from a distance have not changed the essential elements of this image. The message travels faster now and can be received simultaneously by many individuals, but it still is produced by a single person writing alone and still is received as a set of graphic marks that are decoded by individual persons.

The conception of a letter as a graphic inscription produced by the writer whose thoughts it expresses and interpreted by the reader to whom those thoughts are addressed was equally familiar to medieval people, but only as one of several possibilities. Their typical epistolary experience would have encompassed many more instances of letters as events rather than objects, as public, oral performances rather than private, written exchanges. Writing itself was a highly specialized technology that often was delegated to trained scribes. Similarly, special training was required to produce the appropriate language for letters. Most medieval letters would have been dictated to a clerk who would translate them into a structurally and stylistically suitable text that he – or a separate scribe – would then transcribe on parchment or paper. At the other end of the process, the written message might be retranslated into an oral message.

This oral message would be transmitted in one of several ways. It might be read aloud to the designated recipient; or it might be recited from memory by the messenger who delivered it, the physical letter itself remaining sealed as a record for later reference as needed; or it might be paraphrased in the vernacular for the benefit of recipients who could not read or did not understand the letter's Latin.[1]

Like the apostolic Epistles that were read aloud as part of the liturgy, many medieval letters were composed to be read aloud before groups of people. Good examples are the ostensibly personal letters of spiritual love, guidance and encouragement exchanged by cloistered monks and nuns.[2] Abelard's letters to Heloise (and possibly her replies) clearly were meant to be heard by the entire convent of the Paraclete and not merely read in private by its famous abbess.[3]

If anything, the boundary between public and private letters was still more fluid when secular persons were involved. At a time when local communities were more closely knit, literacy was less universal, and communication from the outside less frequent, public reading of what we would consider 'personal' letters was the norm. This oral reception is evident in the frequent and unself-conscious alternation between the terminology of writing/reading and of speaking/listening in medieval discussions of letters. Geoffrey Chaucer could have the Wife of Bath use the apocopated form 'pistel' to designate a spoken, non-epistolary message: 'rowned she a pistel in his ere' (*Canterbury Tales*, III.1,021); but have the Clerk use the same term to designate a written, epistolary text: 'As seith Seint Jame, if ye his pistel rede' (*Canterbury Tales*, IV.1,154).[4]

Long before they were fixed and formalized in the written rules of the *ars dictaminis*, epistolary practices found a place in verbal arts pedagogy.[5] The association between letters and oral discourse is already implicit in C. Iulius Victor's fourth-century *Ars rhetorica*, the only surviving Roman rhetorical treatise that includes a treatment of letter writing. The brief chapter 'De epistolis' that concludes the work is immediately preceded by an equally brief and equally unusual chapter 'De sermocinatione' (on informal discourse, ranging from conversation in a gathering to oral disputation), which includes detailed comments on how the proper delivery of a *sermo* differs from that of an *oratio*. The chapter on letters begins by linking the *sermo* and the *epistola*: 'Many of the precepts that apply to informal discourses also apply to letters'; but the areas of overlap are not specified.[6]

In the late eleventh century, at the precise moment and in the same monastic context that gave birth to the first medieval rhetorical arts of letter writing,[7] the juxtaposition of letters and oral delivery resurfaced in the 'arts of reading', a new genre of textbooks aimed primarily at teaching young monks how to pronounce Latin properly when reading the Bible and other sacred texts aloud. The *Ars lectoria* (1085/6) of Aimeric and the *Ars lectoria* (1087/8) of Siguinus, both written in southwest or west-central France and probably derived from a common ancestor, contain assorted grammatical doctrine, most of it concerned with sound changes resulting from inflection, derivation and compounding, and with the nature and placement of accents in Latin words.[8] At several points, each author interrupts his long series of examples illustrating categories of accentuation in order to address general comments on oral delivery to his reader, and in each of these asides letters are mentioned alongside other varieties of discourse. The best example comes from Siguinus, who first offers a set of precepts to guide 'anyone who wishes to fashion a letter well' and then concludes:

Because if anyone would proclaim something either by heart or from writing-tablets or from a book, either while reading among the public or speaking forth to companions or conversing with friends, he should learn to deliver whatever that may be, whether serious or diverting, by pausing, deliberating, moderating his deportment, not braying with a donkey's voice, not gulping like a greedy sow, not putting word to flight with word, [but] with a free voice, a steady voice, a gentle voice.[9]

Such passages indicate that the same rules applied to the public reading of letters as to the reading of the liturgy in church or texts from the Church Fathers in the refectory, not to mention the recitation of metrical verse in the classroom. However, the sketchy comments in the *artes lectoriae* provide no direct testimony about how monastic letter writers might have applied those rules in practice or whether they were trained in aspects of delivery that were particular to letters.

In the Latin textbooks specifically devoted to letter writing (*artes dictandi*), references to the intended recipients of letters as 'hearers' (*auditores*), to composing letters as 'speaking' (*loqui*), and to epistolary discourse as 'speech' (*oratio*) are quite common. Indeed, orality is built into the technical terms of the medieval art of letter writing. The word for composing texts, including letters, is *dictare* or 'dictate', a professional letter writer or teacher of letter writing is a *dictator*, and the art of letter writing is the *ars dictaminis*.[10] Moreover, it is particularly the case for letters in Latin that the actual words would have been chosen and written down by someone trained in the *ars dictaminis* and not the person whose sentiments they expressed. Finally, much of the training a *dictator* received had to do with making the letter sound right. Guido Faba's *Summa dictaminis*, probably the single most influential letter-writing textbook of the Middle Ages, opens with a discussion of the vices that produce cacophony and goes on to observe that faulty composition not only sounds bad but also impedes oral comprehension: 'that composition is considered faulty which cannot be understood in the first or the second utterance, even if it is read both clearly and well'. Guido adds: 'We also should flee and avoid as a defect a long sequence of words, which tends to hurt both the listener's ears and the speaker's breathing.'[11] Later in the treatise Guido devotes considerable space to the techniques for producing euphony, including the *cursus* – a limited set of approved cadences used to mark clause endings – and the 'colours' of rhetoric, many of which involve auditory effects.[12]

The question I would like to explore is whether this pervasive recognition of a letter's 'aurality', that is, its composition for the ear, translated into a more active concern with instruction in the performance of letters, especially the Latin letters that were the subject of the *artes dictandi*. The challenge in answering this question comes from the nature of the letter-writing textbooks themselves. Like most medieval rhetorical treatises, the *artes dictandi* teach more by demonstration than by precept. A typical treatise will have relatively brief sections in which key terms such as *dictamen* and *epistola* are defined and their varieties and parts are distinguished, but extensive collections of examples, whether of parts of the letter, such as the *salutatio*, or models of entire letters.[13] Since it is difficult to provide a written example of a performance, and since delivery probably was taught by example and imitation more than by written precept, explicit statements about oral performance of letters are hardly to be found in the *artes dictandi*. An important exception to this rule is the *Candelabrum* of Bene of Florence, who taught the *ars dictaminis* at Bologna in the first half of the thirteenth century. The content of Bene's teaching is not unusual for his place and time: the essential points of his doctrine match those of Guido Faba, who was his contemporary at Bologna. Where Bene is unusual is in the exceptional detail he devotes to the theory behind the *ars dictaminis*. One finds the same topics and the same basic instructions in Guido Faba's treatise, but Guido only sketches them out before moving on to the examples. Bene reverses the proportions, providing a few examples but elaborating more fully on the precepts. It is possible that Guido Faba and other teachers of the art provided similar detail in their oral instruction; but that is no more recoverable than his presumed demonstrations of oral delivery.

A brief account of the organizational logic that Bene uses in the *Candelabrum* will help orient my discussion of its treatment of topics related to the oral performance of letters. Bene divides the *Candelabrum* into eight books, the first four of which contain a thorough treatment of the *ars dictaminis* as it was taught at Bologna. Book 5 is a condensed version of Books 1–4, a 'compendium of the entire art'.[14] In Book 6, Bene surveys the French approach to teaching the *ars dictaminis*, while in the final two books he treats a series of topics that apply to all varieties of prose composition, including letter writing. There is a significant amount of repetition, though usually a given topic will receive full treatment only in the most pertinent context.

Bene first mentions delivery (*pronuntiatio*) early in Book 1, while identifying the art of the trivium to which the *ars dictaminis* most properly belongs: 'For grammar enlightens the understanding, logic lends belief, and rhetoric brings about consent. These three things are very beneficial to the letter writer (*dictator*), because his task is to make his hearers understand what he says, believe what they have understood, and consent to what they have believed. However, in its essence it is understood to belong to rhetoric, which considers five aspects of skill in speaking: it discovers and arranges, remembers, is eloquent and delivers gracefully' (*Cand.*, I.4.3–6).[15] He goes on to define the five canons of rhetoric and to identify the quality appropriate to each of them. 'Delivery', says Bene, 'is the attractive management of voice, facial expression and gestures' (*Cand.*, I.4.11),[16] and in the act of delivery the letter writer (*dictator*) should be 'moderate' (*Cand.*, I.4.13).[17] He summarizes these already brief remarks in Book 5, where he says that one who wishes to be an 'accomplished letter writer' must know how to 'deliver with dignity and grace' (*Cand.*, V.3.2–3).[18]

These schematic comments on delivery could be applied to any kind of writing: only my perhaps unduly narrow translation of the term *dictator* as 'letter writer' links them with the performance of letters.[19] More revealing is the fuller treatment of delivery that Bene provides near the end of Book 8. Though these remarks occur in the context of general instruction on composition and derive mainly from the *Rhetorica ad Herennium* (III.11.19–15.27) and Geoffrey of Vinsauf's *Poetria nova* (2,053–4, 2,057–8), they do make some explicit connections to Bene's earlier treatment of specifically epistolary matters. As the most extensive set of comments on delivery in any *summa dictandi*, the passage deserves to be quoted in its entirety:

ON THE THREE METHODS OF PROPER DELIVERY

Delivery likewise concerns itself with three things, namely management of voice, facial expression and gesture, because just as good delivery is worth nothing without the foregoing, so the foregoing are useless without proper delivery. Delivery therefore observes proper management in voice, facial expression and gesture, so that the listener is won over and is led to belief through persuasion, and his passions are kindled.

For voice follows its rules in points, accents, distinctions, subdistinctions and clauses, with all of which we have dealt in the first book, when we treated composition. Although voice, like memory, doubtless comes from nature, it is nonetheless helped by a certain regulating knowledge, because practice preserves the voice and a moderate pace is very beneficial, just as too much dashing ahead weakens and tires the voice. Because of food, drink and certain other things the excellence of the voice is often hindered and, so the doctors say, often helped, and thus the voice should be protected with no little care lest it should suffer a defect when it has been exposed. Excellence of voice consists in clarity, stability and agreeableness, which three are acquired partly from nature, partly from art. The voice, moreover, should harmonize with the subject matter, so that the matter may seem to be expressed in the best fashion.

Facial expressions also should be altered in accord with the quality of the sentiment, preserving in all things a proper moderation, so that the countenance also is taken to be an interpreter of the mind. Likewise, certain moderate gestures should be employed from time to time, by extending the hands, lifting the feet, bowing the neck and doing similar things that seem to suit the subject matter but in no way produce any impropriety in the speaker.

Whence Geoffrey says:

VERSES CONCERNING THREEFOLD DELIVERY

'Let voice represent voice, facial expression facial expression and gesture gesture by little signs. This is a well-managed grace. Let the moderately restrained voice, seasoned with the double savour of facial expression and gesture, feed the hearing.'

These brief remarks are enough about invention, arrangement, style, memory and delivery, because our intent has been to treat thoroughly not civil causes but those things that are more useful for our task. (*Cand.*, VIII.58–9)[20]

As Bene's final comment suggests, he has not dwelt on the general doctrines of the five canons, including delivery, because much of that lore is more relevant to civic oratory than to his more specific concern, which is letter writing. Neither here nor anywhere else in the *Candelabrum* does he indicate the extent or the manner in which facial expression and gesture might figure in the oral delivery of letters. By contrast, although most of his more extensive comments on voice simply distil the general advice to be found in the *Rhetorica ad Herennium*, he begins them by cross-referencing a more specific discussion of voice management in Book I. The passage to which he refers is part of his adaptation of the *Rhetorica ad Herennium*'s discussion of the three features that characterize an accomplished style (*elocutio*) (*RadH*, IV.12.17–56.69) or, in Bene's version, an accomplished piece of writing (*dictamen*), namely taste (*elegantia*), artistic composition (*compositio*) and distinction (*dignitas*), which Bene equates with ornamentation (*hornatus*) (*Cand.*, I.8.2).[21] Composition is the member of this triad that Bene associates most closely with delivery. He also links it directly to epistolary rhetoric, observing that 'composition does not always proceed according to the tradition of the art but sometimes is done according to the wishes of the letter writer' and adding that 'the art of composition is not to be ignored on this account, since it often is necessary because it is honoured by famous authors and philosophers, nor is any letter sent from the Roman See without such ornament' (*Cand.*, I.8.6, 8).[22]

Like the *auctor ad Herennium*, Bene takes composition to mean the artful arrangement of words to produce a uniformly polished discourse (*RadH*, IV.12.18; *Cand.*, I.15.2). However, the Roman rhetorician restricts his treatment of composition to brief strictures against six vices that 'hurt the listener's ears and the speaker's breathing' (*RadH*, IV.12.18), while Bene expands composition to include a variety of positive techniques that will impart a distinctive charm. 'If we wish to attain this charm in our speech', says Bene, 'we need to alter the natural order, so that there is a certain charming and agreeable flow (*cursus*) in the speech and we seem not to speak as the common people' (*Cand.*, I.15.5).[23] All of the techniques that Bene goes on to discuss under artistic composition appeal to the ear and thus constitute evidence that medieval letters were composed to be heard; but one cluster struck him as particularly relevant to the oral performance of epistolary texts. This is because the techniques in question, the *cursus* and the *distinctiones*, not only add charm to the discourse but also assist the speaker in conveying its meaning to a listening audience. The two techniques are inseparable, since the prescribed cadences that constitute the *cursus* are employed to mark the end of a *distinctio* or 'division'. Indeed, Bene discusses the *cursus* under the heading 'On the ending of divisions' (*Cand.*, I.20.1–2).[24]

In order to appreciate the intended effect of the *cursus* in oral performances of letters, therefore, we need first to understand how practitioners of the *ars dictaminis* employed what they called the three divisions or *distinctiones*. The *Candelabrum* again provides more detailed information on this topic than is usual in letter-writing textbooks, including a justification for such attention: 'And because we have referred to divisions frequently, since no speech can please if it is undivided, therefore let us see what a division is' (*Cand.*, I.21.2). 'A division', Bene continues, 'is a complete part of a sentence (*clausule*) that weaves words together in a fitting arrangement and frees meanings from the knot of uncertainty' (*Cand.*, I.21.3).[25] Bene calls the three kinds of division 'dependent' (*dependens*), 'stable' (*constans*) and 'final' (*finitiva*) but in defining them points out that they also are called by the Greek names that designate the punctuation marks appropriate to each, namely 'comma', 'colon' and 'period'. The three divisions differ from one another in their degrees of completeness: a comma presents only part of a thought, a colon contains a complete thought but holds open the possibility that more will follow, and a period concludes the thought decisively. Every sentence comprises at least a period, but in theory there is no limit to the number of commas and colons it might contain (*Cand.*, I.21.5–17).[26]

Along with avoiding the vices that offend the ear, nothing was more important for composing performable texts than skilful handling of the divisions, as Bene had emphasized when he introduced the topic of artistic composition earlier in Book I: 'the art of composition ... brings agreeableness to speech, arranges the divisions, allures the ears of the listeners with artful arrangement and scours away the vices of uncouth eloquence' (*Cand.*, I.14.10).[27] The divisions not only break up the text into distinct segments that help guide aural comprehension but also allure the ear with the pleasing cadences of the *cursus*. A third element contributing to the effect of composing with divisions is implicit in the analogy between the actual divisions and the punctuation marks that set them apart in writing and becomes explicit when Bene next defines and discusses punctuation itself. 'A point', he says, 'is a mark that separates units of meaning and refreshes the breathing of the speaker' (*Cand.*, I.23.2).[28] In other words, divisions are set off acoustically not only by the audible cadences of the *cursus* but also by audible pauses, which are indicated by the punctuation marks following each division in the written text. Pauses also distinguish what Bene calls 'subdivisions' (*subdistinctiones*), in which the pause helps to clarify meaning within a division; but subdivisions are never indicated by punctuation marks (*Cand.*, I.22.11–12, 23.7).

The final aural cue inherent in the divisions and especially in the marks of punctuation associated with each type of division is what Bene calls 'accent', an element of delivery he first addresses under the heading 'On the diversity of punctuating' ('DE DIVERSITATE PUNTANDI', *Cand.*, I.24.1). Because it makes explicit the relationships among the divisions, punctuation and pronunciation, the passage is worth quoting in full. However, Bene's language is difficult to translate because he uses terms such as *punctus*, *coma*, *colon* and *periodus* to refer simultaneously to units of syntax or meaning and marks of punctuation, and the key term *pronuntiatio* can mean 'pronunciation' as well as 'delivery'. For these terms and other technical terms such as *accentus*, I have used the expedient of simply anglicizing the Latin.

I have heard three different things concerning points and the method of punctuating. On the one hand, the Roman Church ends all divisions by pronouncing them with a plain point, uses relatively few written points, and does not write any virgule except when it finishes a concluding sentence. There are others who pronounce in diverse ways just as they also write in diverse ways, saying that all commas should be pronounced with the *arsis*, that is a raising of the voice, and a point with a virgule leading upward shows this; but colons should be ended with a somewhat low accent, which a written point without any virgule designates there; but they maintain that a period should be pronounced with a lower accent, which a point with a virgule leading downward indicates. And this method is followed by almost everybody. But we hold that all divisions, except the final one, should properly end with the *arsis*, but the period with the *thesis*, that is a lowering of the voice, except when we read in church, where the authority of custom should be followed both in the psalms and in other readings. But concerning points we obey the authority of the apostolic see, saying that every point should be without a virgule except when it ends a sermon or letter, because there a double point with a virgule leading downward customarily appears. Also, where there is a question it is quite proper to write above the point a virgule that is somewhat twisty and aimed upward, so that it is evident that it should be pronounced with a high accent. For if we want to vary the written marks of punctuation according to the modes of pronunciation, it will seem like we are neuming the antiphonary; but 'Each has his own will, nor is everyone animated by a single desire. There are a thousand kinds of men, and their habits of life are varied.' (Persius, *Satirae*, V.53, 52; *Cand.*, I.24.2–11)[29]

Bene's preference for the Roman method of punctuating is probably related to his decision to accept the Roman Curia's authority on the rules of the *cursus* (*Cand.*, I.15.12–16, 20.7). However, he does not endorse a uniform accent at the end of every division, which the Roman system of punctuation implies, nor does he endorse what he identifies as the most widespread practice, of raising the voice's pitch at the end of a comma, lowering it slightly at the end of a colon, and lowering it significantly at the end of a period. His preference is to raise the voice at the end of a comma or a colon and to lower it at the end of a period, unless the sentence is interrogative. Finally, Bene understands his rules to apply to the oral performance of letters but not to oral performance of the liturgy, where the Church's own rules for delivery take precedence.

These remarks conclude Bene's treatment of the divisions, which he follows only with some brief rules about sentences, 'since sentences are composed of divisions' (*Cand.*, I.25.2).[30] Here too he is both attentive to the effect a sentence will have on a listening audience and aware of opinions that differ from his own: 'But if a sentence has six or seven or more parts (*membra*) it will seem tiresome. However, it is often supported by the *auctores* and especially the historiographers, and such a sentence is called 'perimonelexis' in the rhetoric of Martianus. Yet many hold that even in an epistolary composition a sentence can be extended as far as the seventh part properly enough' (*Cand.*, I.25.9–10).[31] His final counsel is that 'the letter writer should be very careful in weaving together the sequence of sentences that he not obstruct the ears of the listeners with burdensome words or introduce any prolixity, but let everything appear to move along quickly with fitting words and thoughts so that "each thing keeps the place it has been properly assigned"' (*Cand.*, I.25.20–1).[32]

Bene's expansive treatment of artistic composition, especially the doctrine of the divisions, allows us to glimpse a kind of instruction in delivery that is referenced in almost every medieval *ars dictandi* but usually is described so sketchily that it may not be recognized for what it is.[33] In letters composed according to the rules just described, when read aloud, each division of each sentence would be heard not only through the cadences of the *cursus* that structured its last six or seven syllables but also through the ensuing pause, which would be signalled by a mark of punctuation in the written text, and by the raising or lowering of the voice that preceded the pause. Those trained in this art would compose letters meant to have a distinctive sound and would read them aloud in a manner that accentuated that sound.

We could speculate about and perhaps even try to demonstrate what such a performance might have sounded like; but it is more difficult to assess the visual dimensions of delivery that Bene mentions but discusses in much less detail, namely facial expression and gesture. Detailed comments on gesture are rare in medieval rhetoric textbooks, even in the arts of preaching, where they are most likely to appear. Among the arts of poetry and prose, Geoffrey of Vinsauf's *Poetria nova* is unique in providing brief directions on how to enhance the performance of an apostrophe through tone of voice, facial expressions and gestures with the hands.[34] Bene's *Candelabrum* may be the only letter-writing treatise that speaks directly about physical movements as an accompaniment to oral performance, and its counsel is only that such movements should be appropriate and restrained. Gesture figures more prominently in another thirteenth-century Italian letter-writing treatise, the *Rota Veneris*, by another of Bene's contemporaries at Bologna, Boncompagno of Signa; but there it is represented as an alternative and/or complement to epistolary communication rather than as an element in the oral performance of epistolary texts. As a kind of appendix to this playful art of writing love letters, Boncompagno provides a chapter on 'the gestures of lovers', in which he distinguishes among a 'nod' (*nutus*), an 'indication' (*indicium*), a 'signal' (*signum*) and a 'sigh' (*suspirium*), complete with mock-scholastic definitions and illustrative examples.[35] Although these tongue-in-cheek remarks have more to do with Ovidian comedy than Ciceronian rhetoric, their presence in a work on letter writing may be a sign that facial expression and gesture had a role in dictaminal pedagogy, if perhaps one that was more evident in classroom practices than textbook precepts.

Medieval students typically did not hand in papers but recited their compositions aloud before their teachers and classmates and received criticism and advice orally on the spot. This was as true of the practice letters they composed as of the verse exercises illustrated so profusely in and alongside the arts of poetry and prose by Matthew of Vendôme and Geoffrey of Vinsauf. In the fourteenth century, students at the Oxford grammar schools regularly had to compose verses and letters on the same subject and then recite them from memory to the master; while at St Albans School students were required to compose versions of the same text in quantitative verse, rhythmical verse and epistolary prose as part of their final examinations in Latin composition.[36] There is reason to believe that such performances were seen by teachers and students as opportunities to display the full range of rhetorical skills, including the finer points of delivery. I have written about Geoffrey of Vinsauf's directions for delivering an ironic apostrophe on boys who put themselves forward as masters, and Jan Ziolkowski recently has examined the medieval practice of using musical notation to mark verse passages, such as Dido's lament in the *Aeneid*, for classroom performance.[37] Structurally, medieval letters were modelled on classical orations, and medieval teachers of letter writing may well have exploited their potential for classroom drama through the practice of pairing letters with their responses, as reflected in the surviving collections of model letters. Like the ancient students of rhetoric who sharpened their oratorical skills by declaiming on opposite sides of legal or political issues in their *controversiae* and *suasoriae*, medieval students of letter writing very likely were assigned the roles of initiator and respondent in what often amounted to epistolary debates conducted before an audience of their peers with the teacher as judge. Naturally, no record survives of the precise gestures and facial expressions such students would have employed; but we can be reasonably sure that they would have used more than the resources of voice alone to make their points.

How such schoolroom histrionics might have been transported into the worksphere of the professionally literate is a topic about which I could only speculate. I am reasonably confident that training in the acoustic dimension of performing letters would have informed the actual practice of reading Latin letters aloud in public, whether such training had been received in the context of a specific course on the *ars dictaminis* or as part

of more general training in the *ars grammatica*.[38] I suspect that the degree
to which gestures and facial expressions would have been employed to
enhance such performances would have varied quite a bit, depending not
only on the rank of the dignitary addressed and the formality of the occasion, for example, but also on the dramatic proclivities of the individual reader. One might well expect from the amount of detail (and the
priority of place) that the *artes dictandi* devote to protocols for addressing the highest ecclesiastical and secular dignitaries – popes and bishops,
emperors and kings – that a richly ceremonious and perhaps even 'theatrical' delivery would have been more likely for such letters than for letters addressed to simple monks or even the wealthiest merchants; but the
dictatores are silent on this matter, and even literary representations tend
to focus more on a letter's style or the addressee's reaction to its message
than on the gestures that accompanied its delivery. In any case, since my
goal has been to consider the evidence of formal training in epistolary
delivery, to speculate further about what might have happened outside
the schoolroom would be to exceed my brief.

NOTES

1 Giles Constable, *Letters and Letter-Collections*, Typologie des sources du
   Moyen Âge occidental 17 (Turnhout: Brepols, 1976), 53–5. Also see M. T.
   Clanchy, *From Memory to Written Record: England 1066–1307*, 2nd edn
   (Oxford: Blackwell, 1993), especially 260–72. On the complex relationship
   between oral and written messages in the Middle Ages, especially as it is repre-
   sented in literary texts, see also Martin Camargo, 'Where's the Brief?: The *Ars
   Dictaminis* and Reading/Writing Between the Lines', *Disputatio*, 1 (1996): 1–17,
   and Horst Wenzel (ed.), *Gespräche – Boten – Briefe: Körpergedächtnis und
   Schriftgedächtnis im Mittelalter* (Berlin: Erich Schmidt Verlag, 1997). One
   of the few medieval letter-writing textbooks that discusses the problem of
   Latin letters sent to 'illiterate' recipients is Conrad of Mure's *Summa de arte
   prosandi* (1275–76), in *Die Summa de arte prosandi des Konrad von Mure*, ed.
   Walter Kronbichler (Zurich: Fretz und Wasmuth, 1968), 44. For a translation,
   see 'Where's the Brief?', 5–6. A shorter version of the present essay was read
   at the eighty-third Annual Meeting of the Medieval Academy of America,
   Vancouver, April 2008. I am grateful to the members of the audience for their
   comments, which helped guide my revisions.
2 Jean Leclercq, *The Love of Learning and the Desire for God: A Study of Monastic
   Culture*, trans. Catharine Misrahi (New York: Fordham University Press,
   1961), 220–8.
3 See, for example, Bonnie Wheeler (ed.), *Listening to Heloise: The Voice of a
   Twelfth-Century Woman* (New York: St Martin's Press, 2000).

4   Geoffrey Chaucer, *The Canterbury Tales, Complete*, ed. Larry D. Benson (Boston and New York: Houghton Mifflin, 2000), 101, 134.

5   See, for example, William D. Patt, 'The Early *Ars dictaminis* as Response to a Changing Society', *Viator*, 9 (1978): 133–55.

6   *RLM*, 446–8, quotation from 447: 'Epistolis conveniunt multa eorum, quae de sermone praecepta sunt.'

7   The earliest such treatise is the *Ars dictandi* (c. 1085) by Alberic of Montecassino, though part of the same author's slightly earlier *Flores rhetorici* or *Dictaminum radii* (c. 1080 or earlier) also deals with letters. See Franz Josef Worstbrock, Monika Klaes and Jutta Lütten, *Repertorium der Artes dictandi des Mittelalters*, Teil I: *Von den Anfängen bis um 1200*, Münstersche Mittelalter-Schriften 66 (Munich: Wilhelm Fink Verlag, 1992), 7–18.

8   Harry F. Reijnders (ed.), '*Aimericus, Ars lectoria*', *Vivarium*, 9 (1971): 119–37; 10 (1972): 41–101, 124–76; *Magister Siguinus* Ars lectoria: *Un art de lecture à haute voix du onzième siècle*, ed. C. H. Kneepkens and H. F. Reijnders (Leiden: Brill, 1979). See Kneepkens and Reijnders, xxii–xxxiv, for the authorship, date and interrelatedness of the two treatises.

9   Kneepkens and Reijnders (eds.), *Magister Siguinus*, 91: (a) 'Quisquis epistulam, hoc est "breuem", bene uult fingere'; (b) 'Quodsi quis uel corde uel tabulis uel codice quidlibet edicturus, uel in populo legens uel sociis proloquens uel amicis referens illud immorando, deliberando, habitum moderando, non uoce asinina extonans, non scrofe more gurgitans, non uoce uocem infugans, uoce libera, uoce firma, uoce summissa quicquid illud serium aut ludicrum pronunciare addiscat.' Cf. the related comments in Reijnders, '*Aimericus*', 172. See also Reijnders, '*Aimericus*', 94; and Kneepkens and Reijnders, *Magister Siguinus*, 141, 143. Later 'arts of reading' lack such references to letters, perhaps because the development of the *ars dictaminis* rendered them superfluous. See, for example, Elsa Marguin-Hamon (ed. and trans.), *L'Ars lectoria Ecclesie de Jean de Garlande: Une grammaire versifiée du xiiie siècle et ses gloses*, Studia Artistarum: Subsidia 2 (Turnhout: Brepols, 2003).

10 A. Ernout, 'Dictare "Dicter," allem. Dichten', *Revue des Études Latines*, 29 (1951): 155–61.

11 Augusto Gaudenzi (ed.), 'Guidonis Fabe Summa dictaminis', *Il Propugnatore*, n.s. 3 (1890): part 1, 294–5: (a) 'illud dictamen vitiosum habetur quod in prima vel secunda prolatione non potest intelligi, si bene legatur pariter et distincte'; (b) 'fugere debemus et ut vitium evitare longam verborum continuationem, que et auditoris aures et oratoris spiritum ledere consuevit' (cf. *Rhetorica ad Herennium*, IV.12.18).

12 Gaudenzi (ed.), part 2, 345–70.

13 Martin Camargo, *Ars dictaminis, Ars dictandi*, Typologie des sources du moyen âge occidental 60 (Turnhout: Brepols, 1991), especially 17–28.

14 *Bene Florentini Candelabrum*, ed. Gian Carlo Alessio, Thesaurus Mundi 23 (Padua: Antenore, 1983), 155: 'INCIPIT QUINTUS. DE COMPENDIO TOTIUS ARTIS'. All translations from the *Candelabrum* (*Cand.*) are based

on this edition, which I will reference parenthetically in the text using Alessio's section numbers.

15 Ed. Alessio, 5: 'Nam gramatica illuminat intellectum, logica fidem prestat, rethorica facit velle: que tria multum expediunt dictatori, quia suum est facere ut ea que dicit intelligant auditores, intellecta credant et creditis acquiescant. Substantialiter tamen ad rethoricam spectare cognoscitur; que, in orationis artificio quinque considerans, invenit et disponit, memorat, eloquitur et pronuntiat eleganter.'

16 Ed. Alessio, 5: 'Pronuntiatio est vocis, vultus, gestus moderatio cum venustate.' Bene's source is *Rhetorica ad Herennium* (*RadH*), I.2.3. Guido Faba quotes the same definition: *Summa dictaminis*, ed. Gaudenzi, 296.

17 Ed. Alessio, 5: 'dictator debet esse … in pronuntiando modestus'.

18 Ed. Alessio, 156: 'Qui dictator esse perfectus desiderat est necesse ut … sciat … graviter et venuste pronuntiare.'

19 Broadly speaking, *dictator* meant 'someone who composes', 'an author' or 'a writer', but it also could be used more specifically to designate 'one who formulates documents', especially epistolary documents, or 'a teacher of the *ars dictaminis*'. See, for example, J. F. Niermeyer and C. van de Kieft, *Mediae Latinitatis lexicon minus*, rev. J. W. J. Burgers (Leiden: Brill, 2002), 433.

20 Ed. Alessio, 273–4:

DE TRIPLICI MODO RECTE PRONUNTIANDI.

Pronunciatio similiter ad tria se habet, scilicet ad moderationem vocis, vultus et gestus, quia sicut bona pronutiatio [*sic*] sine precedentibus nichil valet, ita precedentia sine digna pronuntiatione sunt frivola. Pronuntiatio igitur in voce, vultu et gestu dignam moderationem observat, ut concilietur auditor et ad fidem persuasione ducatur, ut animorum motibus incalescat.

Vox enim servat in punctis, accentibus, distintionibus, subdistintionibus et clausulis suas leges, de quibus omnibus fuit in primo libro, cum de compositione tractavimus, expeditum. Vox autem, sicut memoria, sine dubio a natura procedit et tamen, quadam scientia modificante iuvatur, quia usus conservat vocem et moderata deambulatio prodest multum sicut nimia excursio vocem extenuat et fatigat. Ciborum, potus, et aliarum quarundam rerum causa vocis sepe bonitas impeditur et sepe, ut dicunt phisici, adiuvatur et ideo debet vox cautela non modica custodiri ne defectum, cum oportuna fuerit, patiatur. Vocis autem bonitas in claritate, firmitate et suavitate consistit, que tria partim natura, partim artificio acquiruntur. Vox ergo materie consonet, ita quod res exprimi optime videatur.

Vultus quoque secundum dignitatem sententie sunt mutandi, servata in omnibus moderatione decenti, ut interpres animi vultus etiam reputetur. Similiter gestus quidam moderati sunt aliquando adhibendi, extendendo manus, erigendo pedes, inclinando cervicem et similia faciendo que videantur ad materiam pertinere, dum modo nichil in horatore generent inhonestum.

Unde ait Gaufredus:

VERSUS DE TRIPLICI PRONUNTIATIONE.

Vox vocem, vultus vultum gestusque figuret
Gestum, per notulas hec est moderata venustas

Auditum pascat vox castigata modeste
Vultus et gestus gemino condita sapore.
[Citing *Poetria nova*, 2,053–4, 2,057–8.]

Hec de inventione, dispositione, elocutione, memoria et pronuntiatione breviter dicta sufficient, quia non de causis civilibus sed de his que magis operi nostro expediebant habuimus propositum pertractandi.

21 Ed. Alessio, 8: 'sciendum est quod tria in omni exquisito dictamine requiruntur, scilicet elegantia, compositio et hornatus, qui a Tullio dignitas nominatur' (cf. *RadH*, IV.12.17–56.69).

22 Ed. Alessio, 9: (a) 'Compositio tamen non semper secundum artis traditionem procedit sed contingit eam sepe fieri ad libitum dictatoris'; (b) 'sed non est ob hoc compositionis artificium ignorandum, cum sepe sit necessarium quoniam est apud nobiles autores et philosophos in honore, nec a sede Romana sine tali decore aliqua epistola destinatur'.

23 Ed. Alessio, 18: 'Si ergo volumus in oratione assequi hunc leporem, oportet naturalem nos ordinem commutare, ita quod in sermone sit quidam cursus lepidus et suavis ne loqui populariter videamur.'

24 Ed. Alessio, 25: 'DE FINALITATE DISTINCTIONUM'. On the medieval *cursus*, see especially Tore Janson, *Prose Rhythm in Medieval Latin from the Ninth to the Thirteenth Century*, Studia Latina Stockholmiensia 20 (Stockholm: Almqvist & Wiksell, 1975), and on the *cursus* in Italy, see also Gudrun Lindholm, *Studien zum mittellateinischen Prosarhythmus: Seine Entwicklung und sein Abklingen in der Briefliteratur Italiens*, Studia Latina Stockholmiensia 10 (Stockholm: Almqvist & Wiksell, 1963).

25 Ed. Alessio, 27: 'Et quia sepe fecimus de distinctionibus mentionem, cum nulla possit oratio placere, si fuerit indistincta, ideo quid sit distinctio videamus. Distinctio igitur est unius clausule integrum membrum, dictiones digna ordinatione contexens et sententias a nexu dubitationis expediens.'

26 Ed. Alessio, 27–8: 'Tres autem sunt species distinctionum, scilicet dependens, constans et finitiva.' Bene illustrates the three divisions thus: 'Exemplum de his tribus distinctionibus istud detur: "Cum inter omnes virtutes caritas optineat principatum." (ecce coma) "non est sine ipsa virtutum certa possessio." (ecce colum) "in qua est omnium illarum posita certitudo"; (ecce periodus).' In this example, the *coma/distinctio dependens* and the *periodus/ distinctio finitiva* end with a *cursus velox* ($-\cup\cup$ $\cup\cup-\cup$), while the *colum/ distinctio constans* ends with a *cursus tardus* ($-\cup$ $\cup-\cup\cup$). The third type of sanctioned cadence, the *cursus planus* ($-\cup$ $\cup-\cup$), is not illustrated.On the history of the *distinctiones* and the complex relationship among punctuation, syntax, meaning and delivery/oral recitation in the Middle Ages, see especially M. B. Parkes, *Pause and Effect: An Introduction to the History of Punctuation in the West* (Berkeley; Los Angeles: University of California Press, 1993). Also see Jan Ziolkowski, *Nota Bene: Reading Classics and Writing Melodies in the Early Middle Ages*, Publications of the Journal of Medieval Latin 7 (Turnhout: Brepols, 2007), 83–97, on the relationship between punctuation and oral performance of texts.

27 Ed. Alessio, 17: 'artificium compositionis ... orationi suavitatem accommo-
dat, distinctiones ordinat, audientium aures artificiali ordinatione demulcet
et vitia quelibet eloquii rusticantis eliminat'.

28 Ed. Alessio, 30: 'Punctum est signum segregans intellectus et spiritum recre-
ans prolatoris.'

29 Ed. Alessio, 31–2: 'De punctis autem et modo punctandi triplicem differen-
tiam iam audivi. Ecclesia quippe Romana omnes distinctiones in pronuntiando terminat puncto plano et punctis scripturalibus utitur valde paucis
nec ullam virgulam scribit nisi quando clausulam conclusionis finit. Alii
sunt qui diverso modo pronuntiant sicut diversimode quoque scribunt,
dicentes quod per arsin, id est elevationem vocis, omnia sunt comata profer-
enda et hoc ostendit puntum [*sic*] cum virgula sursum ducta; cola vero sunt
accentu gravi aliquantulum finienda: quod denotat punctum sine ulla virgula
ibi scriptum; at periodum censent graviori accentu pronuntiari debere, quod
punctum mostrat cum virgula infra ducta. Et iste modus fere ab omnibus
observatur. Nos vero tenemus quod omnes distinctiones, preter finitivam,
debent per arsin legittime terminari, sed periodus per thesin, id est deposi-
tionem vocis, nisi cum in ecclesia legimus ubi tam in psalmis quam ceteris
lectionibus auctoritas consuetudinis est servanda. De punctis vero distinctionum sedis apostolice auctoritatem servamus dicentes quod omne punctum sine virgula esse debet nisi ubi sermo vel epistola terminatur, quia ibi
geminum punctum cum virgula deorsum ducta fieri consuevit. Ubi etiam
est interrogatio virgula satis digne puncto superscribitur aliquantulum tor-
tuosa et in acutum directa, ut pateat acuto accentu illam pronuntiari debere.
Nam si iuxta pronuntiationum modos puncta scripturalila volumus variare,
antiphonarium videbitur quod neumemus, sed

> Velle suum cuique est nec voto vivitur uno;
> Mille hominum species et rerum discolor usus.'

30 Ed. Alessio, 32: 'De clausulis quoque sequitur ut agamus, quoniam ex distinctionibus clausule compinguntur.'

31 Ed. Alessio, 33: 'Si vero sex vel septem vel plura membra receperit, videbitur
tediosa: tamen apud auctores et maxime istoriographos multotiens toleratur
et talis clausula perimonelexis in rethorica Martiani vocatur. Multi tamen
volunt quod satis honeste usque ad septenarium possit etiam in epistolari
dictamine clausula prorogari.'

32 Ed. Alessio, 35: 'Sit itaque dictator multum diligens in clausularum serie con-
texenda, ne verbis onerantibus aures impediat auditorum neve aliquam pro-
lixitatem inducat, sed tam verbis quam sententiis convenientibus videantur
procedere omnia expedite ut "singula queque locum teneat sortita decenter"
[Horace, *Ars poetica*, 92].'

33 Cf. Guido Faba, *Summa dictaminis*, ed. Gaudenzi, 336–7. Twelfth-
century *artes dictandi* that treat the *distinctiones* include Bernard of
Bologna(?), *Rationes dictandi*, in Ludwig Rockinger (ed.), *Briefsteller und
Formelbücher des eilften* [sic] *bis vierzehnten Jahrhunderts*, 2 vols., Quellen

und Erörterungen zur bayerischen und deutschen Geschichte 9 (Munich: G. Franz, 1863–4; rpt. New York: Burt Franklin, 1961), 25–6; Peter of Blois, *Libellus de arte dictandi rhetorice*, in Martin Camargo (ed.), *Medieval Rhetorics of Prose Composition: Five English* Artes Dictandi *and Their Tradition* (Binghamton: Medieval and Renaissance Texts and Studies, 1995), 45–6; and Transmundus, *Introductiones dictandi*, ed. and trans. Ann Dalzell (Toronto: PIMS, 1995), 52/3–56/7.

34 Martin Camargo, 'Medieval Rhetoric Delivers; or, Where Chaucer Learned How to Act', *New Medieval Literatures*, 9 (2007): 41–62, at 51–3.

35 Ryszard Ganszyniec (ed.), *Polskie listy miłosne dawnych czasów* (Lwów: Drukarnia Ossolineum, 1925), 171–83, at 180–2. This *editio princeps*, like Friedrich Baethgen's 1927 edition of the *Rota Veneris*, is less readily accessible than Boncompagno da Signa, *Rota Veneris: A Facsimile Reproduction of the Straßburg Incunabulum with Introduction, Translation, and Notes*, ed. and trans. Josef Purkart (Delmar, NY: Scholars' Facsimiles and Reprints, 1975). See 64–6 (facsimile) and 92–5 (translation) for the material on gestures.

36 Martin Camargo, 'If You Can't Join Them, Beat Them; or, When Grammar Met Business Writing (in Fifteenth-Century Oxford)', in C. Poster and L. C. Mitchell (eds.), *Letter-Writing Manuals and Instruction from Antiquity to the Present: Historical and Bibliographic Studies* (Columbia: University of South Carolina Press, 2007), 68, 83–4; and Camargo (ed.), *Medieval Rhetorics*, 29–30.

37 Camargo, 'Medieval Rhetoric Delivers'; Ziolkowski, *Nota Bene*, especially 143–72.

38 See, for example, Geoffrey of Vinsauf, *Documentum de modo et arte dictandi et versificandi*, II.3.170–5, in Edmond Faral (ed.), *Les arts poétiques du xiie et du xiiie siècle* (Paris: Champion, 1924), 318–19.

CHAPTER 8

The concept of ductus,

Or journeying through a work of art

Mary Carruthers

The concept that an artistic work is a journey (while certainly to be found in ancient rhetoric) achieves a particular importance – even ubiquity – in medieval analysis. One is said to travel through a composition, whether of words or other materials, led on by the stylistic qualities of its parts and their formally arranged relationships. *Ductus* and its synonyms analyse the experience of artistic form as an ongoing, dynamic process rather than as the examination of a static or completed object. *Ductus* is the way by which a work leads someone through itself: that quality in a work's formal patterns which engages an audience and then sets a viewer or auditor or performer in motion within its structures, an experience more like travelling through stages along a route than like perceiving a whole object. The art of the Middle Ages does not hold up a perfect 'globed fruit' but leads one in a walk along converging and diverging paths.[1] Several closely related Latin words are used in speaking of this dynamic, chiefly *ductus*, *tenor*, *modus* and *color*. My object in this essay is to trace the lineaments of the concept common to all these words in discussions of rhetoric from late antiquity, and the high and late Middle Ages.

THE ITINERARIES OF ART

Geoffrey of Vinsauf begins his *Poetria nova* (the title teases Horace) with an examination of invention, which conceives of *dispositio*, the arrangement of subject matters, as a variety of mapping. He counsels a composer setting out to invent a work, to imagine for himself an internal picture of his composition before he sets hand to tablet:

Let the mind's interior compass first circle the whole extent of the material. Let a definite order chart in advance at what point the pen will take up its course, or where it will fix its Cadiz. As a prudent workman, construct the whole fabric within the mind's citadel; let it exist in the mind before it is on the lips. (lines 55–9).[2]

190

This passage is most famous among literary historians for its invocation of the image of the poet as a master builder, constructing his composition. Often overlooked is the image – equally important – of arrangement as a process of mapping, the composer as mapmaker. Geoffrey's map, circled by his mental compass, is the pattern, the picture (one meaning of medieval Latin *pictura* is 'map') and the general route to be followed in the composition to come. Into such outlines one was able to gather all sorts of materials and still keep clear to oneself and others the 'ways' and 'itineraries' of the whole work.

Having discerned his 'Cadiz' a composer sets out to determine his routes, his *cursus*:

Since the following treatise begins its course [*cursus*] with a discussion of order, its first concern is the path that the ordering of material should follow [*quo limite debeat ordo currere*] ... Order may follow two possible routes [*Ordo bifurcat iter*]. (lines 79–81, 87)

At this point Nims' translation unfortunately obscures the Latin text's stress on the journey analogy by introducing – as Geoffrey does not – the concepts of 'natural' and 'artificial' order. What follows is my more literal translation of lines 88–90: 'The main line of the highway is the leader there, where subject matter and words follow the same route, nor does the order of the speech depart from the order of its subject matters' for 'Linea stratae / Est ibi dux, ubi res et verba sequuntur eumdem / Cursum nec sermo declinat ab ordine rerum.'

Notice how Geoffrey conceives of the 'main line' both as a road and as something that 'leads' one on – *ductus* is an attribute of highways. This may seem a trivial, obvious point but it is at the heart of the matter. Roads are not passive; they have instrumentality and agency because they direct us – they give us our limits – even when we stray from them. One can only be in error (*errare*) from a plainly delineated route (*linea stratae est ibi dux*). Notice as well the metaphor in Geoffrey's first formulation of the dispositive task in composing: one's first concern is to determine *quo limite debeat ordo currere*, 'by which path' one's chosen compositional order should be directed.

Limes, iter, via, cursus – these are the common nouns of medieval argument and of medieval compositions. But the straight path (*limes rectus* or, to use a more common, alternative phrase found in the *Rhetorica ad Herennium, ordo simplex*), though it is a necessary reference, makes for a boring journey: Geoffrey is quite clear about this. The interesting action is found in the paths of artifice, in schemes that do not simply plod along unidirectionally from start to end, but which multiply (though – note – they do not multiply endlessly): 'Ordinis est primus sterilis, ramusque secundus / Fertilis et mira succrescit origine ramus / In ramos, solus in plures, unius in octo' (lines 101–3) [The first way of ordering is sterile, and the second is fertile, from its marvellous origin a branch grows up into branches, the one into many, the single into eight]. Then, with charac-teristic verve, Geoffrey encourages his students: 'Patentem / Ecce viam! ratione viae rege mentis habenas' [Behold the road is open! direct the reins of your mind by means of the rational plan of the route] (lines 110–11).

The road metaphor governs his discussion of the entire composing pro-cess. For Geoffrey, his contemporaries, and the generations he influenced, the two basic ways of composition (*modi agendi*) are by means of the amp-lification or abbreviation of one's matters.[3] Both methods are discussed in terms of roads and journeys. Geoffrey continues:

For the opening of the poem, the art described above has offered a various move-ment or *tenor*. The poem's progress now invites you onward. By means of your pre-visualized image, direct your step further along the road's course. The way [*gressus*] continues along two routes [*viae*]: there will be either a wide path or a narrow, either a river or a brook. You may advance at a leisurely pace or leap swiftly ahead. (lines 203–8)

A bit further on, discussing the trope of digression, Geoffrey observes: 'Sometimes, as I advance along the way, I leave the middle of the road, and with a kind of leap I fly off to the side, as it were; then I return to the point whence I had digressed' (lines 534–6).

This ancient conception of a composition as embedding within itself 'ways' (*gressus, modi*) and 'routes' (*cursus*) also finds expression in common advice to orators to think of the arrangement of their speech as an itiner-ary among set places leading from start to finish, the 'Cadiz' of Geoffrey of Vinsauf's compositional map. In rhetoric, *memoria* is addressed primarily to the task of *ex tempore* speaking, when one will be required to be 'fast on one's feet' in adapting any prepared speech to the vagaries of a particu-lar occasion. Having just described the mnemonic technique of using the rooms of a house as one's outline, and placing in each of them image-cues for matters to be recalled, Quintilian suggests other similarly useful struc-tures: 'Quod de domo dixi, et in operibus publicis et in itinere longo et urbium ambitu et picturis fieri potest. Etiam fingere sibi has regiones licet.[4] [What I said about a house can be done also with public buildings, a long road, a town perambulation, or pictures. One can even invent these set-tings for oneself]. Twelve hundred years later, the technique was still in use, commended in an art of preaching by Friar Francesc Eiximenis (d. 1409), a Catalan Franciscan who was connected with the royal households of Barcelona and then Valencia. In his *Ars praedicandi populo*, he suggests, among other devices, using mental itineraries, such as the pilgrimage road from Rome to Compostela, in order to recall the topics about which one wants to speak as one preaches.[5] Suppose one has eight main topics to speak about – such as clerics, money, merchants, a great bridge, burgesses, olive oil, knights and the apostles. The cities along the way become the distinctive stations in the itinerary of one's composition. So, Rome is the city of clerics, in which one would begin by speaking of clerics. Then one would move mentally to Florence to speak on the topic of money (for Florence 'is a very famous place for money'). Many merchants live in Genoa, there is a great bridge in Avignon (a bridge or *pons* but also, as Kimberly Rivers has suggested, the *ponti*-fex), and in Barcelona live burgesses who have 'huge dwellings and great public buildings'. Saragossa is famous for its oil, Toledo for knights, and Compostela contains 'the body and name' of St James and thus of all the apostles. 'And then I will recall the matters placed along the imaginary route through which my theme runs, remembering them either by going forward starting from Rome or by beginning from Santiago de Compostela and continuing backward to Rome.'[6]

The motif of composing as undertaking a journey with varying routes among its places could extend as well to reading, not only to the activities associated with invention. In a trope that can be found at least as early as Augustine's *De doctrina Christiana*, *lectio divina* was analysed as a procedure of 'grades' or stages along a route.[7] The late-twelfth-century treatise on reading Scripture by Peter of Celle, now called *De afflictione et lectione*, affords a rich description of such medieval reading practices with respect to the biblical texts. Peter gives us a description of reading the Pentateuch very much in terms of a journey, with distinct stations and routes between them.

[T]ravel by your reading all the way to paradise and sigh over what was lost. Drink from the four rivers by imbibing justice, prudence, fortitude and temperance …. Walk with God as Enoch did … In this manner with a deliberate but light step [*Ad hunc modum presso et suspenso pede*] run [*decurre*] through the contents of this book, imitating the good deeds, avoiding the evil ones, interpreting what is obscure, retaining and committing to memory what is straightforward. Whenever you enter a pleasant meadow of prophetic blessings, loosen the folds of your garment, stretch your belly, open your mouth and extend your hand, then depart with mouth, belly, garment, and hands filled …. Then come to Exodus and be saddened by the entry into Egypt. … Observe how the law was given on Mt. Sinai and how it is open to spiritual understanding. Run through the forty-two stopping-places [in the desert] and what they signify in progressions of virtues. Constructing within yourself the tabernacle and its rites with an angelic mind, inhabit the heavenly realms in imitating their sanctity.[8]

As I wrote in *The Craft of Thought*, 'Peter clearly thinks of the matters in Genesis in terms of a map; reading it is for him a series of journeys, a sight-seeing pilgrimage. In each site he commands us to observe the stories and events as mental scenes.'[9] True but not enough. For he does not only observe these mental scenes, he lives in them, with a fully sensory and emotional as well as rational experience. One is asked not just to see, but to 'taste and see' all that is in the textual places encountered in reading. The events of Genesis and Exodus are experienced as though they were stations within an itinerary, places on a world map. For such a reading exercise, to include a map among the front matters of the texts – where one should find study guides and orienting devices – might be quite helpful, and was often done. In all such Bible reading maps, Paradise plays the initiating role, it holds the orienting position. From it one is moved through an itinerary of the other places important in the Genesis–Exodus stories (with the Nile delta and the Red Sea prominently positioned). And there are plenty of stopping-places on the way.

Peter's reading journey culminates in constructing within himself, 'with an angelic mind', the Tabernacle, its furniture and its rites, as described in Exodus 25ff. This ancient Jewish meditational exercise permeates early Christianity as well, nowhere better expressed than in Augustine's meditation (*enarratio*) on Psalm 41, *Quemadmodum desiderat cervus*, which became a touchstone for the life of prayer in the desert. In this psalm (in the version known to Augustine), the psalmist describes his ascent to the house of God, beginning in God's tent, *tabernaculum*, on earth. He walks about it, Augustine imagines, looking at its many embellishments in the form of images of the great saints, and then, led on by sweet music, his route becomes more definite and he travels through the earthly Tabernacle to the heavenly *domus Dei* itself, where he is welcomed amid feasting and celebration. Augustine's commentary underscores how the psalmist is led (*ductus*) by some sounding music (*organum*) which comes from within the structure itself:

Yet it was while he marvelled [*miratur*] at the members of that company in the tent [*membra tabernaculi*] that he was led [*perductus est*] to God's house. He was drawn toward a kind of sweetness [*dulcedinem*], an inward, secret pleasure that cannot be described, as though some musical instrument [*organum*] were sounding delightfully [*suaviter*] from God's house. As he still walked about in the tent he could hear this inner music … drawn to [*or* by] its sweet tones [*ductus dulcedine*], following its melodies and distancing himself from the din of flesh and blood [*strepitu carnis et sanguinis*], until he found his way [*peruenit*] even to the house of God. He tells us about the road he took and the manner in which he was led [*uiam suam et ductum suum sic ipse commemorat*], as though we had asked him, 'You admire the tent on earth, but how did you reach the secret precincts of God's house?'[10]

While the psalmist walks about the tabernacle he hears from within it the melody – voice or instrument – that he follows: it is the sweetness that draws him through and up to the celestial dwelling itself. Augustine focuses on the agency of this movement, the road he took and the manner – *ductus* – in which he was led.

The word he uses, *ductus*, was first analysed as a separate phenomenon of rhetorical art about the same time that Augustine himself was teaching rhetoric prior to his conversion. It was defined in the fourth-century textbook of the Christian rhetorician, Consultus Fortunatianus, whose work reflects the pedagogy of rhetoric that Augustine also knew and taught.[11] Fortunatianus' discussion was then incorporated into Martianus Capella's influential text on the Liberal Arts, *The Marriage of Philology and Mercury* (c. 430?), placed in the discussion of rhetoric. The *ductus* guides what we sometimes now call the 'flow' of a composition – as indeed did Cicero. Unlike Geoffrey of Vinsauf (but like Augustine), Cicero thinks of such movement as audible, like melody, carried in the rhythms of speech and tones of the orator's voice. Famously, in his *Orator* – a work concerned particularly with how various styles sound and thus also with their prose rhythms or *cursus*, their varying internal motions – Cicero describes Herodotus as one who 'flows along like a quiet stream without any roughness', while Thucydides sings of war in a particularly military mode.[12]

The word *ductus* has many more uses than just in rhetoric. Its most frequent use was simply as the past participle of *ducere*, constructed either adjectively or with *esse*, and meaning 'led'. As a masculine noun of the fourth declension it usually means 'guide' or 'command'. The noun also had the meanings of 'course' (often associated with water, as its English derivative, 'duct', still is), 'way' or 'path', and 'directed movement', such as extending a line, and is used often of drawing, whether figures, as in geometry, or letters. *Litterarum ductus* referred to the formalized handwriting for which scribes learned to draw out their lines in a prescribed way.[13] *Ductus* was also commonly extended to motivation; one is said to be 'led' or directed inwardly by some emotion (construed in the ablative) – anger or envy, playfulness or contrition (*penitentia ductu*, an ablative absolute construction, is a common phrase in pastoral writing). And it also occurs in the context of writing about rhetoric, especially after the fourth century. St Ambrose exhorted readers in his exposition of Psalm 118: 'wherefore may faith be your guide for the journey; may Holy Scripture be your path; the way [*ductus*] of divine eloquence is good'.[14] The journey motif is common in other authoritative commentaries on the Psalms. Since these (by Ambrose, Augustine, Cassiodorus and Jerome) formed the basis of all later commentaries on this most widely known of divine writings, their frequent use of this motif provided significant authority for its prominence in later medieval rhetoric. Divine eloquence itself is a journey which has its *ductus*.

So, though in rhetoric *ductus* is an aspect of arrangement or *dispositio*, it pertains always to some guiding movement within and through a work's various parts. Indeed, *ductus* is a principle of movement not stasis, of process rather than product, the con*duct* of a thinking, listening and feeling mind on its *way* through a composition, as one can clearly see in Augustine's account of being *ductus dulcidine* in his comment on Psalm 41, which we just examined. If Geoffrey of Vinsauf thinks of a work's 'courses' in terms of a building and a map or *pictura*, Augustine and Cicero think of it as well in terms of sound and (as we will see) of colour.

DUCTUS AND TENOR AGENDI, MODUS AND COLOR

Fortunatianus analysed compositional movement as having two qualities, one including the other. *Ductus* refers to the overall direction, the governing movement, of the work; for its particular, varying movements section by section he used the word *modus*. 'What is *ductus*? The way in which the case as a whole should be shaped. What is the relationship between *ductus* and *modus*? *Ductus* pertains to the whole oration, *modus* to each particular part in the oration.'[15] Martianus Capella used Fortunatianus' analysis but in altered terms. Where Fortunatianus had only used *ductus*, he also used *tenor*; where Fortunatianus had used *modus* he used *color*. Martianus' words were more common and traditional in rhetorical manuals, but it is Fortunatianus whom he directly adapts:

ductus autem est agendi per totam causam tenor sub aliqua figura seruatus. ... Hi sunt ductus artificiose tractandi et per totam orationem subtiliter diffundendi: qui colore hoc separantur, quod color in una tantum parte, ductus in tota causa seruatur.[16]

[*Ductus* indeed is the *tenor agendi* through the whole composition retained under each particular figure ... [*Martianus then discusses the types of* ductus, *as defined by Fortunatianus.*] These are the *ductus* for composing artfully and skilfully diffusing through the whole oration: these are distinguished by their *color*, for a particular *color* is retained for a single part, the *ductus* for the whole case.]

The vocabulary shifts confusingly among words that are synonymous in rhetoric – *tenor* and *ductus* (as used by these writers) and also *modus, color* and *figura*. Even more confusingly, *modus* in later medieval rhetoric could stand in for *tenor* or *ductus* as in the phrase *modus tractandi*, the way or manner of composing a specific work.

Tenor agendi is a phrase used for the movement of a work as it is in process, both as it is spoken and as it is perceived. In his *Orator*, Cicero says that each style has a distinctive 'flow' – the 'middle style', he says, 'is commonly said to flow with one tenor in speaking'.[17] From the context, it is clear that Cicero is thinking of a speaking voice, whose 'tones' shape both the particular and the sustained movement of the speech. Latin *tenor* is in fact derived from the verb *teneo, tenere*, 'to hold or keep', as a governing movement (the core meaning of *tenor*) keeps the whole together.[18] But Quintilian thought that *tenor* as used in rhetoric was derived from Greek *tonos*, 'tone' of voice and also 'tone', as a finely tuned instrument has 'tone'.[19] It is likely that many ancient and medieval people, trained in oratory and/or in chant and prayer, 'heard' and 'saw' a piece performed in their minds even if they were reading it silently. In the case of ancient oratory, previsualizing exercises and subvocal rehearsals were part of the preparation for speaking (and sometimes these were not so subvocal; Demosthenes famously practised speaking on the shore to be heard over the waves, and also declaimed with pebbles in his mouth). And of course 'tenor' and 'mode', 'colour' and 'figure' are all words that find their way into musical vocabulary as well as into rhetoric. Cicero identified an eloquence of the body, constituted of voice, facial expressions and movements; the speaker's *toni* (or *soni*, 'sounds') are 'like the elegant variety perfected in songs ... There is indeed in speaking a kind of more hidden song.'[20] He is referring not only to the precisely crafted prose rhythms of the *cursus*, used to mark units of meaning like a kind of vocal punctuation, but to the constant modulations of rhetorical delivery as a whole, even the 'plain speaking' of the middle style.

The movement among a composition's parts is not uniform; it can and should vary. Fortunatianus pays most attention to this feature of *ductus*, though before him Quintilian focused at length on the qualities and degrees of movement within a work, for which he frequently used words derived from *ducere, ductus* and its compounds.[21] According to Fortunatianus and Martianus Capella, there are five kinds of *ductus*: simple, subtle, figurative, oblique and mixed. These are distinguished by how direct and easy a path you make for your audience – whether you let them just step along with no obstacles, or whether you want them to work a bit, to look beneath or through your words to another agenda you may have. This is the matter to which Fortunatianus devotes the most attention. His examples are taken from legal proceedings, and they demonstrate how the nature of the charges and the aims of one's client (and oneself) will determine what sorts of figures and colours one may wish to use to persuade the judges.

Fortunatianus admits that the more usual name for what he distinguishes as types of *ductus* is 'figures' (*figurati*) but he dislikes, he says, lumping such variety of movement together in a single term (and he also has reserved *figuratus* for one of his modes of *ductus*). Of interest here is that Fortunatianus evidently recognizes that the variations in movement and direction which he is analysing are among the ornamental properties of a work. Such ornaments are functionally and situationally understood. Thus, switching to an 'oblique' mode acts as a signal that the direction of the work is characterized by a divergence between what is apparently being said and what is meant, in the same way as does an oblique figure like irony or allegory. Stylistic ornaments have both *vis*, or energy/force (fast or slow, measured or lively), and structural function (*ratio*) in the overall scheme. As Fortunatianus writes, 'Other teachers designate all these ways by what [single] name? Figures. Why do we distinguish them by [various] names? Because each single way differs both in force and in rationale, and things ought not be given a single designation whose force and rationale are not the same.'[22] Differences among the ornaments, according to Fortunatianus, are accounted for by variations in these two qualities, *vis* and *ratio*. Notice how the function of an ornament within the overall work, and not how it expresses or 'imitates' something else, determines its character.

What marks out the variation in route(s) of the overall *ductus* are figures, modes and colours of the journey. Fortunatianus reserves the term *modus* for the movement of particular parts of the composition, *ductus* for that of the whole. Martianus Capella uses the word *color* where Fortunatianus uses *modus*: evidently in this context they were at this time synonyms. Since *colores* is a term most commonly used (including by Martianus Capella) for the ornaments of rhetoric (that is, the figures and tropes of style), its adoption by Martianus Capella in connection with way-finding is significant, for it suggests that to Martianus the ornaments played a key marking function for finding one's way through a literary composition.

Lucia Calboli Montefusco has traced the origins, as far as our sketchy sources allow, of Fortunatianus' analysis of the types of *ductus* – plain, oblique, etc – to the much more common idea of rhetorical 'colour', *chroma*, and also to Quintilian, who characterized various strategies of 'figurated discourse' (*figuratae controversiae*).[23] Spoken 'colours' are used as painters use colour, Cicero said, an analogy found also in Aristotle: they give pleasure by offering variety. Moreover for Cicero, *color* like *tonus* can be extended as well to the sounds of delivered speech – indeed he often introduces the word *color* when he is talking about sound and rhythm. For example, in speaking of delivery at the end of *De oratore,* his great theoretical work on the artistry of rhetoric, he focuses on the production of voice, likening *pronuntiatio* to the crafts both of music and of painting. Every emotion, he says, has its own countenance, its tone of voice and expression. The orator's whole body, facial expressions and vocal modulations are like the strings of a lyre which sound to the motions of his mind as though he struck them. All these emotions are drawn out, composed and shaped by his art. 'They are at our disposal to be varied at will in delivery just as colours are in painting.'[24] *Color* is a word shared by all the arts from antiquity onward – it is worth exploring why.

Colour produces variety, and variation is essential for pleasure, both of body and of mind. Artistry, whether of song or painting, architecture or poetry, produces *suavis varietas perfecta*, pleasureful variety made perfect through its agency. It is this pleasure that also persuades. Cicero describes how a successful orator uses ornament abundantly but carefully, each word chosen well. Especially often he should use metaphors 'because such figures by virtue of the comparisons [they make] transport our thoughts, then bring them back, and move them about here and there, and this rapidly changing movement of thought in itself pleases'.[25]

DUCTUS RATIONIS: THE AGENCY OF FORMAL ARRANGEMENT

Though his particular analysis of the types of *ductus* has received the most attention from scholars, Fortunatianus' analysis of the relationship of *consilium* to *ductus* is also a useful addition to current debates about the nature of authors and authority, focusing a profound change in understanding from pre- to postmodern notions of 'author'. The analysis is not unique or original with Fortunatianus, but, as with the nature of *ductus*, he articulated with some precision a commonplace of previous pedagogy.

The concept of *consilium* is invoked often in Cicero's early *De inventione*; as a term in rhetoric it can be rendered best in English as 'plan'. 'Consilium est aliquid faciendi aut non faciendi excogitata ratio' [*Consilium* is one's deliberated plan for doing or not doing something] (Cicero, *De invention,*. I.25.36). It is the aggregate of the rational decisions and selections of the composer as s/he works – the artist's own 'intention'. But this plan is not the same thing as the *ductus* of the finished or delivered work, Fortunatianus states. *Ductus* is born of constant deliberation and various choices: 'Is *ductus* always the same in every part? no. Why? Because *ductus* is generated from the *consilium*, and the *consilium* of all the parts is not always the same.'[26] This mental *consilium* takes shape in the work as its *ductus*, but – a point stressed by Fortunatianus – while his mental plan is of the author's own volition and judgement, *ductus* is a quality of the work itself: 'How is *consilium* distinguished from *ductus*? In that the *consilium* is a matter of [the author's] choice, and *ductus* is part of the work itself. Likewise in that the *ductus* develops from the *consilium*, not the *consilium* from the *ductus*.'[27] Within a work (oration), Fortunatianus also distinguished a work's *ductus* from its *modus* or rather *modi*, and its 'goal', which he termed its *scopus*, 'aim'. *Scopus* basically means the object of a directed gaze, a 'target': the word is unusual in rhetorical manuals but is found more often in Christian meditational writing, including the work of John Cassian. The role of monastic practices of invention and composition needs to be given due weight in the development of rhetorical teaching during the Middle Ages – one cannot look solely to ancient sources and their transmission.[28]

Scopus is not a word found in the rhetorics of Cicero or Quintilian. Augustine feels compelled to gloss it in his *City of God* as an unusual Greek word equivalent to Latin *intentio*. Speaking of the title *episcopus* (bishop), which he says is not only an honorific but defines the post's core duties, he derives the Greek verb *episkopein* from Greek *skopōs*. He emphasizes that these Greek words are unfamiliar to Latin speakers. *Skopōs*, he says, means *intentio* in Latin; the Greek verb for what a bishop does is rendered in Latin as *superintendere*, 'manage, administer'.[29] In his rhetoric, Fortunatianus associates the word *scopus* with the intention or goal of the whole work, and *modus* with the 'way' of each particular part. *Ductus* is thus the direction that 'manages' and supports the whole work (as its synonym, *tenor*, is for Martianus Capella), while *modus* and *scopus* both are aspects of the *ductus*.[30] A work is a journey, with a starting-point and routes directed to an end – what Geoffrey of Vinsauf, centuries later, called its Cadiz, journey's end.

So *ductus* is the way(s) that a composition, realizing the plan(s) set within its arrangements, guides a person to its various goals, both in its parts and overall. This meaning is apparent in a use which Quintilian makes of the general concept. In the preface to his third book on *The Orator's Education*, he speaks of other writers on the subject of rhetoric, all of whom shared the same goal (of making the subject clear) but each of whom constructed different routes to that goal, and drew their disciples along those various ways: 'for so many writers, though all moving towards the same goal, have constructed different roads to it, and have each made their disciples follow their special route'.[31] At times *ductus* seems to mean almost what we think of as literary genre. The Latin version of Theodore of Mopsuestos' commentary on the Psalms (c. 380) speaks of how, in expounding a particular psalm text, a preacher uses a pastoral *ductus* for his audience, one suitable for those who have the care of people's souls: 'et pastorali ductu et moderatione tractamur' [we should compose in a pastoral way and with moderation], in this context referring to the middle style.[32] A monk of the late tenth century, addressing a poem to Abbot Constantine of Fleury, says he has adopted *ductus panegyricus* for it.[33]

Through its formal disposition *the work* in and of itself 'directs' movement. This is a crucial point for any audience or other kind of performer to understand. The work does not transparently 'express the author's intentions'. Its formal arrangements themselves are agents, which cause movements, mental and sensory and – as in the case of architecture – physical. In the *accessus ad auctores*, the standard medieval commentaries on the Poets and other authors (including the Psalms), one required section is called *intentio auctoris*. This is *not* the author's intention in any biographical sense. It is rather an intention within the work itself, considered as an authoring agent and distinguished from the human, historical author: for example, of Ovid's 'Epistolae' [= *Heroides*], the statement of the *intentio auctoris* begins 'intentio huius operis est ...', 'the intention of this work is ...'.[34] In other words, the composition also is an active agent, and once his *consilium* is formed within the work, the human craftsman cedes further control to the work's own *ductus*, colours and modes. The notion that works have some agency in themselves can be found as well in Horace, who attributes agency over an audience to the *poemata* he is characterizing:

Non satis est pulchra esse poemata; dulcia sunto
et, quocumque uolent, animum auditoris agunto. (Horace, *Ars poet.*, 99–100)

[It is not enough for poems to be beautiful – they must be sweet and, *as they may wish*, act on the mind of a listener.][35]

A related aspect of this idea, that the forms of a work themselves act directly on an audience, is found in dialectic. This is the common notion of *ductus rationis*, 'the path of reason', or how the parts of an argument lead one from premises to conclusion.[36] These were classified thoroughly, and are found in medieval curricula with the works of the *Organon*, in particular Aristotle's *Categories* (by way of Porphyry's *Isagoge*) and Boethius' *De differentiis topicis*.[37]

The sharp division made now by scholars between works of dialectic and works of rhetoric was not so firmly observed (or defined) before the advent of separate university faculties, and one finds early secular masters like Abelard using the model of rational *ductus* to speak of matters that traditionally were the province of rhetorical disposition as well. Abelard is known to have taught rhetoric as well as dialectic, though his rhetorical work – during which he famously disputed with his master William of Champeaux (and won, he says) – has received little attention. But recent investigation has begun to correct this imbalance, focusing fully on Abelard's teaching about rhetoric,[38] including a new and corrected edition by K. M. Fredborg of Abelard's lengthy digression on rhetorical argument (as discussed especially in *De inventione)* in his commentaries on the fourth book of Boethius' *De differentiis topicis*.[39] Fredborg has chosen to edit more cautiously than the previous editor did, and is also more apt to respect readings from manuscript A (Paris, MS Arsenal 910) than only to record manuscript P (Paris, Bib. Nat. MS lat. 7493). Manuscript A often uses the language of *ductus* and *ducere* in discussing rhetorical argument (rather than that of *dicere* and *dictus*, 'is called'), thus preserving the fundamental model of thematic *dispositio* as 'leading' one 'through' the various matters of a composition.

So Abelard wrote 'concerning the subject of implied circumstances and about topics' ['De questione circumstantiis implicita et de locis'], that analysis of any question is set forth through thesis and hypothesis: a thesis does not contain the circumstantial topics in itself but a hypothesis does. These *circumstantiae*, he continues, 'are the rhetorical places (topics), whence [*unde*] our conjectures are led out [*ducuntur*], that is conjectural arguments are drawn forth [*extrahuntur*] which generate our supposition/inference [*suspicionem*]'.[40] Notice how Abelard preserves the essentially spatial nature of this ancient model. *Locus* and *topos* both mean 'location, place': the locational model was already basic to the task of argument in Aristotle's *Topics*, and with it the idea of moving from one place to another, or being led from one to another, along a 'path'. Latin *ratio* refers not only to formal algorithms of logic (as now) but is a far broader term referring to 'plan', 'pattern', 'ordered scheme' – in Greek, *logos*. The very verbs for analysis preserve the model: *deducere* and *inducere*. *Ratiocinatio*, 'the activity of reasoning', and its relatives like *ratiocinatiuus* and *ratiocinor*, come into medieval Latin from the context of rhetoric, most notably in *De inventione*, I.31.51ff, the discussion of arguing from inferences, whence it would commonly have made its way into scholars' disputation. And the family of verbs for composition derived from *trahere*, 'move along, drag', has the same model: *tractare, modus tractandi*, etc. As the juvenile Cicero wrote, in a sentence foundational for both dialectic and rhetoric in the schools of the twelfth century: 'Omnis igitur argumentatio aut per inductionem tractanda est aut per ratiocinationem' (*De inventione*, I.51). Both *inductio* (inference) and *ratiocinatio* (deduction) are used in this sentence with reference to rhetorical strategies. 'Ratiocination' is an argument conducted from initial premises, and in *De inventione* refers to a 'rhetorical syllogism', or enthymeme (it is worth remembering that *sullogismos* in Greek just means arguing, and is not restricted to arguments of a particular logical form). 'Induction' is demonstrated at length by Cicero, with reference to composing the *exordium* and the need first to capture one's audience's good will (*captatio benevolentiae*). 'Induction' is a method of succesive inferences whereby a listener is led along, through a series of propositions with which he agrees, to a conclusion which he would have otherwise resisted or disallowed (Cicero identifies this method as used with particular effectiveness by Socrates in Plato's dialogues). It is a method, Cicero says, best used in 'difficult' cases, such as where an orator needs to gain consent for a matter against the interests or common beliefs of the audience, or where his client or cause is odious.

The discussion of induction included a particularly indirect method called *insinuatio*, 'insinuation'. It received much attention in medieval commentaries on both Ciceronian manuals, and in these commentaries the basic idea that an auditor is 'led' or 'drawn' or 'guided' along a determined path by the structures of the speech is still very evident. It was not a meaningless dead metaphor used unknowingly. An example taken from an eleventh-century commentary, known from its first words as 'Ut ait Quintilianus', makes the point:

Likewise 'insinuation' is the beginning of a rhetorical speech secretly seducing [*literally*, crawling under] the minds of the audience. Whence it is termed *insinuatio*. Especially insinuation is secrecy [caused] by the power of the *tenor*, because it greatly bends about and softens up the hearer. For we say 'to insinuate' is 'to curve around'.[41]

This characterization recalls Fortunatianus' and Martianus Capella's *ductus subtilis* (used when one does not intend what one is apparently saying), but with a generous visual addition from that master seducer, the *serpens persuadens* who, in the common iconography of the scene, winds sinuously about the Tree as he talks to Eve in Eden, his very pose the visual counterpart of *insinuatio*. More noteworthy still is the agency, *vis*, attributed in this commentary to the *tenor* of this trope – the *vis tenoris* produces the secrecy (*occultum*) that creeps along under the ostensible words, then 'winds about' and 'softens up' the unwary hearer. *Insinuatio* is a trope for the beginning of a speech – its surreptitious, seductive, duplicitous nature guides the movement of the whole which follows, and when it is used, the auditor (like poor, ignorant Eve) is lost in error before s/he even gets started.

As principles both of analysis and of practice, *ductus* and *tenor*, *modus* and *color* – the sustained movement and its particular variations along the way – are essential to all medieval arts. The terms were employed with full deliberation as components of a theory of artistic practice, though often the terms overlap or even substitute for one another during their long history. *Modus tractandi*, for example, a phrase more common during the later Middle Ages than *tenor agendi*, can be used for both the overall and particular movements in a work.[42] But whatever the conflation of terms, the fundamental concept of a work as a journey to a goal, with a main track and various byways, remained in common use. Two final examples will demonstrate this point. The great Franciscan preacher, St Bonaventura (d. 1274), introduced his method for reading (and preaching) Scripture by likening it to a sort of great building having several formal dimensions: width, length, height, depth. It is, he wrote, 'multiform'. But its multiform nature contains both various ways (or perhaps 'colorations') of discourse and also one original course common to all that runs through the whole:

On Holy Scripture's own way of proceeding:

Wherefore in such multiformity of knowledge, which is contained in the width, length, height and depth of Scripture, there is one common original way of moving forward, within which is contained a narrative way, preceptual, prohibitory, exhortatory, counselling [*for* praedicativus], threatening, promising, blaming and praising [ways]. And all these ways are subsumed within one original direction, and to this certainly, quite directly.[43]

Notice how Bonaventura attributes agency to Scripture itself: there is a *modus procedendi* belonging to the written book (*ipsius scripture*), and it is found by way of its 'original direction' (*modus authenticus*), which in turn contains multiple other textual modes, nine in all. One could think of it (and perhaps Bonaventura did) as a kind of polyphony based on a sustaining *tenor*, or perhaps as a *pictura* formed of many colours and shapes directing us within and through the great building of Scripture. He defines these nine modes of style in terms of their effect on an audience, the different ways in which someone 'is moved by' them (*movetur*), thus underscoring their agency in what he sees as Scripture's core activity of persuading us to believe. Because we are not persuaded to become good by rational consideration alone (*nuda consideratio*) but more by the inclination and direction of our desires and will, 'Holy Scripture must be composed in the way by which we will be most persuaded'.[44]

A courtly French treatise on rhetoric (1463), composed mostly in verse, divides the procedures of rhetoric among twelve handmaids (*dames*), each of whom gives a speech (termed *enseigne*, a rhetorical 'character' or *ethopoeia*), in which she describes her tasks within the whole compositional endeavour. Called *Les douze dames de rhétorique*, it is best known now for its programme of illustrations of the Twelve Handmaids, planned by the authors, who depicted each performing the tasks typical of her assignment.[45] The eleventh in their order is called 'Deduccion loable', 'praiseworthy planning'; she comes just before 'Glorious Achievement', the fully clothed, coloured and achieved work. *Deduccion* is shown (reproduced as the cover image of this book) as a carpenter and a builder – not an academic clerk – with her ruler, T-square, mallet and wedge tools. Beside her is a table with an open book (with another on the floor in front of her), surrounded by a host of small stones, carefully laid out and sorted. Through the opening behind her are two unfinished buildings, one perhaps a church, one perhaps a tower, each with their wooden frames visible. They are complex structures, as complex as the books which *Deduccion loable* has also made. How to translate *deduccion* in this particular context? She is, of course, arrangement, but defined in particular ways that direct her duties precisely. The figure is shown not yet working manually but planning, her finger thoughtfully to her head. She has stopped to previsualize her constructions, to plan and only then to execute (thus heeding the advice of Geoffrey of Vinsauf). Her posture shows rhetorical *consilium*. But she also represents *ductus*, and what is shown in this picture, I think, is just that moment when *consilium* gives birth (as Fortunatianus said) to the governing intention of the whole work, expressed in its formal arrangements, which are shown in the painting as the tesserated stones, the timber-frame structures, and the opened books, each formally laid out and partly written. Her character says this plainly. Her speech begins with a Latin aphorism, derived from Psalm 44:5, 'Et deducet me mirabiliter dextera mea' [and she will lead me in a wonderful way by my right hand]. *Deduccion*'s task is to plan, yes, but she serves as guide to the plan *within the work*; she conducts us through the whole from its start to its end. As she says: 'To speak of my offices / I undertake to sort the essentials, / the diverse, simple things, / into an integrated work ... . /And there [within the framework, as just described] I arrange my ornaments / my flowers, my colours, my green lawns / in order to attain by hard labours / the goal encompassed in my intention [*corage*].[46] *Deduccion* is the spirit of the work, its *corage*, an agent who is both (as *dispositio*) the director who shapes the integral work, and (as *tenor/ductus*) the guide through her creation, as she leads us by the hand within the marvellous particulars of colour and sound she has assembled. As an image of rhetorical *ductus*, *Deduccion loable* belongs also in Bonaventura's scriptural cathedral, providing rational direction through a work always filled with various music, colour and movement, so that we can surely know how it all goes and how it all fits together as it moves us – *satis recte* – to its conclusion.

NOTES

1 My reference is to Archibald MacLeish's *Ars Poetica*: 'A poem should be palpable and mute / as a globed fruit.' Contrast what Geoffrey of Vinsauf says in his *Poetria nova*, discussed below. A similar contrast has been made often before in discussions of the medieval arts, and should make one seriously doubt the reputation they continue popularly to have for being 'static'.

2 Geoffrey of Vinsauf, *Poetria nova* (c. 1202, with additions made after 1212), in E. Faral (ed.), *Les arts poétiques du 12e et 13e siècles* (1924; rpt. Paris 1962); *Poetria nova of Geoffrey of Vinsauf*, trans. by M. F. Nims (Toronto: PIMS, 1967). All further quotations are from this edition and translation.

3 Much has been written about Geoffrey of Vinsauf, the most widely taught of all medieval masters of composition in the curriculum of rhetoric; his treatise was considered as a work of rhetoric and influenced training in dictamen and preaching as well as 'poetry' in the way we now think of it. *Poetria nova's* influence and dissemination began as soon as the text was composed at the start of the thirteenth century and continued into the sixteenth century and later. See M. C. Woods, *Classroom Commentaries: Teaching the* Poetria nova *across Medieval and Renaissance Europe* (Columbus: Ohio State University Press, forthcoming). On Geoffrey's own sources, see E. Gallo, *The* Poetria nova *and its Sources in Early Rhetorical Doctrine* (The Hague: Mouton, 1971).

4 Quintilian, *Inst. orat.*, XI.2.21.

5 There are more details about this treatise in K. Rivers, 'Memory and Medieval Preaching', *Viator*, 30 (1999): 253–84. For editions and further reading, see also K. Rivers, 'Francesc Eiximenis', in M. Carruthers and J. Ziolkowski (eds.), *The Medieval Craft of Memory* (Philadelphia: University of Pennsylvania Press, 2002): 189–204.

6 Translated by K. Rivers, in *The Medieval Craft of Memory*, 200–1.

7 See Augustine, *De doctrina Christiana*, II.7; I discussed this passage, and the underlying procedures which dominated monastic meditation exercises, in *The Craft of Thought: meditation, Rhetoric, and the making of Images, 400–1200* (Cambridge University Press, 1998), 66–81.

8 Peter of Celle, *On Affliction and Reading*, in *La spiritualité de Pierre de Celle*, ed. J. Leclercq (Paris: Vrin, 1946), tran. H. Feiss, *Peter of Celle: Selected Works* (Kalamazoo: Cistercian Publications, 1987), 137–8.

9 Carruthers, *The Craft of Thought*, 109.

10 *St Augustine, Expositions of the Psalms*, trans. M. Boulding, 6 vols. (Hyde Park, NY: New City Press, 2000–4), vol. II, 246–7; from the Latin text ed. E. Dekkers, CCSL 38 (Turnhout: Brepols, 1956). I discussed this passage at some length in *The Craft of Thought*, 251–4.

11 Fortunatianus' exact dates are not known, but he preceded Martianus Capella, who borrowed from his work and who wrote about rhetoric probably in the 430s (St Augustine died in 430). Others among his probable contemporaries were both John Cassian and the rhetoric master C. Iulius Victor. His *Ars rhetorica* was edited in *RLM*, but more recently and authoritatively by L. Calboli Montefusco, *Consulti Fortunati ars rhetorica* (Bologna: Patrón, 1979), who in her preface brings together what little is known about him (5–20), including the evidence for his Christianity, and who argues persuasively that his given name was Consultus, not Chirius (or C. Chirius, or C. Consultus, as various scribes and editors have called him over the centuries). Fortunatianus' theory of *ductus* is described as 'unusual' by G. A. Kennedy, *Classical Rhetoric and its Christian and Secular Tradition* (Chapel Hill: University of North Carolina Press, 1980), 105, but I hope to show that it was more commonplace than Kennedy allows. It was revived, using Fortunatianus' own categories, by George of Trebizond (d. 1486) and became part of a Venetian debate about the practicality of rhetoric as opposed to a doctrinaire 'Ciceronian' humanism which saw rhetoric in more theoretical and academic fashion: see V. Cox, 'Rhetoric and Humanism in Quattrocento Venice', *Renaissance Quarterly*, 56 (2003): 652–94. Fortunatianus' rhetoric was often copied in the Middle Ages together with a work on rhetoric then attributed to St Augustine; thus, it shared the aura of the master (the pseudo-Augustine's rhetoric is also in *RLM*). In addition, Fortunatianus was named by Cassiodorus as a master of rhetoric, especially on *memoria* and delivery. See J. M. Miller *et al.* (eds.), *Readings in Medieval Rhetoric* (Bloomington: Indiana University Press, 1973), in which appears a portion of Fortunatianus' discussion of *ductus*. All Latin quotations are from Calboli Montefusco's edition; I have cited her chapter and section numbers, followed by the page and line numbers in her edition; translations are mine.

12 Cicero, *Orator*, 39: 'Alter [=Herodotus] enim sine ullis salebris quasi sedatus amnis fluit, alter [=Thucydides] … de bellicis rebus canit etiam quodam modo bellicum.' See also the quotation and comments in n. 20 below.

13 As in Quintilian, *Inst. orat*, X.2.2; *ductus* as 'directed movement' of several kinds is a concept well developed in Quintilian; see the citations in *OLD*, under *ductus*, and n. 21 below.

14 Ambrosius Mediolanensis, *Expositio in psalmi cxviii,* ed. L. F. Pizzolato (Rome: Città nuova, 1987): 'sit ergo tibi fides itineris tui praeuia, sit tibi iter scriptura diuina; bonus est caelestis ductus eloquii'.

15 Fortunatianus, *Ars rhet.,* I.6 (71.20–72.2): 'Quid est ductus? quo modo tota causa agenda sit. Quid interest inter ductum et modum? ductus est totius orationis, modus vero partis alicuius in oratione.'

16 Martianus Capella, *De nuptiis Philologiae et Mercurii (De rethorice),* V.470–1; edn. A. Dick (1925; corr. edn Stuttgart: Teubner, 1969), 235.1–235.25. Remigius of Auxerre (d. 908), in commenting on the whole of *De nuptiis* also defines these terms, *ductus, consilium, tenor,* etc. in ways that show that the concepts were understood by and viable for him: see his *Commentum in Martianus Capella,* ed. C. E. Lutz, 2 vols. (Leiden: Brill, 1965), vol., II, 89–92 especially. William T. Flynn applies some of these types of *ductus* to particular medieval liturgies in his essay '*Ductus figuratus et subtilis*', later in this volume.

17 Cicero, *Orator,* 21: 'isque [= the middle style] uno tenore, ut aiunt, in dicendo fluit'. Peter of Celle's characterization of the flow of his emotions as he vividly read Scripture is a medieval case in point, depicting his reading as having a general tenor (moving through Scripture) with several stylistic modes within it, each of which has its own emotional coloration or mood. The essays by Martin Camargo and Jan Ziolkowski in this volume underscore the continuing importance of imagining performance (with speech and movement), even when one looks silently. Dante's *visibile parlare,* 'visible speaking' which he 'hears' from the marble relief figures he gazes on in the Terrace of the Proud (*Purgatorio,* 10.95), draws upon this medieval commonplace.

18 Cf. *OLD,* under *tenor,* with citations from Cicero and others for the meaning 'sustained movement', and citations from Seneca, Ovid, Statius and others for 'way of proceeding'.

19 In a discussion of barbarisms and misspeaking, Quintilian noted that an old spelling of *tenores* was *tonores,* and this, he said, presumably was from the Greek word *tonos; Inst. orat.,* I.5.22. 'Tone' (as of voice) was indeed a meaning of *tenor* in Latin, presumably reflecting this conflation; see *OLD,* under *tenor,* 5.

20 Cicero, *Orator,* 57: 'tam suauis varietas perfecta in cantibus ... Est autem etiam in dicendo quidam cantus obscurior.' He defines rhetorical *actio* (delivery) as 'corporis quaedam eloquentia' in *Orator,* 55. Later in this treatise he develops at length an anatomy of the *cursus* or the metrical figures used in prose; most of this work was known to the Middle Ages, and proficiency in *cursus* became a focus of *ars dictaminis,* training in court, legal and diplomatic speaking, using model letters designed to be performed aloud, as Martin Camargo demonstrates in his essay in this volume. Clark Maines discusses the inscription of the word *ductus* on a tablet marking a processional route within a Cistercian church in 'Word and Image – Meaning and Function: The *Aque Ductus* Relief at Santa Maria de Alcobaça', *Citeaux: Commentarii Cisterciencis,* 57.1–2 (2006): 5–43.

21 See M. Carruthers, 'Late antique rhetoric, Early Monasticism, and the Revival of School Rhetoric', in C. D. Lanham (ed.), *Latin Grammar and Rhetoric: Classical Theory and Medieval Practice* (London: Continuum Books, 2002), 239–57, and the citations to Quintilian therein.

22 Fortunatianus, *Ars rhet*,. I.8 (74.22–75.1): 'Hos omnes ductus plerique quo nomine vocant? figuratos. Nos ergo quare nominibus separamus? Quoniam singuli ductus diversa et vi et ratione consistunt nec debent uno nomine nuncupari, quorum et vis et ratio non una est.'

23 L. Calboli Montefusco, '*Ductus* and *color*: The Right Way to Compose a Suitable Speech', *Rhetorica*, 21 (2003): 113–31. She points as well (122) to several grammatical treatises, including Servius' commentary on Virgil, which employ *ductus* as an analytical category of style – Servius speaks of 'figurati colores' as 'optimus ductus' in reference to a passage of the *Aeneid*. The passage cited later (see n. 32 below) from the Latin translation by Julian of Eclanum (d. 454, Augustine's Pelagian adversary) of the preacher and bishop, Theodore of Mopsuestos' (d. 428, yet another contemporary of Augustine) Psalms commentary makes similar use of the term *ductus*. His phrase *pastoralis ductus* characterizes 'a pastoral way' of composing. Theodore was a student of the great pagan rhetor of Antioch, Libanius, and both he and Julian had a rhetorical education, as did Augustine – these three, like John Cassian, Theodore's friend and fellow student, John Chrysostom, and so many others of the Church fathers, all spoke and composed within the late antique educational milieu that also included Fortunatianus. Calboli Montefusco wants to restrict the meaning of *ductus* solely to Fortunatianus' particular types, based on 'the speaker's intention of being open or not in pleading the entire case'. But Fortunatianus' contemporaries used *ductus* as a term in rhetoric in less restricted ways.

24 Cicero, *De oratore,* III. 217: 'Nam voces ut chordae sunt intentae .... Nullum est enim horum generum, quod non arte ac moderatione tractetur. Hi sunt actori, ut pictori, expositi ad variandum colores.'

25 Cicero, *Orator,* 134: 'Quibus [luminibus] sic abundabit, ut verbum ex ore nullum nisi elegans aut grave exeat, ex omnique genere frequentissimae translationes erunt, quod eae propter similitudinem transferunt animos et referunt ac movent huc et illuc, qui motus cogitationis celeriter agitatus per se ipse delectat.'

26 Fortunatianus, *Ars rhet.,* I.8 (75.8–10): 'Ductus idem semper est utriusque partis? non. Quid ita? quoniam ductus ex consilio nascitur, consilium autem non omnium semper est unum.'

27 Fortunatianus, *Ars rhet.,* I.8 (75.19–21): 'Consilium a ductu quo differt? quod consilium voluntatis est, ductus ipsius orationis. Item quod ductus ex consilio nascitur, non consilium ex ductu.'

28 This was a major argument of *The Craft of Thought*, as I sought to discern a monastic tradition of composition, which certainly owes much to the ancient rhetors but is also distinct. For Cassian's use of *scopus*, as well as other terms found also in Fortunatianus like *ductus* and *modus*, see especially. 69–91.

It may be relevant in considering their use in rhetoric at this time that Fortunatianus was a Christian, and also a (somewhat older?) contemporary of John Cassian as well as of Augustine.

29 Augustine, *De civitate Dei* ed. B. Dombard and A. Kalb, (1921; rpt. Stuttgart: Teubner, 1981, XIX.19): 'Graecum est enim atque inde ductum uocabulum [= episcopus], quod ille qui praeficitur eis quibus praeficitur superintendit, curam scilicet eorum gerens; σκοπως quippe intentio est; ergo επισκοπειν, si uelimus, latine superintendere possumus dicere.' [This word 'bishop' is borrowed from Greek, for he who is set in charge superintends those of whom he is in charge, that is, caring for them; *skopōs* indeed is 'intention'; wherefore *episkopein,* if we like, we may say in Latin is 'to super-intend.'] *Superintendo* is a late-fourth-century neologism, and this instance in *The City of God* is one of the first recorded for it (perhaps it is even Augustine's coinage): see the citations in C. T. Lewis and C. Short, *A Latin Dictionary* (Oxford University Press, 1879), under *superintendo.* Many English translations of this passage render *skopōs* as 'sight', and *superintendere* as 'oversee', thereby erasing Augustine's original understanding of these terms. These translations derive from the late-nineteenth-century translation project supervised by M. Dods, which was adopted in the influential series of 'Nicene and Ante-Nicene Fathers', now readily available online; it is to be hoped that this unfortunate misinterpretation is not perpetuated.

30 Fortunatianus, *Ars rhet.,* I. 8 (75.14–18): 'Quid, cum diversum consilium fuerit utriusque partis? erit diversus et ductus. Quid? modus et scopos similiter ut ductus? non, quoniam modus est ductus *in* parte orationis, scopus autem id quod omnis efficit ductus.' [What occurs when there may be a different plan for each part? The *ductus* will also be diverse. How? Are *modus* and *scopus* the same as the *ductus*? No, for *modus* is the *ductus* of a section of the oration, *scopus* however is that which the whole *ductus* effects.] The essay in this volume by Paul Crossley on *ductus* in Chartres cathedral demonstrates these relationships very well.

31 Quintilian, *Inst. orat,* III.1.5: 'propterea quod plurimi auctores, quamvis eodem tenderent, diversas tamen vias munierunt atque in suam quisque *induxit* sequentes'.

32 Theodore of Mopsuestos (translated by Julian of Erclanum), commentary on Psalm 99:3, in *Expositio in Psalmos*, ed. L. de Coninck, CCSL 88A (Turnhout: Brepols, 1977), 326. See also n. 23 above.

33 'Qua te laude canam? Verbis quibus ora resoluam? / Materia fandi ductus panegyricus extat' [How shall I celebrate you with praise? With what words shall I loosen my lips? / In regard to the material of artful speaking, the *ductus pangyricus* stands out]; H. Hagen (ed.), *Carmina medii aevi maximam partem inedita ex bibliothecis Helveticis* (1877; rpt. Nieuwkoop: B. de Graaf, 1959), 131.15–16. The anonymous poem, beginning 'Constantine, meis opus est non promere uerbis', was composed at St-Rémi in the 980s. Many thanks to Jan Ziolkowski for passing this citation on to me.

34 Examples can be found in abundance in A. J. Minnis and A. B. Scott (eds.), *Medieval Literary Theory and Criticism: The Commentary Tradition, c. 1100– c. 1375* (Oxford University Press, 1988), 12–36, mostly translated from R. B. C. Huygens, (ed.) *Accessus ad auctores* (Leiden: Brill, 1970). The *Physiologus* (or *Bestiary*), for example, which had no author (in our sense of the word) nonetheless has *intentio auctoris* (17); in the case of named authors, the life of the poet (*vita poetae*) is treated quite separately from his different books, each of which is said to possess a distinct *intentio auctoris*. Something of this idea informs M. Baxandall, *Patterns of Intention* (New Haven: Yale University Press, 1985), which considers the role of 'intentionality' in analysing historical artifacts. When considering art objects, Baxandall wrote, intention is a 'purposefulness' or 'intentiveness' not only on the part of the human artist 'but even more in the historical objects themselves' (40–1).

35 Quintilian is the one who most often invokes the agency of words and syntax as something separable from the agency of the speaker or composer, and in the Latin rhetorical tradition he should be credited as its most thorough exponent before Fortunatianus. See V. Cox, 'Rhetoric and Humanism'.

36 In this context, the Latin phrase *via rationis* renders Latin–Greek *methodos/-us*, 'method', a compound formed of *meta–* and *ódos*, 'way'. See the commentary of E. M. Cope, *The Rhetoric of Aristotle*, rev. J. E. Sandys, 3 vols. (Cambridge University Press, 1877), vol. I, 2–3, on Aristotle's use, in *Rhetoric* I. 2, of the verb *ódopoieō*, literally 'to make a road'.

37 E. Stump, *Dialectic and its Place in the Development of Medieval Logic* (Ithaca, NY: Cornell University Press, 1989); see also T. Reinhardt, *Cicero's Topica* (Oxford University Press, 2003), especially 18–35, on understandings of *topos* in ancient rhetoric and dialectic. See also Quintilian, *Inst. orat.*, V.10, for additional discussion of the 'places of argument' and their use in (forensic) rhetoric.

38 C. Mews, 'Peter Abelard on Dialectic, Rhetoric, and the Principles of Argument', in C. Mews *et al.* (eds.), *Rhetoric and Renewal in the Latin West 1100–1540* (Turnhout: Brepols, 2003), 37–53. Wiliam T. Flynn analyses Abelard's teaching on rhetoric and its relation to the liturgy he devised for Heloise's Paraclete in his essay below.

39 'Abelard on Rhetoric', ed. K. M. Fredburg, in Mews *et al.* (eds.),*Rhetoric and Renewal*, 55–80.

40 Ed. Fredborg, 62: 'Sunt autem circumstantiae quidam loci rethorici, unde ducuntur [P dicuntur] coniecturae, hoc est extrahuntur coniecturalia argumenta quae videlicet suspicionem generant.'

41 'Insinuatio itaque est prima pars orationis rethorice animos auditorum occulte subrepens. Unde insinuatio appellatur. Etenim insinuatio est occultum tenoris vi, quia multum incurvat et emollit auditorem. Incurvare enim dicimus insinuare'; in V. Cox and J. O. Ward, (eds.), *The Rhetoric of Cicero in its Medieval and Early Renaissance Commentary Tradition* (Leiden: Brill, 2006), 435.2. The expression *vis tenoris* invokes the idea developed by Fortunatianus (and, via Martianus Capella, knowable as well to the author

of this commentary); see my previous discussion. The analysis of *insinu-atio* 'formed a staple of the ancient and medieval rhetorical schools,' as Cox and Ward point out (430) in their Appendix, in which they include the whole (rather lengthy) discussion of *insinuatio* from 'Ut ait Quintilianus' (430–42).

42 See A. J. Minnis, *Medieval Theory of Authorship* (Philadelphia: University of Pennsylvania Press, 1988), 118–59; many more examples of *modus tractandi*, *modus agendi*, and *tenor agendi*, used interchangeably, can be found in the commentaries discussed by Woods, *Classroom Commentaries*.

43 St Bonaventura, *Breviloquium*, par. 5 in *Opera omnia*, 10 vols. (Quaracchi: Typographia Collegii S. Bonaventurae 1882–1902) vol. 5, 202–8;: 'De modo procedendi ipsius sacrae Scripture.In tanta igitur multiformitate sapientiae, quae continetur in ipsius sacrae Scripturae latitudine, longitudine, altitudine et profundo, unus est communis modus procedendi authenticus, videlicet intra quem continetur modus narrativus, praeceptorius, prohibitivus, exhor-tativus, praedicativus, comminatorius, promissivus, deprecatorius et laudati-vus. Et omnes hi modi sub uno modo authentico reponuntur, et hoc quidem satis recte.'The structural dimensions of Scripture are described in par. 1–4 as *latitudo, longitudo, sublimitas* and *profunditas*. In par. 5, Bonaventura defines his *modus praedicativus* as 'benefit shown to themselves', that is, to the audi-ence: I have rendered this word in this context as 'counselling', though both 'preaching' and 'predicting' would be possible meanings. The editors record two variants of their reading *praedicativus, praedicatorius* and *praedictivus*. The meaning Bonaventura gives the word here is somewhat unusual. My thanks to Dr Christian Leitmeier, who first guided me to this reference. Bonaventura was invoking a standard Christian trope, patristic in origin, of the Church as a building, such as Noah's Ark or as the Tabernacle or as Solomon's Temple. Hugh of St Victor (d. 1141) wrote an ekphrastic descrip-tion of the Church as Noah's Ark: it is translated by J. Weiss in Carruthers and Ziolkowski (eds.), *The Medieval Craft of Memory*, 41–70.

44 Bonaventura, *Breviloquium*, par. 5: 'Quia enim haec doctrina est ut boni fiamus et salvemur et hoc non fit per nudam considerationem sed potius per inclinationem voluntatis ideo scriptura divina eo modo debuit tradi quo modo magis possemus inclinari.'

45 It was edited most recently by D. Cowling, *Les douze dames de rhétorique* (Geneva: Droz, 2002), from Cambridge University Library MS Nn 3.2; all quotations are from this text. This manuscript is the authors' copy, executed by Jean de Montferrant. Cowling has also written extensively about the architecture metaphor for textual production, *Building the Text: Architecture as Metaphor in Late Medieval and Early Modern France* (Oxford: Clarendon Press, 1998). *Les douze dames* is composed as a literary *débat* among the courtiers Jean Robertet and George Chastelain in particular, and also Jean de Montferrant, all associated with the Bourbon court of Jean II and that of Philippe le Bon of Burgundy, among whom there were many family ties. As Cowling notes, this familial matrix shaped the work in important ways,

affording the ground for its ongoing conversations on the nature of rhetoric and poetry. For a different kind of 'familiar rhetoric', expressed through the medium of illuminated books, see the essay in this volume by Lucy Freeman Sandler on the Bohun family's manuscripts.

46 *Les douze dames de rhétorique*, 24.17–20, 29–32: 'Donc, pour parler de mes droitures / Je sers d'assortir les natures, / les diverses especes pures, / En une integrité d'ouvrage; … Et là j'assortis mes parures, / Mes fleurs, mes couleurs, mes verdures, / Jusqu'à partaindre en labeurs dures / La fin comprise en mon corage.' Thanks to Jeanette Beer for help with this translation, though any fault in it is mine alone.

CHAPTER 9

Ductus *and* memoria

Chartres cathedral and the workings of rhetoric*

Paul Crossley

It is a truth universally acknowledged that Chartres cathedral is the supreme example of an ensemble of architecture, sculpture and painting to have come down to us from the Middle Ages. With its myriad sculpted figures, its two thousand square metres of stained glass and its homogeneous architecture – all completed within the comparatively short period of some forty years, from 1194 to around 1235 – Chartres comes closest to our image of the authentic medieval cathedral.[1] Writing just before 1898, Émile Mâle, the grand master of medieval Christian iconography, saw Chartres, and its northern French sister cathedrals, as the flowers of French national art and the lucid embodiments of the scholastic habit of mind: in its organized figures and its encyclopaedic ambition, Chartres was a sacred book, a *summa* in stone, a beautiful catechism of Christian doctrine.[2]

But catechisms, like cathedrals, are not unchanging monuments to absolute truth; they are subject to the contingencies of history, revision and reception. Mâle never questioned how the book of the cathedral might have been experienced as the activator of thought and feeling; what difficulties attended its massive translation of the verbal into the visual; and what wider implications its colossal expansion of imagery might have had for the place of 'the Great Church' – the aisled basilica – in high medieval society.[3] Mâle's monolithic vision was theological, not historical.[4] To him the cathedral was simply a lower form of sacred literature, the passive illustration of texts, what he called 'a sacred writing whose elements every artist had to learn'.[5] And behind Mâle's magnificent *summa* lies the felt presence of some ideal cathedral, existing for Mâle, as it did for Viollet-le-Duc, and much later for Hans Sedlmayr, above the accidents of time and place.[6]

The aim of this essay is to move from the cathedral as text to the cathedral as experience, and to explore the relationship between aesthetics and performance in a thirteenth-century Great Church. This will involve shifting our gaze from author to audience, from *what* is said and shown to *how* and *why* it is shown. It also entails – in the context of the cathedral's presentation of all the arts in a single arena – making connections between various art forms – including architecture, sculpture, metalwork, stained glass and liturgical 'theatre' – and the rules of rhetoric. Analogies between rhetorical practice and the arts are found from the beginnings of ancient writing, and they continued to be employed fruitfully right through the Middle Ages. As categories of ancient rhetoric they offered theorists of art a valid set of analytical terms that could be applied fruitfully to the shaping and working of medieval art and architecture. Two such rhetorical categories are, I suggest, particularly effective in understanding a great cathedral: the concept of *ductus* – flow, movement, direction, a journey, or 'way', and the category of *memoria* – memory, in the broadest sense of cognitive thinking and composing. Because *ductus* is essentially about performance, or what some anthropological theorists call 'performativity', the first part of this paper concentrates on the liturgy of Chartres – 'liturgy' in the broadest sense as all forms of corporate worship or devotion. It is extraordinary that in the vast bibliography of Chartres (in 1989 there were more than 3,464 publications)[7] little or no attempt – with one shining exception – has been made to correlate the imagery of the building with its liturgy.[8] This is an especially odd omission when a new ordinal was written for the cathedral between 1225 and 1235, at the same time as the later stages of the cathedral's construction and the installation of its images. We will suggest that liturgy and imagery at Chartres worked sometimes in concert, mutually enhancing each other's shared meanings; and we want further to underline that in this correlation of image and ritual, liturgical *movement* was critical, for processions and their stations were the symbols of the Church's journey to her celestial home – journeys whose meanings were marked out and ramified by images. The spatial and sequential nature of architecture and its imagery lent itself eloquently to liturgical movement and to the concepts of transformation and culmination which inform all processional liturgies.

The second aspect of this enquiry involves the mechanisms that conditioned the 'reading' of imagery at Chartres. The main educational milieu of the early Middle Ages, the monastic schools, had trained understanding, memory and contemplation – *affectus* – by visual means, that is by placing information and subject matter into visual diagrams, sometimes using geometrical frameworks. Not all such *picturae* were actually drawn – many were meditational 'fantasies': part of the mental memory techniques of the monk, the *memoria spiritalis*. But whether mental or drawn, the important point here was the conflation of memory with visual aids, for it opened up the possibility for art, at first in the more private world of the monastery, and then in the public and lay forum of the cathedral, to assume a vital role in the ordering, contemplating and memorizing of encyclopaedic truth. This activity is closely bound up with the rhetorical faculty of memory, of *memoria* – not just recalling (as we usually think of the term) but in the broad, classical and medieval, cognitive sense of thinking and categorizing.

The notion of *ductus*, of 'con*ducting*' oneself through the spaces of architecture, guided along the way by sacred images or objects, is essential to any experience of a thirteenth-century cathedral. Every great church had its own sacred topography, its 'cognitive map',[9] its altars, chapels, shrines, screens, miraculous images, between which its laity and clergy moved, sometimes informally, at other times in a more or less prescribed order. The golden principle of this cathedral *ductus* is that the imagery on the exterior of the church, in the sculpture of the porches and portals, acts as a preparation for the imagery, the sacred places, and in some cases the ritual, inside the church. Of the sixty-four martyrs and confessors sculpted on the south transept porches and portals at Chartres, all of them appear in the Chartres ordinal or calendar.[10] The three great portals of the south transept at Chartres, the most public entrances to the cathedral since they face the town and the castle of the Counts of Chartres, are dedicated to the martyrs (Figure 9.1, A), the apostles (Figure 9.1, B) and the confessors (Figure 9.1, C) – just the arrangement we find for the three deep radiating chapels of the chevet (Figure 9.1, F = martyrs, G = apostles, E = confessors).[11] The right hand portal of the south transept, the confessors portal (Figure 9. 1, C), provides another example of this principle of interior and exterior integration. Its sculpture shows the stories and statues of St Nicholas of Bari, St Martin of Tours and St Gilles (Figure 9.2) – themes which reappear inside the cathedral as three altars: St Martin (Figure 9.1, D), St Gilles (? Figure 9.1, P) and St Nicholas (Figure 9.1, E) and two windows: St Nicholas (Figure 9.1, no. 14), and St Martin (Figure 9.1, no. 20).[12] And this arrangement introduces us to a second facet of *ductus*: the power of a group of related images to form a sequence or 'pathway' in front of, through and within the church: in this instance a pathway from the portal to the altar of St Martin in the south aisle of the choir (9.1, D), then to the altar of St Gilles (probably in the southernmost radiating chapel (9.1, P)), followed by the altar of St Nicholas in the next, easterly, chapel, an altar on which was placed a statue of the saint (9.1, E).[13] This 'pathway' must have been one of the busiest in

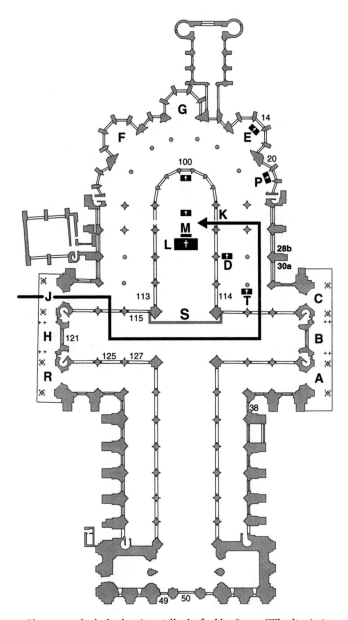

Figure 9.1 Chartres cathedral, plan (specially drafted by Stuart Whatling). A = martyrs portal, B = apostles portal, C = confessors portal, D = altar of St Martin, E = altar of St Nicholas, F = martyrs chapel, G = apostles chapel, H = Coronation of the Virgin portal, J = Infancy portal, K = putative entrance in choir screen from south aisle to sanctuary and feretory, L, M = high altar and shrine of the tunic, P = ? altar of St Gilles, R = Job portal, S = choir screen, T = altar of Our Lady of the Snows

Figure 9.2 Chartres cathedral, Confessors portal, tympanum

the medieval cathedral, for it marks the shortest route between the exterior of the church and the goal of the Chartres pilgrimage, the *sancta Camisa,* the sacred tunic supposedly worn by the Virgin at the birth of Christ, and displayed in a reliquary (the so-called *scrinium*) behind the high altar (Figure 9.1, M). The special associations of this route with pilgrimage are underlined by the importance of St Martin's and St Gilles' shrines on the routes to Santiago de Compostela, and by the sculpture in the tympanum of the confessors portal, showing pilgrims being healed by the curative oils flowing from the shrine and body of St Nicholas (Figure 9.2). The animated statues of this portal – hunting, confessing, blessing, listening – are like the Church's 'Living Stones' of St Peter's first Epistle (1 Peter 2:4–9); and they begin a sequence of related images or *loci* which accompany us – even guide us – on our way to the shrine.[14]

A more complicated pilgrims' pathway, marked out also by images, can be reconstructed in the north aisle of the crypt of Chartres. The starting point here may well have been the right hand portal of the west front, a portal belonging to the so-called Portail Royal, the triple

Figure 9.3 Chartres cathedral, Portail Royal, general view

portal ensemble of *c.* 1140–5 which survived the fire of 1194, a fire which destroyed the eleventh-century cathedral and ushered in the construction of the present High Gothic church[15] (Figures 9.3 and 9.4). As we will see, the central portal of the Portail Royal was, like other tripartite cathedral entrances, opened only for major ceremonial events; the side portals were the entrances and exits for everyday use. The right hand, 'Incarnation' portal has a tympanum dominated by one of the iconic leitmotifs of Chartres, the sculpture of the *Sedes Sapientiae*, the 'Throne of Wisdom', where the infant Christ is hierarchically enthroned in the lap of his mother[16] (Figure 9.4). This image is repeated – like a musical variation – in different places and materials throughout the cathedral. Its most ancient and mythic manifestation was the late eleventh- or early twelfth-century wooden cult statue of the Virgin (once containing relics and surviving only in the form of seventeenth-century copies and engravings) placed in the eleventh-century crypt, in the chapel of Notre-Dame-sous-Terre, a chapel extensively rebuilt in the seventeenth century, and at present situated towards the eastern end of the crypt's northern

Figure 9.4 Chartres cathedral, Portail Royal, Incarnation portal

corridor (Figure 9.5). This, however, was the general site of the medieval
chapel, which lay on the north side of the crypt,[17] and also of the mythic
altar of the Druids and the sacred well, the 'Puits des Saints Forts', into
which some of the earliest Chartres martyrs were supposedly thrown to
their deaths (Figure 9.6, A). In keeping with this emphasis on the early
Christian history of Chartres, an altar to Saints Savinien and Potentien,
first-century evangelists of Gaul and of Chartres, was positioned in the
crypt near the altar of Notre-Dame-sous-Terre. Access to and exit from
this cluster of *loci* and images were varied, but one sequence can partially
be reconstructed by the imagery that marks it out. From the west end
of the cathedral the pilgrim could have moved through the right hand
western portal, with its *Sedes Sapientiae*; down a set of steps in the south
western tower (Figure 9.6, B) into spaces that Sebastian Rouillard in
1609 emphasized as suitable for processions:[18] along the long south aisle
of the crypt and round its ambulatory, moving now westwards along
the north aisle and then visiting the well, the altar of the early evangelists, and the chapel and image of Notre-Dame-sous-Terre (with another

Figure 9.5 Chartres cathedral, Notre-Dame-sous-Terre. Engraving by Leroux, *c.* 1700, Paris, Bib. Nat. MS fr. 32973

Sedes Sapientiae). A thirteenth-century mural of the *Sedes Sapientiae* was installed near the chapel to enhance the cult and aura of its Romanesque archetype and to compensate for the translation of the cult image to the main altar after the 1194 fire.[19]

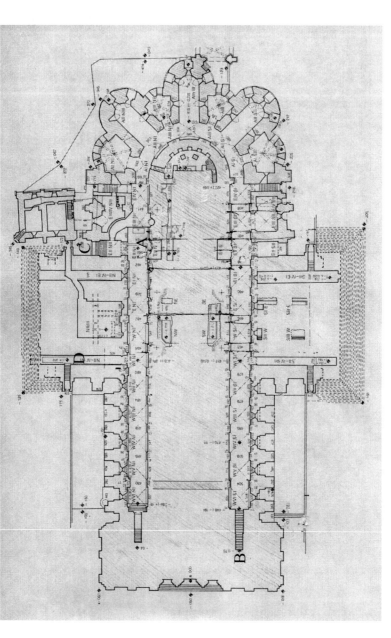

Figure 9.6 Chartres cathedral, ground plan of crypt. After Jan van der Meulen and Jürgen Hohmeyer, *Chartres: Biographie der Kathedrale*, with slight alterations by P. Crossley; the lettering and captions A–D as in the original list. A = Probable site of chapel of Notre-Dame-sous-Terre and the sacred well; B = Steps leading from southwestern tower to south aisle of crypt; C = steps from chapel of Notre-Dame-sous-Terre to northeast corner of the north transept; D = Corridor leading to the above-ground portal at northwest corner of the north transept

If pilgrims then wanted to gain access quickly to the cathedral above, they did not need to move back to the western towers; they could take one of two short cuts, the first northwards directly from the altar of Notre-Dame-sous-Terre along a tunnel and up a set of steps, bringing them out and onto the northeastern corner of the north transept porches,[20] and then to a view of the portals of the whole facade (9.6, C). Here they were greeted by a gigantic display of Marian imagery: St Anne and the Virgin on the trumeau of the central portal, and the Dormition, Assumption and Coronation of the Virgin on its lintels and tympanum (Figure 9.1, H) – all this accompanied by the Nativity portal on the left, which celebrates with doll-like realism the 'pilgrim-friendly' story of the Infancy of Christ (Figure 9.1, J). Consistent with the *ductus* principle that imagery on the exterior mirrors themes and images experienced inside the building, the ancient associations of the Virgin at Chartres are sublimated into a glorification of the Virgin as the Church, though it amounts here to its most ambitious celebration in Western imagery.

The hagiographical and historical implications of the crypt are developed in the second short cut out of it. Four bays westwards, also from the crypt's north aisle, a corridor leads northwards to a small portal in the northernmost buttress on the west side of the north transept (Figure 9.6, D). There the visitor was immediately greeted by standing figures on the porch, placed as close to the crypt door as possible (Figure 9.7). They are the figures of St Potentien and St Modeste, the latter converted to Christianity by the companions of St Savinien, and martyred by being thrown into the well. Once again, as in the confessors portal, saints venerated or remembered within the church come alive in their sensuous images outside it. The principle of repetition which we noted earlier as crucial to the *ductus* of images could not be clearer in this long sequence – with the *Sedes Sapientiae* at its beginning and almost at its ending; with the Virgin cult image of the crypt brought to life in the extended narratives of the north porch and portal sculpture; with the evangelists and martyrs of early Christian Chartres embodied as real figures in the porch that lies above their altar and their grave.

And now, for pilgrims intent on entering the cathedral via the north portals, another odyssey with imagery begins, this time on a dramatic scale. Stepping from west to east, the first (right hand) portal is dedicated to Job (Figure 9.1, R), where on Maundy Thursday the penitents received public absolution and were admitted into the church. Lying on his dung hill, tormented by the devil and his wife, Job was, from the twelfth century, the exemplar of patience and *poenitentia*.[21] The imagery of the other

Figure 9.7 Chartres cathedral, northwest corner of the north transept, figures of
St Potentien and St Modeste

two portals of the north transept has already been indicated: the central one devoted to St Anne and the Child Mary, and the Dormition, Assumption and Coronation of the Virgin (Figure 9.1, H), the left one to the Birth and Infancy of Christ, the most likely entrance to the church (Figure 9.1, J). Once inside the north transept the law of *ductus* as direction via repetition takes hold. The theme of the Virgin, St Anne and the Infancy is repeated insistently: St Anne and the Virgin in the central lancet of the north transept terminal window, crowned by the Apotheosis of the Virgin in the rose above it (Figure 9.1, no. 121, and Figure 9.9). Windows with Infancy themes dominate the north transept and the

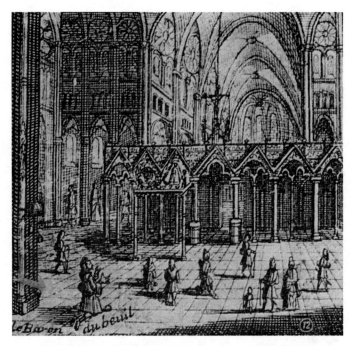

Figure 9.8 View of the choir screen by Nicolas de Larmessin. Detail from the engraving
'Triomphe de la Sainte Vierge dans l'Église de Chartres', 1697

crossing of nave and transepts (Figure 9.1, nos. 125, 127, 115, 114). Moving
from the transept into the crossing, visitors would soon find themselves
confronted by the sculpture on the western face and return sides of the
choir screen (*jubé*), demolished in the eighteenth century but surviving
in enough fragments accurately to reconstruct the placement of the figures and their narrative sequence (Figure 9.1, S; Figure 9.8). Its northern, return face probably contained a sculpture of Anne and Joachim
at the Golden Gate, or the Birth of the Virgin, particularly apt themes
for the cluster of Marian subjects in the north portals and transepts.[22]
The screens' front face proceeded, from left to right, with the narrative
of the Incarnation: the Annunciation, the Nativity, the Annunciation to
the Shepherds, the Magi before Herod, the Dream of the Magi and the
Presentation in the Temple (Figure 9.8).[23] Carried by the narrative drive
and touching detail of these images from north to south across the crossing, the pilgrim would have found the closest route to the shrine to be
along the south aisle of the choir, where the Marian themes are taken
up by the glass, one window showing scenes from the life of the Virgin
(Figure 9.1, no. 28b), while its neighbour showed another *Sedes Sapientiae*

Figure 9.9 Chartres cathedral, north transept rose window and lancets

vision, known popularly as 'Notre Dame de la Belle Verrière' (Figure 9.1, no. 30a). In front of the latter stood the altar of Our Lady of the Snows (Figure 9.1, T).[24] From here it was a short step to the entrance to the shrine space through a putative southern door in the southern flank of the old choir screen (Figure 9.1, K and M).

All these 'pathways' or 'journeys' are hypothetical reconstructions based on the evidence of images, entrances and likely circulation patterns; they are not prescribed in the Chartres ordinal. In any case, pilgrims were allowed into the sanctuary only in special circumstances, either because they sought miracles, or because they were of privileged social status. Nor are we fortunate enough to possess a processional for thirteenth-century Chartres. But with the help of the researches of Margot Fassler it is possible to reconstruct from the ordinal, as well as from tropes, sermons, commentaries and hymns, one type of important liturgical *ductus* in the Chartres calendar, namely the ceremonial entrance of the bishop (and more occasionally of the king) into the cathedral on the major feasts of the year: Nativity, Epiphany, the Holy Innocents, the Purification, Palm Sunday, Easter, the Ascension, Pentecost and the Assumption of the Virgin.[25]

These entrance processions took place through the central portal of the Portail Royal, moved up the central aisle of the nave, entered the choir through the central portal of the screen, and came to a close when bishop and clergy were seated to the right of the high altar. What is intriguing for the art historian is the correlation of the liturgy of this procession with the images which formed its backdrop. The triple-portal Portail Royal, before which the bishop paused before entering the cathedral through the central portal, is the story of human salvation, indeed of biblical time (Figure 9.3). The Old Testament is represented by the prophets, whose elongated bodies seem literally to hold up the New Testament in the lintels and tympana above them. On the right hand portal New Testament time begins with the Incarnation (Figure 9.4); on the left it ends in the Ascension and Mission to the Apostles; and in the centre time itself ends with the Apocalyptic God and his disciples in the court of heaven.[26] Especially relevant to the general meaning of the processional liturgy and to the imagery inside the church is the Incarnation portal, with the Annunciation, the Visitation and the Nativity in the lower lintel and the Presentation in the Temple in the lintel above, with Christ's eucharistic body placed, with a unique prominence, on the central altar, like a ritual sacrifice, flanked by the Virgin and the high priest Simeon. Both lintels are crowned by the *Sedes Sapientiae* in the tympanum. As Fassler has shown, the Introit tropes sung or said in front of the portals, and during the entrance to the nave, are all to do (not surprisingly) with entering, with the coming of the Messiah into time, into his Church and at the end of time. At the feast of the Purification the trope ran: 'Behold, Christ born from the virgin comes to his holy/Temple: let us rejoice saying/We have received your mercy O God/Whom the righteous old man Simeon received with rejoicing.' For the third Mass of Christmas the Introit hymns included: 'Let us rejoice today, because God descended from Heaven /And to earth for our sakes /A boy is born to us/Whom long the prophets predicted.' At the Epiphany they sang: 'He descended from the starry heavens to the *throne* (*solio* – my italics) of his own kingdom.'[27] The living poetry of the hymns and the mute imagery of the portals join to re-enact Christ's *adventus* into our world and into his Church. And true to the principle of *ductus*, whereby interior imagery repeats, or enlarges on, the themes of the exterior, so the three western lancet windows take up the themes of the portals below them. Seen from inside, we have the Stem of Jesse to the right (Figure 9.1, no. 49), and the Life of Christ in the centre (Figure 9.1, no. 50), whose two climactic upper panels show another *Sedes Sapientiae*, above a prominent image of Christ entering Jerusalem on Palm Sunday. The *Sedes Sapientiae* image effects the *ductus* from exterior to interior by the 'law' of similarity; the Palm Sunday image is Christ's most famous *ductus*, and a reminder of the liturgical *ductus* itself. On Palm Sunday the responsory *Ingrediente domino* was sung by the bishop and his procession at the southwest gate of the city, the Porte Cendreuse, and again when he entered the cathedral.[28] Church and city were transformed into Jerusalem, and the bishop into Christ. As the Palm Sunday procession moved down the central aisle of the nave, overshadowed on the same axis by the glazed image of Christ entering Jerusalem, there could be no doubt about the meanings of this re-enacted biblical history – liturgy and image conspired to underline them.

The next station in the procession, the choir screen, amplified these themes, particularly the eucharistic and incarnational iconography of the right hand portal of the Portail Royal, the so-called Infancy portal. The screen develops the theme of the infancy portal with touching detail and a new monumental scale. It enlarges the portal's unique eucharistic imagery by playing on the theme of the Rood, which as a mighty silver-gilt crucifix once rose above the central vault of the screen (Figure 9.8). In the same eucharistic tenor the screen showed two images of the Agnus

Dei – the sacrificial Lamb of God – both placed on the all-important central axis of the church: one as a vault boss over the screen's central entrance to the liturgical choir, and the other as a medallion above that entrance, but on the back, inner wall of the choir.[29] Four further inter- ior images of the Virgin and Child repeated the *Sedes Sapientiae* format of the Incarnation portal, two on side windows (Figure 9.1, nos. 38, 113), and two on the church's longitudinal axis: the first (sheathed in silver) was a new cult statue, of 1200, placed on the high altar,[30] and the second, in glass, still dominates the axial eastern window of the clerestory of the choir, and (like the western Incarnation portal) rises out of scenes of the Annunciation, Visitation and the gathering of the eucharistic bread (Figure 9.1, no. 100).[31]

The longitudinal spine of the cathedral, moving from west to east, is the all-important structure in this controlled *ductus*. Christ's incarnation beneath the *Sedes Sapientiae* had opened the journey at the west facade, and now closes it on the central axis of the apse. From portal sculpture to stained glass, from screen to altar imagery, climaxing in the glazed clerestory in the apse, we are confronted with the repetition and ampli- fication of key themes and motifs, strung out along a pathway, defined by a sequence of images, a pathway that provides the direction for the images' theatrical equivalents, the liturgy of entrance and salvation. The bishop as Christ comes into the world through the western portals, stands in his nave under the image of Christ's entry into Jerusalem, reas- serts his Incarnation, assumes the role of suffering redeemer as he passes through the double Agnus Dei of the screen and its crucifix, and then gains his symbolic paradise to the right of the high altar (Figure 9.1, L), an altar on which sits the familiar image of the *Sedes Sapientiae*, but now enriched from wood to silver, and finally repeated in the high clerestory of the apse, directly above the altar and the shrine.

Such correlations of image and performance should hardly surprise the modern historian of medieval liturgy or theology. The leading motive for church building in the Middle Ages was liturgical: the decorous inter- section of past and present in quasi-theatrical form: the persuasive power of performance. Most of Abbot Suger's descriptions of his famous new church at St-Denis are part of a liturgical context, while the final sec- tion of his *De consecratione* describes in proud detail a series of liturgical processions.[32] In that sense liturgy – particularly processional litur- gies – belonged to the rhetorical category of *ductus*, a concept known to ancient rhetoric, but first used as a separate textbook term by Consultus

Fortunatianus and then rooted in Christian monastic meditation by his probable contemporary, St Augustine. The *ductus* of architecture has clear parallels with the *ductus* of rhetoric. In its literary and classical form *ductus* delineates the conduct of a mind moving towards a goal; it is a literary composition (*dispositio* – the rational and proper arrangement of words) set in flow, and it joins the elements of *dispositio* into a route or pathway which gives that composition an active meaning, as much dependent on the sequence as on the elements disposed. Did the 'artistic advisors' at Chartres draw the evident parallels between the *ductus* of literary rhetoric and the contrived flow of liturgical performance?[33]

Much circumstantial evidence suggests that they did, though any attempt to reconstruct the 'artistic policy' of the cathedral chapter, or to discover the cathedral's notional 'programme', involves a hazardous journey from the visual to the verbal. But rhetoric, or 'rhetorics' (for the term refers to different experiences and techniques) is never far from the public art of images and architecture. The famous formulation of the purposes of Christian art, attributed to Thomas Aquinas – to instruct, impress and stimulate contemplation – echoes Cicero's classic definition of rhetoric: to instruct, to delight, to move: *docere, delectare, permovere*.[34] From Cicero and Quintilian to Hugh of St Victor and Geoffrey of Vinsauf, the architect was likened to the orator. *Dispositio* – the building blocks of *ductus* – furnishes some of the closest analogies to architectural practice. It is, says Quintilian, as important in laying out a building as in putting together the elements of speech.[35] Its medieval derivation, *despositio*, figures universally in architectural description. In the famous ninth-century plan of the abbey of St Gall, Abbot Heito of Reichenau, its author, dedicates it to Abbot Gozbert and self-deprecatingly calls it 'a few designs (*exemplata*) for the layout (*de posicione*) of a monastery.'[36] *Dispositor* was a term sometimes used to describe what an architect (*architectus*) does.[37]

To apply this general affinity to the specific analogies between *ductus* and architectural space, and to root both in Christian monastic meditation, was the achievement of St Augustine. For Augustine and his contemporary theoretician of *ductus*, Fortunatianus, *ductus* was a manner of literary composition, in the form of movement: a 'way', articulated by 'modes' (*modi*) and 'colours' (*colores*), which are the ornaments of rhetoric, and which light the path to the goal or final aim of the movement: the *scopus*, the climax which the whole *ductus* has presupposed.[38] Augustine applied this kinetic system to the idea of conversion and meditative prayer, and within that meditative envelope, to a mental experience of architecture. In his commentary on Psalm 41, on 'The Place of the Tabernacle' (*locus tabernaculi*), Augustine constructs a mental journey to a building, the Tabernacle of Moses – one whose general 'tenor' (the overall direction of the composition) is laid down for him, but whose particular ways can be chosen by him. *Ductus* is directed motion and it expresses authorial choice – the *tenor agendi* – but it also allows the viewer to choose his own way within its possibilities. First he stands outside the tabernacle, consumed with restless disorientation, 'blundering about' (*errabo quarens Deum*). Then he steps inside, where he perambulates (*ambulare*), admires, looks, sees grouped figures of 'faithful men' (*homines fideles*) and marvels at their 'disciplined physique ... in the service of God' ('animae servienti Deo membra corporalia militare admirer'), physiques which 'show their attributes'. They are virtues, disposed like standing actors in the *loci* of his mental building. He still 'walks about the place of the tabernacle' ('sed adhuc in loco tabernaculi ambulo') as if postponing his entrance to the *scopus*. But only by admiring these membra – these men with their disciplined figures – can the soul ascend to paradise, for he finally steps across the last threshold (*transibo*), and reaches the *scopus*, the house of God, the *domus dei*.[39]

The parallels between the psychological stations of this mental pathway and the liturgical and axial movements at Chartres hardly need emphasis. First, at Chartres, comes the preparation outside the portals, often noisy, disorienting and crowded (this is the 'blundering about'); then the entrance into the cathedral to find freedom of movement within an overall sense of direction; then the 'modes' and 'colours' along the way: the imagery of the screen, the brightness of the altars and glass – all catching the eye and disposing our thoughts in distinct directions, all demarcating the chosen pathway; then what Augustine calls 'the figures of the virtuous' standing in the *loci* of his mental building like the monumental standing figures of the saints on the portals and in the glass. And finally, the curving ambulatory and its chapels (*ambulare*), leading to the threshold (*transibo*), through the choir gate of the south aisle or the *jubé* into the sanctuary, the holy of holies, the shrine of the Virgin, marked out by the *Sedes Sapientae* on the high altar. She is the *scopus* itself, the point to which everything has been ultimately directed – a point crowned in the clerestory with a final burst of Marian imagery (Figure 9.1, no. 100), and accompanied directly below by a devotional catharsis, expressed in the prayers, often shouted and pleaded, of the pilgrims at the shrine.[40]

If architecture, space, sequence and imagery offer rhetorical parallels to the directed motion of *ductus*, could the second guiding concept of this essay, *memoria* – the rhetorical capacity not only to recall but to think and to order – inform the stress on order, clarity and geometric harmony which dominates the aesthetic of the early-thirteenth-century French cathedral? Mâle may have seen the cathedrals as nostalgic images of a world order that never existed, but he was right to recognize, in the cathedrals' colossal ensembles of imagery, a pressure towards visual order and didactic clarity that became more insistent with each new enterprise.[41] The portals at Chartres balance tympana and archivolts, capitals and column figures, with a lucidity unprecedented in twelfth-century sculpture. Its terminal facades are dominated by the ordered unfolding of rose windows, their presence more insistent in Chartres than in any cathedral before it (Figure 9.9).[42] With their hierarchies of figures devolving from centre to circumference and mapping the categories of the heavens and the earth, roses bring to the cathedral the twin notions of cosmic order and pedagogic clarity. And in the narrative windows in the side aisles of Chartres the stories of the Bible and of saints' lives are disposed within the complex armatures of the windows in such a way as to invert, extend or emphasize the main themes of the narrative itself. In the famous St Lubin window in the north aisle of the nave, the narrative sequence of the bishop's life, placed in foiled figures, surrounds a central spine of circular scenes which act as a moral and didactic sublimation of the narrative, for if read from bottom to top, they describe the transformation of earthly wine into the wine of the eucharist, a transformation effected by the bishop-cellarer himself.[43] We are confronted by a kind of 'writing in geometry', where the structure of the window allows us diagrammatically to emphasize, repeat or confront the special elements of the story, thus taking us beyond simple narrative sequences into the domain of instruction and meditation. As Wolfgang Kemp rightly claimed, 'this whole process was one of the greatest achievements of the twelfth century'.[44]

These windows involved the organization of images into geometric frameworks in such a way as to teach, edify and stimulate memory. Preaching to nuns in France, Bonaventura compared a well-ordered sermon, beautifully spoken, to the crystalline clarity of a well-designed stained-glass window.[45] Medieval memory was not simply a method of recall; it had, as Mary Carruthers emphasizes, a cognitive role, as a way of thinking and composing, often in pictorial and architectural terms. Medieval monastic thinking was a branch of seeing, a method of visualizing thought as cognitive 'pictures' (*picturae*), memorizing them (since such structures were designed to be memorable) and then using them for further thinking.[46] The ingredients of these mental pictures could be figures and schemes from the Bible (the Temple of Ezekiel, or the Tabernacle of Moses), or they could resemble diagrams or schematic structures, like wheels, or map-like figures or genealogical trees or trees of virtue, usually geometrical in design.[47] Many of these memory structures were architectural or quasi-architectural. In their compartments and stories, letters, associations and meanings could be placed, retrieved, combined with other associations and finally returned to where they belonged. Buildings of the mind as machines for meditation appear (as we have seen) in Augustine's 'The Place of the Tabernacle', in Adam of Dryburgh's later-twelfth-century 'Triple Tabernacle, together with a Picture' (*De tripartite tabernaculo*), and 'The Book of Breads' (*Liber de Panibus, c.* 1175), by Peter of Celle, bishop of Chartres.[48] All applied theological exegesis to quasi-architectural mental structures, thereby opening the door to the visual in the representation of higher truths.

Among the most influential twelfth-century exercises in the architectural mnemonic were the two treatises on Noah's ark written in the 1120s by Hugh of St Victor, 'The Moral Ark of Noah' and 'The Mystical Ark of Noah' – works central to our topic since Hugh's vision of the Church, in both its institutional and architectural forms, was readily adaptable to artistic programmes. Hugh's didactic and cognitive *picture* – his mental model of the ideal Church – was an ark, a boat consisting of square compartments like architectural bays, and with a central 'crossing' in the form of a square cubit, decorated at its centre by an image of the Lamb of God. It also had three storeys, divided into smaller and larger seats, all mnemonic *loci* into which Hugh placed images of the prophets, apostles and popes – in effect the lineage of the heavenly hierarchy.[49] The cleric had to memorize this structure, open its compartments and meditate on their contents (what Hugh called 'a variety of all delights'[50]), compare them to other subjects in other compartments, and then return them to their rightful places in the whole. Like Augustine, or Adam of Dryburgh, Hugh's architectonic visions were probably mental; he may never have drawn or painted his visionary ark as a real picture. In fact, monastic mnemotechniques rely almost wholly on fictive buildings and frameworks, not on the real spaces of the monastery itself. It is surely no coincidence that designs for real buildings, such as Malachy of Armagh's for his new church at Saul in Ireland,[51] or Gunzo of Baume's for the third church at Cluny, originated in visions.[52] The St Gall plan was sent to Abbot Gosbert so that he might 'exercise [his] wits on it' (*sollertiam exerceas tuum*), not build it. There is no evidence that it was, indeed, ever built.

But the fictive character of monastic architectural memory systems did not stand in the way of representing theological truth via visual patterns;

indeed, it positively encouraged it. Hugh of St Victor's architectural descriptions come startlingly close to the details and structures of later-twelfth-century architecture. His Lamb of God crowning the central 'crossing' of his ark is echoed, not only in the central bay of the Chartres choir screen, but also in the Agnus Dei boss at the centre of the eastern crossing of the new Gothic choir of Canterbury cathedral (1180).[53] In his short treatise on practical geometry Hugh explores the nature of the cosmos as if it were a rose window: 'measurement of the cosmos starts at its centre, evaluates the diameters and circumferences of the celestial sphere and its inner orbits with the help of proportion theory, and ... sets a specific ratio and value for each distance. Our discussion, accordingly, must start at the centre, and move, in fixed order, to the other parts.'[54] He goes on to note that 'the celestial hemisphere is rotated in twelve integral equinoctial hours, the entire celestial sphere in twenty four'.[55] All three of Chartres' roses are composed of twelve spokes! If Hugh's neo-Platonic speculations on numbers and the Christian cosmos could find later realizations in the real pictograms of the rose window, so too could Christian ethics be shaped by the visual geometry of numbers. The thirteenth-century manuscripts of his 'On the Five Sevens or Septenaries' (*De quinque septenis seu septenariis*), show the sevens and fives of Christian truth and practice in the form of *rotae* which closely resemble rose windows, even down to the way in which the figures are generated visually from the centre, but ascend theologically in importance from the circumference.[56]

All this does not suggest that if Hugh had committed his mental ark to visual form it would have assumed the shape of a Gothic cathedral and its geometries. Despite the parallels between Hugh's mental constructs and the real church, it has been notoriously difficult to find a direct link between Hugh's theology and the appearance of Gothic architecture in northern France, despite sterling attempts to do so.[57] The real visual parallels with Hugh's *picturae* may be identified with a pre-Christian and neo-Platonic tradition of visual ordering whereby cosmic, moral and divine themes were organized into visual diagrams, drawn or painted: signs of the zodiac, labours of the months, vices and virtues, liberal arts – all contained within wheels or maps or schematic trees. Indeed, there seems to be a real affinity between these 'images of divine order', as Madeline Caviness called them,[58] and the Tree of Life, marking off and defining the men and women of biblical history at the centre of Hugh's ark.[59] Grover Zinn has drawn our attention to a now lost drawing, described in Hugh's *De arca Noe mystica*, showing Christ holding a disc, on which was represented the cosmos, the six days of creation, the twelve months of the year, the signs of the zodiac, etc.[60] But rather than seeing this notional drawing as a blueprint for the Last Judgement tympanum of Suger's new St-Denis, it would be more germane to our argument to note the wider implications of Victorine teaching for the presentation of ordered *memoria* in the northern French cathedral. Nothing suggests that Hugh wanted artists to take up his writings as models for their designs; but that does not mean that his works, which were original and influential, could not have been exemplary in their general principles.

Hugh's two treatises on Noah's ark are nothing less than extended meditations on the proper nature of the institution of the Christian Church, a theme which runs through all his writings. The connections with the later cathedrals of northern France lie in Hugh's use of a single visual and architectonic model for his ideal Church: the ark of Noah. Ark and cathedral are not literal copies of each other – indeed the latter is 'real' and the former almost certainly mental – but they occupy the same metaphorical territory, as architectonic structures, for they stand as single images allowing the mind to focus inwardly on their significance. Indeed, as models for contemplation, their principal point of comparison is their visual character. Both present complicated theological ideas through visual means. For Hugh, learning begins with looking. His vision of the Church/ark is therefore well-adapted to comparisons with artistic programmes – with building and with art. Once these similarities are secured, the Ark and the cathedral represent fundamentally similar notions of the church – its clergy, its history, its sacramental functions, its liturgy, its structure and organization, its symbolism. Though Hugh is writing too early to appreciate the parallels between his vision and those of the cathedrals of northern France in the half-century either side of the year 1200, hindsight can easily assemble the similarities. The ark is the whole of biblical history, including the patriarchs, prophets, apostles and popes, who witness the faith (the cathedral is the Old and New Testament, together with Christ and the saints, made manifest). The ark must be presented in its ideal form since only in this way can its purposes be known (the cathedral is the Heavenly Jerusalem peopled by the Living Stones of the community of saints). The ark gathers up the truth from its diverse sacred sources and draws them into the one meaning of Christ himself (the cathedral gathers the saints and their teaching into the company of Christ and the apostles). The ark/Church is the outer shell for the inner significance of its contents – people, clergy, eucharist and liturgy (the cathedral is brought to sacred life by the *ductus* and diversity of its liturgies). The ark is a machine for teaching and for self-transformation, leading the soul upwards from beauty and history to allegory, tropology and final illumination (the cathedral's images lead their viewers from literal meaning to anagogical wisdom). The ark celebrates the achievements of Gregorian reform: a secure, hierarchical clergy, well-educated, freed from secular control and fulfilling their role as the successors of the apostles and the central witnesses of the heavenly hierarchy (Chartres celebrates clerical power, where the saints [most of them clerics] come together around the dominant images of the apostles, both in the south transept portals and in the radiating chapels).[61] Such tallies could be extended almost indefinitely.

In only one respect does the ark differ fundamentally from the cathedral: it belonged to the private, contemplative world of the regular canons; its public, educational function was indirect and limited. While there is still some debate on the precise nature of the Augustinian mission and Rule in the first half of the twelfth century and its relations with traditional monasticism, there can be little doubt that one of the spiritual goals which separated the regular canons from the reformed monks was their vocation to teach their fellow men 'through word and example',[62] in town, city and parish. But it is equally clear that Hugh's ark belonged to a specifically monastic genre of spiritual meditation, in which focused mental imaging stimulated intellection and emotion.[63] The artistic and pedagogic challenge to the secular canons of the twelfth century – those who were singled out as 'living among the world' and who were seen as most in need of reform[64] – was to apply these schemata of contemplation and understanding to the public art of the cathedrals, and thus to appeal to 'the world': to the public domain of the laity, the secular canon and the university-trained bishop. The didactic and representational needs of this new audience triggered a colossal change in the scale and position of sacred imagery. The ark and similar schematic 'images of divine order' had, until the early years of the twelfth century, led a sequestered life, as discrete schemata, whether in the manuscript form of pictograms, palindromes and monograms, or as diagrammatic mosaic pavements, usually decorating the sanctuary.[65] In the 'open' world of the cathedrals these images had now to be enlarged, made visible to all, and given various tectonic frameworks. One example will have to suffice. The *opus sectile* pavement of the Trinity chapel at Canterbury cathedral (before *c.* 1220), seems to come straight from the repertory of monastic mnemotechniques or 'images of divine order': a pattern of diagonally laid squares, intersected by circles, and surrounded by the conventional imagery of the cosmic diagram – the Labours of the Month and the Signs of the Zodiac. The closest parallels to this scheme, as Christopher Norton has surmised, are to be found in cosmological schemata, such as the Diagram of the Macrocosm and Microcosm on folio 17^v of Byrhtferth's *Computus* (c. 1100).[66] This schema, or something very similar to it, shapes the design of the iron armature of the north rose window of Canterbury's eastern transept – a design which is in turn translated into stone: in the plate tracery of the rose window of the south transept of Lausanne cathedral,[67] whose glass is filled with cosmic and terrestrial themes. It is as if the 'monastic' diagram was enlarged, up-ended and made into a memorable *pictura* for a public audience. The whole process implies a migration from fictive and mental architectures to real structures and spaces.

Evidence that such architectural thinking had infiltrated into the chapter and 'school' at Chartres during the construction of the cathedral is provided by a treatise on the Church written by the Chancellor of the cathedral school at Chartres, Peter of Roissy during his period of office (1204–11/13). His two versions of 'The Manual of the Mysteries of the Church' (*Manuale de mysteriis Ecclesiae*) offer intriguing glimpses into the ethical and pictorial imagination of a cleric whose training and outlook may have made him responsive to the rhetorical implications of the cathedral's imagery, and to the frameworks that articulate its figures. The simple Latin of the 'Manual', aimed at the half-educated lower clergy, follows the 'popular' thrust of contemporary Parisian preaching, but in this case explains, in a characteristically Victorine way, the mysteries of the faith by what can be *seen* – namely the church and its furnishings. Peter certainly knew the abbey of St Victor in Paris since he plagiarized entire passages of the *Poenitentiale* of Robert of Flamborough, canon of St Victor.[68] Peter arrived in Chartres too late to influence the cathedral's overall architectural design, or to play a part in salvaging the mid-twelfth-century west front. But he presided over the completion of the nave and the beginning of the transepts and choir, and in those years there are hints to suggest that he developed an interest in the cathedral's fabric and glass. The Church of the manual consists of an allegorical interpretation of the Christian basilica, with the conventional and mystical commentary expected of such formulae. But more than other contemporary ecclesiologists of Church symbolism, Peter of Roissy was a keen observer of architecture. He does not mention Chartres by name, but his long descriptions of the Christian Church – its portals, columns, screens, thrones, vestments, hangings and precincts – amount to a more systematic and detailed discussion of architecture than most of his contemporaries offered.[69]

And this suggests that his manual may have been founded on a real engagement with actual architecture, not just with mental or allegorical

Figure 9.10 Chartres cathedral, interior of the nave looking west

diagrams. For instance, when he speaks, in the section on the shape of the Church, of churches with three stories (*tria tabulata*) like that of Noah's Ark (*in archa Noe secundum*), he may have remembered Hugh of St Victor's picture of the ark as a three-tiered set of rectangular boxes, but he could also be reconciling that fictive image with the three-storey elevation that made Chartres such a novel experience in twelfth-century France (Figure 9.10).[70] And when he speaks of the church that has 'major' (*maiores*) and 'minor' (*minores*) columns, does he mean the alternating pier systems of Early Gothic churches, or is he noticing another novelty of Chartres, its new *cantonné* pillars, with minor shafts surrounding a major core?[71] And is it coincidence that in the manual's section on the Church's portals (*de hostio*) he describes a church with doors facing north and south, both open to the people (*populo*), when Chartres is unique among Great Churches of the early thirteenth century in having extensive sculpted portals in north and south transepts, both open to pilgrims and visitors?[72] And when Peter comes to the stained glass and windows of the Christian Church, which is of major interest to him, one senses a response to the unique emphasis given to glazing at Chartres in the first decade of the thirteenth century. Not surprisingly, his descriptions of the glass are mostly in the form of conventional allegory: glass signifies Scripture by keeping out evil weather but admitting light. Its windows are wide inside and narrower outside because their mystical sense is greater than their literal meanings, etc.[73]

It is only when he comes to the geometrical framing of figures – also in a discussion of the Church's precious hangings – that he betrays an awareness of the 'geometry of the mind'. Figures placed in round frames, he says, signify the original and infinite love of God; the triangle suggests the Trinity; the square signifies the four-sided virtues. In the same vein he describes the windows as square-rectangular below to contain the 'moral virtues of great prelates', and circular above because 'they must be perfect and serve God always who is alpha and omega'.[74] He could be describing, in his ekphrastic language, the novel forms of the Chartres clerestory: the plate tracery windows, their lancets containing huge standing figures of 'great prelates', crowned by a single oculus ('circular above'). 'We should', he concludes in his section on Easter hangings, 'diligently consider how to do the same for all images (*picture*) and diagrams (*figure*),' from images of plants to those of animals to humans ('Similiter alie figure et picture diligenter debent considerari').[75] Clearly, Peter understands that the status and meaning of things represented in art (*picture*) must be organized and presented appropriately in their proper frames (*figure*), and that this should be done for *all* art, across the multiplicity of imagery in his sacred Church. Here is evidence, from the very heart of the building enterprise at Chartres, that images can be understood in terms of schemata, and that both can be made literally manifest in the ordered masses of figures presented by the great secular cathedrals of the reforming Church.

If Peter of Roissy hints at an understanding of one rhetorical instrument which informs the design of Chartres – memory and its frameworks – my second text provides conclusive evidence that Gothic cathedrals of the thirteenth century acted as channels for *ductus* and *memoria* together. It comes, however, from outside Chartres, indeed outside northern France, and it dates to the very end of the Middle Ages. Laurent Fries from Alsace, geographer, astrologer and doctor, was born about 1480, studied in Colmar, lived and worked in Strasbourg, and died in Metz sometime before 1533. In 1523 he published a treatise in Latin and German on memory, his *Ars memorativa*.[76] His purpose was to enrich natural memory by cultivating artificial memory, and his technique, which went back to Cicero and Quintilian, was to visualize an ensemble of significant places – *loci*, pigeon holes – and then mentally to place in them words or images. The technique is so conventional that it would hardly detain us but for the fact that Fries chose a cathedral – that of his native Strasbourg – as his memory landscape. In it he situates twenty-four sites, remembers their positions, and attaches to each letters, words, concepts and associations. The sequence in which these elements appear in his notional orator's speech is constructed by the orator remembering to go in his memory to each of these *loci* in the order he has established. In fact, only ten of the orator's twenty-four places were identified by Fries in the cathedral, but their order is enlightening (Figure 9.11). The sequence starts in the north transept and moves into the eastern bay of the nave. More specifically, it begins with the altar of St Laurence (1), goes to the font (2), then to the stairs leading from the north transept to the choir (3), then the stairs to the crypt (4), to the big pier of the crossing (5) and then to the statue and altar of St Anne (6) and (7), placed probably above the thirteenth-century choir screen (8). The ninth and tenth stations were identified by the iconography of the images on the screen's gables: St Leonard visiting prisoners, and the feeding of orphans. The transepts of Strasbourg, where all this took place, were under construction in the 1230s or 1240s, and decorated with sculpture by an atelier coming straight from Chartres,[77] though there is no way of knowing if the masons brought with them this architectural and spatial mnemonic and whether it remained there as a purely oral technique until written down by Fries. What is clear are the astonishing similarities between Fries' memory engine and the 'pathway' that I identified at Chartres from the north transept entrance to the screen. In both, a set of images or objects – of moderate size, clearly lit, distinct but interrelated (as all memory diagrams are instructed to be), are deployed to guide a sequence of meditations or associations – a *ductus* brought from the mental landscape of monastic meditation to the public theatre of high medieval art.

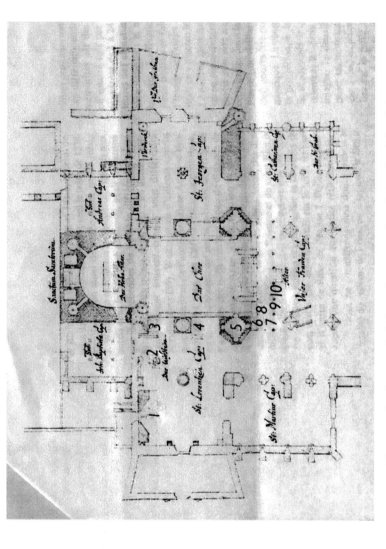

Figure 9.11 Strasbourg cathedral, north transept, plan of J. J. Arhardt (1643), (SUB Göttingen, 2 Cod. Ms Uffenbach 3, B1.12)

These two texts, and the textual evidence which supports them, suggest that the rhetorical modes of *ductus* and *memoria* could be brought into the domain of medieval aesthetics, and that their special qualities of movement and ordering had parallels to, and even consequences for, actual buildings. But the relationship between rhetoric and cathedral is not a simple causative one; rather, it was loose and 'open' and in that sense creative. The purpose of this paper is not to argue that the Chartres chapter sat down in 1194 and prepared a rigid 'programme' for the new cathedral, a sort of Wagnerian *Gesamtkunstwerk*, which legislated for the conduct of the liturgy and the presentation of its imagery down to the last detail. Even a building as homogeneous as Chartres shows clear improvisations and changes of mind in the design of its architecture and the placement and quantity of its sculpture:[78] there were plans, but plans that suffered major alteration. And the visitors to a great cathedral could themselves shape their own *ductus*, just as they could meditate on the combinations of *locus* and framework in their *memoria*. In his comments on Adam of Dryburgh's *The Triple Tabernacle*, its patron, Abbot John of Kelso, notes how contemplation of Adam's mental image or 'picture' of the Tabernacle of Moses in Exodus enlarges the literal text intellectually and morally. The reader/viewer takes on the qualities of inventive co-author.[79] In a similar way the architecture of Chartres acts as the 'common place' in which clergy and pilgrims can move backwards and forwards from image to image – inventing, as it were, their own meditations, enlarging and reshaping them in a kind of rhetorical dilation. Such is the implication of Manhes-Deremble's exegesis of the narrative windows of Chartres, where a cat's cradle of patristic and biblical reference underpins the 'programme' of the windows, and could only have been understood by the viewer in a long process of informal assimilation: of referring back and forth, of returning and repeating, sometimes adding to or correcting what was felt to be incomplete.[80]

Such informalities worked, however, within a more or less careful integration of ceremony, movement, image and contemplation. Integration of this kind is a rare phenomenon in monumental ensembles, but it is consistent with the little that we know about the creation of High Gothic Chartres in and after 1194. All art historians recognize that Chartres was a new beginning: a new kind of Gothic architecture with a vastly enlarged range of images organized with a new clarity of exposition. Like all beginnings it presupposes careful thought: a rehearsal of motives, perhaps an inquest on how best to realize the Gregorian principle of learning by seeing. Its huge windows and extensive sculptural ensembles – more ambitious than any in contemporary Christendom – suggest a self-conscious enterprise: a statement from its school and chapter on the proper uses and display of Church art. Chartres offered clergy and laity instruction via *memoria* and exploration via *ductus*; it taught them how to learn and how to move: to learn with their eyes and move with their minds.

NOTES

* I would like to thank Paul Binski, Kathleen Doyle, Stuart Whatling, Andreas Puth and Beth Williamson for their invaluable help in the preparation of this article.

1 The literature on Chartres is legion. Most of the published work up to 1989 is listed in the remarkably full J. van der Meulen, with R. Hoyer and D. Cole, *Chartres: Sources and Literary Interpretation: A Critical Bibliography* (Boston: G. K. Hall, 1989). For more recent references, see J. van der Meulen and, J. Hohmeyer, *Chartres: Biographie der Kathedrale* (Cologne: DuMont, 1984); B. Kurmann-Schwarz and P. Kurmann, *Chartres. La Cathédrale* (Auxerre: Zodiaque, 2001). Since this article went to press, a fundamental study by Claudine Lautier of the sacred topography of Chartres cathedral has appeared: 'The Sacred Topography of Chartres Cathedral: The Reliquary Chasse of the Virgin in the Liturgical Choir and Stained-Glass Decoration', in E. S. Lane, E. Carson and E. Shortell (eds.), *The Four Modes of Seeing: Approaches to Medieval Imagery in Honor of Madeline Harrison Caviness* (Ashgate: Farnham, 2009), 174–96.

2 E. Mâle, *L'art religieux du XIIIe siècle en France* (Paris: E. Leroux, 1898), 1–21; and *Religious Art in France: The Thirteenth Century: A Study of Medieval Iconography and its Sources*, tr. M. Mathews: (Princeton University Press, 1984), 1–26. All further references will be to the Princeton translations and editions.

3 The term 'Great Church', referring to large basilicas, either cathedrals or abbey churches, was coined by P. Kidson, *The Medieval World* (London: Hamlyn, 1967), 65–74, 98–112.

4 Critical discussions of Mâle's approach to cathedral art can be found in M. Camille, *The Gothic Idol: Ideology and Image-Making in Medieval Art* (Cambridge University Press, 1989), xxvii; P. Kurmann, 'Die gotische Kathedrale – Ordungskonfiguration par excellence?', in B. Schneidmüller, (ed.), *Ordnungsfigurationen im Hohen Mittelalter*, Konstanzer Arbeitskreis für mittelalterliche Geschichte 64 (Osfildern: J. Thorbecke, 2006), 279–80; and E. Emery, *Romancing the Cathedral: Gothic Architecture in Fin-de-Siècle French Culture* (Albany: State University of New York Press, 2001), 41–3, 116–17, 146–9, 168–9.

5 Mâle, *Religious Art*, 3.

6 P. Kurmann, 'Viollet-le-Duc und die Vorstellung einer idealen Kathedrale', in H. Hubach, B. von Orelli-Messerli and T. Tassini (eds.), *Reibungspunkte. Ordnung und Umbruch in Architektur und Kunst: Festschrift für Hubertus*

Günter (Petersburg: Imhof, 2008), 159–68; and 'Viollet-le-Duc und die ironisierte Kunstgeschichte', in *Geschichte der Restaurierung in Europa*, 2 vols. (Worms: Wernersche Verlagsgesellschaft, 1993), vol. II 53–62; Hans Sedlmayr, *Die Entstehung der Kathedrale* (Zürich: Atlantis, 1950).

7 Van der Meulen, *Sources and Literary Interpretation*, *passim*.

8 That exception is the work of Margot Fassler; see 'Liturgy and Sacred History in the Twelfth-Century Tympana at Chartres', *Art Bulletin*, 75 (1993): 499–520, and 'The Disappearance of the Proper Tropes and the Rise of the Late Sequence: New Evidence from Chartres', in *Cantus Planus* (Budapest: Hungarian Academy of Sciences, 1990), 324–6 (not available to me). All definitive discussion of the relationship between liturgy and imagery at Chartres must wait until the appearance of her study on the west facade and its liturgical sources; see 'Liturgy and Sacred History', 540 n. 42.

9 The phrase comes from C. P. Graves, 'Social Space in the English Medieval Parish Church', *Economy and Society*, 18 (1989): 297–322, at 303.

10 W. Sauerländer, 'Reliquien, Altären und Portale', in N. Bock, S. de Blaauw *et al.* (eds.), *Kunst und Liturgie im Mittelalter: Akten des internationalen Kongresses der Bibliotheca Hertziana und des Nederlands Instituut te Rome, 1997* (Munich: Hirmer, 2000), 121–34.

11 A point first made by P. Kurmann and B. Kurmann-Schwarz, 'Chartres Cathedral as a Work of Artistic Integration', in V. C. Raguin *et al.* (eds.), *Artistic Integration in Gothic Buildings* (University of Toronto Press, 1995), 138–9.

12 The altar of St Martin and its visually cognate windows are discussed by C. Lautier, 'Les vitraux de la Cathédrale de Chartres: Reliques et images', *Bulletin Monumental*, 161 (2003): 397, at 21, 40, 41. I am indebted to her reconstruction of the altar placements and dedications at Chartres.

13 According to Sebastian Rouillard's 1609 testimony. See Kurmann-Schwarz and Kurmann, *Chartres*, 144–5.

14 I am referring to notional 'pilgrims' here though I am aware that the traditional view of Chartres as a centre of international pilgrimage has been severely qualified by A. Chédeville, *Chartres et ses Campagnes XIe – XIIIe siècles* (Paris: Klincksieck, 1973), 506–25, who defined its Virgin cult as predominately local. See also J. Van Herwaarden, 'Pilgrimage and Social Prestige: Some Reflections on a Theme', in H. Kühnel (ed.), *Wallfahrt und Altag in Mittelalter und Früher Neuzeit (International Round Table Gespräch, Krems an der Donau 8 Oktober 1990)* (Vienna: Austrian Academy of Sciences, 1992), 32.

15 W. Sauerländer, *Das Königsportal in Chartres: Heilsgeschichte und Lebenswirklichkeit* (Frankfurt: Fischer Taschenbuch, 1984).

16 I. Forsyth, *The Throne of Wisdom: Wood Sculptures of the Madonna in Romanesque France* (Princeton University Press, 1972), 105–11.

17 Van der Meulen and Hohmeyer, *Chartres: Biographie*, 185–98, argues, largely on the basis of the wording of Louis XI's gift of a tabernacle, that the original chapel was in the central part of the crypt, directly 'under the choir'

(i.e., the liturgical choir), and not in the north aisle of the crypt. I am not convinced by this, given the generalized nature of medieval descriptions of place and the devotional imperative of placing the new chapel in the area of the old. Note also the reliable late-seventeenth-century source, Canon Claude Estienne, who described the marbled seventeenth-century chapel as occupying the same place as its predecessor ('on a dispose ce lieu en une très belle chapelle de marbre' – see L. Merlet (ed.), *Catalogue des reliques et joyaux de Notre-Dame de Chartres* (Chartres: Garnier, 1885), 174 ; Lautier, 'Les vitraux', 37.

18 Van der Meulen and Hohmeyer, *Chartres: Biographie*, 194.

19 A. Prache, *Chartres Cathedral: Image of the Heavenly Jerusalem* (Paris: Centre national de la Recherche Scientifique, 1993), 18–19; M. Caviness, 'Stained Glass Windows in Gothic Chapels and the Feasts of the Saints', in N. Bock, S. De Blaauw *et al.* (eds.), *Kunst und Liturgie im Mittelalter: Römisches Jahrbuch der Bibliotheca Hertziana*, 33 (1999/2000): 135–148, at 146.

20 Much of this tunnel dates from the late sixteenth century up to 1905, but it probably reflects a medieval pathway. See R. Hoyer, 'Documents primordiaux de l'archéologie chartraine: les plus anciens plans connu de la cathédrale Notre-Dame', *Bulletin de la Société archéologique d'Eure-et-Loir, Mémoires*, 31:1, suppl. 19 (1988): 1–57.

21 Y. Delaporte, *L'Ordinaire Chartrain du XIIIe siècle*, Société Archéologique d'Eure-et-Loir, Mémoires 19 (Chartres: Société Archéologique d'Eure-et-Loir, 1953), 46–7; A. Katzenellenbogen, *The Sculptural Programs of Chartres Cathedral: Christ, Mary, Ecclesia* (New York: Norton, 1964), 67–78; B. Abou-el-Haj, 'The Urban Setting for Late Medieval Church Building', *Art History*, 11 (1988): 17–41, at 25ff. The north transept portal was also used for the penitents at Saint-Lazare at Autun; see O. K. Werckmeister, 'The Lintel Fragment Representing Eve from Saint-Lazare, Autun', *Journal of the Warburg and Courtauld Institutes*, 35 (1972): 1–30.

22 A convincing case for such a scene is made by K. McCarthy, '"Both a Barrier and No Barrier": The Jubé of Chartres Cathedral', unpublished MA thesis, Courtauld Institute of Art (1998), 17–20; see also J. Mallion, *Le jubé de la cathédrale de Chartes* (Chartres: Société Archéologique d'Eure-et-Loir, 1964), 87.

23 J. Mallion, *Le jubé*; L. Pressouyre, 'Pour une reconstitution du jubé de Chartres', *Bulletin Monumental*, 125 (1967): 419–29.

24 Lautier, 'Les vitraux', 21.

25 It is beyond the scope of this paper to consider in detail the liturgy of thirteenth-century Chartres and its extensive manuscript sources. Lists of more than twenty manuscripts of Chartrian usage relevant to the study of the Chartrian liturgy were published by Delaporte, *L'Ordinaire Chartrain*, 203–13. An updated list of the extant manuscripts can be found in Fassler, 'Liturgy and Sacred History', especially 518–19; and Fassler, 'The Disappearance'. I will confine my main sources to the ordinal made for Chartres *c.* 1225–35 (Chartres Bib. municipale, MS 1058), destroyed by fire

in 1944 but transcribed, edited and published by Y. Delaporte, *L'Ordinaire Chartrain*, and to references to the twelfth-century ordinal, the *Ordo veridicus* (Châteaudun, Archives hospitalières, MS 13) lost but copied – though not published – by Delaporte, and now in the Diocesan Archive in Chartres.

26 For the Portail Royal, see Sauerländer, *Das Königsportal in Chartres*; Katzenellenbogen, *Sculptural Programs*, 7–49.

27 Fassler, 'Liturgy and Sacred History', 503–7.

28 For the Palm Sunday procession, see C. Wright, 'The Palm Sunday Processions in Medieval Chartres', in M. Fassler and R. Baltzer (eds.), *The Divine Office in the Latin Middle Ages* (Oxford University Press, 2000), 344–71.

29 Mallion, *Le jubé*, 86–7, 161–6, 170–1.

30 Delaporte, *L'Ordinaire Chartrain*, 32; and Y. Delaporte, *Les trois Notre-Dame de la cathédrale de Chartres* (Chartres: E. Houvet, 1955), 36–9.

31 J. W. Williams, *Bread, Wine and Money: The Windows of the Trades at Chartres Cathedral* (University of Chicago Press, 1993), 37–68.

32 A. Speer, 'Is There a Theology of the Gothic Cathedral? A Re-reading of Abbot Suger's Writings on the Abbey Church of St.-Denis', in J. Hamburger and A.-M. Bouché (eds.), *The Mind's Eye: Art and Theological Argument in the Middle Ages* (Princeton University Press, 2006), 65–83; E. Panofsky (ed.), *Abbot Suger On the Abbey Church of St. Denis and its Art Treasures* (Princeton University Press, 1979), 115–21.

33 For *ductus*, see M. Carruthers, *The Craft of Thought: Meditation, Rhetoric, and the Making of Images, 400–1200* (Cambridge University Press, 2000), 77–81, 266–9 and her essay in this volume. Its meaning in relation to allied disciplines, and to thirteenth-century music, is discussed by N. van Deusen, *Theology and Music at the Early University* (Leiden: Brill, 1995), 37–53.

34 J. Tripps, *Das handelnde Bildwerk in der Gotik* (Berlin: Gbr. Mann, 2000), 223–32. Cf. Cicero, *Orator*, 69; Quintilian, *Inst. Orat.*, XII.10.59.

35 Quintilian, *Instit. Orat.*, VII, proem., and II.13.9–11. These and other passage are discussed in C. Van Eck, 'Architecture, Language and Rhetoric in Alberti's *De re aedificatoria*', in P. Crossley and G. Clarke (eds.), *Architecture and Language: Constructing Identity in European Architecture c. 1000c.1650* (Cambridge University Press, 2000), 72–81, at 75.

36 W. Braunfels, *The Monasteries of Western Europe* (London: Thames & Hudson, 1972), 46; W. Horn and E. Born, *The Plan of St Gall*, 3 vol. (Berkeley; London: University of California Press, 1979), vol. I, 9; L. Ness, 'The Plan of St. Gall and the Theory of the Program of Carolingian Art', *Gesta*, 25 (1986):1–8.

37 See N. Pevsner, 'The Term "Architect" in the Middle Ages', *Speculum*, 17 (1942): 549–62, referring particularly to Benno of Osnabrück who is described by his biographer as both *architectus* and *dispositor* in connection with his building of Speyer.

38 For the use of these terms in Fortunatianus, Martianus Capella and Augustine, see Carruthers, *The Craft of Thought*, 77–9, and her essay above.

39 For a full discussion of 'The Place of the Tabernacle' see Carruthers, *The Craft of Thought*, 251–4, 355 n. 80, for excerpts from the Latin text of *Enarrationes in Psalmis.*

40 See particularly the miracle of the man with paralysed hands, where the men of the parish shout, weep and plead to God, the Virgin, St Germanus and St Lubin, and to St Thomas, to cure him. A. Thomas (ed.), *Miracula B. Marie Virginis in Carnotensi ecclesia facta*, Bibliothèque de l'école de Chartres 42 (Paris, 1881), miracle 26, 548–9.

41 For the problem of 'order' in the cathedral, see P. Kurmann, 'Die gotische Kathedrale', *passim.*

42 Except perhaps Laon. For roses, see R. Suckale, 'Thesen zum Bedeutungswandel der Gotischen Fensterrose', in K. Clausberg *et al.* (eds.), *Bauwerk und Bildwerk im Hochmittelalter: Anschauliche Beiträge zur Kultur- und Sozialgeschichte* (Giessen: Anabas, 1981), 259–294; and P. Cohen, *The Rose Window: Splendour and Symbol* (London: Thames & Hudson, 2005).

43 C. Manhes-Deremble, *Les vitraux narratifs de la cathédrale de Chartres: Études Iconographique*, Corpus Vitrearum: France, Études 2 (Paris: Léopard d'or, 1993), 52–6, 98–107.

44 W. Kemp, *The Narratives of Gothic Stained Glass*, trans. C. Salzwedel (Cambridge University Press, 1987), 42.

45 J. Hamburger, 'The Place of Theology in Medieval Art History: Problems, Positions, Possibilities', in Hamburger and Bouché (eds.), *The Mind's Eye*, 11–31, at 14.

46 M. Carruthers, *The Book of Memory*, 2nd edn (Cambridge University Press, 2008); Carruthers, *The Craft of Thought*; M. Carruthers and J. Ziolkowski (eds.), *The Medieval Craft of Memory: An Anthology of Texts and Pictures* (Philadelphia: University of Pennsylvania Press, 2002).

47 M. Evans, 'The Geometry of the Mind', *Architectural Association Quarterly*, 12 (1980): 32–55; and M. Caviness, 'Images of Divine Order and the Third Mode of Seeing', *Gesta*, 22 (1983): 99–120.

48 All these authors are discussed in Carruthers, *The Craft of Thought*, 251–4, 246–50, 205–9, 238–9.

49 M. Fassler, *Gothic Song: Victorine Sequences and Augustinian Reform in Twelfth-Century Paris* (Cambridge University Press, 1993), 211–40; Carruthers, *The Craft of Thought*, 243–6; G. R. Zinn, 'Hugh of St. Victor and the Art of Memory', *Viator*, 5 (1974): 211–34. A translation of *De arca Noe mystica* has been made by Jessica Weiss in Carruthers and Ziolkowski (eds.), *The Medieval Craft of Memory*, 41–70.

50 Carruthers, *Book of Memory*, 45.

51 Carruthers, *The Craft of Thought*, 224–6; R. Stalley, *The Cistercian Monasteries of Ireland* (New Haven: Yale University Press, 1987), 11–13.

52 Braunfels, *Monasteries of Western Europe*, 58–9, and Document IX, 240–1.

53 Carruthers, *The Craft of Thought*, 243–4; Fassler, *Gothic Song*, 220–2; P. Binski, *Becket's Crown: Art and Imagination in Gothic England 1170–1300* (New Haven: Yale University Press, 2004), 8. Sometime before the

fourteenth century Christchurch possessed a copy of *De arca Noe*. See M. R. James, *The Ancient Libraries of Canterbury and Dover* (Cambridge University Press, 1903), 36. The copy appears in the list of books during Prior Henry of Eastry's period of office. It does not appear in the Fragmentary Catalogue of the library dated *c.* 1170. I am grateful to Paul Binski for alerting me to this source.

54 *Hugonis de Sancto Victore opera propaedeutica: Practica geometriae, De Grammatica, Epitome Dindimi in philosophiam*, ed. R. Baron, Publications in Medieval Studies 20 (Notre Dame University Press, 1966); and Hugh of St Victor, *Practical Geometry*, trans. F. A. Homann (Milwaukee, WI: Marquette University Press, 1991), 57.

55 Hugh of St Victor, *Practical Geometry*, 60–1. I am grateful to Laura Cleaver for advice on rose windows and their Victorine connections.

56 Suckale, 'Thesen zum Bedeutungswandel', 280–4. See especially plate 13, showing the early-thirteenth-century Septenarrota, Oxford, Bodleian Library MS Lyell 84.

57 C. Rudolph, *Artistic Change at St-Denis: Abbot Suger's Program and the Early Twelfth-Century Controversy over Art* (Princeton University Press, 1990), 36–47, 58–62; G. Zinn, 'Suger, Theology and the Dionysian Tradition', in P. Gerson (ed.), *Abbot Suger and Saint-Denis: A Symposium* (New York: Metropolitan Museum of Art, 1986), 37–40. For an anti-textual critique of Rudolph, see Speer, 'Re-Reading of Abbot Suger', 66–7.

58 Caviness, 'Images of Divine Order'. See also Evans, 'Geometry of the Mind'.

59 Fassler, *Gothic Song*, 220.

60 Zinn, 'Suger, Theology', 37.

61 Most of these summaries on the meanings of Hugh's ark are indebted to Fassler, *Gothic Song*, 211–40.

62 C. Walker Bynum, 'The Spirituality of Regular Canons in the Twelfth Century: A New Approach', *Medievalia et Humanistica*, n.s. 4 (1973): 3–24. For a summary of the debate, see also Fassler, *Gothic Song*, 187–97.

63 'A Little Book About Constructing Noah's Ark', in Carruthers and Ziolkowski, *The Medieval Craft of Memory*, 42–3.

64 The distinctions come from the anonymous twelfth-century treatise, *Libellus de diversis ordinibus et professionibus qui sunt in aecclesia*, discussed by Fassler, *Gothic Song*, 192–7.

65 For mosaic pavements, particularly Italian and Augustinian, see L. Donkin '"Ornata Decenter": Perceptions of Fitting Decoration amongst Augustinian Canons of Sant'Orso in Aosta in the Mid-Twelfth Century', *Journal of the Warburg and Courtauld Institutes*, 71 (2008): 75–93.

66 Oxford, St John's College MS 17, fol. 17ᵛ; C. Norton, 'The Luxury Pavement in England before Westminster', in L. Grant and R. Mortimer (eds.), *Westminster Abbey: The Cosmati Pavements*, Courtauld Research Papers 3 (Aldershot: Ashgate, 2002), 7–27.

67 A comparison first made by Christopher Wilson: see 'Lausanne and Canterbury: a "Special Relationship" Re-considered', in P. Kurmann and

M. Rohde (eds.), *Die Kathedrale von Lausanne und ihr Marienportal im Kontext der europäischen Gotik* (Berlin: De Gruyter, 2004), 89–124, at 97; also Cohen, *Rose Window*, 208–13.

68 S. Kuttner, 'Pierre de Roissy and Robert of Flamborough', *Traditio*, 2 (1944): 492–9.

69 The claim is made by M.-Th. d'Alverny, 'Les mystères de l'Église d'après Pierre de Roissy', in P. Gallais and Y.-J. Riou (eds.), *Mélanges offerts à René Crozet*, 2 vols. (Poitiers: Société d'études médiévales, 1966), vol. II, 1,085–104, at 1,088. She also gives a French translation of parts of the text.

70 *Ibid.*, 1,097.

71 *Ibid.*, 1,096. The point was first made by O. von Simson, *The Gothic Cathedral: Origins of Gothic Architecture and the Medieval Concept of Order*, 2nd edn (New York: Pantheon, 1962), 196.

72 D'Alverny, 'Les mystères de l'Eglise', 1,096.

73 *Ibid.*, 1,095–6.

74 *Ibid.*, 1,096.

75 *Ibid.*, 1,103.

76 J. M. Massing, 'Laurent Fries et son "Ars Memorativa": La cathédrale de Strasbourg comme éspace mnémonique', *Bulletin de la Cathédrale de Strasbourg*, 16 (1984): 69–78. Reprinted in J. M. Massing, *Studies in Imagery*, 2 vols. (London: Pindar Press, 2004), vol. I, 251–74.

77 Y. Gallet, 'La nef de la cathédrale de Strasbourg, sa date et sa place dans l'architecture gothique rayonnante', *Bulletin de la Cathédrale de Strasbourg*, 25 (2002): 49–82, for a discussion of the latest attempts to date the end of the transept construction and the beginning of the nave.

78 Büchsel, *Die Skulptur des Querhauses der Kathedrale von Chartres* (Berlin: Gebrüder Mann, 1995) *passim*, and 166–7; see additional and dissenting conclusions by Kurmann-Schwarz and Kurmann, *Chartres*, 287–302.

79 Carruthers, *The Craft of Thought*, 247.

80 Manhes-Deremble, *Les vitraux narratifs*, 37–73.

CHAPTER 10

Ductus figuratus et subtilis

Rhetorical interventions for women in two twelfth-century liturgies*

William T. Flynn

Whether one characterizes the twelfth century as a period of intellectual and cultural renaissance, of emerging scholastic and monastic cultures, or of ecclesiastical reformation in both secular and monastic institutions, it is clear that the century saw a tenfold increase in the number of, if not in the relative status of, women's institutions.[1] Both of the principal figures treated here – the self-styled deaconess of the Paraclete, Heloise, and the prioress (though functionally abbess) of Rupertsberg, Hildegard – contributed to an ongoing critical dialogue about the nature of monasticism and founded monastic communities. Both made cogent observations about the Benedictine Rule and contributed to the creation of liturgies about and for women. While Hildegard's explanation of the Rule emphasized the *discretio* given to the abbot or abbess that allowed them to adapt it to changed circumstances,[2] Heloise's critique ended with a request for a new Rule specifically designed for her nuns, a request met by Abelard,[3] though, so far as one can tell, never fully implemented (and very gradually abandoned) at the Paraclete.[4]

Such innovations were by no means limited to women's institutions. For example, Abelard, responding in typically impolitic fashion to Bernard of Clairvaux's criticism of the novel phrasing of the Lord's Prayer used at the Paraclete, pointedly listed the numerous liberties the Cistercians had taken with their new hymnal.[5] However, the burgeoning of women's institutions raised the issue of their proper constitution and governance and created the opportunity at the Paraclete for writing a new Rule (and consequently a radically reformed liturgy) that (in Heloise's words) 'should be proper for women, and which should prescribe anew (*ex integro*) the arrangement and ethos (*statum habitumque*) of our profession'.[6] Elsewhere I have described in some detail the radical effects that the liturgical adaptations at the Paraclete had on the most solemn feasts of the year, the Easter Triduum.[7] Given that a feast's solemnity often militates against liturgical change, it is astonishing that one can count no fewer than fifty-five

items in the Paraclete's Ordinary and Breviary for the services from the
Second Vespers of Maundy Thursday through to the Mass of Easter Day
that are rarely found elsewhere; most of these changes are likely to have
been instituted during Heloise's abbacy.[8] Although Hildegard's additions
to the liturgy were more outwardly conforming, the sheer number and
length of her additions (seventy-seven substantial items) suggest that her
programme of liturgical innovation was no less thorough-going than that
of the Paraclete. It would not be too much of an exaggeration to say that
most of Hildegard's liturgical music is designed, at least in part, to help
justify and celebrate the particular form of women's monasticism practised at her convents.

Such redirecting of liturgies towards specific institutional concerns
was part of the wider twelfth-century reconstruction of religious life.
The sense that the old orders needed to be reformed brought rhetorical
concerns to the fore: old liturgies seemed to need clarification and focus,
and the specific vocation of women monastics needed to be reflected
within them. Indeed, Abelard's later writings reflect a new concern with
rhetoric, and may be read as a theoretical response to his production of
liturgies for the Paraclete. By paying attention to his reflections on rhetorical method, scattered throughout these later works, I will demonstrate
Abelard's largely conscious application of rhetorical method in his analysis of his inherited liturgy and in his reformation of liturgical rites, and
suggest that this approach to the liturgy treats it as if it is a new rhetorical
form: persuasive action.

ABELARD'S THEORY OF SACRED LITERATURE

According to his own account, early on Abelard studied rhetoric with
William of Champeaux and interrupted William's rhetoric classes to dis-
pute about matters usually reserved for dialectic.[9] As Constant Mews has
pointed out, the texts being disputed were likely Cicero's *De inventione*
and perhaps the fourth book of Boethius' *De differentiis topicis*, and it
was specifically the common ground of argument analysis, covered both
in rhetoric and dialectic, that concerned Abelard.[10] Mews has traced the
development of Abelard's reflection on the use of argumentation in rhetoric and dialectic throughout Abelard's career, and demonstrated that he
gradually came to the view that the truth or falsehood of an argument
could be judged solely through a specific dialectical analysis, whereas an
analysis of its persuasive power was principally the domain of rhetoric.
Such a view preserved what Abelard considered the specific role for formal

logic, which he maintained should be applied to any given proposition (which must be treated as hypothetical), in order to test its validity and to move towards greater certainty. Abelard therefore formulated 'a definition of rhetoric that emphasizes its instrumentality, rather than issues of truth or falsehood'.[11] In his excursus on rhetoric, Abelard says: 'Indeed, rhetoric exists chiefly for persuasion. And to persuade is to rouse [*commovere*] and draw out [*trahere*] people's dispositions [*affectus*] so that, with us, they desire or reject the same thing.'[12] The consequence of this bold view of dialectic as an exclusive realm was that the contested classification of rhetoric as a branch of ethics was both clarified and strengthened. Although this definition of rhetoric supported his early preference for dialectical argument, Abelard demonstrated, in his later work, a growing concern with rhetorical technique. I will first describe the rhetorical theory that can be gleaned from Abelard's theoretical works, and then will link these to his composition of hymns and sermons designed to produce a more convincing, effective and affective liturgy.

Abelard's most developed statement on rhetoric comes in the prologue to his *Commentaria in Epistolam Pauli ad Romanos*.[13] This, along with Abelard's philosophical and theological reflections on language, provides what Peter van Moos has described as a serendipitous development of a 'medieval concept of literature' arising through 'reflection in the twelfth century on the logic of language'.[14] Since the rhetorical theory espoused within this prologue was written directly after Abelard's most sustained period of activity on the Paraclete Rule and liturgy, it provides a window into what may have been his *modus operandi* when devising his liturgical compositions.

Abelard's prologue controversially defines all Scripture as rhetorical speech that intends not only to teach but also to exhort. Scripture not only lays out what ought to be done in precepts, but uses exhortation (*admonitiones*) and good and bad examples that move one's desire (*voluntas*) towards the good things that it teaches.[15] Moreover, three specific types of rhetorical speech may be found in Scripture: while New Testament fulfils the Old, Abelard maintains that, in both, the Lord teaches through precepts that are laid down principally in the books of law and the Gospels. He suggests it is the intention of the Gospel (*intentio Evangelii*) to proclaim these precepts, and this implies that they form (for Abelard) the *materia* for much sacred literature. Precepts, however, require a secondary persuasive elaboration in the form of exhortation (*admonitio*) so that they will be put into practice, and exhortation is supplied largely by the books of the prophets in the Old Testament and by the Epistles and Apocalypse in the New. Not only does exhortation persuade, but examples (*exempla*) of good and bad conduct and their consequences persuade: these are found in the histories (and other writings) of the Old Testament and in the Acts of the Apostles in the New.[16]

All three types of rhetorical speech are essential for effective proclamation, because the precepts necessary for salvation (which communicate the *intentio Evangelii*) can be taught and even learned without provoking the disposition (*affectus*) to obey them. Citing Cicero's *De inventione* (II.56.168–9), Abelard argues that the general intention of the Gospel should be supported for the beauty (*decor*) of the Church and the increase (*amplificatio*) of its wellbeing. This requires a supporting literature that uses the persuasive techniques of rhetoric designed to move the disposition of its hearers to assent to, and follow, the evangelical precepts. Abelard defines this rhetorical role as the *intentio generalis* of the Epistles and (albeit briefly) justifies all new sacred composition (including the writings of the holy Fathers, canons, decrees, monastic Rules and saints' lives) as writings that serve the same rhetorical ends.[17]

The prologue concludes by placing Paul's Epistle to the Romans within this overarching classification of sacred literature, identifying within it an *intentio propria*; in other words, a specific aim of this letter is to support the specific evangelical precepts concerning humility and fraternal concord. This *intentio propria* is linked to specific topics (*materia*) and specific persuasive devices (*modi tractandi*) in a passage so replete with technical rhetorical terms that it is worth quoting in full:

And so, since, as was said, the intention of the Gospels [*euangeliorum intentio*] is to teach us the things which are necessary for salvation, the Epistles support this intention, so that they might move us to obey the evangelical teaching, and indeed some of them transmit salvation to amplify or develop [*ad amplificandam uel … muniendam*] it more securely. And clearly this is the general intention [*generalis intentio*] of all the Epistles.

But for each Epistle, it is appropriate that specific intentions [*propriae intentiones*] be sought, whether topics [*materiae*] or modes of treatment [*tractandi modi*], as in this very Epistle, whose intention clearly is to call the Romans who had been converted from the Jews and the gentiles back from the arrogance of controversy to true humility and brotherly concord, as each group had been preferring itself before the other.

Indeed it brings this about in two ways [*modi*], namely as much through amplifying [*amplificando*] the gifts of divine grace as through diminishing [*extenuando*] the merits of our works, so that nobody may presume to boast in himself about works, but should assign the whole, whatever he is able to do, to divine grace, consequently, one should indeed recognize that he has received whatever good he holds. And so in these two things, namely, as much in our works as in divine grace, consists the summary of the entire matter [*materia*].

But the mode of treatment is in the diminishing [*attenuatio*] of our works, as was said, and in the exaggeration [*exaggeratio*] of grace, so that now nobody should presume to boast about works, but 'Let anyone who boasts, boast in the Lord'.[18]

Abelard's analysis of the rhetoric of Romans attends to the specific problem of identifying a work's overall rhetorical strategy. Any specific work should have an identifiable *intentio propria* (its specific goal). This is reached through the progressive interplay among the *materia* (topics) that are treated, its specific *modus tractandi* (mode of treatment) and the rhetorical *modi* or *colores* (techniques) employed to discuss the *materia*.

This analysis calls to mind the theory of *ductus* first found in the fourth-century rhetor Fortunatianus but transmitted to the Middle Ages by way of Martianus Capella.[19] Fortunatianus defined a rhetorical mode as the directed motion (*ductus*) in a part of a composition, but all of the directed motion (*ductus*) produces the goal (*scopus*). The term *ductus*, which I am translating as 'directed motion', is therefore equivalent to Abelard's *modus tractandi*, suggesting that Abelard may indeed have encountered the concept of *ductus* through Capella, whose discussion associates the term with skilful treatment (*artificiose tractandi*).[20] What Abelard calls the *intentio propria* is therefore analogous to Fortunatianus' *scopus*, and what he calls the *modus tractandi* is analogous to *ductus*, and both use the term *modus* to refer to specific rhetorical devices.

However, Abelard's analysis of Romans not only uses the theory of *ductus* but also refines the theory by demonstrating connections between *materia* (topics) and *ductus*. In fact, one may determine what kind of *ductus* is being deployed by comparing the work's *scopus* (goal, Abelard's *intentio*) to its topics (Abelard's *materia*). Thus, although Abelard considers the pride of the two factions within the Church of Rome that leads each to stress the validity of its own practice to the detriment of fraternal concord to be the central problem that the letter to the Romans was written to address, he notes that the letter does not criticize this pride directly by identifying it as a sin and calling for repentance, but addresses it indirectly through a discussion of two topics: merit and grace. The specific technique of *attenuatio* (diminishing) is employed to minimize the merits of 'our works', and *exaggeratio* (exaggeration) to emphasize the role of God's grace; together these form what Abelard calls the *modus tractandi* (i.e., *ductus*) of the whole Epistle. Capella had defined this particular strategy as *ductus subtilis*, in which the mind wants one thing and the speech pleads another ('cum aliud vult animus, aliud agit oratio'), but Abelard's analysis makes it clear that such a strategy is not simply a matter of disguising one's real aims, but could succeed by gaining assent to less controversial topics that could not logically be conceded without requiring assent to the work's more controversial *intentio*.

As von Moos has pointed out, Abelard's characterization of the various *intentiones* within Scripture comes from

a quite positive understanding of rhetoric ... Development (*amplificatio*) refers less to extent than to intensity. Since ... all parts of the Bible ... are composed in the manner of rhetorical speech ..., the admonitory parts are not an addition but a pedagogical deepening, an achievement of the same linguistic intention. In terms of speech-act theory, we could say that the message passes consequently from a simply 'informative' mode to a more elaborate 'illocutive' mode of presentation.[21]

Von Moos rightly states that although Abelard's defence of the rhetorical nature of Scripture is novel, it is focused on the homiletic aspects of Scripture, and that one must look elsewhere (especially in his theological and philosophical writings discussing the theory of language) for Abelard's 'deepest justification for a rhetorical approach to the Bible':

[This] lies, for Abelard, in the paradox that God is inexpressible, indeed unfathomable, but that revelation nevertheless speaks about him, in a language that can be best understood with the aid of the descriptive repertoire made available by the art of eloquence.[22]

While von Moos is correct in identifying the problem of describing the ineffable God as the deepest justification for employing rhetorical analysis, Abelard's contribution to this discussion was to give it greater philosophical precision. The literary appreciation of the 'hermeneutic' passages of the Bible that employ figures and tropes had formed the backbone of grammar instruction since Origen and Tychonius, and were transmitted through Augustine's *De doctrina Christiana*, perfected by Cassiodorus in his *Expositio Psalmorum* and had become part of the standard pedagogy of grammar and rhetoric through works such as Bede's *De schematibus et tropis*.[23]

Moreover, the originality of Abelard's analysis of Romans does not lie in its approach to interpreting Scripture's 'illocutive' as opposed to its 'hermeneutic' passages, but in its recognition that there is a need for a literature within and beyond Scripture that supports both what Scripture reveals and what it teaches, a literature which therefore has the *intentio generalis* of helping specific audiences in specific circumstances to assent to, and affirm, either what is commanded (in Scripture's moral and homiletic writings) or what is revealed (in Scripture's prophetic and poetic writings). Rhetorical analysis is equally useful for both categories of writings: it can reveal both the 'illocutive' strategies designed to produce assent to Scripture's precepts and it can demonstrate 'hermeneutic' strategies that allow an appreciation of the special language adopted in Scripture (which is also the special language of the medieval liturgy).

In Romans, the 'illocutive' strategy required the deployment of a *ductus subtilis* through which a gradual assent to a controversial claim might be gained. As will be shown below, the 'hermeneutic' strategy (especially of Hildegard's prophetic voice, but also in the Paraclete Easter liturgy) requires what Capella had called a *ductus figuratus*. In legal rhetoric, *ductus figuratus* was deployed because of modesty, when metaphors and other tropes were used to avoid naming indecencies directly, but a *ductus figuratus* was inevitable when the already poetic speech of Scripture was the only revealed access to the ineffable topics under discussion. As Mary Carruthers has demonstrated, the hermeneutic strategy served by *ductus figuratus* was inextricably linked to monastic practices of meditation in which the very difficulty of probing the figurative language of Scripture was thought to produce the deepening awareness of its essential mystery:

> In the monastic Middle Ages, the way of meditation was initiated, oriented, and marked out especially by the schemes and tropes of Scripture. Like sites on a map, these functioned cognitively as the 'stations' of the way, to be stopped at and stayed in mentally before continuing. ... All figurative language can function for a reader in this way, but for monastic composition, the 'difficult figures' were particularly important intellectually, providing what St Augustine called *obscuritas utilis et salubris* 'productive and health-giving difficulty'.[24]

As shown above, Abelard's analysis of the rhetorical techniques employed within Scripture justified the use of such techniques in any attempt to respond to new audiences and circumstances: new sacred literature, although it can never claim the *auctoritas* of Scripture, may be judged along with the writings of the councils, the Fathers, the writers of monastic Rules, hagiographers and liturgists, and (to the extent that it proves inspired) take its place among them.

THE RHETORIC OF THE PARACLETE LITURGY

My previous work on the Paraclete brought out one of Abelard's most important rhetorical choices in fashioning its reformed Easter liturgy: it was directly and concretely adapted so that it would be made more effective for a women's community.[25] Abelard used the women followers of Christ (especially Mary Magdalene) as the dominically sanctioned models for his reconstruction of the nature and purpose of women's monasticism, which he locates principally in a continuation of the diaconal ministry towards Christ of the women who followed him.[26] In the fundamental text in Abelard's Letter 5, he developed the idea of a special connection of nuns to the Easter story, offering an allegorical reading of the Song of Songs specifically addressed to the Paraclete community:

'I am black, but comely, O daughters of Jerusalem. Therefore the king has loved me and has led me into his chamber.' And again: 'Do not consider that I am brown because the sun has discoloured me' [Song of Songs 1:4–5]. While the contemplative soul, which is specially [*specialiter*] called the bride of Christ, may generically [*generaliter*] be described through these words, nevertheless they apply more precisely [*expressius*] to you: indeed, your very habit speaks them outwardly. For that same outward appearance of blackness or of low dress, in likeness to the mourning garb of good widows lamenting for their dead husbands, whom they had loved, makes you truly manifest in this world, according to the Apostle, as widows and abandoned, who should be supported by the contributions of the Church [cf. 1 Timothy 5]. Indeed, Scripture[27] recalls the grief of these widows over the slaying of their bridegroom, saying: 'The women sitting at the tomb were mourning, weeping for the Lord.'[28]

In this extremely complex cluster of references, Abelard makes two contrasts: one between the application of the term *sponsa Christi* in species (*specialiter*) to the 'contemplative soul' in genus (*generaliter*) and the second to the even more precise (*expressius*) application of the term to Heloise and her nuns, equating the 'blackness' of the *sponsa* with the nuns' outward garb that marks them as 'good widows ... in this world'. It is the rhetorical fittingness (*aptum*) of its gendered application and the literal and allegorical connections made between widows, Jerusalem, and brides that makes it more precise (*expressius*) when applied to nuns. To support this claim, Abelard refers to 1 Timothy 5, where good widows who have no worldly obligations are organized into what he would claim were proto-monastic communities devoted to a life of constant prayer and diaconal ministry.[29] Moreover, he refers to the Gospel narrative by quoting the Holy Saturday Gospel antiphon for Lauds. Its text not only emphasizes that women followers of Christ were widows mourning (in reality) the loss of their metaphorical *sponsus*, but its *versus* (not quoted, but certainly understood) supports the notion of their special diaconal ministry: 'And these women had followed him from Galilee, ministering to him.'[30] Finally, the letter contains an allusion to the anagogical meaning of the office of widow by reminding the reader that the *sponsa* of the Song of Songs is speaking about her blackness to the Daughters of Jerusalem, connecting the personification of Jerusalem as a widow in Lamentations to the *sponsa* of the Song of Songs, and (though this is never explicitly stated) to the heavenly Jerusalem 'descending from heaven from God prepared [*ornata*] as a bride for her husband' in the Apocalypse 21:2.[31]

Abelard's Letter 5 concludes by characterizing the Easter season as particularly meaningful and, indeed, the principal narrative that a women's community should reflect on, and the cluster of images he builds there again refers to Lamentations. He explicitly links the theme of women's lamentation to the texts of the Good Friday liturgy, especially to the Reproaches of Christ from the cross, featuring Lamentations 1:12:

Stand by his tomb in your mind always, and lament and grieve with the faithful women, about whom, as I have already mentioned above, it is written: 'The women sitting at the tomb were mourning, weeping for the Lord.' Prepare with them ointments for his burial, but better, indeed spiritual, not bodily, ointments; for he who did not receive the ointments [i.e., from the women at the tomb] seeks these perfumes again. Feel remorse over these things, with a complete sympathy of devotion. Towards this, indeed towards compassion's remorse, he himself also exhorts the faithful through Jeremiah, saying: 'O all ye that pass by the way, attend, and see if there is any sorrow like unto my sorrow' [Lamentations 1: 12] ... Now, he is the way through which the faithful pass over to the fatherland. He indeed raised the cross (from which he cried out in this manner) as a ladder for us towards this purpose ... Grieve over him alone; share in his suffering by your grieving. And fulfil what Zechariah the prophet foretold about devout souls: 'They shall strike up', he said, 'a lament as over the only-begotten son, and they shall grieve over him as it is customary to grieve at the death of a first-born son' [12: 10] ... This is your lament, sister; may this be your wailing, you who have been joined in blessed matrimony to this bridegroom.[32]

Given Abelard's emphasis on the women followers of Christ as the dominical model for nuns, one might expect to find a particularly elaborate *visitatio* ceremony having the *Quem queritis* dialogue at its core. The more fully developed of such ceremonies include laments for the women at the tomb and would seem to fit well with Abelard's desire to provide a special connection of the Easter season to the *affectus* of women. However, even though the extant sources for the Paraclete record both the *depositio* of the cross on Good Friday and its *elevatio* during the third nocturn of Easter Matins,[33] they are completely silent about the *visitatio*, which would, if it formed part of the rite, normally require commentary.

Although it is possible that the *visitatio* ceremony's absence may simply be due to the incomplete record we have of the Paraclete liturgy,[34] it seems to me just as likely that it was intentionally left out of Abelard and Heloise's revised rites. The whole of the Paraclete's provisions for the Easter Triduum seem to have been reconfigured as a huge *visitatio* ceremony played out at literal, allegorical, tropological and even anagogical levels, so that the women followers of Christ, and therefore the nuns' are always at the centre. For example, at the Adoration of the Cross on Good Friday, the Paraclete Ordinary gives the *incipit* for two responsories not found elsewhere that demonstrate how the rite was adapted *ad status*, i.e., shaped for the assembled virgins and widows of the Paraclete. The Adoration rite would normally consist of the antiphon *Ecce lignum* followed by its *versus* from Psalms 66:20 and 118:1, followed by the antiphon *Crux fidelis* sung antiphonally with verses of the hymn *Pange lingua ... proelium*. However, the Paraclete rite stipulates that two responsories should be sung before *Crux fidelis* and its hymn. The first of these, although we have only the enigmatic *incipits* of its antiphon, *versus* and *repetendum*, suggests a close connection to Abelard's discussion of Lamentations 1:12 in Letter 5 (given above):

Mulieres. V. Attendite vos. R. Non enim[35]
    ([Antiphona.] The women ... V[ersus]. You! Behold. R[epetendum]. For ... not ...)

Waddell has suggested that the Crucifixion narrative (Matthew 27:55–6; Mark 15:40–1) is the most likely source for the first part of the antiphon.[36] In context, these passages contrast the complete abandonment of Jesus by the male disciples with the women who had ministered to him and who were present (although a long way off) at Jesus' death on the cross. More speculatively, I would add that of the 139 occurrences of *non enim* in the Vulgate that could provide a possible biblical source for the *repetendum*, Romans 3:22–3 would work best, since it is the only one that provides a fitting conclusion to both the antiphon and *versus*. The whole text reconstructed might read:

A. Mulieres multae ibi erant, aspicientes a longe, non enim est distinctio, omnes peccaverunt, et egent gloria Dei. V. Attendite vos et videte si est dolor sicut dolor meus. R. Non enim est distinctio, omnes enim peccaverunt, et egent gloria Dei.
    [A. Many women were there, looking on from afar, for there is no difference: all have sinned and fall short of the glory of God. V. You! Behold and see whether there is any sorrow like my sorrow! R. For there is no difference: all have sinned and fall short of the glory of God.]

Whether or not one accepts this reconstruction, the few surviving words of the *incipit* are enough to show that the rite of the Adoration of the Cross had been reshaped so that women (*Mulieres*) were placed at its centre: placed within hearing distance of the *vox Christi* (according to Abelard's comments in Letter 5) saying the words of Lamentations 1:12 (*Attendite vos*).

The second responsory text is signalled in the Ordinary by a single word, *Egredimini*, but its source (as Waddell pointed out) is most likely Song of Songs 3:11, which describes the Daughters of Zion going forth to meet their king (Solomon) as he is crowned at his betrothal:

> Go forth, O Daughters of Zion, and see King Solomon in the diadem with which his mother crowned him on the day of his betrothal and on the day of his gladness of heart.

Abelard had used this verse as the *thema* for his third sermon for Palm Sunday and had described the 'procession' of the Daughters of Zion as symbolic of their 'taking up the cross' to follow Christ, interpreting Solomon's 'diadem' as the crown of thorns.[37]

Thus the additions to the Adoration Rite are apparently limited to the words of the Scripture without any moral or allegorical commentary on them. This careful presentation of uninterpreted New Testament narrative and Old Testament typology is part of an overall rhetorical strategy that Abelard hints at in the prefaces to his hymnal and to his sermonary. Abelard makes a distinction in his second hymnal preface between the *materia* suitable for nighttime and that suitable for the day:

> [The hymns] which are in the night office should contain the events of their days. But the daytime hymns should hand down the allegorical or moral understanding of the same events. And it is done in this way, so that the obscurity of history may be reserved for the night, but the light of understanding may be reserved for the day.[38]

Although this passage refers specifically to the *cursus* of hymns, an examination of the distribution of texts at the Paraclete shows that the same rule applies to the whole of the liturgy. For example, Abelard's Rule forbids the reading of Gospel homilies in Matins and assigns them only to meals and the *collatio*.[39] The principal reason for this is that their explanations of the allegorical and tropological meanings of the texts of Scripture would occur in the night instead of the day (weakening the effect he tries to create with his hymn cycle).[40] Moreover, his sermon cycle regularly treats and (what is most important) regularly explains the allegorical types developed in his hymns and in the rest of the Paraclete liturgy for the same feasts.[41]

The full application of this method to the Easter liturgy is made more complex because Abelard considers the three days of the Easter Triduum to be a single liturgical celebration, depicting the *transitus* from sorrow to joy liturgically through two days of mourning (commencing after the Mass on Holy Thursday) and a day of rejoicing (starting with the combined first Vespers and Vigil of Easter).[42] As a result, the first two days of the Triduum are arranged so that a unique hymn written for each liturgical hour commemorates the events of the Passion at the times they are mentioned in the Gospel, while the antiphons and responsories are chosen because of their allegorical associations with the events. The explanation of these associations comes only on the third day, so that instead of a single night there is a two-day period of uninterpreted quotation of Scripture followed by the explanation of allegories and types in daytime hymns and commentary of Easter Day.[43] On Easter, the texts develop the theme of rejoicing, employing types that foreshadow the Resurrection events and continue to highlight women's roles. For example, rather than focusing on the Exodus and explaining it as a type of the Resurrection that culminates in the canticle sung by Moses and the children of Israel (Exodus 15:1–14), Abelard's Matins hymn *Da Mariae Timpanum* treats the canticle's repetition in a choral dance led by Miriam (Exodus 15:20).[44] The hymn's last two stanzas allude to Mary Magdalene (without naming her); during the daytime Easter sermon Abelard discusses her as the New Testament fulfilment of Miriam.

Abelard's Lauds hymn *Golias prostratus est* functions quite differently, with allusions to various Old Testament types for Christ (David, Samson, the Lion of Judah), followed by the refrain: *Resurrexit Dominus*, which functions like a biblical gloss. The second stanza of this hymn continues the *ad status* address to the Paraclete nuns by describing the Daughters of Zion as 'singing praises', i.e., singing *laudes*, the service for which the hymn was most likely intended. The refrain's quick identification of each of the Old Testament types serves to explain the allegories of many of the earlier readings and songs in the *cursus*.

The examples given so far should give a fairly good idea of the ways that the Paraclete liturgy was rhetorically shaped *ad status monialium*. They also demonstrate not only that this shaping mined the Old and New Testament for models of women's participation (whether allegorically or historically) in the Passion and Resurrection events, but also that the exposition of the *materia* was carefully staged according to its allegorical type and whether it was to be placed in the night office or during the day.

Most important of all, as Abelard's characterization of the season in Letter 5 suggests, the entire series of types and events offered in Scripture heightens the connection of the Passion and Resurrection narratives with the *affectus* of women. This is stated explicitly in the opening of his Easter Sermon (preached during the day and therefore the key point at which the purpose of the whole of the liturgical *cursus* is discussed): 'The pages of the Old as much as of the New Testament bear witness to how great a degree the rejoicing of the Paschal solemnity applies to the devotion and honour of women.'[45] Three examples of the liturgy's emphasis on women's *affectus* will suffice to show the intensive development of themes of lament and joy, and of the Easter season as a time of *transitus* from one emotion to the other. First, the Adoration ceremony described above enacts the relationship that Abelard had described in Letter 5 by means of a liturgical rite. Second, the extraordinary cycle of fourteen hymns that Abelard wrote to mark each liturgical hour on Good Friday and Holy Saturday adopts an illocutive strategy that is made explicit in the lines with which each of the fourteen hymns concludes: the singers pray to experience directly the appropriate transition of *affectus*:

> Tu tibi compati
> sic nos fac, domine,
> tue participes
> ut simus glorie,
> sic presens triduum
> in luctu ducere
> ut risum tribuas
> paschalis gratie.

[Make us, O Lord, suffer with you in such a way that we may be partners in your glory, and thus the present three days are to be conducted in sorrow, so that you may bestow the laughter of Paschal grace.]

Third, the unusual choice of the sequence *Epithalamica* for the Easter Day Mass enables a similar ritualizing of joy through the singing of a bridal song in the *species* of the *sponsa* and *filiae Sion* of the Song of Songs. In my investigation of the function of this sequence within the Paraclete liturgy, I suggested that its unusual poetic and musical form places it closer to the style of Abelard's *planctus* than to any known sequence, indicating that it makes use of the ambiguity of form between sequence and *planctus*, to turn the *planctus* form into a song of joy. This is made explicit in the concluding lines of its main section where the singers sing about the song itself: 'mestis reddita sponsi presentia convertit elegos nostros in cantica' [the bridegroom's presence, restored to the despondent, turns our elegies into canticles].[46]

The rhetorical strategy adopted in the Paraclete's Easter liturgy can thus be seen to be constructed along lines consistent with the theory of rhetoric that Abelard developed in his Romans commentary and theological writings. Its *intentio generalis*, like that of all sacred literature, is to help specific audiences in specific circumstances to assent to, and affirm, what Scripture reveals and commands. The *intentio propria* of the Paraclete Easter liturgy is to call the nuns to claim as their own the love of God and neighbour foretold throughout the Scriptures, revealed by the path taken by Jesus in the Passion and Resurrection narratives, and by his passing-over (*transitus*) from death to eternal life.[47] As was shown above, Abelard conceived of *ductus* (his *modus tractandi*) as being essentially related to the choice and disposition of topics (*materia*). Even in the few examples from the Paraclete liturgy discussed here, it is clear that the choice of *materia* highlights the participation of women in narratives that foreshadow the Easter narrative, in the Passion narrative itself, and in narratives read as a moral allegory of the nuns' purpose and vocation, especially the Song of Songs. At each stage the specific *modus* employed is *exaggeratio*, here deployed to emphasize the depth of lamentation and height of joy. In its disposition it uses 'hermeneutic' strategies (*ductus figuratus*), carefully working out the Old Testament types that gradually shift the focus from the abandoned widow (Jerusalem) in Lamentations to the joyful *sponsa* of the Song of Songs, and relating these (and other types) to a careful working through of the Passion narrative. Moreover, at each stage, 'illocutive' strategies (*ductus subtilis*) are employed, worked out in the form of ritualized acts of women's lamentation, such as the newly shaped Adoration of the Cross, in hymns marking each hour of the Passion that provide the words to pray for a change of *affectus*, and ritualized acts of women's joy, such as the unusual sequence *Epithalamica*, in which the nuns as the *sponsa* and Daughters of Jerusalem find the *sponsus* at the Easter Day High Mass. *Epithalamica* leads directly to the Easter Day Gospel in which the women followers of Christ (the dominical model for nuns) discover the empty tomb and are commanded to proclaim that the Lord has risen.

Although Heloise was describing how the new Rule for the Paraclete should be written when she requested that it 'should be proper for women, and ... should prescribe anew the arrangement and ethos of our profession',[48] the strategies adopted to reshape the Paraclete's Easter liturgy use exactly the same approach, accomplished through a profound and conscious application of rhetorical technique, extending beyond the words to the action of the rites.

THE RHETORIC OF HILDEGARD'S PROPHETIC VOICE

In contrast to Abelard, whose rhetorical thinking has been reconstructed (in part) from his theoretical statements and his rhetorical analysis scattered throughout his writings, Hildegard minimized her debt to the liberal arts in order to stress the divine origins of her works, and derived her rhetorical voice and much of her imagery and language from the prophetic books of the Bible. However, as noted above, the quantity of her practical contributions to the liturgy rivals his, and they use a distinctive rhetoric based on the key images developed in her visionary experience and prophetic expression of them. Not only did Hildegard write seventy-seven substantial chants that carry rubrics indicating their liturgical use, and her *Ordo Uirtutum* (her procession of the virtues), she also wrote a substantial *De tempore* collection of fifty-eight sermons.[49]

However, the strategy she adopted towards reshaping the liturgy appears at first to be less radical than the changes introduced at the Paraclete. Even though the rubrics to many of Hildegard's seventy-seven chants indicate their liturgical genre clearly, most have no absolutely clear assignments to specific feasts. The collection as a whole seems to provide the additions around the margins of the liturgy rather than a radical overhaul. For example, much of the new material may have been destined for votive offices, such as those for the Virgin, the Holy Spirit and the Angels, all of which were growing in popularity in the twelfth century, and although this new material could also replace older chants for regular feasts (e.g., the several Marian feasts, Pentecost, St Michael and All Angels), there is nothing to prove (or disprove) any specific assignments. Other pieces, such as the *symphoniae* for virgins and widows, may have been written for the common, and much of the rest, for locally important saints, e.g., the monastery's patron St Rupert and the newly revitalized cult of St Ursula.[50] Nevertheless, taken together, these additions recapitulate and (according to Hildegard's statements about the purpose of music) perfect through music all of the key concepts covered in Hildegard's major writings.[51] Moreover, as the analysis of Hildegard's hymn for the Lauds of St Ursula (*Cum uox sanguinis*) given below will demonstrate, Hildegard's texts are often structured by the liturgical *cursus* itself and in turn provide her commentary on it.

The great number of items that Hildegard provided for St Ursula suggests that Ursula's cult was of particular importance at Rupertsberg, and its story of a charismatic woman gathering an army of women around her offered a particularly fine opportunity for an acting abbess to write an office that would speak to the *status* of her nuns. Hildegard's chants for Ursula are the only pieces that carry a rubric for a specific liturgical office, Lauds. Since there is seemingly more repertory provided than could be used within Lauds, the precise reconstruction of this office is contested. Nevertheless, any reconstruction of the festal Lauds service would place the hymn *Cum uox sanguinis* directly after the psalmody. It is therefore worth noting that the antiphon series as a whole narrates the *historia* of Ursula and her 11,000 companions up to the point at which they are martyred and ends with the devil scoffing at them. The hymn takes up the narrative at precisely this point, with the 'voice of their blood' crying out to God. The complete antiphon series could have been sung at Lauds if the very rare variation of splitting the last item of the psalmody (Psalms 148–50 sung under one antiphon) into its constituent parts were followed. This would preserve the narrative, and because it provides appropriate intertext for each antiphon, I think this the most appropriate disposition of the repertory for Lauds.[52] Whether or not one accepts this possibility, the antiphon series as one encounters it in the manuscripts narrates the story up to the martyrdom and provides a coherent setting for the hymn.

The text of the hymn (given in the first column of Table 10.1) is devoted almost entirely to the presentation of a set of arresting images, such as *uox sanguinis* (1a), *radix mambrae* (1e), *sacrificium uituli* (5a), *incombustus rubus* (10b).[53] Some of these images, such as *uox sanguinis*, are particularly striking since they must be read metaphorically: blood does not literally have a voice. Furthermore, whether metaphorical or not, almost all of these images refer to passages within Scripture that traditionally prompted commentary or elaboration when they were quoted or interpreted in other passages of Scripture, in patristic and medieval commentary, or in liturgical songs and homily. For example, the phrase 'arietem in spinis pendentem' (3b) [the ram hanging upon thorns] comes from the Vetus Latin translation of the story of Abraham and Isaac found in a commentary by Ambrose.[54] The Vulgate reading is 'arientem herentem inter vepres' 'a ram caught among the briars'. Although Hildegard's use of the older Latin wording does not obscure the biblical locus in any significant way, it reinforces its traditional allegorical application to Christ, since 'pendens in spinis' more readily suggests the cross, its nails and (somewhat more remotely) the crown of thorns.

The multivalency of such images was likely to have been particularly clear to Hildegard's own nuns since they were steeped not only in the sources Hildegard drew upon, but also in Hildegard's particular ways of connecting and weaving the traditional materials together in her

Table 10.1 *Edition, and biblical/liturgical references of Hildegard of Bingen's Cum uox sanguinis*

(1)	**CVM** uox sanguinis ursulae	(a)	As the voice of the blood of Ursula	Gen. 4:10 (cf. Heb. 12:24)
	et innocentis turbae eius	(b)	and of her innocent throng	cf. Apoc. 7:9–10
	ante thronum dei sonuit.	(c)	resounded before the throne of God,	CAO 7804 Ubi est Abel frater tuus (Septuagesima)
	antiqua prophetia uenit	(d)	the ancient prophecy came	
	per radicem mambrae	(e)	through the root of Mamre,	CAO 6563 Dumstaret Abraham ad radicem Mambre (Quinquagesima)
	in uera ostensione trinitatis	(f)	in a true manifestation of the Trinity,	Gen. 18:1–2
	et dixit.	(g)	and said:	Patristic interpretation of Gen. 18:1–2
(2)	**I**ste sanguis nos tangit	(a)	"This blood touches us;	Apoc. 7:13–17; 22:14
	nunc omnes gaudeamus.	(b)	now let us all rejoice."	
(3)	**E**t postea uenit congregatio agni	(a)	And then came the congregation of the lamb	Apoc. 7:9–11, 13–17;
	per arietem in spinis pendentem	(b)	through the ram hanging on the thorns,	19:1, 6–9; Gen. 22:13
	et dixit.	(c)	and said:	(VL – Ambrose)
				CAO 7762 Tentavit Deus Abraham (Quinquagesima)
(4)	**L**aus sit in ierusalem	(a)	"Praise be to Jerusalem	Apoc. 21:1–4 (New Jerusalem)
	per ruborem huius sanguinis.	(b)	through the redness of this blood."	Apoc. 7:14; 12:11; 22:14 (Colour is unique to Hildegard)

(5)	**D**einde uenit sacrificium uituli quod uetus lex ostendebat	(a) Next came the sacrifice of the calf, (b) which the old law revealed	Gen. 8:20; Ex. 24:5–8; Heb. 9:6–7, 11–14, 16, 18–20; cf. Lev. 7:1–2
	sacrificium laudis	(c) as a sacrifice of praise,	Ps. 49:9–10, 14, 23; 106:22 (23); 115:15–17; Heb. 13:11–15
	circumamicta uarietate et quae faciem dei moysi obnubilabat dorsum illi ostendens.	(d) a law veiled with variety, (e) and which screened God's face from Moses, (f) showing his back to him.	Ps. 44:10; cf. 44:14–15 Ex. 28:11 (also 39:13); 33:20–3
(6)	**H**oc sunt sacerdotes qui per linguas suas deum ostendunt et perfecte eum uidere non possunt.	(a) In this, there are priests, (b) who, through their tongues, make God known, (c) and him, they cannot fully see.	Acts 2:6–11 1 Cor. 13:9–12
(7)	**E**t dixerunt.	(a) And they said:	
(8)	**O** nobilissima turba uirgo ista quae in terris Ursula uocatur in summis columba nominatur quia innocentem turbam ad se collegit.	(a) "O most noble throng: (b) That virgin, (c) who in all the world is called the bear, (d) in the heights is named the dove, (e) for she gathers an innocent throng to herself.	Cant. 2:14; 5:2; 6:8 cf. Ps. 44:15–16
(9)	**O** ecclesia tu es laudabilis in ista turba.	(a) O Church: (b) you are praiseworthy in that throng."	Heb. 12:22–3

CAO 6055 Aedificavit Noe altare (Quinquagesima)

CAO 7762 V. Immola Deo sacrificium laudis (Quinquagesima)

CAO 7340 V. Astitit ... circumamicta (Assumption)

CAO 7484 Qui sunt nubes ... quasi columbae (Is. 60) (Assumption)

Table 10.1 (*cont.*)

(10) Turba magna	(a) The great throng –	Apoc. 7:9–10	CAO 6131 V. Rubum quem viderat
quam incombustus rubus	(b) this is what the unburnt bush	Ex. 3:2–3	moyses incombustum, conser-
quem moyses uiderat significat	(c) (that Moses had seen) signifies,		vatam, agnovimus tuam
et quam deus in prima radice	(d) and what God had planted in the first root,	Gen. 2:8	laudabilem virginitatem
plantauerat			(Assumption)
in homine quem de limo formauerat	(e) in the human being whom he had formed	Gen. 2:7	CAO 6928, 6739 Formavit ...
	from clay,		Dominus hominem de limo
ut sine commixtione uiri uiueret	(f) so that without a man's commingling he	(Hildegard)	(Septuagesima)
	might have life		
cum clarissima uoce clamauit	(g) – this throng cried out with the clearest voice,	Ex. 25:11, 17, 24, 29, 39;	CAO 1532 ... titulus ... pudoris ...
in purissimo auro thopazio et saphiro	(h) in the purest gold, topaz and sapphire,	28:17–20; 39:10–13;	fundata sapphiris (Purification)
circumamicta in auro.	(i) veiled with gold:	Apoc. 21:19–21	
(11) Nunc gaudeant omnes celi	(a) "Now let all the heavens rejoice,	Apoc. 21:1–2	CAO 7877 Vidi ... Jerusalem
et omnes populi cum illis ornentur.	(b) and may all the peoples with them be		... ornatam tanquam sponsam
	adorned.		(2 p. Easter)
amen.	(c) Amen."		

Variant readings:

(D = Dendermonde St-Pieters & Paulusabdij Cod 9; R = Wiesbaden, Landesbibliothek Hs. 2, 'Riesenkodex')

1a: D has 'CVM' uppercase and rubricated; R has 'Cum', only the 'C is rubricated; 1c: R adds 'sonuidei' (crossed out) after 'dei'

2b: R punctuates with ':'

3a: D omits uppercase rubricated 'E'

4b: R punctuates with ':'

5a: R reads 'uirtuli'; 5e: R reads 'que' (no e cedilla)

6c: D reads 'perfectae' (has e cedilla)

8b: D reads 'virga'

9a–b: R omits

sermons and writings, and it is striking that all of the images cultivated in this song are extensively developed in her visionary trilogy of theological works.

In *Cum uox sanguinis*, the images are presented in a particularly compact and enigmatic form, and the rhetorical emphasis provided by the musical setting produces a *ductus figuratus* that speaks to those already initiated into the deeper meanings that the images convey and who delight in meditating upon 'the productive and health-giving obscurity' of Scripture.[55] As we have seen above in the Paraclete liturgy, the careful deployment and explanation of such imagery could organize a whole liturgical celebration, or, indeed, a whole liturgical season. However, Hildegard's hymn takes the opposite approach, producing a procession of the images themselves linked in such a way that the relationships between them are recapitulated and completed through the music. The opening image of the hymn, *uox sanguinis*, is particularly important to the structure of its chain of figurative associations. It has two biblical loci: the first is from the Old Testament (Genesis 4) where Cain has murdered Abel because the Lord had found Abel's sacrificial offerings acceptable while rejecting Cain's own. In Genesis 4: 9–10 the phrase is used verbatim as the Lord questions Cain about the murder of his brother Abel: 'And the Lord said to Cain: Where is your brother Abel? And he answered, I do not know: am I my brother's keeper? And he said to him: What have you done? The voice of your brother's blood [*vox sanguinis fratris tui*] cries out to me from the earth.' The second scriptural reference, from the New Testament Letter to the Hebrews, is more subtle, since the phrase 'uox sanguinis' is not used verbatim, but it is clear that Hebrews 12:24 concludes with an allusion to the phrase to end a long discussion about martyrdom (the 'great cloud of witnesses', *tanta nubes testium*, mentioned in 12:1). In 12:18–24, Abel's death foreshadows Christian martyrdom, contrasting the old covenant received by Moses on Mount Sinai (cf. Exodus 19–20) with the new covenant effected by the sacrificial death of Christ:

For you have not come to a passable mountain, and a burning fire, and a whirlwind, and darkness, and storm, and the sound of a trumpet, and the voice of words, from which they who heard absolved themselves, so that the word would not be spoken to them: For they did not endure what used to be said: 'And if even a beast touches the mount, it shall be stoned.' And what was seen was so terrible that Moses said: 'I am frightened, and tremble.'

But you have come to mount Zion, and to the city of the living God, the heavenly Jerusalem, and to the company of many thousands of angels, and to the church of the firstborn, who are enrolled in the heavens, and to God the judge of all, and to the spirits of the just made perfect, and to Jesus the mediator of the new testament, and to the sprinkling of blood which speaks better than that of Abel [*et sanguinis aspersionem melius loquentem quam Abel*].

Hildegard explicitly built upon this allusion to Abel's murder in Hebrews when providing her own commentary on Genesis 4:10 in her last great visionary work, *Liber divinorum operum*, interpreting martyrdom as a particularly acceptable sacrifice that anticipates future heavenly glory:

Indeed, the blood-red voice of the martyrs [*sanguinea … vox martyrum*], who knew neither sins, nor why they were killed, ascended to God; but the splendour of divinity shines upon them in such a way that it foreshadows the future innumerable multitude with the same splendour of divinity. For the brightness of eternal life is given to them, in which they know the answer that has been made known to them; and their cry has not been covered over with base works of sinners, because they were innocent, and because their blood was poured out according to the Incarnation of the Son of God, when they declared that the Lamb would pour out his own blood.

And these are called companions, they who were killed on account of faith and justice … For the voice of the blood poured out of a human being ascends on high through his soul crying out and complaining, that it has been expelled from the individual body in which God had placed it: and then the same soul receives the merits of its works either in glory or in punishments. Indeed, the first voice of blood began to cry out to God in Abel, for Cain recklessly and wantonly destroyed the building of the works of God.[56]

Hildegard's text not only gathers up all of the associations from Genesis and Hebrews, but alludes to the Apocalypse (chapters 7 and 22 in particular) and (in the last line) delicately touches on the metaphor of the body as a tabernacle or temple, a favourite metaphor of monastic authors. The song alludes to all of these themes and so could serve (like the songs at the end of *Scivias*) as a summary and powerful re-presentation of the vision Hildegard is interpreting in *Liber divinorum*.

It is not only the opening image that is deeply implicated in the song text, along with its biblical intertext and Hildegard's theological interpretation: each image draws upon a similar range of biblical associations which are deployed over the whole text of this song. The third column of Table 10.1 lists the biblical references that undergird the imagery, and indicates that the progression of imagery is set up in such a way that the song text refers to Old Testament *historiae* or types that alternate with their New Testament analogues.

In the first stanza, the Old Testament images are principally drawn from Genesis and alternate with material from, or related to, the Apocalypse. The martyrs' blood in the song text (1a) calls to mind Abel's blood, while Ursula's throng (1b) calls to mind the multitude of martyrs in heaven (1b and c). The ancient prophecy (1d) comes through the root or foot of the mountain Mamre (1e), where three angelic visitors appeared to Abraham to announce that Sarah would conceive in her old age, and in line 1f the traditional interpretation of the three visitors is supplied: it is a revelation of the Trinity (and therefore of last things). Stanza two begins with images that allude to the Apocalypse: the blood which 'touches us' (2a) and the rejoicing (in 2b) indirectly suggest the elders washing their robes in the blood of the Lamb in the Apocalypse. These references are explicitly called to mind when the 'congregation of the lamb' enters (3a), and, as stated earlier, line 3b refers to the ram that substituted as a sacrifice for Isaac, one of several Old Testament types for Christ the Lamb of God. Stanza four again shifts to the New Jerusalem of the Apocalypse, where the red blood of the martyrs is praised (4a–b).

Although stanzas 5 and 6 continue to alternate allusions to Old Testament narratives with their intepretations within the New Testament, the Old Testament source shifts from the first book of the Pentateuch, Genesis, to the second, Exodus. The 'sacrifice of the calf' (5a) is a reference to Moses' sanctification of the book and people of the covenant, named here as the old law (5b). The sections of the Letter to the Hebrews given above as sources for lines 5b and c, explicitly explain the images from Exodus as types signifying Christ's sacrifice. The 'sacrifice of praise' (5c) is found in several Psalm verses. For example, the whole of Psalm 49 argues that priestly sacrifices are meaningless without an interior sacrifice of praise, and Hebrews 13:15, using the term *hostia laudis*, defines the sacrifice of praise as 'the fruit of the lips confessing Christ's name'. Line 5d uses a distinctive phrase from Psalm 44, an epithalamium that was used allegorically at many Marian feasts and feasts for virgins.[57] In Psalm 44 the words *circumamicta uarietate* describe the bride's clothing, and since its lexical range includes the ideas of disguising and covering, I suggest a translation that combines the bridal theme with these nuances. Thus the phrase 'sacrifice of praise, a law veiled with variety' (5c–d) turns the sacrifice of Ursula's virgin martyrs into their bridal procession, even though the images have been carefully chosen in order to conjure up the context of the Song of Songs without using the traditional *sponsus/sponsa* imagery. In Psalm 44 itself the phrase *circumamicta uarietate* is echoed later on by a similar phrase, *circumdata in auro* [set in gold] and line 10i of Hildegard's song conflates these two passages, in the construction *circumamicta in auro*. Moreover, these images have a double edge, since they are similar to the language used to describe Aaron's priestly vestments and the ornamentation of the ark and tabernacle in Exodus 24–5. The progression of the images thus relates Abel's acceptable sacrifice to the sacrifice of the temple, to the moral sacrifice of praise, as well as to the bodily sacrifice of the virgin martyrs, and identifies all of them as priestly. The opening of stanza 6 then acts as a gloss for the whole section: 'Hoc sunt sacerdotes' [In this (series of sacrificial actions), there are priests]. Even though these priests may make God known through preaching (through their tongues), they, like Moses, have only a partial vision of God (6c).

The final section of the song (stanzas 8–11) connects Ursula's throng of virgin martyrs (8) to the merits of the Church (9) and to the Apocalypse's great throng of martyrs (10) through a series of linked images. Stanza 8 also develops the bridal imagery, since Ursula, the leader of the 'noble throng' of virgin martyrs, receives a symbolic name: *columba*, the dove, which is used as a pet name for the *sponsa* in the Song of Songs; nevertheless, the text again avoids direct reference to the terms *sponsus* and *sponsa*. In stanza 10 the 'turba magna' [great crowd of martyrs] is revealed as the reality prefigured by the burning bush from which God spoke in Exodus and as the significance of the virginal creation of Adam from clay in paradise. Finally, the crowd cries out in purest gold, topaz and sapphire set in gold. Although, as mentioned above, all of these images come from Aaron's priestly vestments and the ornamentation of the ark, tabernacle and temple, they are also used in the Apocalypse to describe the construction of the New Jerusalem. Thus the prayer asking that all the people be adorned along with the heavens is yet another veiled allusion to bridal imagery, calling to mind Apocalypse 21:2 without quoting it directly, in which the New Jerusalem, representing the redeemed Church, descends from God 'adorned like a bride – *sponsa ornata* – for her husband.'

The extensive use of biblical imagery in *Cum uox sanguinis* can thus be seen to operate in two ways. First, images are acquired through the verbatim quotation of short phrases of Scripture which, since they are distinctive and occur only rarely in the Bible, can serve as mnemonic loci that call to mind their larger biblical context. Examples of these are *uox sanguinis* (1a); *sacrificium uituli* (5a); *sacrificium laudis* (5c); *circumamicta uarietate* (5d); *columba* (8d); *turba magna* (10a); and *in purissimo auro* (10h). Second, clever paraphrases of Scripture, whether created anew or borrowed from older readings embedded in commentary, are constructed so that not only the biblical locus may be evoked but also the wider context of quotation in commentary, presumably including Hildegard's own preaching and teaching, may be called to mind. Examples of these are *per radicem mambrae* (1e); *congregatio agni* (3a); *per arietem in spinis pendentem* (3b); *per ruborem huius sanguinis* (4b); *dorsum illi ostendens* (5f); *per linguas suas deum ostendunt* (6b); *incombustus rubus* (10b); *in prima radice plantauerat* (10d); and *circumamicta in auro* (10i).

The deployment of this imagery (its *ductus*) is carefully controlled throughout the poem. While the principal technique used is to provide arresting images that call to mind the more difficult and enigmatic of the 'saving obscurities of Scripture', they are not simply piled up upon each other haphazardly. Instead, they are introduced and linked with terms and phrases used in Scripture that introduce revelation of mysteries, and with terms and phrases used in Scripture commentary that promise explanation of obscurities. For example, the image of the 'root (or foot) of Mamre' is glossed 'in a true manifestation of the Trinity' (1f). Although both the location and the explanation are traditional, the song text omits the detail of the three angelic visitors that makes its traditional interpretation function. Similarly, the 'sacrifice of the calf' is glossed as an image which the old law revealed (5b), but omits any of the narrative detail that connects the sacrifice to Moses' anointing the book and people of the covenant.

The following stanza borrows a standard phrase used in commentary, *Hoc sunt* or *hoc est* [In this, there are/is]. The ablative *hoc* is used to signal that it is all of the previous discussion that is being glossed, not an individual term that would normally use an *id est* gloss (or somewhat confusingly a *hoc est* gloss where *hoc* is neuter nominative). The opening of stanza 6 thus promises an explanation of the foregoing obscurities, but the precise referent of *hoc* is ambiguous. Is it the reference to sacrifices that reveals the presence of priests, or their role in anointing (which is part of the missing narrative context), or the more proximate images of the imperfect law that obscures Moses' vision of God?

Stanza 8 also promises clarification, offering an alternative name for Ursula (using the rhetorical figure *etymologia* often found in commentary to explain Hebrew names and places and to reveal a deeper symbolic meaning). In lines 8c–d, the earthly name Ursula (little bear) is given its heavenly meaning *columba* (dove), but, as has already been pointed out, the new name creates yet another level of allegory, rather than clarifying an allegorical term with its literal signifier. Finally, in Stanza 10a–c, it is 'the great multitude that the unburnt bush signifies [*significat*].' The verb *significo* is a favourite in biblical commentary and a key term in

Augustine's discussion of figurative language in *De doctrina Christiana*, but here and in the following lines the explanatory glosses link Old Testament imagery and metaphors to New Testament imagery and metaphors, although they never explain the connections being made. To sum up: although the text constantly seems to work exegetically by juxtaposing Old Testament *figurae* with New Testament *res*, it actually jumps over the New Testament narrative to substitute a set of New Testament images that turn out to be another set of *figurae* (at the anagogical rather than allegorical level of interpretation). Since all of these New Testament images are left obscure in the hymn text itself, the hymn, as a whole, is a tour de force of monastic *ductus figuratus*, offering a structured presentation of the obscure imagery of the Bible that (for an initiate) provides the stages for an entry into its deeper (though no less obscure) meaning.

However, it is also a tour de force of *ductus subtilis* ('in which the mind wants to plead one thing, but the speech pleads another'). The *intentio hymni* is to celebrate the feast of Ursula and her companions, but the progression of imagery places their sacrifice within the whole history of sacrifices that authorizes and creates the redeemed Church, only without ever mentioning the Passion and Resurrection narratives that were considered to have revealed the *res* behind all of the imagery.

While it is certainly the case that these foundational narratives were so well-known that they formed a backdrop against which all of the more difficult images could be projected, the specific deployment of the images in this hymn is at the very least informed by, and perhaps even inspired by, an even deeper level of the patterned appropriation of biblical narrative presented by the liturgy itself. The fourth column of Table 10. 1 lists the series of liturgical items that have *materia* in common with the key images used in *Cum uox sanguinis*. It will probably suffice simply to translate their *incipits* in order to demonstrate how much Hildegard's choice of imagery has been influenced by them: 'Where is your brother Abel?', 'While Abraham stood at the foot of Mambre', 'God tempted Abraham', 'Noah built an altar', 'Offer God a sacrifice of praise', 'She stood, veiled', 'What clouds are these [...] like doves', 'The bush which Moses had seen, unburnt, preserved, we acknowledge to be your praiseworthy virginity', 'The Lord formed man from clay', 'A tablet of chastity, founded on sapphires', and 'I saw Jerusalem, adorned like a bride'. However, the influence of the liturgy does not end there. As can be seen in the liturgical assignments given for each of the antiphons and responsories, much of the ordering and deployment of the images follows the progression of the long season of Lent, starting from Septuagesima rather than Ash Wednesday, when the prescribed readings in Matins were the first books of Scripture, Genesis and Exodus, before moving on to readings that were topically arranged around the temptations of the senses and designed to provoke systematic self-examination and contrition. The whole season of Lent was a prolonged period of preparation, meditation and mortification, leading to the celebration of Easter, and it is not by chance that the Easter season responsory *Vidi ... Jerusalem* concludes the set of references. The remaining allusions to the liturgy are all taken from Marian feasts, largely the Assumption, pointing to the association of Mary with the new Ecclesia, so popular in twelfth-century Song of Songs commentaries, but also bringing in the perfection of the body in chastity from the feast of the Purification. Hildegard's liturgical structure can thus be seen to be almost identical to that at the Paraclete. It closely associates, and supports the connection of, women's monasticism with the liturgical progression from Lent to Easter, during which the fundamental narratives of salvation are represented.

During the twelfth century the same societal changes that created new opportunities for a revival of women's monasticism also caused a sustained debate about the proper ways to live out a Christian vocation and a sense of disconnection between the professed beliefs and the desires voiced by many men and women in monastic institutions. Abelard, at Heloise's instigation and with her oversight, contributed to her reform of the Paraclete liturgy by attempting to shape the liturgy itself into a rhetorically convincing act, adapting the *materia* so that it would be systematically addressed to the nuns *ad status*, and specifically addressing the gap between belief (*intentio*) and feeling (*affectus*) by providing ritual celebrations of women's religious lament and joy. Hildegard, in addressing the same gap, reshaped the liturgy with words and music that enabled her community to participate as directly as possible in her own visionary experience. This experience was strongly shaped by the traditional words and images presented in the liturgy, but newly offered back in Hildegard's charismatic and prophetic voice.

NOTES

* I would like to thank Margaret Bent for the opportunity to present my initial analysis of Hildegard's *Cum uox sanguinis* at her Seminar for Medieval and Renaissance Music, All Souls College, Oxford, November 2005.

1 G. Constable, *The Reformation of the Twelfth Century* (Cambridge University Press, 1996); B. L. Venarde, *Women's Monasticism and Medieval Society: Nunneries in France and England, 890–1215* (Ithaca, NY: Cornell University Press, 1997), 52–88.

2 See Hildegard of Bingen, *De regula Sancti Benedicti*, ed. H. Feiss, in *Hildegardis Bingensis Opera Minora*, ed. P. Dronke *et al.*, CCCM 226 (Turnhout: Brepols, 2007), 67–97. See also C. Mews, 'Heloise and Hildegard', *Tjurunga*, 44 (1993): 20–9, at 23.

3 In citing the Letters of Abelard and Heloise, I follow the numbering of the letters in PL 178, cols. 113A–340D, making use of these editions: *Historia calamitatum*, ed. J. Monfrin (Paris: Vrin, 1967) (Letter 1, 62–109); J. T. Muckle, 'The Personal Letters between Abelard and Heloise', *Mediaeval Studies*, 15 (1953): 47–94 (Letter 2, 68–73; Letter 3, 73–7; Letter 4, 77–82; Letter 5, 83–94); J. T. Muckle, 'The Letter of Heloise on Religious Life and Abelard's First Reply', *Mediaeval Studies*, 17 (1955): 240–81 (Letter 6, 241–53; Letter 7, 253–81); T. P. McLaughlin, 'Abelard's Rule for Religious Women', *Mediaeval Studies*, 18 (1956): 241–92 (Letter 8, 242–92); and Peter Abelard, *Letters IX–XIV*, ed. E. R. Smits (Groningen: Rijksuniversiteit, 1983) (Letter 9, 219–37; Letter 10, 239–47). Letter 6 contains Heloise's critique of the Benedictine Rule. See L. Georgianna, '"In Any Corner of Heaven": Heloise's Critique of Monastic Life,' in B. Wheeler (ed.), *Listening to Heloise: The Voice of a Twelfth-Century Woman* (New York: St Martin's Press, 2000), 187–216.

4 Replacing the Rule had a profound impact on the Paraclete liturgy. C. Waddell has demonstrated that many of the elements of the altered liturgy persisted in later sources. See his editions and commentaries of *Nationale Ms français 14410, and the Paraclete Breviary: Chamont, Bibliothèque Municipale Ms 31: Introduction and Commentary*, CLS 3 (1985); *The Old French Paraclete Ordinary: Edition*, CLS 4 (1983); *The Paraclete Breviary: Edition*, 3 vols., CLS 5–7 (1983); and *Hymn Collections from the Paraclete*, 2 vols., CLS 8–9 (1989); hereafter cited as CLS and volume number. See also J. Szövérffy, *Peter Abelard's Hymnarius Paraclitensis*, 2 vols. (Albany: Classical Folia, 1975). The Paraclete Institutions (*Institutiones nostrae*) were most likely compiled by Heloise and are printed as part of the appendix to Letter 8 in PL 178, cols. 313–17B. Abelard's sermons are in PL 178, 379–610. See also *I sermoni di Abelardo per le monache del Paracleto*, ed. P. de Santis (Leuven University Press, 2002). Although the two most important liturgical sources, edited by Waddell (CLS 4 and 5), exist only in manuscripts dating from the late thirteenth century (the Ordinary) and the late fifteenth (the Breviary), Abelard's influence can be confirmed from the hymns and sermons assigned, and other unique features of the liturgy that are first mentioned in Letters 3, 5–8 and 10.

5 Abelard, Letter 10. See also C. Waddell, 'Peter Abelard's *Letter 10* and Cistercian Liturgical Reform', in J. R. Sommerfeldt (ed.), *Studies in Medieval Cistercian History II*, Cistercian Studies Series 24 (Kalamazoo, MI: Cistercian Publications, 1976), 75–86.

6 Heloise, Letter 6, 242.

7 W. T. Flynn, 'Letters, Liturgy, and Identity: The Use of *Epithalamica* at the Paraclete', in G. Iversen and N. Bell (eds.), *Sapientia et Eloquentia: Meaning and Function in Liturgical Poetry, Music, Drama, and Biblical Commentary in the Middle Ages*, Disputatio 11 (Turnhout: Brepols, 2009), 301–48.

8 On the stability of solemn feasts, see A. Baumstark, *Comparative Liturgy*, rev. B. Botte, trans. F. L. Cross (London: Mowbray, 1958), 26–30. On rare and unique texts found at the Paraclete, see C. Waddell, 'Peter Abelard as Creator of Liturgical Texts', in R. Thomas (ed.), *Petrus Abaelardus (1079–1142): Person, Werke und Wirkung*, Trierer Theologische Studien 38 (Trier: Paulinus Verlag, 1980), 267–86.

9 Abelard, Letter 1, 65–6.

10 C. Mews, 'Peter Abelard on Dialectic, Rhetoric, and the Principles of Argument', in C. Mews *et al.*, (eds.), *Rhetoric and Renewal in the Latin West 1150–1540: Essays in Honour of John O. Ward*, Disputatio 2 (Turnhout: Brepols, 2003), 37–53. The rest of this paragraph depends upon Mews.

11 Mews, 'Peter Abelard on Dialectic', 47–8.

12 Aberald, *Super topica glossae*, excursus on rhetoric, I.3.1. Edited in K. M. Fredbrog, 'Abelard on Rhetoric', in Mews *et al.*, (ed.), *Rhetoric and Renewal*, 55–80, at 66. All translations of Latin are my own throughout.

13 All versions of the commentary are thought to date either from around 1133 or 1135/6. Abelard's thinking about ethical *intentio* seems to grow out of his rhetorical concerns, so I would incline towards the later date, closer to his *Scito te ipsum*.

14 P. von Moos, 'Literary Aesthetics in the Latin Middle Ages: The Rhetorical Theology of Peter Abelard', in *Rhetoric and Renewal*, 81–97, at 87–9, 95–6.

15 In his later writing Abelard uses the word *voluntas* with a meaning that is better translated as 'desire' than 'will'.

16 For his categorization of Scripture, Abelard relies on Augustine, *De Genesi ad Litteram*, ed. J. Zycha, CSEL 28 (Wittenberg: F. Tempsky, 1894), I.1.3.

17 Abelard reports criticisms that Heloise made about the arrangement, authorship and authority of hymns (at a time when the Cistercians had also strongly criticized the hymnal) in order to authorize his own more rationally arranged hymnal; see his first preface, CLS 9, 5–9.

18 Abelard, *Commentaria in Epistolam Pauli ad Romanos*, in *Opera Theologica I*, ed. E. M. Buytaert, CCCM 11 (Turnhout: Brepols, 1969), 43.

19 On *ductus* theory, see L. Calboli Montefusco, '*Ductus* and *color*: The right way to compose a suitable speech', *Rhetorica*, 21 (2003): 113–31.

20 Martianus Capella, *De nuptiis Philologiae et Mercurii*, ed. J. Willis (Leipzig: Teubner, 1983), 165. See the discussion of the uses of *ductus* in medieval rhetoric in the essay by M. Carruthers, Chapter 8 above.

21 Von Moos, 'Literary Aesthetics', 88–9.

22 *Ibid.*, 89.

23 For a discussion of the appreciation of the figurative language in Scripture and its practical application to works written for the liturgy, see W. T. Flynn, *Medieval Music as Medieval Exegesis* (Lanham, MD: Scarecrow Press, 1998), chapter one, 'Reading and Proclaiming: Ornate Language in Grammar, Rhetoric and Liturgy', 9–56.

24 M. Carruthers, 'Late Antique Rhetoric, Early Monasticism, and the Revival of School Rhetoric', in C. D. Lanham (ed.), *Latin Grammar and Rhetoric: From*

Classical Theory to Medieval Practice (London: Continuum, 2002), 239–57, at 245. The quotation at the end of this passage is from Augustine, *De doctrina Christiana*, IV.8.22.

25 Some of the arguments here can be found in a more fully developed form in Flynn, 'Letters, Liturgy, and Identity'.

26 M. M. McLaughlin first set out Abelard's theory that women involved in religious life have a special dignity because of the historical and allegorical connection that they have to Christ, in 'Peter Abelard and the Dignity of Women: Twelfth-Century "Feminism" in Theory and Practice', in *Pierre Abélard, Pierre le Vénérable: les courants philosophiques, littéraires et artistiques en Occident au milieu du XIIe siècle* (Paris: Centre National de la Recherche Scientifique, 1975), 287–333. See also G. Macy, 'Heloise, Abelard and the Ordination of Abbesses', *Journal of Ecclesiastical History*, 57 (2006): 16–32.

27 This is not a biblical quote, but is from the Holy Saturday liturgy for Lauds.

28 Abelard, Letter 5, 83–4.

29 Abelard, Letter 7, 264–5. Since the passage from Letter 5 quoted above contains, *in nuce*, Abelard's whole theory of women's monasticism, one suspects that the letter corpus as it has been transmitted is a thoroughly redacted exchange designed to reinforce the Paraclete's constitution and liturgy. For more information, see my 'Letters, Liturgy, and Identity'. See also M. Powell, 'Listening to Heloise at the Paraclete: Of Scholarly Diversion and a Woman's "Conversion"', in *Listening to Heloise*, 255–86.

30 The antiphon is always assigned to the Gospel canticle (*Benedictus*) for Lauds of Holy Saturday; see *Corpus antiphonalium officii*, ed. R.-J. Hesbert, 6 vols., Rerum ecclesiasticarum documenta, series maior Fontes 7–12 (Rome: Herder, 1963–79), vol. 3, CAO no. 3,826. The dominical ministry of these women followers (with a special emphasis on the several accounts of a woman anointing Christ in anticipation of his burial – all of which are attributed to Mary Magdalene) is treated in Abelard's Letter 7, 254–8.

31 It is perhaps possible that this theme was explicitly developed in the Paraclete Easter liturgy. Although the sequence of Matins readings and responsories cannot be fully reconstructed, it is clear that it is a unique series beginning with a reading starting at Genesis 49:9 (which treats the lion of Judah), and answered with a responsory based on Apocalypse 5:5 (in which the lion of Judah opens the book of life). If the series continued to pair allegorical types from the Old Testament with their analogues in the Apocalypse, the culmination of the series may have paired Jerusalem as widow with the Apocalypse's *sponsa ornata*. The series was then followed by another unique series of canticles from the Song of Songs. See CLS 4, 30; CLS 5, 386–7.

The traditional link between the earthly *Lamentationes lamentationum* and the heavenly *Cantica canticorum* through the personae of the *vidua* and *sponsa* can be seen in Gilbert the Universal, *Glossa ordinaria in Lamentationes Ieremie Prophete, Prothemata et Liber I*, ed. with introduction and translation by A. Andrée, Studia Latina Stockholmiensia 52 (Stockholm: Almqvist & Wiksell, 2005), 162.

32 Abelard, Letter 5, 91–2.

33 CLS 4, 25 and 30.

34 Waddell gives a good account of the problems of the records, in his introduction to the Ordinary in CLS 3, the gist of which is that the Ordinary is a not always successful Old French translation of a Latin Ordinary now lost, and it may also inadequately represent or intentionally omit rites given by the exemplar that had since passed out of use.

35 CLS 4, 28.

36 CLS 3, 112–13.

37 Abelard, Sermon 10, PL 178, 448B.

38 CLS 9, 49. J. M. Ziolkowski gives a good orientation to these prefaces and a convenient translation in *The Letters of Peter Abelard: Beyond the Personal* (Washington: Catholic University Press, 2008), 24–51.

39 Abelard, Letter 8, 263.

40 The patterns of reading indicated in the Paraclete Ordinary show that Gospel readings at Matins were indeed replaced, at least in part, and that a century and a half later the new pattern persisted for thirty-nine principal feasts. See CLS 3, 365.

41 Its preface states (in extremely flowery rhetoric) that his sermons will focus on plain explanation, which (in the main) they do. For the text of the preface, see *I sermoni di Abelardo*, 85, and Ziolkowski, *Letters of Abelard*, 64–72.

42 For Abelard's comments on the Triduum and the full Lent–Easter season, see his Easter Sermon, PL 178, 486C–D.

43 Abelard considered the narrative of the Passion itself to be more convincing and compelling than any allegories foretelling it or founded upon it; see his Sermon 11, PL 178, 453C.

44 CLS 9, 64. The liturgical assignments are complex, since none of the patterns of assignment suggested in Abelard's hymnal prefaces is consistently retained in the surviving Ordinary and Breviary. In my suggested assignments, I have followed the pattern given in the prefaces that corresponds most closely to Abelard's preference for having the uninterpreted words of Scripture at night and the explanation of allegory in the day.

45 Abelard, Sermon 13, PL 178, 484B.

46 T. J. Bell has investigated the relationship between two sequences (*Epithalamica* and *Virgines castae*) that Waddell controversially attributed to Abelard and Abelard's other writings, in *Peter Abelard After Marriage: The Spiritual Direction of Heloise and Her Nuns through Liturgical Song*, Cistercian Studies Series 211 (Kalamazoo, MI: Cistercian Publications, 2007); 261–74 treat *Epithalamica* directly. However, Dronke, among others, is convinced that neither sequence displays Abelard's poetic voice. See P. Dronke and G. Orlandi, 'New Works by Abelard and Heloise?', *Filologia mediolatina*, 12 (2005): 123–77. What can be stated with certainty, and what I have demonstrated in my 'Letters, Liturgy, and Identity', is that *Epithalamica* is so implicated in the Paraclete liturgy and forms such an important ritual highpoint in it, so thoroughly coordinated with revisions known to be Abelard's, that it

must have been part of Heloise's and Abelard's plans for its reformed liturgy from the beginning. Judging by the sources uncovered by Bell, the same case might be made for *Virgines castae*.

47 See Abelard's Easter Sermon 13, PL 178, 485C.

48 Heloise, Letter 6, 242: 'quae feminarum sit propria et ex integro nostrae conversionis statum habitumque describat'.

49 The most recent text editions of all of these are available in *Hildegardis Bingensis, Opera minora*. The three works cited here are the song collection, *Symphonia armonie celestium reuelationem*, ed. B. Newman, 373–477, *Ordo uirtutum*, ed. P. Dronke, 505–21, and the sermons, *Expositiones euangeliorum*, ed. B. Kienzle, 187–333.

50 Unfortunately, Newman's edition of *Symphonia* creates a series of section titles that are similar to festal rubrics and that undergird her (possibly correct) argument that the overall arrangement in Dendermonde, St-Pieters & Paulusabdij MS Cod. 9 is closest to an authorial archetype. This means that the existing assignments, both generic and festal, conveyed by the rubrics are relegated to the apparatus, and the precise location of the festal rubrics (which are, of course, entered only at the beginning of the relevant group of chants) cannot be accurately reconstructed from her edition.

51 Hildegard specifically states that the music of the songs concluding *Scivias* completed her understanding of the meaning of all that went before; see Hildegard of Bingen, *Scivias*, ed. A. Führkötter, CCCM 43 (Turnhout: Brepols, 1978), III.13, 632. For the full argument, see W. T. Flynn, 'Singing with Angels: Hildegard of Bingen's Representations of Celestial Music', in J. Raymond (ed.), *Conversations with Angels*, (Palgrave Macmillan, forthcoming).

52 A full analysis of the possible reconstruction of this service and the possible liturgical uses for all of Hildegard's repertory forms a chapter of my monograph in preparation, '*Veiled with Variety': Hildegard of Bingen's Office for Saint Ursula and the Rhetoric of Twelfth-century Women's Monasticism*.

53 In my edition, I have paid particular attention to the rubrication and to the musical phrases to determine where to indicate verses and line breaks. For this reason, it differs slightly from Newman's edition, particularly in creating an entire stanza (my stanza 7) out of the words 'Et dixerunt', and in the line divisions in the later stanzas.

54 Ambrose of Milan, *Epistulae et Acta*, vol. 2, ed. M. Zelzer, in *Sancti Ambrosii opera*, CSEL 82 (Wittenberg: Hoelder-Pichler-Tempsky, 1968–90), Epistle 55.3.78.

55 Augustine, *De doctrina Christiana*, IV.8.22.

56 Hildegard of Bigen, *Liber divinorum operum*, ed. A. Derolez and P. Dronke, CCCM 92 (Turnhout: Brepols, 1996), III.4.13, 430.

57 Psalm 44 also supplies imagery used at the Paraclete in the unusual Easter sequence *Epithalamica*, and in the equally unusual sequence for feasts of virgin martyrs, *Virgines castae*.

CHAPTER II

Terribilis est locus iste

The Pantheon in 609

Susan Rankin

'St Boniface was the fourth bishop of Rome after St Gregory. He obtained for the Church of Christ from the Emperor Phocas the gift of the temple at Rome anciently known as the Pantheon because it represented all the gods. After he had expelled every abomination from it, he made a church of it dedicated to the holy Mother of God and all the martyrs of Christ, so that, when the multitudes of devils had been driven out, it might serve as a shrine for a multitude of saints.'[1]

Bede's account of the consecration of the Pantheon as a Christian church dedicated to the holy Mother of God and all the martyrs of Christ was composed in the early 730s, but depends directly on the *Liber pontificalis* for the period of Boniface IV's papacy, between 25 August 608 and 5 May 615.[2] Boniface's dealings with the Byzantine Emperor Phocas must predate his deposition and execution (at the hands of Heraclius) in October 610. Nevertheless, the occasion of the building's rededication could have been any year between 609 and 615, but is conventionally set in 609 or 610.[3]

The building known as the Pantheon – a temple dedicated to all the gods – was begun early during the reign of the Emperor Hadrian, possibly as early as 118 and finished between 125 and 128.[4] While the name of the architect is unknown, the 'conception of the building and the motivating personality behind its creation' were entirely Hadrian's.[5] This second-century building replaced a sanctuary of the same dedication constructed by Agrippa *c.* 25 BC, which had burnt down twice before Hadrian's accession.[6] That Hadrian, replacing Agrippa's building but maintaining its function, should reinstate the wording of an older inscription – M · AGRIPPA · L · F · COS · TERTIUM · FECIT[7] – underlines the significance in imperial Rome of such monuments as a connection between the present and the past.[8]

From the moment of its construction the design and symbolism of Hadrian's monumental building has brought it iconic status. Originally approached by a flight of five steps leading up to a colonnaded porch supported by Egyptian marble columns, it unites the disparate shapes of rectangle and circle. This enormous porch leads to an inner building shaped as a cylinder, covered with a dome, itself of the same height as the cylinder. Light streams into this inner building through an oculus at the top of the dome. This was an innovative conception in more than one sense, above all in the combination of rectangular and circular shapes (based on a sphere enclosed within a cylinder),[9] and in the use of an oculus in a building of this scale.[10]

Not only the size, but the rich treatment of surfaces would have impressed. A pavement designed in large alternating squares and circles within squares was made from coloured granites, marbles and porphyry. Arranged with a circle at the centre of the whole, the lines and diagonals created by these floor tiles help to articulate the circular design of the whole domed edifice. The vibrancy of colour on the floor was continued in the handling of the walls, with marble columns and marble panels, some cut from quarries in far distant corners of Hadrian's empire,[11] and thus very deliberately selected. The division of the floor was mirrored by coffering in the dome: here five rows of niches cut in steps (corresponding to the number of planets recognized in ancient astronomy), each consisting of a circle of twenty-eight (analogous to the phases of the moon), rose towards the oculus.[12]

The design of this inner building around a central *vertical* axis stretching through an oculus and the hemispherical shape of the dome, combined with the astronomical numbers used to articulate the inner surface of the dome, all reveal a cosmographically orientated intention. In this the building sits within an established tradition for the creation of representations of the heavens through symbolism or cosmological images (allowing that representation was generally achieved through images rather than physical magnitude).[13] In addition, the effect of movement of the sun's rays around the building during the day, and the incorporation into the dome of a twenty-eight phase pattern to mirror the moon's orbit around the earth, as well as a series of five progressively more distant circles standing for the revolving planets, point to a concern with marking out the cyclical movement of time, a developing characteristic of monumental decorative art in the second century. Writing in the third century, the Roman historian Dio Cassius speaks of the dome as a symbol of the heavens: 'it has this name [Pantheon], perhaps because it received among the images which decorated it the statues of many gods, including Mars and Venus; but my own opinion of the name is that because of its vaulted roof, it resembles the heavens'.[14]

Sited in the centre of the Campus Martius – a swampy area within a bend of the Tiber river – the Pantheon was angled to face and to sit on the same axis as the Mausoleum of Augustus.[15] Through this orientation, and the retention of the inscription referring to Agrippa, Hadrian publicly honoured his Augustan model.[16] Hadrian's building was not simply a temple to the gods, designed as a 'closed, self-contained cosmic space',[17] but one in which the dominion of the Roman empire might be celebrated as an aspect of the relation of its people with its gods.[18] The building openly commemorates Roman rule, just as it presents an epitome of the cosmos. In a later period, that area of the city became more inhabited; the connecting line between the Pantheon and the Mausoleum of Augustus could hardly have been visually experienced, because of the number and height of the surrounding structures. Yet the orientation of the Pantheon on an axis not quite exactly north–south could always have been read in relation to the older Augustan building.

The Pantheon is last mentioned in antique literature in a passage in the Theodosian code related to 368/370 (recording the text of a law publicly read in the Pantheon);[19] in a period after its use as a temple,[20] this was a place where the emperor conducted business. In 391–2 the Emperor Theodosius decreed the closure of pagan temples. In the five centuries between its construction and its rededication as a Christian temple in 609, the whole architectural landscape of Rome had changed. During the fourth century, the building of churches, shrines and other Christian centres had been concentrated on the edges of the city and beyond the walls. But from early in the fifth century, notwithstanding invasions and other crises, the topographical map of Rome began 'increasingly [to] reflect the city's Christian character'.[21] The construction of Santa Maria Maggiore on the summit of the Esquiline hill exemplifies a new trend to build large basilicas in more central situations; in addition, older public buildings were taken over as churches. By the end of the sixth century, places of Christian worship in Rome could be divided into three kinds: the large basilical churches, the 'tituli' (private houses and new buildings within the city used for worship) and the shrines of martyrs, sitting outside the city walls.[22] In a long period of decline from the glories of imperial Rome, the Christian Church first consolidated but eventually transformed the city:[23] Rome became the city of the apostles and St Peter, the principal Christian city in the west, 'urbs urbium et totius mundi caput'.[24]

In the newly revived Rome of the early seventh century – a city in which the Christian faith was widely perceived as the only foundation for future stability – the old, imposing edifice of the temple of all the pagan gods, the Pantheon, was rededicated. While the moment of its consecration as a Christian church belongs to the papacy of Boniface IV, the third pope to succeed Gregory the Great (590–604), it is likely that the impetus to achieve this transformation, and the civic understanding which underpinned the enterprise, derive from Gregory's reign.[25] For it was as a result of Gregory's policies, above all through his support of 'simple faith and practical tasks', that the decline of Rome's economic and social fabric was finally arrested.[26] Nevertheless, we should consider just what kind of event was taking place. Although common in the east, the taking over of pagan temples had not been sanctioned by the Roman papacy until late in Gregory's life.[27] In Rome, existing public buildings had been converted for use as Christian churches, but never a pagan temple.[28] It is, in fact, Gregory's own words which provide the most important clues to contemporary ecclesiastical understanding of the conversion of buildings from pagan to Christian use: writing to Abbot Mellitus, after his departure for England, Gregory advised 'the idol temples of that race should by no means be destroyed, but only the idols in them. Take holy water and sprinkle it in these shrines, build altars and place relics in them. For if the shrines are well built, it is essential that they should be changed from the worship of devils to the service of the true God. When the people see that their shrines are not destroyed they will be able to banish error from their hearts and be more ready to come to the places they are familiar with, but now recognizing and worshipping the true God.'[29] Gregory's letter eloquently expresses the need to remove symbols of pagan worship: in large and magnificent form the Pantheon was certainly that. But, crucially, Gregory recognizes that the change of meaning of these shrines is not to be roughly imposed: the supplanting of significance of existing, familiar buildings with the new Christian message involves more than instant alteration. Therefore it is to be undertaken as a process of persuasion: when the people to be converted 'see' (that their shrines are not destroyed but transformed), they will be able to recognize the true God and therefore have the confidence to worship him in those places. The situation in Rome was not exactly parallel – in the dual sense that the Pantheon had not been used for a long time and the people of Rome hardly needed conversion; yet it was surely necessary to demonstrate for the Romans the Christian sanctity of the Pantheon building, so that they could feel confidence in its power as a Christian space, one in which they could petition God, rather than one in which evil spirits could be summoned.[30]

Gregory's approach was innovatory only in respect of architecture: this was no more than the familiar Christian habit of overwriting previous cultural meanings. The institution of Christian feasts on specific days with previous associations (of which Christmas Day is the most celebrated), and the appropriation of iconographic schemes for Christian images,[31] offer two other groups of examples, both well-established since the fourth century. And yet the process of altering the cultural meaning of a building cannot have been quite as simple and direct as all that. On the day before its rededication the Pantheon was not a new building, waiting to be endowed with significance, but an old one,[32] constructed in a past about which Roman Christians may have had mixed feelings – remembering not only the long and glorious history of their city, but also the martyrdom of many Christians. The Pantheon had housed the statues of what were now regarded as pagan gods: indeed, its whole design was visibly inspired by a cosmological theme, eloquent in its symbolism of a pantheon of gods chosen at the inception of the building *c.* 120. That Boniface IV and other Church officials recognized the complexities of the situation is suggested by the new dedication, to Mary and all the martyrs. It is not so much that the decision to include 'all the martyrs' might be explained as an attempt to mirror the previous dedication to all the gods, as that it should have the strength – through multiplicity of resonances, especially in Rome – to comprehensively replace the older meaning: the themes of universality and cosmological unity designed into the building would respond equally well to the new dedication. Yet the patronage of the martyrs may not have been considered enough to bring confidence to the people in their worship: for alongside them was added Mary, mother of God. By the early seventh century, the cult of Mary – with its dual themes of Christology and virginity – was well-established in Rome:[33] this new dedication sat alongside two previous Roman church dedications to Mary, St Maria Maggiore (built under Sixtus III, 432–40) and St Maria Antiqua (dating from the third quarter of the sixth century). By this time, the cycle of Marian feasts had begun to develop, with the adoption in the late sixth century of a feast of the Assumption.[34] The main unresolved question, in examining the history of the Pantheon, is to establish why at this specific moment a dedication to Mary was chosen, and whether it resulted from Byzantine influence (in which negotiation with the Emperor Phocas may have played a part).

As the first pagan temple in Rome to be converted to Christian use, the occasion of the Pantheon's consecration must have held enormous significance for the people of Rome. Pagan temples in the city had been officially closed in the late fourth century, a law forbidding their spoliation passed less than a decade later by Emperor Honorius revealing one

of their possible fates.[35] Yet the importance of public buildings in the city,
in the fourth and fifth centuries at least, is underlined by the financial
resources dedicated to their preservation and restoration, even if attempts
to keep monuments in good repair were likely to fail.[36] In view of the
important cultural role of building in Roman society, and the didactic
function of monuments,[37] we cannot conceive of the Pantheon as representing a forgotten past, with an easily swept aside significance, even in
the early sixth century. Not least through the multiple texts inscribed on
the entablature of the building's front, concerning the original building
on that site, and then subsequent campaigns of building and restoration,
this was a monument which wore its history openly.[38]

As late as 538 the Roman practice of dedicating a church involved only
the celebration of the eucharist.[39] By the end of the sixth century, the
deposition of relics in the new building seems also to have become crit-
ically important, as revealed in the writings of Gregory the Great himself.[40] What materials were brought to Sancta Maria ad Martyres, and
how they were situated once there is entirely unknown: however, there
can be no doubt of the availability of many martyrs' relics, taken from
the tombs surrounding the city.[41] For Mary there could be no bodily relics: what stood in their place, as a site of veneration, was a large and very
fine icon.[42] Wolf has argued that, in the context of the transformation of
a temple in a period of calamities and in a part of Rome subject to con-
tinuous flooding, the 'Madonna of the Pantheon could ... [have] become
a sacred protector of the *Populus Romanus* in the heart of the early medieval *urbs*'.[43] The means by which the older pagan associations of this very
striking space would be obliterated, superseded by a Christian conceptualization and organization, thus involved the physical presence of the
relics of the martyrs – their closeness to those who wished to 'remember'
them and to be remembered by them – and ritual. It is with that ritual
that this study will be concerned.

SOURCES OF LITURGY FOR AN ANNUAL 'DEDICATIO BASILICAE SANCTAE MARIAE AD MARTYRES' FEAST

A chant book copied in the area of modern northeast France and Belgium
in the late eighth century includes the rubric 'III id*us* Mai*as* dedicatio
basilicae *sanctæ* Mari*æ* ad mart*yres*', followed by four Proper chants
(omitting an Alleluia).[44] The surviving books of mass chants copied in the
ninth and early tenth centuries maintain the tradition of copying proper
chants for this essentially Roman feast:[45]

Monza (mid 9th c.):	Dedicatio basilicae sanctae Mariae
Corbie (mid 9th c.):	III. Idus Maias dedicatio basilicae sanctae Mariae
Compiegne (870s):	III. Idus Maias dedicatio basilicae sanctae Mariae ad martyres
Senlis (c. 880):	III. Idus Maias dedicatio basilicae sanctae Mariae ad martyres
Laon (end 9th c.):	III. Idus Maias dedicatio sanctae Mariae
Albi (c. 900):	
Chartres (end 9th c.):	III. Idus Maias dedicatio basilicae sanctae M[ariae]
SG 359 (early 10th c.):	Dedicatio basilicae sanctae Mariae ad martyres

These chant books are consistent with the Gregorian and some Gelasian sacramentaries copied in Carolingian Francia, which include either the longer rubric identifying the date 'III Idus Maias id est XIII die mensis Maii natale sanctae Mariae ad martyres' or the shorter 'Dedicatio basilicae Mariae ad martyres';[46] and the form 'Die xiii mense mai. Dedicatio ecclesiae sanctae Mariae ad martyres' appears in Carolingian lectionaries.[47] The two forms of reference which appear in sacramentaries reflect the confusion of liturgists faced with a feast which celebrated a group of saints who did not share a day of birth into heaven. Plainly the day of Mary's heavenly birth was celebrated at another time of year,[48] while the martyrs whose relics were collected for the church were unnamed, and thus lacking single or collective dates of death/heavenly birth. Some liturgists simply proceeded in the usual manner, naming the feast 'natale sanctae Mariae ad martyres'; in view of the less comprehensible aspects of that expression, others adopted a phrase which referred to the building, recognizing the feast as a celebration of the building's consecration. (It is worth noting that the *Liber pontificalis* for 608–15 refers to a church of the blessed virgin Mary *and* all the martyrs;[49] it is only in the Life of Pope Vitalian, 657–72, that the church is named 'sancta Maria ad Martyres'.[50]) Whether both Carolingian forms of reference depend on Roman exemplars cannot be determined: at least the sharing of the simple 'dedicatio' form between chant books and sacramentaries suggests a Roman model.

Were chants copied under these rubrics composed for the Pantheon's rededication in 609? For knowledge of the liturgy of the Roman church in the late sixth and early seventh centuries, we depend more or less entirely on later sources copied elsewhere, since Roman liturgical books of this date do not survive. For the chants, for example, the earliest surviving books copied in Rome date from the eleventh century: in these the set of chants associated in Carolingian liturgical books with the dedication of Sancta Maria ad Martyres are included under the rubric 'In dedicatione ecclesiae' – matching contemporary northern practice.[51] What does survive, however, is the evidence of books copied north of the Alps which contain a liturgy named as Roman – or simply associated with Pope Gregory the Great: that is, books which were copied after the Carolingians decided to use Roman liturgical practice throughout their empire.[52] Of particular relevance to this consideration of the Sancta Maria ad Martyres dedication feast is the replication in those books of the Roman pattern of papal stational liturgy: well into the tenth century northern scribes continued to copy rubrics naming the churches where the pope should celebrate mass on feast days. Such instructions related essentially to the topography, buildings and seasonal ritual of Rome itself.[53] How such instructions could have been enacted as ritual in those places where the books were copied is difficult to clarify:[54] nevertheless, the consistency of their presence in northern books compels us to read their inclusion as more than facile copying from exemplars of something which would then be ignored.

The Carolingian directive, that Roman liturgy should become the model for northern practice, came from the central seat of power – the kings, later emperors, above all, Pippin III and his son, Charlemagne: Rome was to be a model for spiritual and daily liturgical life. It could thus be argued that it was the whole system of Roman liturgy that they aspired to recreate, not only the detail of ritual during the mass and offices but also the fundamental concept of a public system of celebration, during which a central figure (the pope) should circulate, responding to the need to petition saints for intercession at those physical places with which they were themselves associated. Yet the stational system of worship in Rome developed because of the multiplicity of Christian centres in a large urban situation, and the need to link many diverse communities. The organization of the scheme was not rooted in theological considerations, but in the topographical and social history of the city itself.[55] To understand why those stational details were copied in the north, we need to recognize the importance of Rome in the world of Western Christianity, known as the eternal city and *caput mundi*. Many people living in far-flung parts of Europe would have visited Rome, and been directly aware of the sheer number of Roman churches housing the relics of saints and martyrs. A number of guides recorded routes along which pilgrims to Rome could progress, visiting the shrines of saints to collect relics of those who had once fought for the Christian church.[56] The church of Sancta Maria ad Martyres featured prominently in those guides. The commemoration in Carolingian books of the holy shrines which studded the Roman landscape – an element often separated from the commemoration of the saints themselves on their titular feast days – reflects a deliberate appropriation of a detailed Christianized narrative of the past, a past which could be remembered through reference to a topographical model and itineraries through it. It is this appropriation which connects the later northern books with earlier Roman practice, and which underlines the veracity of their record of earlier practice. As long as the ritual enacted elsewhere sought to encapsulate the Roman papal stational visits, then the feast celebrating the consecration of the Pantheon in the name of Mary and the martyrs would remain within the scheme: the transfer of chants to a mass 'In dedicatione ecclesiae' coincides with a loss of interest in the Roman stational scheme (evident in books copied from the second half of the tenth century on).

That the liturgical materials copied in Carolingian books under such headings as 'Dedicatio sancta Maria ad martyres', whether prayers for the priest or chants for cantor and choir, were themselves Roman in origin is thus demonstrable: what is more difficult to demonstrate is a direct line from those materials back to 609. Although interested in the chants, McKinnon used evidence from the transmission of readings to raise the possibility that liturgy for the dedication feast of Sancta Maria ad Martyres was not composed for the occasion of its first Christian consecration but dated from after 645, observing that Boniface IV, despite the fact of his consecration of the Pantheon, 'appears not to have instituted a permanent annual commemoration of the event on 13 May'.[57] McKinnon made his argument on the basis of a reconstruction of a set of Gospel readings in use in Rome *c.* 645 (Π-type evangeliary).[58] However, in the case of the 13 May dedication feast, the evidence of the manuscripts on which Klauser based his reconstruction of a Π-type set of Gospel readings (of *c.* 645) is mixed: the earliest source, copied in the mid eighth century in Northumbria, is itself internally inconsistent,[59] while the next example of this reconstructed Π-type evangeliary, copied in western Germany *c.* 800, does indeed have 'Die xiii mens. Maias Dedicatio ecclesiae Scae Mariae ad martyres'.[60] The evidence of these lectionaries is confusing and cannot be so straightforwardly imposed: Frere pointed out the haphazard quality of his early Π-type and Chavasse noted the diversity of records related to practice in seventh-century Rome.[61] In the field of chant studies McKinnon's radical reading of the evidence has also been rejected: in particular Peter Jeffery has proposed other ways of reading the absence of the feast from seventh-century Roman records, that is, even supposing the hypothesis of its absence to be correct.[62] Perhaps the most useful way of summarizing the situation is to say that none of the liturgical sources from which arguments are drawn was copied before 750; none of the sources on which these arguments are based is itself Roman (until centuries later); in the vast majority of sources of Roman liturgy copied in the eighth and ninth centuries, excepting the Gelasian sacramentaries, the dedication feast of 13 May does appear.

It is only in chant books copied in the later tenth and eleventh centuries that mention of the dedication feast of Sancta Maria ad Martyres begins to disappear (in the north) – at the same time as the Proper chants associated with the feast reappear under the typical rubric 'In dedicatione ecclesiae', revealing an alternative usage which was of more specific local relevance. From at least this period, if not earlier, the mass chant set became standard not only for church consecrations, but also for an annual commemoration of that consecration.[63] In this transfer from the specific 13 May feast to the Common, the history of this set of Proper chants sits in contrast to prayers for 13 May. It has already been noted that the Gelasian sacramentaries copied in the Carolingian period have no 'Sancta Maria ad Martyres' feast: of course, they do have prayers 'in dedicacione basilicae nouae' and 'ad missas in dedicacione basilicae novae', and even a subsequent set 'Item alia missa'.[64] The first set begins:

Deus, qui loca nomine tuo decata sanctificas, effunde super hanc oracionis domum graciam tuam, ut ab omnibus hic inuocantibus te auxilium tuae misericordiae senciatur.

[O Lord, who by your name sanctify places, pour out your favour upon this house of prayer, so that here the succour of your mercy may be felt by all calling upon you.]

Likewise the Carolingian Gregorian sacramentaries include a prayer 'in dedicatione ecclesiae':

Domum tuam quaesumus domine clementer ingredere et in tuorum tibi corda fidelium perpetuam constitue mansionem, ut cuius aedificatione subsistit, huius fiat habitacionis praeclara.[65]

[We beseech you, O Lord, mercifully to enter into your house, and to establish a perpetual dwelling for yourself in the hearts of your faithful people, so that whatever remains in its construction, it might become the most splendid [edifice] of this dwelling.]

In the form transmitted from Rome, representing the papal liturgy, the Gregorian sacramentary had no other material designated for the dedication of churches: its lack is signalled by the presence in a supplement composed in the north of the rather precisely titled 'Missa in anniversario dedicationis basilicae'.[66] Between these various sets of prayers and those for 13 May there is no overlap. What these sets of mass prayers clarify, in a way that had not been absolutely made clear by the Proper chant sets, is that, outside of Rome, the mass prayers for the dedication of churches were quite independent from those for the 13 May feast. While there is no evidence about which chants were to be sung with the mass prayers for a church dedication somewhere north of Rome *c.* 800, it is certainly not possible to argue that the Proper chants associated with 13 May were created 'not as the Proper of a particular date but as the Common for the dedication of a church'.[67] The Common was not the point of departure of this chant set but its destination.

One other challenge to the relation of the chants copied under the 'Dedicatio sancta Maria ad Martyres' heading to the consecration in *c.* 609 can be more quickly set aside: this concerns their lack of mention of either Mary or the martyrs. In McKinnon's description of the chants: 'This is a Mass Proper about temples and churches, a dedication formulary; it is totally lacking in reference to Mary (or for that matter to martyrs).'[68] It was on this basis that McKinnon moved to his most definitive statement about the set of chant Propers: '[the *Terribilis est* Mass Proper] cannot have originated at the time that Boniface IV (d. 615) dedicated the Pantheon to Mary and all the martyrs. Rather it was composed when it was no longer necessary to honor Mary with a 13 May festival because the four great Marian festivals were already in place.'[69] It is certainly true that Mary and the martyrs are noticeably absent from the Proper chant texts, and, indeed, largely from the prayers (where the martyrs get but a brief notice). The argument advanced by McKinnon simply assumes that Mary and the martyrs *would* have had a place in the mass of consecration celebrated in 609; yet prayers in the Gelasian and Gregorian sacramentaries for dedication masses beyond that associated with Sancta Maria ad Martyres do not respond to that expectation. In tune with the prayers presented above, these sets are concerned with the sanctification of the building, with the presence of God in it, with the need for a supplicant to find God in that place. None of these prayers has any place for the naming of a titular patron saint. By analogy then, the argument against the relation of the chants to the original consecration in *c.* 609 falls away. Nevertheless, it remains unclear why Mary and the martyrs remain unmentioned in the chants – and I will return to this issue once the chants have been examined in detail.

PROPER CHANTS FOR THE CEREMONY
OF CONSECRATION IN 609

In view of the lack of source material from seventh-century Rome, it is impossible to prove a direct relation between the chants preserved in later books under the rubric 'Dedicatio basilicae sanctae Mariae ad martyres' and the act of consecrating the Pantheon as a Christian church in *c.* 609: yet arguments against such a relation are not convincing. The final part of this study rests on the basis that that hypothesized relation can be trusted.

Before the early seventh century, there is little sign of the orderly composition of chants for individual feasts, that is, of the composition of groups of chants of different genres at the same moment. Since individual parts of the mass ceremony developed at different times, and in different ways, it is more likely that older layers of chant developed within genres, and then became associated with individual feasts; sets of Introit, Gradual, Alleluia (or Tract), Offertory and Communion chants for specific feasts could then have been crystallized and fixed at some point – so far untraced, but probably not before the pontificate of Gregory the Great.[70] In being called for at a relatively late stage in relation to much of the Gregorian repertory, the dedication chants were probably composed as a set:[71] that this was probably the case is implied by continued use exclusively as a set, and without transferral to other feasts, with the exception of *Alleluia V. Adorabo ad templum* (which may predate this period of composition). One notable characteristic of the set, which appears deliberate (and could thus support the proposition that they were composed as a group) is the way in which they draw on biblical sources in an ordered series:

Introit	Genesis 28:17–22
Gradual	IV Ezra 8:21–4
Alleluia	Psalm 137:2
Offertory	1 Chronicles 29:16–18 and 2 Chronicles 7:8–12; 7:1–3
Communion	Matthew 21:13; 7:8

Besides the fact of beginning with Genesis, and ending with a text from one of the Gospels, we can note that this set uses a New Testament text *only* for the Communion antiphon. Such patterns are not at all usual among sets of Proper chants for individual feasts. Although the Old Testament dominates as a source for chant texts, it is by no means standard that the Communion antiphon should be isolated as the only New

Testament text, nor do other sets seem to follow any kind of biblical order. What the order of the dedication set emphasizes is not so much a sequence related to books of the Bible, as the possibility of a narrative designed into the set of Proper chants from the outset. The relation of this narrative to the function of this specific mass of consecration will be discussed further below.

Let us imagine that the building has been cleaned and renovated, and the day of the consecration has arrived. How the mass started is surprisingly easy to reconstruct, since the conduct of the papal stational mass for Easter Day is described in considerable detail in *Ordo Romanus* I:[72] the processional ceremonial might be less elaborate on this day, but it is unlikely that the structure differed. The pope would be preceded by a procession of his own clergy, with crosses and reliquaries: they would be greeted outside the building by local clergy. On arrival, the pope would go to a sacristy to vest.[73] Once ready to proceed, he would signal that the singers should begin the Introit, and while this was sung, acolytes with lighted torches, led by the thurifer, would conduct him into the central aisle of the church. The choir would bring the Introit to an end once they had received a further signal from the pope, who would then move to his seat somewhere near the main altar. For the Pantheon, we can imagine that the pope came through the porch to the door of the rotunda, and that the choir inside began singing the Introit as he stood at the door. As the pope and his entourage gazed inside, aware of the enormous dome rising above, the words 'Terribilis est locus iste' would have rung around the building. The Introit antiphon continued: 'hic domus dei est et porta caeli et vocabitur aula dei'.[74] That the space within which worship was performed should be called 'a house of God' and the 'gateway to heaven' is not unexpected, and yet these statements seem peculiarly apposite for an occasion when the function of the building needed to be so radically altered.

Beyond this first level of description and naming, there were more layers of textual meaning, easily read into the moment by anyone familiar with a well-known biblical story. As in the case of many chants, the text was compiled from a series of biblical extracts, formulated to make a short and clear statement. For this Introit antiphon the extracts were drawn from one chapter of Genesis, from the passage which describes Jacob's dream:[75] Jacob had found himself far from home and had collected stones and lain down to sleep under the open sky. In his dream a ladder had stretched from earth to heaven, with angels ascending and descending, and then God had spoken to Jacob, assuring him of His presence with him. When Jacob woke in the morning, his first words were 'Surely the Lord is in this place, and I knew it not', continuing 'How awe-inspiring is this place: this is none other but the house of God, and this is the gate of heaven.' Through the words 'Terribilis est', the Introit chant thus evoked a story in which a previously unrecognized holy place was discovered, and named as the gateway to heaven. But there is also an appeal – through the Genesis story – to the conception of this building as a universe in itself: the earth below, the heaven above. Jacob lay under the stars: the pope, gazing upwards from the door into the rotunda, would have seen light streaming through the central oculus, and bronze tiles set into the coffered niches, like stars twinkling above.[76]

This chant text was easily fixed, through its relation to its biblical sources, and its own internal syntax. While the identity of the psalm verse sung between repetitions of the Introit antiphon varies from one source to another – and now sits beyond detection – the antiphon text itself never varies, and, most significantly, survives in both Gregorian (Roman-Frankish, from the late eighth century and later) and Old Roman (Roman, from the eleventh century and later) chant books in the same, unchanged form. Musical delivery of the text may have been less fixed, more fluid: the distance between the original musical moment and the musical material as it reaches us is potentially greater than that of the text. That at least is the direct implication of the Gregorian and Old Roman melodies for *Terribilis est locus iste* (Example 11.1).[77] Yet there is no doubt that these two melodic settings are related: once the individual stylistic rules of each are recognized, the common features of the two stand out clearly. The modality of this melody is shaped by D as the point of beginning and ending, and F above as a point of recitation: when the notes on either side of this minor third, C below and G above, are reached, they usually project movement back into the central third. (Only in the Gregorian version, C is strengthened and elaborated by the A below, which can only be approached and departed from via C.) The techniques by which the two melodic dialects effect textual articulation are quite different: in this Old Roman melody, there is a noticeable concentration of melismatic development on specific words ('iste', '[de]i est', 'celi', 'dei'), always at the ends of textual phrases. In the Gregorian version, this linking of melisma with text phrase endings is almost completely reversed, with more elaboration within the phrases, and cessation of movement at the ends. Here the melody is more strongly shaped by modal thinking, the beginnings and ends of musical phrases marked by the interaction of the pitches D and C. Against this background of different procedures for

Example 11.1 Gregorian and Old Roman melodies for the Introit *Terribilis est locus iste*

the melodic articulation of the text, both melodies divide the text into short sections, thereby helping to project textual syntax:

Terribilis est locus iste : hic domus dei est : et porta caeli : et uocabitur aula dei.

After the Introit, the mass continued with the singing of the Kyrie and Gloria, and the reading of the Epistle, followed by the second Proper chant, the Gradual. Associated with meditation on the reading which it followed, the Gradual chants were highly melismatic, allowing soloists to elaborate the chosen words in long musical phrases. For this consecration

mass, the Gradual opens with a phrase which links it to the Introit antiphon, followed by words from the apocryphal book IV Ezra:

Responsory
Locus iste a deo factus est, inaestimabile sacramentum, irreprehensibilis est.

Verse
Deus cui adstat angelorum chorus, exaudi preces servorum tuorum.[78]

In contrast to the Introit antiphon, for which more or less the whole textual formulation can be traced back to one scriptural source, the text of
the Gradual's responsory and verse involved combining material from
more than one scriptural source, in addition to significant reshaping. The
opening phrase draws the words 'Locus iste' from the same passage as
the Introit (Genesis 28), whereas as a syntactical group the words 'a deo
factus est' are not scriptural. Nevertheless, they do appear to refer back to
the Genesis story: immediately before uttering 'Terribilis est locus iste',
Jacob had exclaimed 'uere Dominus est in loco isto et ego nesciebam'.[79]
The value of 'in Deo factus est', in the liturgical context of dedicating
a church to God, is the extent to which the phrase renders the relation
between the place of dedication and God more direct, more substantial.
The rest of the text, responsory as well as verse, depends on IV Ezra.[80] In
this passage, the most interesting alteration of the scriptural model is the
addition of the word 'sacramentum'. In its famous (Augustinian) sense of
'a visible sign of an invisible reality', sacrament is here made to apply to
the space inside the Pantheon, thus strengthening the substantiation of
a relation to God: this place is the visible sign of the invisible God (and
therefore it is beyond reproach). These affirming words are then followed,
in the verse, by a petition to God.[81]

Both musical settings of the Gradual, Gregorian and Old Roman, are
closely related, pointing to a common ancestor (Example 11.2). In the
responsory these melodies have the following structural pattern:

1 *begins F, rise to a   a to c, recitation around a   recitation around a, ends F*
   Locus iste   a deo   factus est

2 *recitation on c falling to a[82]   movement around G, between F and b*
                                        flat/c, ends G
   inaestimabile   sacramentum

3 *rise from a to c, recitation on c, fall to F   begins F, ornamental melisma*
                                                    (F–d/e), ends F
   irreprehensibilis   est

Example 11.2 Gregorian and Old Roman melodies for the Gradual *Locus iste*

Apart from demonstrating the closeness of the two melodic formulations, this brief description of structure underlines their common rhetorical behaviour vis-à-vis the text. In each the first text phrase, 'Locus iste a deo factus est', is set in a closed melodic passage; after this, each of the three words 'inaestimabile', 'sacramentum', 'irreprehensibilis' becomes the object of considerable elaboration, while the last word can be heard as set to one note (*F*) – which closes the tonal trajectory of the whole, followed by a melisma which decorates the whole. In the verse, the passage 'Deus cui adstat angelorum chorus' is sung through without any sense of musical caesura, the melody intoned from *F* rising through *a* to *c*, with recitation there ('angelorum'); most striking here is the melismatic treatment of 'chorus', as if the listeners could hear the music of the angels surrounding God. In the second part each word in the petition is given its own emphasis (as in the second part of the responsory),[83] thereby delivering the petition 'hear the prayers of your servants' in prolonged and forcible manner.

The Gradual was immediately followed by another elaborate soloist's chant, the Alleluia. This was sung with the verse

Adorabo ad templum sanctum tuum : et confitebor nomini tuo[84] (Psalm 137:2).

There can be no question of the relevance of this text in this context, the singer worshipping God in God's holy temple through the beauty of his (the singer's) ornate singing. Yet it cannot with confidence be proposed that this Alleluia was composed for the occasion of the Pantheon's consecration, since it is associated with other feasts besides that of the dedication of Sancta Maria ad Martyres. Notable among these is the Marian Purification feast on 2 February. Even if that feast was not officially fixed before the middle of the seventh century, the underlying layer of 'Hypapante', the presentation of Christ in the temple to Simeon, may already have been in place,[85] itself meriting the *Adorabo* text.

After the Alleluia the Gospel was read, possibly followed by a homily, although there is no surviving identified text for that. Then came the offering of gifts, during which the Offertory chant was sung. This has the longest text of all the Proper chants, with two verses, and would have taken longer to sing than any of the others:

Domine Deus in simplicitate cordis mei laetus obtuli uniuersa :
et populum tuum qui repertus est uidi cum ingenti gaudio :
Deus Israel custodi hanc uoluntatem, Domine Deus.

V1   Fecit Salomon solemnitatem in tempore illo :
fecit Salomon solemnitatem in tempore illo :
et prosperatus est et apparuit ei Dominus.

[Deus Israel custodi hanc uoluntatem, Domine Deus.]
V2   Maiestas Domini aedificauit templum :
uidebant omnes filii Israel gloriam Domini descendentem super domum
et adorauerunt et collaudauerunt Dominum dicentes :
[Deus Israel custodi hanc uoluntatem, Domine Deus.][86]

The source of all of this textual material is Chronicles, all of it concerned with the one biblical story which relates to the dedication of a church – the dedication of Solomon's temple. In the Bible the opening words came from the mouth of King David, speaking about the gold and silver he had given for the temple. In this Christian consecration mass they could have been understood to come from the emperor (whose presentation of gifts was recorded in the *Liber pontificalis*), if he was at the mass, or from the pope. Indeed, the Offertory may be imagined as voicing the pope's own address to God, expressing his position as an earthly intercessor between the people of Rome – God's people – and the deity.

The Offertory verses report first about the occasion of the dedication of Solomon's temple, here used as an *exemplum*, and then what actually happened at it: 'the majesty of the Lord filled the temple', and even more important for the occasion of the Pantheon's rededication, 'all the children of Israel *saw* the glory of the Lord come down over the house'. Through the singing of this chant, not only is that older act of dedication recalled, but the present moment of dedication is rendered vivid and effective: the worshippers have named the building as a house of God, and now God has responded with an overwhelming presence in the building. Above all, the people of Rome have witnessed that response.

After the offerings were made, preparations for the eucharist would have begun; the Sanctus was sung, the *Pater noster* and other intercessions said. While the eucharist was offered to the people, the Communion antiphon was sung. This consisted of a statement by Christ (or God), followed by three invitations:

Domus mea, domus orationis uocabitur, dicit Dominus :
in ea omnis qui petit accipit : et qui quaerit inuenit : et pulsanti aperietur.[87]

Those invitations must have been heard in relation to their context: this building, the old Pantheon, the new Sancta Maria ad Martyres, will be a house of prayer, in which those who ask for God's help will receive it. The text has resonances beyond this, since the first of its two sources, in the Gospel of Matthew, immediately follows the description of Jesus chasing moneychangers out of the temple. By choosing this text, those who formulated the chant referred to a biblical story about the cleansing

of a temple of worship, with the further implication that it is Christ himself who has acted as the moving force in ridding the Roman Pantheon
of its pagan idols. Finally, the second part of the text offers the words of
God, inviting them to petition him in this place. The idea of introducing the voice of God at the moment when the eucharist was offered was
surely inspired: God responded to the petitions of the worshippers, and
accepted the physical situation in which the mass was being celebrated as
his house. It is the first time in the set of five chant Propers that his voice
is heard, and the change underlines the decision to use Old Testament
texts for all the previous chants, with the New Testament – the new law –
at the moment of eucharistic meeting between people and God.

Indeed, the choice of texts and articulation of voices in all five Proper
chants is striking, from the moment of the pope's arrival with the statement – as if by all present – 'this place is awe-inspiring, and it is a house
of God', through the establishment that the building itself represents the
invisible reality of God, and the petition 'hear the prayers of your servants',
the Alleluia singer's offering of beautiful, joyful song to the Lord in this
temple, the pope's offering and petition, to the sense of presence of the Lord
in the building, around the worshippers, and finally, the Lord's own voice
during the Communion: 'My house will be called a house of prayer – and
in it all who ask will receive.' It is as if the set of five chants was conceived
of as one medium of communication with God during the mass, and that
through this medium could be heard a dialogue during which a dynamic
process of discovery, naming and conviction of the holiness of the place
was established by/for the people of Rome, followed by petition and praise
of God, to all of which came the response of first the presence of God, and
then his own voice, recognizing, accepting and inviting prayer.

Writing over a century later, Bede understood the ritual conversion of this
monumental pagan temple to a Christian church to have been effective: the
fact that he made mention of an event which had nothing directly to do
with Anglo-Saxon England is a measure not only of his interest in Gregory's
views about the rededication of pagan temples, but also of the success of the
ritual carried out on that 13 May. The achievement of a new identity can also
be read directly in Roman sources: more or less immediately, the church of
Sancta Maria ad Martyres became part of the Roman stational system, visited by the pope on three days during the liturgical year.[88]

Of course, the change from pagan temple to Christian church belongs
in a much longer narrative context than just this one day: it has especial force as one moment in a period of strongly developing Christianity,

centred around the pope as spiritual leader of the city. Nevertheless, the change of use and of meaning of a pagan building which represented a now lost imperial past was effected on one day. This is where a simple distinction proposed by the French historian Nora becomes useful. He divides all sites of memory into those which have meaning 'imposed' and those for which meaning is 'constructed', thereby separating, on the one hand, places and/or objects for which symbolic and memorial intention is inscribed in the place or object itself, and, on the other, places and/or objects for which 'circumstances, the passage of time, human effort, and history itself' has transformed them into places of memory.[89] In those terms the meaning of the Pantheon was 'imposed' on the day before the consecration; and the meaning of Sancta Maria ad Martyres was 'imposed' on the day after. Nora's examples of *constructed* memory deal with the collective imposition of readings developed over long periods of time, sometimes centuries, yet I see no reason not to appropriate the idea of 'constructed memory' to describe the process of the Pantheon's transformation from one 'imposed' symbolic meaning to another. Perhaps the most audible way in which that new memory of the Pantheon was constructed was through the filling of this resonant space with the distinctive sound of Roman chant: to sing and to hear such unmistakeable music, sometimes recitational, sometimes rhapsodic, would make a simple and direct statement about identity. Yet the musical chants composed for this occasion and arranged in a specific order also reveal an active process of change, one in which the actions undertaken in the mass, including – through the Proper chants – a dialogue between the people of Rome and God, suggest, shape and confirm a new intention for the building: the people of Rome present the building to God as his house, and God, at the moment of the eucharist, recognizes it as such. The metamorphosis in perception of the building was not the result of celebrating any old mass, with its distinctive music, within the walls of the building, but the result of celebrating a specially composed mass, one in which a dynamic process had to follow its course to achieve that recognition by God. That dynamic process constituted a finely constructed rhetorical exercise in persuasion, designed not only to achieve God's acknowledgement, but, above all, to shift the attitudes of the Roman people, to develop their faith in the building as a holy Christian site. The mass chants became a vehicle for that persuasive exercise, and through it the refocusing of perceptions of the building towards a different set of memories: for a building extraordinarily rich in memories, this was how the Romans used ritual to change the meaning of the monumental and centuries-old Pantheon.

Postscript

The chants make no direct reference to Mary or the martyrs. It would be possible, through a typological reading, to hear most of the chants as referring to Mary – as 'house of God', 'gateway to heaven', 'a mystery beyond comprehension'.[90] Nevertheless this is a reading which, when the chants were sung in the Pantheon, would have sat beyond the most obvious. What is especially interesting then, if these chants were indeed composed for this occasion, is the directness of the communication from the people of Rome to God, their only intercessor the pope.

NOTES

1 'Hic est Bonifatius quartus a beato Gregorio Romanae urbis episcopo, qui inpetrauit a Focate principe donari ecclesiae Christi templum Romae, quod Pantheon uocabatur ab antiquis, quasi simulacrum esset omnium deorum; in quo ipse, eliminata omni spurcitia, fecit ecclesiam sanctae Dei genetricis atque omnium martyrum Christi, ut, exclusa multitudine daemonum, multitudo ibi sanctorum memoriam haberet.' *Bede's Ecclesiastical History of the English People*, ed. B. Colgrave and R. A. B. Mynors (Oxford: Clarendon Press, 1969), II.4, 148–9.

2 Louis Duchesne, *Le liber pontificalis: Texte, introduction et commentaire*, additions and corrections by Cyrille Vogel, 2nd edn, 3 vols. (Paris: De Boccard, 1955–7); *The Book of Pontiffs (Liber Pontificalis)*, trans. with an introduction by Raymond Davis (Liverpool University Press, 1989).

3 For a recent summary of arguments, see Martin Wallraff, 'Einheit und Vielfalt des Göttlichen in der Spätantike', *Jahrbuch für Antike und Christentum*, 47 (2004): 128–43, at 139 n. 55.

4 Bibliography on the Pantheon is extensive, and can only be suggested here by a small number of representative studies: W. L. MacDonald, *The Architecture of the Roman Empire*, 2 vols. (New Haven: Yale University Press, 1965), vol. I, 94–101; Kjeld de Fine Licht, *The Rotunda in Rome: A Study of Hadrian's Pantheon*, Jutland Archaeological Society Publications 8 (Copenhagen, 1968); W. L. MacDonald, *The Pantheon: Design, Meaning and Progeny* (Cambridge, MA: Harvard University Press, 1976); Edmund Thomas, 'The Architectural History of the Pantheon in Rome from Agrippa to Septimius Severus via Hadrian', *Hephaistos*, 15 (1997): 163–86; Edmund Thomas, *Monumentality and the Roman Empire: Architecture in the Antonine Age* (Oxford University Press, 2007), 68–9.

5 MacDonald, *The Pantheon*, 12.

6 *Ibid.* On Agrippa's building, see especially Thomas, 'Architectural History', where he refutes the argument that Agrippa's building was only a temple 'in the widest possible sense, since it is unlikely that its purpose was primarily religious': for this proposal see Paul Godfrey and David Hemsoll, 'The Pantheon: Temple or Rotunda?' in Martin Henig and Anthony King (eds.), *Pagan Gods and Shrines of the Roman Empire* (Oxford: Oxford Committee for Archaeology, 1986), 195–209, at 205.

7 'Marcus *Agrippa* Lucii Filius Consul *tertium fecit'* [Marcus Agrippa, son of Lucius, consul for the third time, built this]. Renovations undertaken in AD 202 were noted in further inscriptions (including 'pantheum vetustate corruptum cum omni cultu restituerunt'), across the architrave: Thomas, 'Architectural History', 165–6.

8 MacDonald, *The Pantheon*, 84. On the significance of monumental buildings in ancient Rome as historical markers, see especially Thomas, *Monumentality*, 168–70.

9 Thomas, 'Architectural History', 178.

10 MacDonald, *The Pantheon*, 88.

11 *Ibid.*, 35–6.

12 Thomas, *Monumentality*, 68.

13 On this in general, see Karl Lehmann, 'The Dome of Heaven', *Art bulletin*, 27 (1945): 1–27; rpt. in W. Eugene Kleinbauer (ed.), *Modern Perspectives in Western Art History* (New York: Holt, Rinehart and Winston, 1971), 227–70.

14 Dio Cassius, LIII.27.3 as translated by MacDonald, *The Pantheon*, 76.

15 On the siting of the Pantheon in relation to the mausoleum, see Thomas, 'Architectural history', 174–5, with a useful sketch-plan.

16 *Ibid.*; MacDonald, *The Pantheon*, 84.

17 Thomas, *Monumentality*, 68.

18 MacDonald, *Architecture*, 119.

19 Codex Theodosianus, XIV.3, 10.

20 Visiting Rome in 357, Constantine II remarked on the images of former emperors in the niches, implying that statues of the pagan gods had by that time been removed: Ammianus Marcellinus, XVI.10.14.

21 Richard Krautheimer, *Rome: Profile of a City, 312–1308* (Princeton University Press, 1980), 33.

22 *Ibid.*, 71–5 and John F. Baldovin, *The Urban Character of Christian Worship*, Orientalia christiana analecta 228 (Rome: Pontifical Institute, 1987), 106–18.

23 This is a recurring theme in Krautheimer, *Rome*, chapter 2; it would be insufficient, however, to portray imperial and Christian power and achievements in a simple opposition to each other. For a more nuanced view, and the argument that 'late antiquity was a period when the authority of the bishop of Rome was only one of several shaping the city', see Mark Humphries, 'From Emperor to Pope? Ceremonial, Space, and Authority at Rome from Constantine to Gregory the Great', in K. Cooper and J. Hillner (eds.), *Religion, Dynasty, and Patronage in Early Christian Rome 300–900* (Cambridge University Press, 2007), 21–58.

24 'City of cities and head of the whole world' – thus Gregory of Tours, in the preface to Book V of his *History of the Franks*, ed. B. Krusch and W. Levison, MGH Scriptores rerum merovingicarum 1.1 (Hannover, 1951), 193–4. In a recent study the first composition of this passage is dated *c.* 576: see Guy Halsall, 'The Preface to Book V of Gregory of Tours' Histories: Its Form, Context and Significance', *The English Historical Review*, 122 (2007): 297–317.

25 Krautheimer, *Rome*, 72.

26 *Ibid.*, 61. But see also Humphries, 'From Emperor to Pope?'

27 On Gregory's attitude to the conversion of pagan temples, see F. J. Niederer, 'Temples Converted into Churches: The Situation in Rome', *Church History*, 22 (1953): 175–80; and Bruno Judic, 'Le corbeau et la sautelle: L'application des instructions de Grégoire le Grand pour la transformation des temples païens en églises. Études de cas', in Lionel Mary and Michel Sot (eds.), *Impies et païens entre antiquité et moyen age*, UMR Textes, images et monuments de l'antiquité au haut Moyen Âge (Paris: Picard, 2002), 97–125.

28 Although it might seem that this could be challenged it is commonly asserted, presumably on the grounds that this was the first building previously used as a temple not to be physically built for its Christian use: see Pierre Jounel, 'Le culte collectif des saints à Rome du VIIe au IXe siècle', *Ecclesia orans*, 6 (1989): 285–300; and Sible de Blaauw, 'Das Pantheon als christlicher Tempel', *Boreas*, 17 (1994): 13–26.

29 *Bede's Ecclesiastical History*, I.30, 106–7: 'uidelicet quia fana idolorum destrui in eadem gente minime debeant, sed ipsa quae in eis sunt idola destruantur, aqua benedicta fiat, in eisdem fanis aspergatur, altaria construantur, reliquiae ponantur. Quia, si fana eadem bene constructa sunt, necesse est ut a cultu daemonum in obsequio ueri Dei debeant commutari, ut dum gens ipsa eadem fana sua non uidet destrui, de corde errorem deponat, et Deum uerum cognoscens ac adorans, ad loca quae consueuit familiarius concurrat.'

30 On the shaping of a process to change the function of the Pantheon see further below; on the construction of collective memory, especially in relation to Christian Rome, see M. Carruthers, *The Craft of Thought: Meditation, Rhetoric, and the Making of Images, 400–1200* (Cambridge University Press, 1998), *passim* and especially 54–7.

31 See T. F. Mathews, *The Clash of Gods: A Reinterpretation of Early Christian Art* (Princeton University Press, 1993), xx.

32 That is, notwithstanding the fact that preparations – restoration of the exterior and cleaning of the interior – would have had to have been undertaken for some time previously.

33 On the cult of the Blessed Virgin Mary in the late antique period, see M. Fassler, 'The First Marian Feast in Constantinople and Jerusalem: Chant Texts, Readings, and Homiletic Literature', in P. Jeffery (ed.), *The Study of Medieval Chant: Paths and Bridges, East and West* (Woodbridge: Boydell and Brewer, 2001), 25–87; A. Cameron, 'The Cult of the Virgin in Late Antiquity: Religious Development and Myth-Making', in R. N. Swanson (ed.), *The Church and Mary* (Woodbridge: Boydell and Brewer, 2004), 1–21; and M. Vassilaki (ed.), *Images of the Mother of God: Perceptions of the Theotokos in Byzantium* (Aldershot: Ashgate, 2005).

34 While the establishment of Marian feasts is difficult to pin down, in the West the feast of the Assumption seems to have emerged first. On this, and on liturgy for the celebration of Marian feasts in Constantinople and Jerusalem, see Fassler, 'The First Marian Feast'.

35 The other fate being re-use – through which a good number of Roman pub-
    lic buildings were converted into Christian churches. On spoliation and re-
    use of Roman buildings in this period, see B. Ward-Perkins, *From Classical
    Antiquity to the Middle Ages: Urban Public Building in Northern and Central
    Italy* AD *300–850* (Oxford University Press, 1984), 89–91, 203–23.

36 *Ibid.*, 38–48.

37 Thomas, *Monumentality*, 168–70.

38 The texts of these inscriptions are set out in Thomas, 'Architectural History',
    165–6.

39 Pope Vigilius (537–55) to Profuturus of Braga: 'De fabrica vero cujuslibet
    ecclesiae, quae diruta fuerat, restauranda, et si in eo loco consecrationis
    solemnitas debeat iterari in quo sanctuaria non fuerunt, nihil judicamus
    officere, si per eam minime aqua exorcidiata jactetur; quia consecrationem
    cujuslibet ecclesiae, in qua sanctuaria non ponuntur, celebritatem tantum
    scimus esse missarum. Et ideo si qua sanctorum basilica a fundamentis etiam
    fuerit innovata, sine aliqua dubitatione, cum in ea missarum fuerit celebrata
    solemnitas, totius sanctificatio consecrationis implebitur. Si vero sanctuaria
    quae habebat ablata sint, rursus eorum repositione et missarum solemnitate
    reverentiam sanctificationis accipiat': PL 84 (Paris, 1850), 832. For further ref-
    erences, see also A. G. Martimort, *L'église en prière: Introduction à la liturgie*
    (Paris: Desclée, 1961), 179–80; and M. Andrieu, *Les ordines romani du haut
    moyen age*, 4 vols. Spicilegium sacrum Lovaniense 11, 23, 24, 28 (Louvain,
    1931–56), vol. IV, 359–84.

40 Andrieu, *Les ordines*, IV, 360ff., with multiple citations from Gregory.

41 *Ibid.*, 366; also Alan Thacker, 'Rome of the Martyrs: Saints, Cults and Relics,
    Fourth to Seventh Centuries', in É. Ó Carragáin and C. N. de Vegvar (eds.),
    Roma Felix – Formation and Reflections of Medieval Rome (Aldershot: Ashgate,
    2007), 13–49, *passim*.

42 Gerhard Wolf, 'Icons and Sites: Cult Images of the Virgin in Mediaeval
    Rome', in Vassilaki (ed.), *Images of the Mother of God*, 23–41, at 25. On icon
    as relic see also Maria Andaloro, '376: Icona con l'hodighitria', in S. Enjoli
    and E. la Rocca (eds.), *Aurea Roma: Dalla città pagana alla città cristiana*
    (Rome: L'Erma di Bretschneider, 2000), 661–2; and 'Vom Porträt zur Ikone',
    in M. Andaloro and S. Romano (eds.), *Römisches Mittelalter: Kunst und
    Kultur in Rom von der Spätantike bis Giotto* (Darmstadt: Wissenschaftliche
    Buchgesellschaft, 2002), 23–54, with a reproduction (no. 23); for another
    reproduction, see R. Cormack and M. Vassilaki (eds.), *Byzantium 330–1453*
    (London: Royal Academy of Arts, 2008), no. 47.

43 Wolf, 'Icons and Sites', 30.

44 Brussels, Bibliothèque royale de Belgique MS 10127–10144, fol. 105ʳ. The text
    of the chant book is edited by Dom René-Jean Hesbert, *Antiphonale mis-
    sarum sextuplex* (Rome: Herder, 1935).

45 The manuscript sources are as follows: Monza: Monza, Tesoro della Basilica
    MS CIX; Corbie: Paris, Bib. Nat. MS lat. 12050; Compiègne: Paris, Bib.
    Nat. MS lat. 17436; Senlis: Paris, Bibliothèque Ste. Geneviève MS 111;

Laon: Laon Bibliothèque municipale MS 239; Albi: Bibliothèque municipale Rochegude MS 44; Chartres: Chartres Bibliothèque municipale MS 47, destroyed in 1944, reproduced in *Le codex 47 de la bibliothèque de Chartres*, Paléographie musicale 11 (Solesmes, 1912); SG 359: Sankt Gallen Stiftsbibliothek MS 359, reproduced in *Cantatorium de Saint-Gall*, Paléographie musicale series 2, 2 (Solesmes, 1924). The sources from Monza, Corbie, Compiègne and Senlis are edited in Hesbert, *Antiphonale*; Albi is edited in J. A. Emerson and L. Collamore, *Albi, Bibliothèque municipale Rochegude, manuscript 44: A Complete Ninth-Century Gradual and Antiphoner from Southern France*, Musicological studies 77 (Ottawa: Institute of Mediaeval Music, 2002).

46 Jean Deshusses (ed.), *Le sacramentaire grégorien: ses principales formes d'après les plus anciens manuscrits*, 3rd edn, 3 vols., Spicilegium Friburgense 16, 24, 28 (Fribourg: Éditions universitaires, 1988–92), vol. I, no. 107 (p. 118).

47 W. H. Frere, *Studies in Early Roman Liturgy II: The Roman Gospel-Lectionary*, Alcuin club collections 30 (Oxford University Press, 1934), under no. 129 (12, 42).

48 A celebration of Mary's Nativity was decreed by Pope Sergius I (*Liber pontificalis* for Sergius I, 687–701); it is unclear at what stage this took the form of a fully-fledged feast, with its own liturgy.

49 *Liber pontificalis* for Boniface IV, 608–15: 'in quo fecit ecclesiam beatae Mariae semper virginis et omnium martyrum'.

50 *Liber pontificalis* for Vitalian, 657–72.

51 In Vatican City, Biblioteca Apostolica Vaticana MS lat. 5319, fol. 135 (a Roman gradual of c. 1100), and Vatican City, Bibliotheca Apostolica Vaticana, Archivio San Pietro MS F22 (a gradual from St Peter's of the thirteenth century); the texts are collected in P. F. Cutter (ed.), *Musical Sources of the Old Roman Mass* (Neuhausen-Stuttgart: American Institute of Musicology; Hänssler Verlag, 1979), under nos. 295, 297; the melodies from Vat. lat. MS 5319 are transcribed by M. Landwehr-Melnicki in B. Stäblein (ed.), *Die Gesänge des altrömischen Graduale Vat. Lat. 5319*, Monumenta monodica medii aevi 2 (Kassel: Bärenreiter, 1970), at 14, 140, 341, 426.

52 As decreed in, for example, the Admonitio generalis of 789: A. Boretius (ed.), *Capitularia regum Francorum I*, MGH Legum Sectio 2 (Hannover: Impensis Bibliopolii Hahn, 1883), 52–62.

53 The Roman stational system is one of several examples used to demonstrate the significance of itineraries (such as the route of liturgical processions) in creating maps in collective memory, which could then become the basis for further layers of thought, in Carruthers, *The Craft of Thought*, 40–57.

54 For a possible way of reading the use of Roman stational liturgy in a northern monastery, see A. A. Häussling, 'Liturgie in der Karolingerzeit und der St. Galler Klosterplan', in P. Ochsenbein and K. Schmuki (eds.), *Studien zum St. Galler Klosterplan II*, Mitteilungen zur vaterländischen Geschichte 52 (St. Gallen: Historischen Verein des Kantons St. Gallen, 2002), 151–83.

55 For the detail of the stational system, see Baldovin, *Urban Character*, 106–41.

56 On the cult of martyrs in Rome, and the interest this aroused elsewhere, see Thacker, 'Rome of the Martyrs'; on Carolingian engagement with relics, see also Julia Smith, 'Old Saints, New Cults: Roman Relics in Carolingian Francia', in J. M. H. Smith (ed.), *Early Medieval Rome and the Christian West: Essays in Honour of Donald A. Bullough* (Leiden: Brill, 2000), 335–9; and R. McKitterick, *Charlemagne: The Formation of a European Identity* (Cambridge University Press, 2008), 326–30.

57 J. McKinnon, *The Advent Project: The Later Seventh-Century Creation of the Mass Proper* (Berkeley: University of California Press, 2000), 187; see also 155–6, 166–7, 187–90.

58 *Ibid.*, 167, 187. For reconstruction of early states of the Roman epistolary and evangeliary, see Frere, *The Roman Lectionary*, and Theodor Klauser, *Das römische Capitulare Evangeliorum*, Liturgie geschichtliche Quellen und Forschungen 28 (Münster: Aschendorff, 1935). For a useful guide to sources and their relationships, see Cyrille Vogel, *Medieval Liturgy: An Introduction to the Sources*, rev. and trans. W. G. Storey and N. K. Rasmussen (Washington: The Pastoral Press, 1981), 339–54.

59 Würzburg, Universitätsbibliothek codex M.p.th.f.62: *Facsimileausgabe des Codex M. p. th. f. 62 der Universitäts-Bibliothek Würzburg*, ed. H. Thurn, Codices selecti phototypice impressi 17 (Graz: Akademische Druck-und-Verlagsanstalt, 1968); see also Vogel, *An Introduction*, 339, 342–3. Although copied by one scribe, the Epistle and Gospel lists recorded in this source do not depend on the same festal calendar, and present conflicting evidence: the Epistle list includes a reference to a station at Sancta Maria ad Martyres on the Friday after Easter, while the Gospel list does not (and neither has the feast on 13 May).

60 Vatican City, Biblioteca Apostolica Vaticana MS Pal. lat. 46; edited in Theodor Klauser, 'Ein vollständiges Evangelienverzeichnis der römischen Kirche aus dem 7. Jahrhundert, erhalten im Cod. Vat. Pal. Lat. 46', *Römische Quartalschrift für christliche Altertumskunde und für Kirchengeschichte*, 35 (1927): 113–34.

61 Frere, *The Roman Lectionary*, 88; A. Chavasse, 'L'épistolier romain du codex de Wurtzbourg: Son organization', *Revue bénédictine*, 91 (1981): 280–331, at 280.

62 P. Jeffery, 'Rome and Jerusalem: From Oral Tradition to Written Repertory in Two Ancient Liturgical Centres', in G. M. Boone (ed.), *Essays on Medieval Music in Honor of David G. Hughes*, Isham Library Papers 4 (Cambridge, MA: Harvard University Press, 1995), 207–47, at 215–16.

63 To what extent that same mass liturgy, even if rubricated for the Dedicatio Sancta Maria ad Martyres feast, had already been in use for church consecrations north of the Alps, is impossible to tell.

64 L. C. Mohlberg (ed.), *Liber sacramentorum Romane aeclesiae ordinis anni circuli*, Rerum ecclesiarum documenta Fontes 4 (Rome: Herder, 1981), nos.88, 89, 90.

65 Deshusses (ed.), *Sacramentaire grégorien*, vol. I, no.195 (p. 303).

66 *ibid.*, no. 63 (p. 423).

67 McKinnon, *The Advent Project*, 189.

68 *Ibid.*, 188.

69 *Ibid.*, 189.

70 The issue of the period when the repertory of Gregorian chant took its defini-
    tive shape is explored on various levels in Jeffery, 'Rome and Jerusalem'. It was
    also central to McKinnon's *The Advent Project*; on McKinnon's conclusions,
    however, see the reviews by J. Dyer in *Early Music History*, 19 (2000): 279–
    309; S. Rankin in *Plainsong and Medieval Music*, 11 (2002): 73–98; and
    P. Jeffery in *Journal of the American Musicological Society*, 56 (2003): 169–79.

71 J. McKinnon, 'The Emergence of Gregorian Chant in the Carolingian Era',
    in McKinnon (ed.), *Antiquity and the Middle Ages: From Ancient Greece to
    the Fifteenth Century* (London: Macmillan, 1990), 88–119, at 106–7; Jeffery,
    'Rome and Jerusalem', 215; McKinnon, *The Advent Project*, 155.

72 Andrieu, *Les Ordines*, vol. II, 67–108. It is unlikely that the Roman model
    for this ordo was compiled before 700; nevertheless, the relation between the
    pope's arrival and the beginning of the mass is unlikely to have been han-
    dled differently at an earlier date.

73 It is unclear where such a sacristy might have been sited in the Pantheon.

74 'This place is awe-inspiring : this is the house of God and the gateway to
    heaven : and it will be called the court of God.' For the text in Gregorian
    books, see Hesbert (ed.), *Antiphonale*, no. 100; for the text in the later 'Old-
    Roman' books, see Cutter, *Musical Sources*, nos. 295, 297.

75 Genesis 28:17–22 (with the words extracted for the chant in italics): 'cumque
    evigilasset Iacob de somno ait . vere Dominus est in loco isto et ego nesci-
    ebam. pavensque quam *terribilis* inquit *est locus iste* . non est *hic* aliud nisi
    domus Dei et porta caeli. surgens ergo mane tulit lapidem quem subposuerat
    capiti suo et erexit in titulum . fundens oleum desuper … *et* lapis iste quem
    erexi in titulum *uocabitur domus Dei*'.

76 The removal of these bronze tiles in 663 by Emperor Constantine II is
    recorded in the *Liber pontificalis* (for Pope Vitalian, 657–72).

77 The melodies shown in Examples 1 and 2 are taken from Stäblein (ed.), *Die
    Gesänge* (see n. 51 above), and the *Graduale triplex* (Solesmes: Desclée, 1973),
    397–8. In these examples only the melodic pitches are reproduced, without
    information about rhythm and articulation, typically preserved in early neu-
    matic notations.

78 'This place was made by God : a mystery beyond comprehension, above
    all reproach.' V. 'O God, around whom a chorus of angels stands, hear the
    prayers of your servants.' OR (= Old Roman): 'a Deo factum est'; 'astant
    angelorum chori'. The passage is drawn from IV Ezra 8:21–4: 'Domine qui
    habitas in seculum, cuius oculi elati et superna in aerem, et cuius thronus
    inaestimabilis et gloria incomprehensibilis, cui adstat exercitus *angelorum* cum
    tremore … *exaudi* domine *orationem serui tui* et auribus percipe precationem
    figmenti tui, intende uerba mea.'

79 Genesis 28:16: 'Surely the Lord is in this place, and I knew it not.'

80 On the relation between the chant text and IV Ezra, see Louis Brou, 'Le IVᵉ livre d'Esdras dans la liturgie hispanique et le Graduel Romain *Locus iste* de la messe de la dédicace', *Sacris erudiri*, 9 (1957): 75–109. Brou's argument for the primacy of the Spanish use of a liturgical text 'Locus iste' over the Roman ignores both the derivation of the first phrase from Genesis, and the presence in the Roman version of the word *sacramentum*.

81 In the petition the words from Ezra 'exaudi domine orationem serui tui' are rendered in the plural, and with 'orationes' changed to 'preces'. Pointing out the exact relation between the closing phrase of the verse and that of the Gradual *Protector noster* (for Monday in the first week of Lent), Peter Jeffery traced this text back to Psalm 83:10 + 9 ('Rome and Jerusalem', 216 n. 24). However, while that responsory text is clearly drawn from the Psalm, the formulation of the verse is less straightforward: it reads 'Domine deus virtutum exaudi preces seruorum tuorum' against the Psalm text 'Domine deus uirtutum exaudi orationem meam.'

82 Here a typical difference between the Gregorian and Old Roman formulations of this melody can be seen: in the Old Roman, the phrase begins immediately on the recitation pitch, while in the Gregorian, the melody intones to that pitch (using a standard formula).

83 In this specific sense there is variation between the Gregorian and Old Roman settings, the latter making a pair of 'exaudi preces', the former pairing 'seruorum tuorum'.

84 'I will worship at thy holy temple : and I will confess thy holy name.'

85 Writing at the end of the fourth century, Egeria reports on a procession on this day in Jerusalem; at least by 600 such processions were also practised in Byzantium: for this day Pope Sergius I (687–701) officially ordered a procession in honour of Mary: see Martimort, *L'Église*, 752.

86 'O lord God, in the simplicity of my heart I have joyfully offered all things: and I have seen with great joy your people gathered here: God of Israel, preserve this good intention, O Lord God.' V1 'In those days Solomon kept the feast : in those days Solomon kept the feast : and he was favourable and the Lord appeared unto him. [God of Israel, preserve this good intention, O Lord God.]' V2 'The majesty of the Lord filled the temple : all the children of Israel saw the glory of the Lord come down over the house : and they adored and worshipped the Lord, saying: [God of Israel, preserve this good intention, O Lord God].' These texts are drawn from 1 Chronicles 29:16–18; 2 Chronicles 7:8–12' 7:1–3.

87 'My house will be called a house of prayer (says the Lord): in it all who ask will receive, and he who seeks will find, and to him who knocks it will be opened.' Matthew 21:13: 'Et dicit eis : scriptum est *domus mea domus orationis uocabitur* ... (22) et omnia quaecumque petieritis in oratione credentes accipietis.' Matthew 7:8: 'omnis enim *qui petit accipit et qui quaerit inuenit et pulsanti aperietur*'.

88 On 1 January (as the octave of Christmas, a day on which Mary was cel-
    ebrated in the Roman liturgy in this period); Friday after Easter; 13 May.
89 See the introduction by Pierre Nora to *Realms of Memory: Rethinking the
    French Past*, under the direction of Pierre Nora, ed. with a foreword by L. D.
    Kritzman, trans. A. Goldhammer, 3 vols. (New York: Columbia University
    Press, 1996–8), vol.III, xx.
90 I thank Dr Alex Lingas for his suggestion that the chant texts might be read
    this way.

Index

CAMBRIDGE STUDIES IN MEDIEVAL LITERATURE

CPSIA information can be obtained at www.ICGtesting.com
Printed in the USA
LVOW05s0447211213

366092LV00013B/378/P